The Atlas of
North American Exploration

The Atlas of
North American
Exploration

From the Norse Voyages to the Race to the Pole

William H. Goetzmann
Glyndwr Williams

Prentice Hall General Reference

New York • London • Toronto • Sydney • Tokyo • Singapore

Prentice Hall General Reference
15 Columbus Circle
New York, New York, 10023

Library of Congress Cataloging-in-Publication Data

Goetzmann, William H.
    The atlas of North American exploration / William Goetzmann and
Glyndwr Williams.

        p.   cm.
    Includes index.
    ISBN 0-13-297128-3
    1. North America — Discovery and exploration — Maps. 2. Explorers —
North America — History — Maps.   I. Williams, Glyndwr.   II. Title.
    G1106.S12G6   1992   <G&M>
    911.7 — dc20   92-8573
                                                                    CIP
                                                                    MAP

Artwork: Swanston Graphics Limited,
Vernon House, Vernon Street, Derby DE1 1FR

Cartographic director: Malcolm Swanston
Maps created by: Isabelle Lewis and Jacqueline Land
Assisted by: Pamela Hopkinson and Andrew Bright

Editorial: Swanston Publishing Limited,
The Fitzpatrick Building, 188-194 York Way,
Kings Cross, London N7 9AX

Editorial director: Anne Benewick
Editor: Chris Schüler
Assisted by: Cathy Jones, Elizabeth Wyse,
George Wilkes, Alex de Berry
Picture research: Suzanne O'Farrell
Additional design: Albert Kueh, Ian Cockburn

Consultant: G. Malcolm Lewis,
Amerindian and Inuit Maps and Mapping Programme,
University of Sheffield

Printed and bound in Hong Kong
Produced by Mandarin Offset Ltd.

10   9   8   7   6   5   4   3   2   1

First Edition

Contents

Preface

The story of the explorers of North America begins many thousand years before Columbus, with the crossing by Mongoloid hunters of the land bridge from Asia. In the intervening millennia before the coming of the Europeans the trickle of migration from the north broadened until it spread a thin layer of settlement over much of the continent. As they adapted to their new environments, the migrants settled into what the European arrivals would find a bewildering variety of culture types: the Inuit of the far north, the elusive Beothuk of Newfoundland, the farming Algonquians of the northeast, the elaborate temple-mound cultures of the southeast, the fishing communities of the west coast, the buffalo hunters of the plains, the pueblo-dwellers of the southwest.

These societies developed in almost unbroken isolation from Europe. Despite the forays westward across the Atlantic of the pre-Columbian area, notably by the Norsemen, whose sagas, reports to the Vatican and even maps alerted few beyond fisherman and the Hanseatic League. Despite the mighty voyages of Columbus and Magellan, America did not exist as a separate entity until Amerigo Vespucci gave it a name and gold poured into Europe as a result of Cortés's conquest followed by those of many other Spaniards. North America remained relatively neglected in the light of these glittering finds and did not bulk large in the European consciousness until the 16th century. To the end of his life Columbus himself assumed that his discoveries were part of Asia, and only after his death was there general acceptance of the existence of a previously unsuspected continent.

From that exciting period of realization, four hundred years were to pass before Europeans completed their exploration and mapping of the main features of North America. It is their endeavors which are represented in this volume. As far as possible we tell the story through their own maps and drawings, their journals and letters, to capture some of the immediacy of their reaction to the new lands. But what was new to the first Europeans was old to the existing inhabitants, and we have tried to set the narrative of European exploration against the Amerindian response. The clash of cultures which followed the European arrival in North America has been told many times, usually in the context of Indian hostility to white settlement. Here, we have stressed the importance of the Indian in influencing the course of European exploration. Indian friendship could pull the new arrivals in one direction, Indian hostility push them in another. As carriers, guides and hunters the Indians were essential to the newcomers once they moved away from their ships. Indian methods of travel became standard for the Europeans – the snowshoe in winter, the birchbark canoe or dugout boat in summer. Where the evidence exists, we show how the mysterious land beyond the river or over the hills was often familiar terrain to the Indians who made crucial maps for explorers like Lewis and Clark or Jedediah Smith. We would not wish to understate the courage and endurance of the explorers from Europe, but it needs to be remembered that their "discoveries" were often the formalization and recording of knowledge already held by the indigenous inhabitants.

The spreads in this atlas follow a common pattern. They include an analysis of the particular exploration; a modern map; one or more historical maps or illustrations; and an extract from the explorer's own record. The modern maps show the explorers' routes in relation to Indian and European settlements at the time. Important modern boundaries and cities are shown in grey.

A word of caution is needed here. By its very nature a map implies certainty, but often the explorers' routes can only be plotted by informed guesswork. Some of the earlier explorers in particular had only rudimentary navigational and surveying instruments, and their journals have sometimes disappeared or survived in mangled form. Indian tribal boundaries were rarely formal or precise, and in any case fluctuated with migration and dispersal. European forts, missions and trading posts also shifted, and quite often an old name would be reused in a new location.

The bibliography is both a guide to further reading and an acknowledgement of our debt to the work of many fine scholars. We specifically wish to acknowledge the help of G. Malcolm Lewis, who advised on the names and locations of Indian and Inuit peoples; Professor Charles Hudson, whose recent researches have greatly advanced our knowledge of the route taken by de Soto; Professor Louis De Vorsey; Mary Marmon; Ann Gaines; Chris Schüler; John Morris; and William Pugsley. The latter two are in large measure responsible for the Arctic maps at the end of this book, while Morris also located the routes eastwards from Santa Fé across the Llano Estacado of Texas.

W.H.G.
G.W.

America: Found, Lost, and Found Again

BY
DAVID BEERS QUINN

America was far from being a "new country" when seafarers from Europe reached its shores in the 15th century. The continent was discovered not once, but several times. Firstly, by nomadic hunters crossing from Siberia in prehistoric times; then by Norse seafarers from Greenland who established a fragile colony on Newfoundland; and only much later, by Columbus and his successors.

For each new set of arrivals, the continent represented something different. For the first pioneers who made the icy crossing from Asia, it was an extension of their hunting grounds. For the Norse seafarers, it was Vinland. For Columbus, it was the Asian mainland. Only after his death did the idea of America – the continent – materialize on European maps.

The land-bridge with northeast Asia that existed some 50,000 years ago allowed human emigrants to reach America for the first time. Joined by successive waves of reinforcements, they spread over the two halves of the continent and developed into many widely differentiated cultures. Native American society had developed a long way before Europe had consolidated to any meaningful degree. Consequently, European notions about the "primitive" condition of the indigenous peoples in eastern North America were very wide of the mark. Most of these societies had highly developed agriculture or horticulture; specialized hunting areas and group divisions; and lived a satisfactory social life, in places with highly developed and widespread religious practices.

MYTHS AND LEGENDS
Europe and America developed in ignorance of one another for millennia. The westward expansion of Europe came only after centuries of epic myths, legends and tentative explorations of the vast ocean which fringed its western lands.

The oldest of these legends was probably that of the Seven Cities. When the Moors invaded Portugal in the 8th century, it claimed, seven bishops and their flocks fled across the ocean to establish Seven Islands (or Cities) far to the west. The story, which seems to have flourished orally in Portugal, surfaced in the sea charts of the 15th century, and was current at the time Columbus sailed. When Spanish conquistadors in the early 16th century heard reports of the pueblos of New Mexico, the Seven Cities shifted their location and began to appear on maps of this region.

A reconstruction of an Irish curragh of the 6th century, of the type St Brendan may have used.

THE LEGEND OF ST BRENDAN
The second legend was that of St Brendan, bishop of Clonfert in Ireland, who died in 577. His reputation as a traveler took shape about 900 in a "Life" which circulated widely

in manuscript from then onward. This credited him with making voyages into the ocean to islands later identified as, in particular, the Fortunate Islands (the Canaries). About 1000, this was followed by the "Navigatio," a fine tale of his voyages to the ultimate western limits of the known world. The lands Brendan was supposed to have visited have been identified in modern times as the Faröes, Iceland and America; and in the 1970s Tim Severin made a successful attempt to cross to Newfoundland by the same route in a replica of an Irish ship of the period. Later charts placed St Brendan's Isle on varying parts of the northern Atlantic. No serious scholars now consider that Brendan did any of these things apart from probably cruising up the western Scottish islands; but Irish monks did reach Iceland well before the Norse invasion of the later 9th century.

THE LEGEND OF MADOC
The last legend to obtain widespread publicity was that of the Welsh Madoc (Madog ab Owain Gwynedd). Late medieval Welsh poets had characterized Madoc as a sea rover; but between 1578 and 1584, Queen Elizabeth's astrologer John Dee and the writer on exploration Richard Hakluyt resurrected this mythical figure and concocted a story that he had discovered America long before Columbus. At a time when Francis Drake and Walter Raleigh were staking a claim to North America, the story lent an air of legitimacy to English territorial ambitions. The authenticity of this claim was not finally exploded until the mid-19th century.

Throughout the late 14th and 15th centuries, sea charts (portolan charts) incorporated these and other legends. From 1424 a great rectangular island, named Antilia, far to the west, was equated with the mythical Seven Cities. Columbus himself believed in its existence, and was amazed he did not encounter it in 1492.

Above left: Several imaginary islands were located in the Atlantic by 15th-century cartographers. The Paris Map of c.1490 (redrawn) shows the Island of Brasil and the Seven Cities to the west of Ireland.
Above: Martin Behaim's 1492 globe (detail redrawn above) shows the rectangular island of Antilia midway between Europe and Japan (Cipangu).

THE NORSE SETTLEMENTS
Late in the 9th century, Norse adventurers discovered Iceland, and by AD 900 they had established a substantial colony there. It soon outgrew the island's limited resources. When Eirik the Red was temporarily exiled for a crime there, he sailed southward and westward and discovered Greenland in 983. The climate was milder than in modern times, and he returned to Iceland with tales of fine open lands. In 986 he succeeded in bringing out a colony there, founding the Eastern Settlement (Julianehåb). A little later the Western Settlement (Godthåb) developed, and soon thrived by exploiting the rich fishing and sea-mammal resources of the area, together with a limited range of grazing for livestock.

Bjarni Herjolfsson, on his way to Greenland in 985, had sighted further land to the west and south of Greenland, so that about 1000, Leif Eiriksson undertook a voyage from Eirik's home at Brattahlid in the Eastern Settlement. He traveled first to the northwest, finding a rocky land he called Helluland (Baffin Island), and farther south another he named Markland (Labrador) and finally a land (Newfoundland, or some other farther south) he called Vinland, where he wintered. All we have as a record of his voyage are the sagas, oral accounts which were not written until the 13th century. They state that Vinland was the residence of a sequence of would-be colonists from Eirik's extended family, some with women and children, over the next twenty years or so. They all moved back to Greenland or came to a tragic end, and if other settlements were

The Vikings in North America,
985- c.1020

Bjarni Herjolfsson, 985

Leif Eiriksson, c1000

Conjectural Norse voyages

Norse settlement

Godthåb (Western Settlement)

Julianehåb (Eastern Settlement)

GREENLAND

Davis Strait

Baffin Island

ARCTIC CIRCLE

HELLULAND

Hudson Strait

985
Bjarni Herjolfsson, blown off course from Greenland, sights land and follows coast

c.1000
Leif Eiriksson investigates Herjolffson's sightings. Founds settlement somewhere along coast

MARKLAND

DORSET

INUIT

LABRADOR

NORTHERN LIMIT OF TREES

L'Anse aux Meadows

Strait of Belle Isle

VINLAND

BEOTHUK

NEWFOUNDLAND

Gulf of St Lawrence

Prince Edward Island

ALGONQUIAN

Cape Cod

Atlantic Ocean

SOUTHERN LIMIT OF SALMON

N
E
S
W

Above: A
reconstruction of a
Viking ship of the 9th
century, based on the
Oseberg ship, found in
Norway in 1905. Leif
Eiriksson would
perhaps have made his
voyage in a similar
craft.

made they have not yet been located. By 1020, or a little later, the Vinland voyages were discontinued, except for occasional expeditions to Markland for timber.

The Vinland of the sagas cannot be identified as such. The grapes brought with their green branches by Leif in the spring sound unlikely. Finally, after much search, a Norse site was found at L'Anse aux Meadows, on the Newfoundland side of the Strait of Belle Isle. It was excavated between 1961 and 1968 by Anne Stine Ingstad and her husband, Helge, and subsequently by Parks Canada. The archaeologists found house sites which could have accommodated about 80 persons, evidence of iron-smelting and, more recently, indications of ships being repaired. The absence of cattle byres and of a substantial midden has called in question the wintering of cattle there and of over-winter residence by colonists, but Inuit looting of the site may well explain these anomalies.

There is little doubt that expeditions were made from the site to Prince Edward Island, possibly up the St Lawrence, and even the long haul to New England, where summer grapes can be freely found. Yet history and legend have not yet been wholly reconciled. The climate deteriorated, and after Greenland became subject to Norway in the late 13th century, the Norse outposts became more and more isolated. The Western Settlement succumbed to the advance of the Inuit, while the Eastern Settlement eventually .withered through isolation and attrition. By the time John Cabot coasted the area in 1497, the forgotten Norse settlements had dwindled away.

PORTUGUESE EXPLORATION

The second European venture to pave the way to the Americas was the Portuguese maritime exploration of the western Atlantic in the 15th century. First Madeira was discovered and colonized between 1419 and 1435. Then the far-flung chain of the Azores was found in three groups between 1427 and 1452, and all colonized by about 1460. The farthest of these islands, Flores, was 1000 miles west of Portugal. A vigorous fishery centered on Terceira led to many attempts to discover islands or mainland farther west, but no clear evidence that the Corte Réal family, which dominated the island, discovered land before Columbus has been found.

THE INFLUENCE OF MAP-MAKERS

Material, technical and academic developments in the 15th century not only improved the capacity of seamen to make long voyages, they also encouraged visionary theorists and

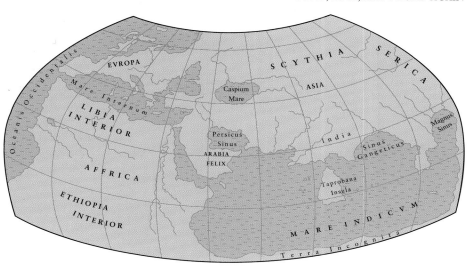

Above: The geographer Claudius Ptolemy produced his "Geographia" in Alexandria around AD150. In the early 15th century a Byzantine copy found its way to western Europe, where it was widely reproduced (the version redrawn above was printed in Ulm in 1486). It stimulated much discussion about what lay beyond the point where Asia runs off the edge off the map.

even practical sailors to make fresh calculations about the accessibility of distant parts of the globe. Asia was the subject of much speculation, even if it was Guinea gold which promoted most economically-motivated ventures in the 1470s and 1480s.

At the academic level, the circulation of Ptolemy's "Geographia" in manuscript, and later in print, set out a clear, if antiquated, picture of the world. The 2nd-century Alexandrian geographer's maps were sectionalized by a grid of latitude and longitude. Ptolemy thought there was an equal distribution of land and water eastward and westward round the globe; but his map of furthest Asia was obligingly left unterminated, which permitted those with interests in reaching out from Europe to the East by the Atlantic Ocean free reign for their theories. Pierre d'Ailly's "Imago Mundi" (c.1415) was also widely copied, and raised doubts in its readership about the potential distance westward of Asia from Europe. It, too, circulated widely in print during the 1470s.

The third influence was the vivid narrative of Marco Polo on eastern Asia (Cathay in particular) in the late 13th century, which also circulated in manuscript and was printed shortly after 1480. He gave the impression that Cipangu (Japan) was 1500 miles to the east of Quinsay (Hangchou) and so a milestone on the way to Europe, even though conservative academic theory correctly placed Cathay at least 10,000 miles from Europe. It was on such material that Columbus, John Cabot and others such as the Florentine doctor Toscanelli, were to build theories which seemed to bring Asia much nearer to Europe than had ever been considered.

The influence of these works on Portuguese scholars and administrators, and probably even on a few seamen such as Columbus, was considerable. It contributed to the almost unending search, aided by trade in gold and slaves, for a sea route southward and then eastward to Asia, until the final turning of the southern tip of Africa by Dias in 1488.

THE REVOLUTION IN SHIPPING

Such feats could not have been accomplished without much improved shipping. During the 15th century there was a Europe-wide movement away from the round ship towards longer, narrower and higher vessels. In some respects the Portuguese led the way. Their adoption of light, narrow caravels powered by two, three or more lateen sails, enabled them to penetrate coastal inlets and to cover considerable distances at greater speed than hitherto. For longer voyages they built larger ships which combined the traditional mainmast with its great square sail with the lateen which added maneuverability to the driving power of the older types of sailing vessel. This type of ship, with local variations, was also being used in other parts of western Europe, including England, well before 1500.

Navigation also improved. To the compass was added the astrolabe (adapted from the astronomer's instrument), and the quadrant, which enabled noon sun-sights to be taken with some approach to accuracy in calm weather. These could be checked by the observation of the Pole Star (a routine known as "the Regiment of the North Star" was in

During the 15th century, the essentially Mediterranean round ship (top) gave way to more oceanworthy craft such as the carrack (above). In such vessels, the Portuguese reached out into the Atlantic as far as Madeira and the Azores.

vogue before the end of the century), and latitude tables were also beginning to appear. Speed could, in most cases, still only be calculated by expert observation by skilled navigators (though the log and line, with half-hour glasses, is thought to have been available before 1500).

But sailors still had no way of estimating the distance they had traveled from east to west except by dead reckoning: sailing along a specific latitude and roughly calculating their speed. Despite its limitations, the method enabled European sailors to reach the southern tip of Africa and to reach out into the Atlantic to discover the Caribbean islands and, eventually, America.

THE EARLY VOYAGES OF COLUMBUS

In 1574 Paolo Toscanelli of Florence wrote to an influential friend in Portugal to propose that the distance westwards from Europe to Asia was much less than had previously been proposed. He communicated this to King Manuel who had an expedition sent westward in 1474 to locate Antilia, at least, if not Cipangu. The expedition came back without result, but it paved the way for Christopher Columbus a few years later.

Columbus indeed may have had some ideas about exploration in the north or west before he left Genoa for Portugal or the north in 1476. After being shipwrecked in southern Portugal he was picked up by a Genoese fleet and brought to England early in 1477.

The English had been the pioneer venturers into the northwest Atlantic, both for fishing and trading off Iceland, since before 1400. Bristol had joined east coast ports in trading in air-dried cod (*bacalhau*) and train oil, for English foodstuffs and cloth, from 1424 onwards. Columbus made his way to Bristol, where he joined a ship bound for Iceland. If one is to believe his own muddled account given near the end of his life, he must have transfered to a fishing vessel to round the westward end of Iceland and sail some way along the north coast, finding the water open but being warned of long months of icebound waters. If Columbus had any notion of exploring over the North Pole it was ended then. He returned by way of Galway, where he saw two strange bodies cast up by waves in the remains of a boat, which he afterwards decided were orientals from Cathay.

By 1479 at the latest, Columbus was back in Portugal and had settled in Lisbon. He then moved to the Madeiras, and took part in at least one voyage to West Africa. But he was also learning navigation and studying books and manuscripts relevant to westward exploration. By 1481 he had learned about the

Toscanelli letter. He wrote direct to its author and when he may have received an encouraging reply, prepared his grand design of sailing westward to Asia.

BRISTOL MARINERS

Meanwhile in England, Bristol merchants, frustrated in the Iceland trade by Danish competition, were searching for new fishing grounds. If, as seems highly probable, Columbus used Bristol vessels to make his first voyage of exploration to Iceland in 1477, it is probable that he also conveyed to them up-to-date portolan sea charts, which showed many islands in the Western Ocean. We know that the Bristol merchants had such charts by 1480 at the latest. In that year, Thomas Lloyd set out to search for the Isle of Brasil, which was, confusingly, shown twice on some charts, one version close to Kerry, the other far in the west.

Lloyd failed to find the island, and had to put back to Ireland. He was probably the agent of a syndicate which had received permission from Edward IV to make unusual voyages into the ocean. One member of this group was Thomas Croft. As collector of customs in Bristol, he was not allowed to trade. The government commissioners suspected him of breaking this prohibition and, on 24 September 1481, they questioned him about his activities. He was alleged to have owned shares (one-eighth) in two ships which sailed earlier in that year, and to have supplied salt towards their lading. His defense (which was accepted) was that the *George* and the *Trinity* had gone to " 'search' and find the Isle of Brasile" and were not engaged in trading. The phrase, the only reference we have, is ambiguous, but it could mean that land across the ocean was at least sighted. If so, this could have been Newfoundland.

As we do not have any evidence of further Bristol maritime activity in the Atlantic before 1490 or 1491, this vague suggestion that land was found has been treated with considerable scepticism. However, in 1955, the late L. A. Vigneras found in Spain a letter of December 1497 or January 1498 from the Bristol merchant, John Day, to Columbus. It gave a detailed account of John Cabot's successful voyage to eastern North America, adding the mysterious comment that they had found this land before "in times past" (*en otros tiempos*), "as your Lordship knows." This raised the question whether the 1481 expedition, or some intermediate voyage, had found land in the west, had indeed found land before 1492. This has been argued back and forward ever since. No conclusive evidence has yet appeared, but there is at least a possibility that Bristol may have been the starting point of a pre-Columbian discovery of America.

THE GRAND DESIGN

By 1484 Columbus had his grand design worked out. He had convinced himself that from the western Canary Islands he could reach Marco Polo's Cipangu (Japan) by a voyage of 2400 miles, which was within the capacity of sailing ships by this time. From there he believed he could reach Quinsay (Hangchou) after another voyage of 1150 miles. We now know these distances to be 10,600 and 11,766 miles respectively.

Columbus attempted to sell this scheme to John II of Portugal in 1484, but without success, and in 1486 he turned to Ferdinand and Isabella of Spain. They gave him some slight encouragement, but postponed their decision indefinitely. In 1488 Columbus returned to Portugal in time to observe the return of Bartholomew Dias from his triumphant rounding of southern Africa. This achievement irrevocably committed Portugal to planning ocean voyages round Africa to the eastern Indies, and led to a final rejection from Spain.

In despair of getting Iberian support for his project, Columbus sent a modified version to his brother Bartholomew, a cartographer in Lisbon, in the hope of selling the project to Henry VII of England. His plan was to construct a sea chart which would place the Island of the Seven Cities, not opposite Morocco or the Iberian lands as on other sea charts, but in the low 50s of north latitude opposite Ireland, approximately where Newfoundland was to be defined not so long after, and with a convenient stopping place in mid-Atlantic, named as the Isle of Brasil. Henry VII rejected the scheme in 1489; Bartholomew then attempted to sell the

project to France, but was again unsuccessful. He returned to England in 1492, where it appears (though evidence is far from conclusive) that Henry VII eventually accepted the plan. If Henry did so, he may have been influenced by the knowledge that from about 1490 Bristol ships were known to be making western voyages once more, either for exploration or trade.

Returning by way of France in 1493, Bartholomew learned that not only had his brother won the support of Spain at last, but had set out and returned with news of his discovery of the western Indies. Yet Bartholomew, on returning to Spain, was chagrined to learn that Christopher, now honoured as Admiral of the Ocean Sea, had already set out once again with a large fleet for the new islands and, it was expected, the Asiatic mainland.

Christopher Columbus had returned to Spain in 1490, only to learn the details of the long inquiry into his project which had ended unfavorably for him. He was, however, informed by the Queen that when the war with the Moors of the Kingdom of Granada was over he might apply again. This he did by appearing at court, then established outside the city of Granada, the last besieged remnant of the Moorish kingdom. After the fall of the city in January 1491 he was finally refused by King Ferdinand, but, through the intercession of an official, Isabella recalled him and at last agreed to his project in principle. In the enthusiasm of the conquest she felt generous enough to gamble.

Columbus made hard terms, demanding and obtaining the prospective title of admiral and governor of any lands he found, with a share of their revenues, together with the fitting out of his squadron by the crown. He had made maritime friends at Palos in 1486, so it was there that he went for his ships and

their crews. The Pinzon family furnished him with two small Portuguese-type caravels – the *Niña* and *Pinta* – and agreed to provide officers for them. A larger Galician ship – the *Santa Maria* – then in port at Palos, was hired. The three ships were fitted out for a long voyage.

They set out from Palos for the Canaries on 1 August 1492. Columbus believed that Antilia lay on the parallel of 28°N (which would have brought him to Florida), so he decided to sail down that latitude, setting out from Gomera on 6 September. He expected to reach Antilia after some 12 or 13 days' sailing, and expressed some surprise when he did not. On the 19th he said he was certain that to the north or south there were some islands, though they never appeared, but he sailed ahead on his westward course, with some minor variations, until 7 October (by which time his men were very restive), when, attracted by a flight of birds to the southwest, he changed course in that direction.

COLUMBUS'S FIRST LANDFALL

On the night of 11 October, lookouts reported what they regarded as clear signs of land ahead and the ships made a landfall at the island the natives called Guanahani on the 12th. They solemnly annexed it to the king and queen of Spain. Columbus believed that it lay off the coast of Cipangu (Japan) as it was close to his estimate of the distance of that country from the Canaries.

The land which Columbus reached on 12 October 1492 is generally reckoned to have been Watlings Island in the Bahamas. So firmly established has this attribution become that since 1926 the island has been called San Salvador, the name Columbus gave to his landfall. It formed the centerpiece of the 1992 quincentenary, but the attribution has not satisfied everyone. In scholarly circles, minute

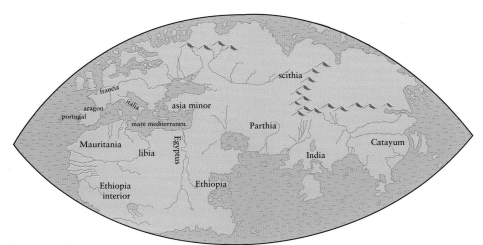

The 1457 Florence "Mappemonde" (redrawn left) anticipated Columbus's views on the proportions of the globe and the distance westwards from Europe to Asia. Such maps, which placed Asia much closer to Europe than had previously been thought, encouraged mariners such as Columbus and Cabot to seek a westward route to Cathay.

Martin Waldseemüller's globe of 1507 (redrawn right) correctly identified the lands found by Columbus, Cabot and Vespucci as part of one continent. From the first name – Amerigo – of the latter explorer, the German cartographer named the entire southern part of the landmass "America." The name stuck and by 1520 applied to North America also.

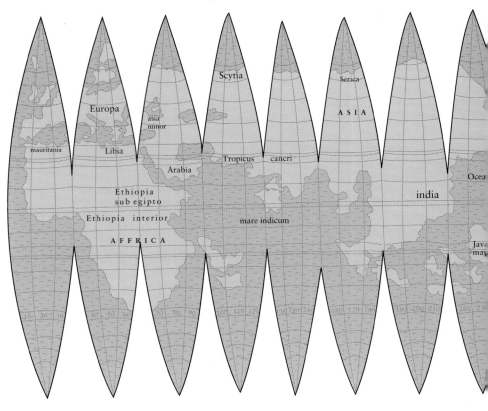

examination of the surviving materials on the voyage has produced a number of alternative landfalls, although none of them has ousted San Salvador from popular esteem. The closest studies, however, have concluded that while Columbus's first landfall was in the Bahamas, or not very far south of them, the evidence is insufficient to make an entirely positive identification with any particular island.

Columbus passed a further series of islands before making a crucial landfall on what he regarded as an outpost of Asia. He named the island Hispaniola. His opinion was confirmed by the discovery of the north coast of Cuba which must, in his view, be part of Asia itself. He turned back, ran the *Santa Maria* aground on the north of Hispaniola, and left her crew to set up the first Spanish colony in the West. They were never seen again.

Columbus was fortunate in his return voyage in the *Pinta*. When he entered Seville on 31 March 1493 he found he had to follow the Spanish sovereigns to Barcelona. There, on 20 April 1493, he presented his version of his discovery of the Indies, describing the Tainos (male and female) whom he had captured as "Indians." This letter to the king's treasurer, which he had sent ahead of him,

was printed for the information of courtiers and officials before the end of April. He was ennobled and regranted all and more of the privileges and powers which he obtained on paper at Granada. His sovereigns and he were soon to receive from Pope Alexander VI the Bull Inter Caetera confirming his "conquests" to Spain and enshrining for all time the description of the land and people as the "Indies" and the people as "Indians."

THE "NEW" AMERICAN CONTINENT

What was to follow was a more complex and very different story. Columbus died in 1506, still believing he had found Asia. But the events of 1492 and those which followed produced the most remarkable shift in European, and indeed world, perceptions of the layout of the globe; and in 1507 the American continent appeared as such on a German map.

In the year that Columbus set out, Ferdinand and Isabella had completed the reconquest of Spain from the Muslims. This, and the techniques of colonial administration developed in the Canary Islands between 1479 and 1492, enabled the Spanish to begin the exploitation of the new islands at once. A great expedition was dispatched to the

orientalis

America

Oceanus Occidental

260 270   280 290 300   310 320 330   340 350 360

Caribbean in 1493; the conquests of Mexico and Peru followed in 1521 and 1533. Within a few decades Spain had acquired a colonial empire that astounded 16th-century Europe, and helped to dominate large parts of it. It was not until the 17th century that Spain began to run out of impetus, and countries like England, France and the Netherlands were able to challenge its monopoly position in the New World.

All this was brought about at great cost to the peoples Columbus took to be "Indians." The complexity and sophistication of the indigenous societies was to be only slowly, in fact much too slowly, appreciated by the European intruders, and in much of North America, European interventions, far from bringing "civilization" to backward peoples, destroyed highly organized, if simply equipped, societies.

A three-masted ocean-going caravel of around 1480. The front and middle masts are square-rigged, while the rear carries a lateen sail. Columbus and Cabot's ships, the Santa Maria *and the* Matthew, *would have been very similar.*

Part I : A Continent on the Edge of the World

In search of a new route to the East, European seafarers were hindered and often confused by the unknown lands which stood in their way. At first these lands appeared disconnected, but by the second decade of the 16th century it was generally accepted that there existed a vast new continent, previously unsuspected and still shrouded by ignorance: North America. European explorers clung to their dream of finding a route to the riches of Cathay. Only gradually, as they searched the rivers, bays and frozen northern straits for a navigable route to the Pacific, and the Spaniards probed deep into the southern interior, did they begin to grasp the size of the continent they had stumbled upon.

While Cabot and the Corte-Réals skirted the coastlines of Newfoundland and Nova Scotia, Spanish exploration of the Caribbean north of Cuba led to the gradual appearance on the maps of the Florida peninsula. Between these two areas lay a huge gap of 1500 miles. This was bridged by Verrazano's expedition in 1524, which showed that the Atlantic coast of North America extended from Florida to Nova Scotia.

The more of the new shoreline was revealed, the more urgent to Europeans became the need to find a way through this barrier to the lands of the East. By the 1530s the Frenchwere searching for such a route in the region just beyond Verrazano's farthest north. Sailing into the St Lawrence River, Cartier reached a thousand miles into the continent, only to be informed by Indians that he was still three months' travel from the western ocean.

For the first time some comprehension emerged of the massive dimensions of the North American continent, and efforts grew to find a way around rather than through the great landmass. Repeated voyages to northern waters explored the complex maze of the Arctic archipelago. The endeavor was heroic as small sailing vessels battled, and failed, to find a way through its ice-choked channels.

To the south, the Spaniards had roughly charted the outline of the Gulf of Mexico. They now attempted to conquer the interior, launching a series of expeditions on a scale not to be repeated for another two centuries. Cabeza de Vaca covered a large area west of the Mississippi with a handful of companions. De Soto, with mailed soldiers and chained Indian bearers laid a bloody trail across 3000 miles of what is now the southern United States. Coronado led a great and ambitious expedition in search of fabulous cities which lay, according to a potent mix of legend, folklore and Indian information, somewhere north of Mexico. Spanish ships, meanwhile, set out from their Mexican ports to explore the west coast as far north as Oregon.

The amount of knowledge gained by the early European explorers was vast, but much of it was half-remembered, carelessly recorded, and distorted. Nowhere was this more so than in the response to the native peoples encountered. These had emerged in a bewildering variety of culture types, from the Inuit of the far north to the pueblo-dwellers of the upper Rio Grande. Although the nature of contact differed, collaboration was as usual as violence. At this stage settlement was not a preoccupation of the European newcomers, so a major cause of later tension rarely arose. The dominant European motives were the search for a route to the East through the continental barrier, and the hopes of finding gold and silver on the scale found by the Spaniards in Mexico and Peru. Neither route nor riches was found and an air of frustration and failure hangs over early European explorations.

The Country of the Grand Khan

THE VOYAGE OF JOHN CABOT, 1497

As Columbus explores the Caribbean and its shores, far to the north John Cabot seeks a different route to Asia.

Right: An ocean-going caravel of the same period and type as Cabot's ship, the Matthew. *A relief from Tiverton church, Devon, dated 1489.*

In 1496 the Spanish ambassador in London reported home that "uno como Colón" ("one like Columbus") was trying to interest the English king, Henry VII, in a voyage across the Atlantic. The seafarer was John Cabot, a Venetian who had settled in Bristol some time between 1493 and 1495. He sailed from Bristol in May 1497 in a single small vessel, the *Matthew*, and sighted land within a month. No maps or latitudes survive to identify his landfall, which may have been anywhere between southern Nova Scotia and northern Newfoundland; most scholars favor the midway point around Cape Breton. Cabot ventured inland only a bowshot's distance, and saw no inhabitants; but snares, a fire-site, and a painted stick convinced him that they were not far off.

Like Columbus, Cabot thought that he had reached Asia, the land of the Great Khan. The king's modest award of £10 was simply and more realistically, "to hym that founde the new Isle." A larger expedition set out the following year, but ended in disaster: one ship turned back, the other four vanished, and with them John Cabot. "He is believed," wrote a contemporary some years later, "to have found the new lands nowhere but on the very bottom of the ocean."

News of Cabot's discovery reached Portugal, where preparations were being made for voyages to the same region. In 1500, Gaspar Corte-Réal probably sighted the southern tip of Greenland at Cape Farewell. In 1501 he seems to have reached Labrador, Newfoundland, and possibly as far south as Maine. Gaspar and his ship were lost, but his brother Miguel, in another vessel, kidnapped 50 Micmac or Beothuk and sold them as slaves in Lisbon.

Further expeditions from Bristol are shrouded in even more obscurity. John Cabot's son Sebastian may have been involved; in 1505 he was rewarded by Henry VII for "the fyndinge of the newe founde landes." Three North American "savages" were presented to the English court in 1502. But the cod banks John Cabot had crossed in 1497 were soon attracting more interest (▶ *page 50*) than a mainland which, it was slowly being realized, was not a part of Asia.

All that is known about John Cabot's 1497 voyage comes from these two contemporary accounts.

That Venetian of ours who went with a small ship from Bristol to find new islands has come back and says he has discovered mainland 700 leagues away, which is the country of the Grand Khan, and that he coasted it for 300 leagues and landed and did not see any person; but he has brought here to the king [Henry VII] certain snares which, were spread to take game and a needle for making nets, and he found certain notched trees so that by this he judges there are inhabitants.

Letter from Lorenzo Pasqualigo, August 1497

He [John Cabot] landed at one spot of the mainland, near the place where land was first sighted... they found tall trees of the kind masts are made, and other smaller trees, and the country is very rich in grass... they found a trail that went inland, a site where a fire had been made, manure which they thought to be of farm animals, and a stick half a yard long pierced at both ends, carved and painted with brazil, and by such signs they believed the land to be inhabited. Since he was with just a few people, he did not dare advance inland beyond the shooting distance of a crossbow, and after taking fresh water he returned to his ship.

John Day's letter to the Grand Admiral (Christopher Columbus), 1497-98

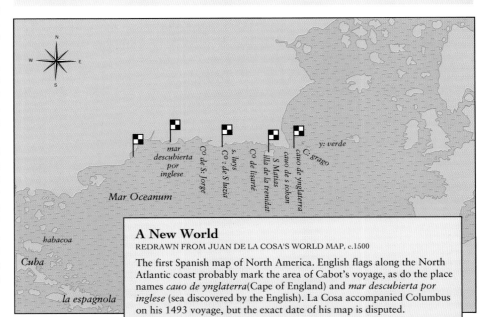

mar descubierta por inglese

Cº de S. Jorge

s. luys

Cº. de S lazia

Cº de lisarie

S Matias

Illa de la trenidat

cauo de s iohan

cauo de ynglaterra

y: verde

C. grago

Mar Oceanum

habacoa

Cuba

la espagnola

A New World

REDRAWN FROM JUAN DE LA COSA'S WORLD MAP, c.1500

The first Spanish map of North America. English flags along the North Atlantic coast probably mark the area of Cabot's voyage, as do the place names *cauo de ynglaterra*(Cape of England) and *mar descubierta por inglese* (sea discovered by the English). La Cosa accompanied Columbus on his 1493 voyage, but the exact date of his map is disputed.

1501
The Corte-Réals' three ships from Portugal meet "huge masses of solid snow floating upon the sea"

June 24 1497
Cabot sights land. He goes ashore nearby, and raises "the banners... of the Holy Father and the King of England"

July 20 1497
Cabot returns to England

"Following the shore [Cabot's crew] saw two forms running... but could not tell if they were human beings or animals"

"Cabot finds the sea "swarming with fish, which can be taken not only with the net, but in baskets let down with a stone""

2/ Spain in the New World, 1497

Spanish territory

Known to Europeans

Unknown to Europeans

Corte-Réal's men "made their way about a league inland, where... they found... pines of such measureless height and girth, that they would be too big as a mast for the largest ship." They kidnap 50 inhabitants

Gaspar Corte-Réal's vessel continues exploring southward. It is not seen again. The two other ships return to Portugal, where the captives are sold as slaves

1/John Cabot and the Corte-Réals 1497-1501

◀‑‑ Possible route of John Cabot, 1497

◀‑‑ Possible route of the Corte-Réals, 1501

Limit of spring ice

Cod banks

⚓ Landing

⚑ Formal act of possession

Kidnapping

ATLANTIC OCEAN

NEW

L A B R A D O R

P E N I N S U L A

NEWFOUNDLAND

BEOTHUK

Newfoundland Banks

NASKAPI

MONTAGNAIS

QUEBEC

HURON

ABENAKI

MALISEET

NEW BRUNSWICK

PASSAMAQUODDY

MICMAC

PRINCE EDWARD ISLAND

NOVA SCOTIA

PENNACOOK

PENOBSCOT

ME

They Named It La Florida

PONCE DE LEÓN TO AYLLÓN, 1513-26

The Spanish explore the Florida coast and found their first, short-lived settlement on the North American mainland.

In the two decades that followed Columbus's first voyage, the Spanish strengthened their hold on Hispaniola and conquered and settled Cuba, Puerto Rico and Jamaica. To the north, near Cuba and the homeward track of Spanish ships, lay further undiscovered lands, and, from 1502, the projecting snout of the Florida peninsula began to appear on maps.

In 1512, Juan Ponce de León, the conqueror of Puerto Rico who had sailed with Columbus on his second voyage, was granted a royal licence "to discover and settle the island of Bimini," one of the "marvelous countries" to the north. In 1513 León set sail from Puerto Rico and landed on the east coast of the peninsula. It was Easter Week – "Pasqua Florida" – and the name soon became attached to an area of the southeast considerably larger than the modern state of Florida.

The inhabitants of the region attacked the Spanish, wounding two of them. The expedition then sailed south against the Gulf Stream, which bore against them so strongly as they rounded Cape Canaveral, that León named the spit *Cabo de las Corrientes*.

> Of the 500 men who set off on this mission, only 150 returned. Oh Captains, you who preach of those lands you are going to settle or to attack and destroy, preaching conversion and baptism, destroying the land wherein you go and the natives with it, taking the Christians, who were deceived and misled by the promises you gave them, to their deaths... May God forgive you!
>
> from Oviedo's *History of the Indies*, 1535

Skirting the Florida keys, León finally landed on the west coast at a natural harbor he called San Carlos Bay – almost certainly Charlotte Harbor or Tampa Bay. Here too the inhabitants attacked, launching fleets of canoes against the Spanish ships.

The expedition then returned to Puerto Rico. León had traced the southeast corner of the North American mainland, although he may not have realized it; in 1521 he wrote to the king of Spain that he had discovered "the island of Florida and others in its district." He returned to San Carlos Bay that year with a colonizing venture of 250 men, but was driven off by the fierce resistance of the inhabitants and died of his wounds a few days later.

But another colonizing expedition was already under way, sponsored by Lucas Vásquez de Ayllón, a judge on Hispaniola. The expedition's commander, Francisco Gordillo, teamed up with the slave-hunter

Above: A suit of armor of the type worn by the early Spanish conquistadors. The kettle hat, bevor (chin plate) and leg-guards are Spanish, the breast and back plates German.

Pedro de Quexos, and landed around Winyah Bay. They explored the region, took formal possession of it for Spain and, disobeying Ayllón's orders, enslaved 50 native people.

One of them, baptized Francisco de Chicora, accompanied Ayllón to Spain, and gave glowing descriptions of his homeland. Ayllón was granted a licence to settle between the latitudes 35°N and 37°N, and in 1526 left Hispaniola with six vessels and 500 men, women and children, including a number of African slaves. The ships reached the area of Winyah Bay before turning south to find a more promising site, probably at the mouth of the Savannah River. Here Ayllón founded San Miguel de Gualdape, the first Spanish municipality in North America. But the settlement came under repeated attack from the native people of the region, the slaves revolted, and the settlers were racked by hunger and disease. Ayllón died of fever, the survivors returned to Hispaniola, and the east coast of Florida was left to its inhabitants for another 40 years. Only the maps recorded the ambitions of these frustrated conquistadors.

The Florida Peninsula
REDRAWN FROM JUAN VESPUCCI'S WORLD MAP, 1526

For the first time, Florida is shown correctly as a peninsula, not an island as had previously been thought. The coast on either side is also mapped in detail, and *Trá. nueva de Ayllón* (New land of Ayllón) marked with a Spanish flag. From there, no further land is shown until *Trá. de los bacallaos* (Land of Cod, or Newfoundland).

Trá de los bacallaos

Trá nueva de Ayllón

R: Jordán

C: de sáta elena

baya de sa maria

Rio de sa terazanos

Trá Floryda

Cuba

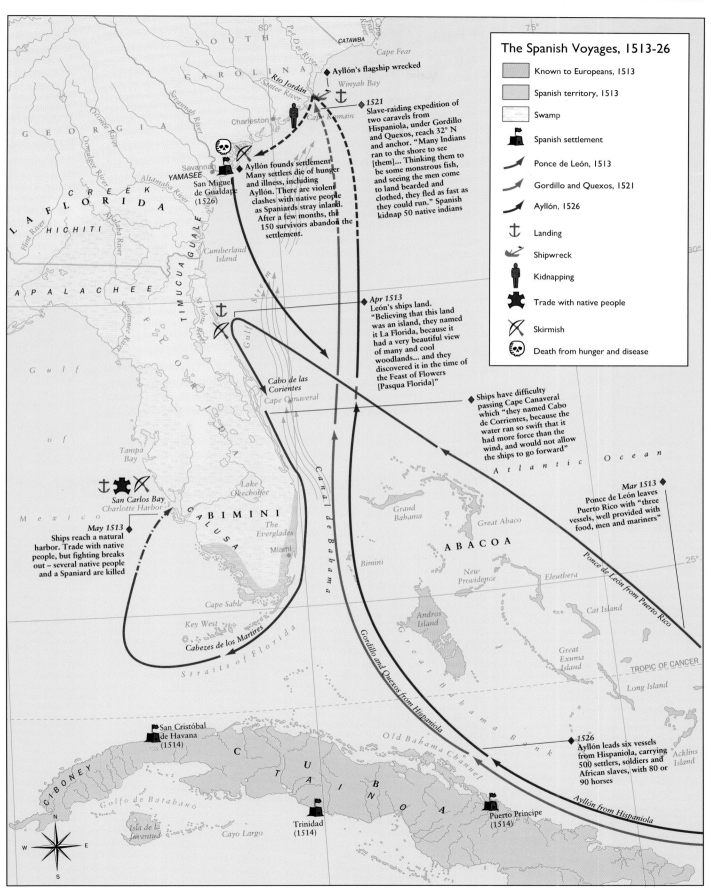

The Spanish Voyages, 1513-26

	Known to Europeans, 1513
	Spanish territory, 1513
	Swamp
	Spanish settlement
	Ponce de León, 1513
	Gordillo and Quexos, 1521
	Ayllón, 1526
	Landing
	Shipwreck
	Kidnapping
	Trade with native people
	Skirmish
	Death from hunger and disease

Ayllón's flagship wrecked

1521
Slave-raiding expedition of two caravels from Hispaniola, under Gordillo and Quexos, reach 32° N and anchor. "Many Indians ran to the shore to see [them]... Thinking them to be some monstrous fish, and seeing the men come to land bearded and clothed, they fled as fast as they could run." Spanish kidnap 50 native indians

Ayllón founds settlement. Many settlers die of hunger and illness, including Ayllón. There are violent clashes with native people as Spaniards stray inland. After a few months, the 150 survivors abandon the settlement.

San Miguel de Gualdape (1526)

Apr 1513
León's ships land. "Believing that this land was an island, they named it La Florida, because it had a very beautiful view of many and cool woodlands... and they discovered it in the time of the Feast of Flowers [Pasqua Florida]"

Ships have difficulty passing Cape Canaveral which "they named Cabo de Corrientes, because the water ran so swift that it had more force than the wind, and would not allow the ships to go forward"

Mar 1513
Ponce de León leaves Puerto Rico with "three vessels, well provided with food, men and mariners"

May 1513
Ships reach a natural harbor. Trade with native people, but fighting breaks out — several native people and a Spaniard are killed

San Carlos Bay
Charlotte Harbor

1526
Ayllón leads six vessels from Hispaniola, carrying 500 settlers, soldiers and African slaves, with 80 or 90 horses

Ponce de León from Puerto Rico
Gordillo and Quexos from Hispaniola
Ayllón from Hispaniola

San Cristóbal de Havana (1514)
Trinidad (1514)
Puerto Principe (1514)

CATAWBA
Cape Fear
Rio Jordán
Winyah Bay
Charleston
Cape Romain
SOUTH CAROLINA
GEORGIA
Savannah
YAMASEE
CREEK
LA FLORIDA
HICHITI
Cumberland Island
APALACHEE
TIMUCUA GUALE
Gulf Stream
Cabo de las Corientes
Cape Canaveral
Gulf of Mexico
Tampa Bay
BIMINI
CALUSA
Lake Okechobee
The Everglades
Miami
Cape Sable
Key West
Cabezes de los Martires
Straits of Florida
Grand Bahama
Great Abaco
ABACOA
Bimini
New Providence
Eleuthera
Andros Island
Atlantic Ocean
Cat Island
Great Exuma Island
TROPIC OF CANCER
Long Island
Acklins Island
Canal de Bahama
Great Bahama Bank
Old Bahama Channel
GIBONEY
CIBONEY
TAINO
Golfo de Batabanó
Isla de la Juventud
Cayo Largo

Pee Dee River
Santee River
Oconee River
Ocmulgee River
Altamaha River
Flint River
Savannah River
St Johns River
Suwannee River
Chatahoochee River
Apalachicola River
Cape Fear River

80°
75°
30°
25°

A New Land Never Seen Before

THE VOYAGE OF GIOVANNI DA VERRAZANO, 1524

In his search for the "eastern sea," the Italian navigator Giovanni da Verrazano traces the 1500-mile eastern coastline of North America.

Balboa's sighting of the Pacific from a peak in Darien in 1513 and Magellan's voyage of 1519-22, the first round the world, had established that America was a separate continent. Coastal explorers now began to seek a way through the landmass which blocked the way to the Pacific and Asia. Magellan had found one such route far to the south through the strait named after him, but a northern passage would be quicker. In 1524 Giovanni da Verrazano led a French expedition to the Atlantic coast of North America in hope of finding such a route.

Above: Probably Verrazano's ship, La Dauphine. *This 100-ton vessel of the French navy was built in Le Havre in 1519 and carried a crew of 50. Detail from Gerolamo da Verrazano's world map, 1529.*

Making his landfall probably somewhere to the south of Cape Fear, Verrazano sailed for about 150 miles along the coast of South Carolina before turning back north. His ship coasted along the Outer or Carolina Banks which enclose Pamlico and Albemarle sounds. From the masthead a wide expanse of water could be seen across the sandy spit of land with no hint of a farther shore. Probably

because of the shoal water he made no attempt to reach this "sea," but it was to appear in all its illusory glory on maps and globes of the period.

After keeping north, too far offshore to spot the entrances to Chesapeake and Delaware bays, Verrazano turned back towards the coast where he anchored near the Narrows of what became New York Bay, the first European to do so. But, with the wind blowing onshore, the expedition stayed there only a day. It was not until the ship reached Narragansett Bay, where it anchored in Newport Harbor, that Verrazano stayed long enough – 15 days – to see much of the country and its inhabitants. Men from the ship went some miles inland, and found wide clearings "adapted to every branch of cultivation – grain, wine, oil... of such fertility that a seed in them would produce the best crops." Verrazano's description of the inhabitants of this region – the Narragansett and Pokanoket – provide the earliest detailed account of the

Coasting south for 100 -150 miles, Verrazano looks in vain for harbor

Turning north, Verrazano makes first landing and meets people of Cape Fear

Mar 1 1524
Verrazano sights land: "There appeared a new land which had never been seen before by any man..."

Mar 25
Verrazano anchors. Waves topple member of his crew. Mainland inhabitants rescue him. From masthead, Verrazano thinks he can see "the eastern sea... which goes round the tip of India, China and Cathay"

Spending three days offshore, Verrazano calls region Arcadia because of its beauty. Kidnaps native child

Apr 17
Verrazano anchors near narrows, is greeted by friendly native peoples, and from a small boat probably sights river mouth

Apr 20 - May 5
Verrazano at anchor. "Makes friends" with native people. Travels 30 or 40 miles inland and finds fertile country "suitable for cultivation"

native peoples of the northeast.

Farther north, the Indians – probably Eastern Abenaki or Penobscot – were much warier, evidence perhaps of contact with European fishing vessels. Verrazano then sailed on past Cape Breton and Newfoundland before returning to France.

Verrazano's voyage was followed by a Spanish expedition in 1525 commanded by a Portuguese pilot, Estevão Gomes, who paid particular attention to the coast of southern New England, and by an English ship under John Rut which in 1527 ran down the Atlantic coast from north to south. What little is known of these voyages confirmed Verrazano's report that North America extended from Florida to Cape Breton without any obvious break in the coastline. Verrazano also realized that the new continent had potential of its own, but at the time this was overshadowed by the fact that it barred the way to the Pacific.

The people of Cape Fear "go completely naked except that around their loins they wear skins of small animals like martens, with a narrow belt of grass around the body, to which they tie various tails of other animals which hang down to the knees; the rest of the body is bare, and so is the head. Some of them wear garlands of birds' feathers. They are dark in color, not unlike the Ethiopians, with thin black hair, not very long, tied back behind the head like a small tail. As for the physique of these men, they are well proportioned, of medium height, a little taller than we are."

The Narragansett "are the most beautiful and have the most civil customs that we found on this voyage... we made great friends with them... When we were lying at anchor one league out to sea because of unfavourable weather, they came out to the ship with a great number of their boats; they had painted and decorated their faces with various colors, showing us that it was a sign of happiness. They brought us some of their food, and showed us by signs where we should anchor in the port for the ship's safety, and accompanied us all the way until we dropped anchor."

Two extracts from Verrazano's letter to
King Francis I of France, 1524

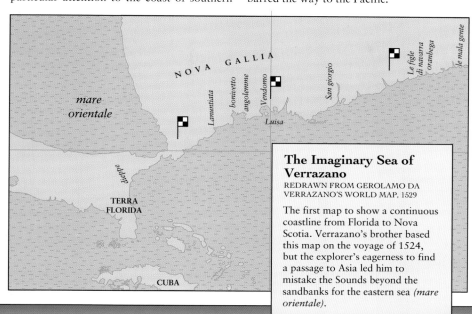

The Imaginary Sea of Verrazano

REDRAWN FROM GEROLAMO DA VERRAZANO'S WORLD MAP, 1529

The first map to show a continuous coastline from Florida to Nova Scotia. Verrazano's brother based this map on the voyage of 1524, but the explorer's eagerness to find a passage to Asia led him to mistake the Sounds beyond the sandbanks for the eastern sea (*mare orientale*).

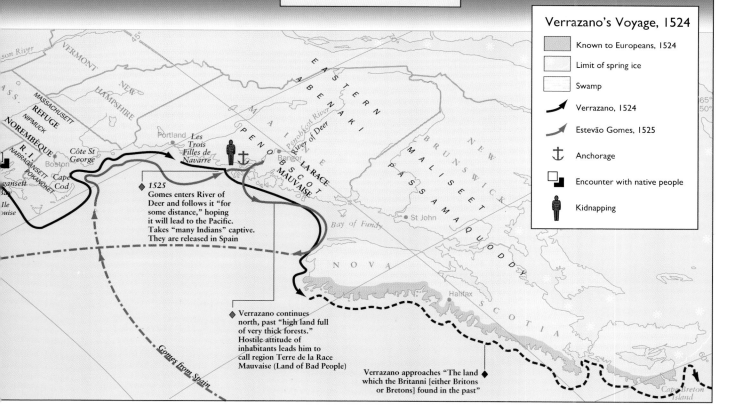

Verrazano's Voyage, 1524

- Known to Europeans, 1524
- Limit of spring ice
- Swamp
- Verrazano, 1524
- Estevão Gomes, 1525
- Anchorage
- Encounter with native people
- Kidnapping

1525
Gomes enters River of Deer and follows it "for some distance," hoping it will lead to the Pacific. Takes "many Indians" captive. They are released in Spain

Verrazano continues north, past "high land full of very thick forests." Hostile attitude of inhabitants leads him to call region Terre de la Race Mauvaise (Land of Bad People)

Verrazano approaches "The land which the Britanni [either Britons or Bretons] found in the past"

St Lawrence, the River of Canada

THE EXPLORATIONS OF JACQUES CARTIER, 1534-36

The Breton seafarer Jacques Cartier finds one of North America's great rivers and travels a thousand miles into the interior of the continent.

Verrazano had shown that the lands discovered by Cabot and the Spanish were linked by a continuous coastline, but explorers did not give up hope of finding a westward passage further north. One possibility was an opening known to French fishermen in Newfoundland-Labrador waters as the "Baye des Chasteaux" (the Strait of Belle Isle).

Cartier left St-Malo in 1534 with two ships and a commission from King Francis I to investigate the area. Ice floes made the going difficult, but they entered the strait and landed on its northern shore. The region was so desolate that Cartier dismissed it as "the land God gave to Cain." He continued in a clockwise course around what seemed to be a great inland sea, missing the entrance to the St Lawrence River. On the Gaspé Peninsula he met 300 Iroquois from the St Lawrence valley, and took two of them back to France, together with descriptions of birch-bark canoes, and the first recorded references to fur trading.

Cartier returned the following year with three ships. On the northern shore, Cartier named a bay after St Laurens on that saint's day, August 10. The name would soon apply to the whole gulf and eventually to the river, which he discovered and entered on this journey. He took his ships to the spot on the river's north shore where the Iroquois village of Stadacona huddled underneath the great rock ramparts where Québec would later be built. From there Cartier followed the river farther west, in the last stages by boat, until he reached the fortified Iroquois village of Hochelaga, with its long-houses sheltering as many as a thousand inhabitants. From a nearby hill, Mont Réal (the future Montréal), Cartier could see the Laurentian Highlands to the north, the Adirondacks to the south, and in between "the most beautiful land, arable, smooth and plain." Unable to pass the Lachine Rapids, Cartier retraced his route and wintered near Stadacona, where his men suffered from scurvy and the intense cold. When the ice broke up in the spring, the expedition left the gulf through a new southern route, later named Cabot Strait after an explorer who never set eyes on it.

In 1541 Cartier returned with an advance guard of settlers, but after enduring another winter near Stadacona and failing to get his boats through the rapids above Hochelaga, he returned to France. In 1543 the last settlers were evacuated.

Cartier had staked France's claim to a huge expanse of North America far removed from Spanish activities. His findings became an established feature on European maps, as did the names he gave them: New France, the St Lawrence and, most prophetically, the Iroquois name which Cartier had heard in 1535 on his second voyage, then refering simply to the region farther west along the great river – Canada.

From the middle of November until the fifteenth of April we lay frozen up in the ice, which was more than two fathoms in thickness, while on shore there were more than four feet of snow, so that it was higher than the bulwarks of our ships... All our beverages froze in their casks... and the whole river was frozen where the water was fresh up to beyond Hochelaga.

Winter on the St Lawrence, from the journal of Cartier's second voyage

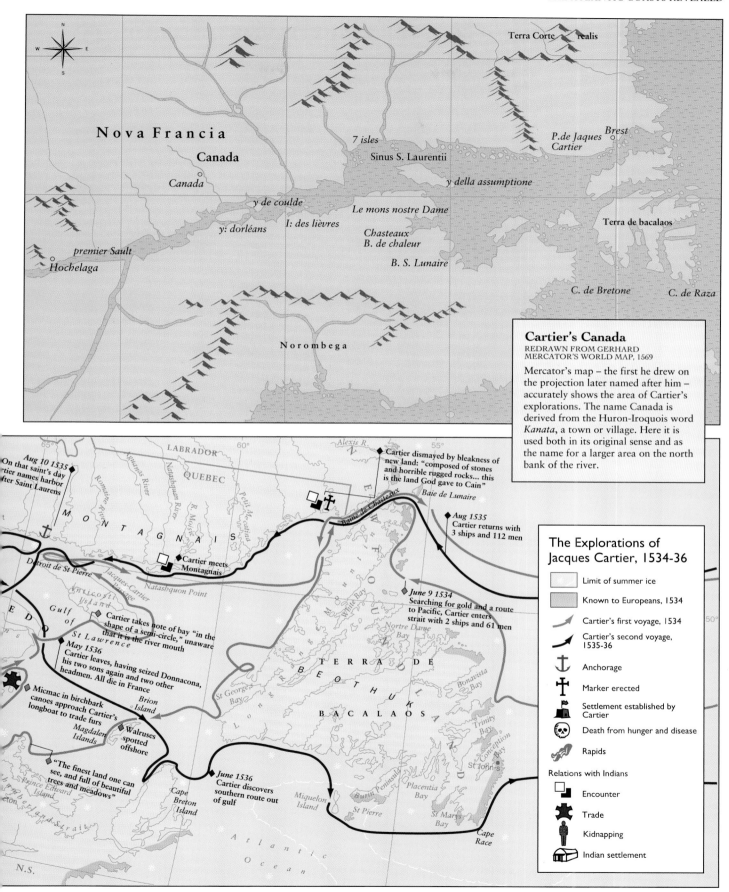

Nova Francia

Canada

Canada

y de coulde

y: dorléans   I: des lièvres

premier Sault
Hochelaga

7 isles

Sinus S. Laurentii

y della assumptione

Le mons nostre Dame

Chasteaux
B. de chaleur

B. S. Lunaire

Norombega

Terra Corte realis

P. de Jaques   Brest
Cartier

Terra de bacalaos

C. de Bretone   C. de Raza

Cartier's Canada

REDRAWN FROM GERHARD
MERCATOR'S WORLD MAP, 1569

Mercator's map – the first he drew on
the projection later named after him –
accurately shows the area of Cartier's
explorations. The name Canada is
derived from the Huron-Iroquois word
Kanata, a town or village. Here it is
used both in its original sense and as
the name for a larger area on the north
bank of the river.

LABRADOR
QUEBEC

Alexis R.

Aug 10 1535
On that saint's day
Cartier names harbor
after Saint Laurens

Cartier dismayed by bleakness of
new land: "composed of stones
and horrible rugged rocks... this
is the land God gave to Cain"

Baie de Lunaire

Aug 1535
Cartier returns with
3 ships and 112 men

M O N T A G N A I S

Detroit de St Pierre

Cartier meets
Montagnais

Natashquon Point

June 9 1534
Searching for gold and a route
to Pacific, Cartier enters
strait with 2 ships and 61 men

Anticosti
Island

Gulf of
St Lawrence

Cartier takes note of bay "in the
shape of a semi-circle," unaware
that it is the river mouth

Nortre
Dame
Bay

May 1536
Cartier leaves, having seized Donnacona,
his two sons again and two other
headmen. All die in France

Brion
Island

St Georges
Bay

T E R R A   D E

B E O T H U K A

Bonavista
Bay

Micmac in birchbark
canoes approach Cartier's
longboat to trade furs

Magdalen
Islands

Walruses
spotted
offshore

B A C A L A O S A

Trinity
Bay

Conception
Bay

St John's

"The finest land one can
see, and full of beautiful
trees and meadows"

Prince Edward
Island

Cape
Breton
Island

June 1536
Cartier discovers
southern route
out of gulf

Miquelon
Island

St Pierre

Burin
Peninsula

Placentia
Bay

St Marys
Bay

Cape
Race

Cumberland Strait

N.S.

Atlantic
Ocean

The Explorations of
Jacques Cartier, 1534-36

Limit of summer ice

Known to Europeans, 1534

Cartier's first voyage, 1534

Cartier's second voyage,
1535-36

Anchorage

Marker erected

Settlement established by
Cartier

Death from hunger and disease

Rapids

Relations with Indians

Encounter

Trade

Kidnapping

Indian settlement

First Searches for a Northwest Passage

THE VOYAGES OF FROBISHER AND DAVIS, 1576-87

English adventurers place the great opening of Davis Strait on the map and bring back the first descriptions of Baffin Island. The existence of the Hudson Strait eludes them.

All attempts to find an opening in the eastern coastline had failed, leading explorers to look for a navigable route to the north, around the continent. This was probably an objective of the Corte-Réals' voyages in the early 16th century (▶ *page 20*) and there is evidence that in 1508 and 1509 John Cabot's son, Sebastian, may have ventured as far as what is now known as the Hudson Strait. But it was another 70 years before London's financial, court and mercantile circles became interested in the route which the English called the Northwest Passage.

In 1576 Martin Frobisher set out northwest in the tiny ship *Gabriel* with a crew of 18. After battling with tremendous seas off Greenland, he reached the southeast coast of Baffin Island, where he found an opening which seemed to divide "two maynelands or continents asunder." The strong tides led Frobisher to believe that this was "the West Sea, whereby to pass to Cathay." Back in England, interest in this prospect faded when news circulated that ore picked up by Frobisher's men contained gold.

Frobisher's expeditions of 1577 and 1578 were therefore directed more towards mining than exploration. In 1578 Frobisher's 15 ships, facing fog and snow, in error entered an

opening to the south. This was the opening to the great waterway of the Canadian north but after 20 days Frobisher turned back, ruefully naming Hudson Strait "Mistaken Strait." Nor was the expedition's mining successful for the minerals they found proved to be iron pyrites or "fool's gold." The Company of Cathay, which had promoted the enterprise, collapsed amid financial loss and mutual recrimination.

The next decade saw three more voyages, under the master mariner John Davis. In 1585 Davis found Cumberland Sound, a mighty opening which he thought might lead to the Pacific. On his return he insisted that "The northwest passage is a matter nothing

doubtful, but at any tyme almost to be passed, the sea navigable, void of use, the air tolerable, and the waters very deep."

During his next voyage, in 1586, Davis explored the west coast of Greenland, crossed the strait which would bear his name to Baffin Island, and worked later his way south to the Labrador coast. On his final voyage, Davis explored Cumberland Sound to its head. He then failed to identify Frobisher Bay, naming it Lord Lumley's Inlet, and to the south crossed "a very great gulfe." This was the entrance of Hudson Strait, but it was yet again to be ignored.

Passage to the Pacific
REDRAWN FROM MICHAEL LOK'S MAP OF THE NORTHERN HEMISPHERE, 1582

This map (*right*) reflects European hopes of finding a sea passage through the North American landmass to Asia. It shows Verrazano's imaginary sea (▶ *page 23*), and interprets Frobisher Bay as a strait leading to the Pacific between Queen Elizabeth's Foreland (R. ELIZABETH) and Lok's Land (LOK). The mapmaker was one of Frobisher's sponsors, and the explorer duly named an island after him.

They are men of a large corporature and good proportion: their colour is not much unlike the Sunne burnte Countrie man... They weare their haire somethinge long and cut before, either with stone or knife, very disorderly... They eate their meate all rawe, both fleshe, fishe, and foule, or something perboyled with bloud & a little water, whiche they drinke. For lacke of water, they will eate yce, that is hard frosen, as pleasantly as we doe Sugar Candie.

Description of Baffin Island Inuit on Frobisher's second voyage

Left: On Frobisher's 1577 journey, fighting broke out between his men and the Inuit at Bloody Point in Frobisher Bay. The scene was captured by the artist John White, who may have been an eye-witness. His painting accurately shows the clothes, kayaks and skin tents of the Inuit.

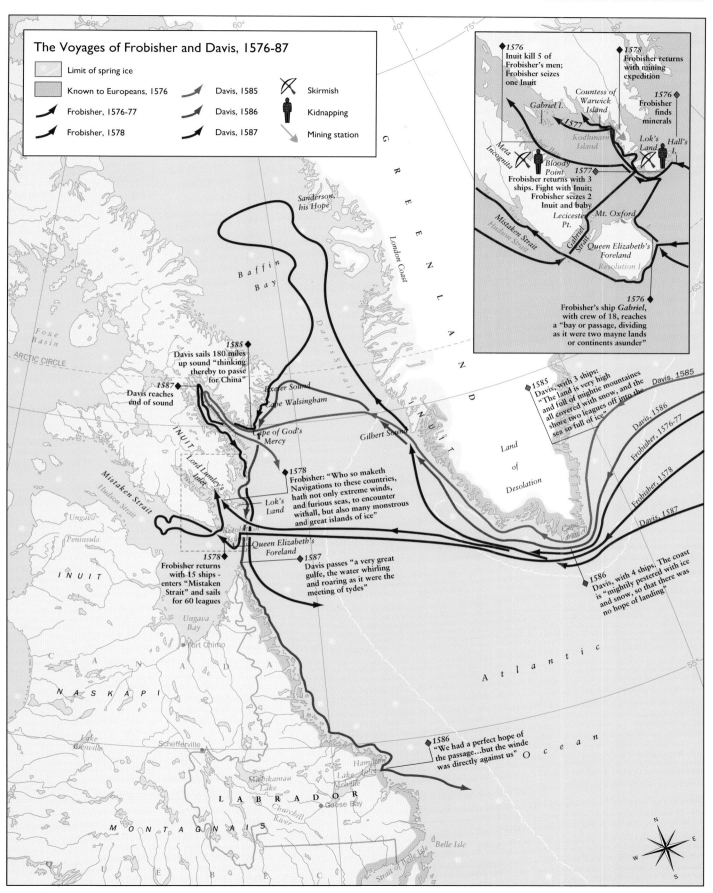

The Voyages of Frobisher and Davis, 1576-87

- Limit of spring ice
- Known to Europeans, 1576
- Frobisher, 1576-77
- Frobisher, 1578
- Davis, 1585
- Davis, 1586
- Davis, 1587
- Skirmish
- Kidnapping
- Mining station

1576 Inuit kill 5 of Frobisher's men; Frobisher seizes one Inuit

1578 Frobisher returns with mining expedition

1576 Frobisher finds minerals

1577 Frobisher returns with 3 ships. Fight with Inuit; Frobisher seizes 2 Inuit and baby

1576 Frobisher's ship *Gabriel*, with crew of 18, reaches a "bay or passage, dividing as it were two mayne lands or continents asunder"

Countess of Warwick Island

Gabriel I.

Kodlunarn Island

Lok's Land

Hall's I.

Meta Incognita

Bloody Point

Lecicester Pt.

Mt. Oxford

Mistaken Strait / Hudson Strait

Gabriel Strait

Queen Elizabeth's Foreland

Resolution I.

G R E E N L A N D

London Coast

Sanderson, his Hope

Baffin Bay

Davis Strait

Foxe Basin

ARCTIC CIRCLE

Baffin

1585 Davis sails 180 miles up sound "thinking thereby to passe for China"

1587 Davis reaches end of sound

Exeter Sound

Cape Walsingham

Cape of God's Mercy

Gilbert Sound

INUIT

1585 Davis, with 3 ships: "The land is very high and full of mightie mountaines all covered with snow, and the shore two leagues off into the sea so full of ice"

Land of Desolation

Davis, 1585

Davis, 1586

Frobisher, 1576-77

Frobisher, 1578

Davis, 1587

1578 Frobisher: "Who so maketh Navigations to these countries, hath not only extreme winds, and furious seas, to encounter withall, but also many monstrous and great islands of ice"

Lok's Land

"Lord Lumley's Inlet" / Frobisher Bay

Mistaken Strait / Hudson Strait

Ungava Peninsula

INUIT

Queen Elizabeth's Foreland

1578 Frobisher returns with 15 ships - enters "Mistaken Strait" and sails for 60 leagues

1587 Davis passes "a very great gulfe, the water whirling and roaring as it were the meeting of tydes"

1586 Davis, with 4 ships, The coast is "mightily pestered with ice and snow, so that there was no hope of landing"

Ungava Bay

Fort Chimo

C A N A D A

N A S K A P I

Lake Bienville

Scheffervillle

Michikamau Lake

Lake Melville

Hamilton Inlet

1586 "We had a perfect hope of the passage...but the winde was directly against us"

Atlantic Ocean

L A B R A D O R

Goose Bay

Churchill River

M O N T A G N A I S

Q U E B E C

Belle Isle

Strait of Belle Isle

The Great Bays of the North

THE VOYAGES OF HUDSON AND BAFFIN, 1610-16

*The English explore Atctic waters in search
of a Northwest Passage to Asia. They find no
passage but become skilled in the art and
science of navigating these dangerous waters.*

At the turn of the 17th century the route to
Asia lay around the Cape of Good Hope and
was dominated by the Portuguese and the
Dutch. In 1602, in search of a new route to
Asia, the East India Company of London
organized and financed a voyage to the
northwest by George Waymouth. Neither
Waymouth nor his immediate successors
made any real progress.

In 1609 Henry Hudson explored what was
to become the Hudson River. Then in 1610 he
set out on a new and dramatic voyage. Early
in August he arrived at the great bay that
would also take his name and was described
by one of his crew as "a spacious sea." Hudson wintered in the south at today's James
Bay. The following summer his crew mutinied
and Hudson was cast adrift, along with his
son and seven crew members. They all died.

A new company was set up in search of the
supposed new route to Asia, "The Governor
and Company of the Merchants of London,
Dicoverers of the North-West Passage."
Almost 300 investors sponsored, among
others, the voyages of Thomas Button, 1612-
13 and William Baffin in 1616. Button
explored 600 miles of the unknown west and

*Baffin's own chart from his logbook, of his journey
through Hudson Strait in 1615. The red dotted line
shows his route; the flags mark his landings; while the
coasts outlined in green are those he saw himself.*

north shores of Hudson Bay, including the
estuaries of the Churchill and Port Nelson
rivers, later important in the European fur
trade. He found no sign of a passage west; nor
did Robert Bylot, a survivor of Hudson's final
voyage, who was sent out in 1615 with Baffin
as his pilot.

The search shifted farther north. In 1616
Bylot and Baffin sailed again, pushing
through heavy ice in Davis Strait to open
water, the "North Water" of Baffin Bay as

whalers later knew it. At their farthest north
they reached Smith Sound, not entered until
the mid-19th century, and on the west side of
Baffin Bay "another great Sound," which
Baffin named Lancaster Sound. In the 19th
century it proved to be the entrance to the
Northwest Passage, but Baffin noted a "ledge
of ice" along the coast, and later that "there is
no passage in the north of Davis Straights."

The search was virtually over. In 1619-20
Jens Munk led a Danish expedition but when
he wintered at Churchill River only three men
survived. There were further English attempts
by Luke Foxe in 1631 and Thomas James,
1631-32.

Off the shore of Hudson Bay, east of Port
Nelson, Foxe and James actually met. A disagreement occurred over protocol. Foxe
wrote: "I did not thinke much for his keeping
out his flagg... To this was replide, that hee
was going to the Emperour of Japon, with
letters from his Majestie...'Keep it up then',
quoth I, 'but you are out of the way to Japon,
for this is not it'."

All their searches for a strait to the Pacific
from Hudson Bay were futile and their
voyages provided little new geographical
information. But a tradition of English Arctic
navigation was established. English explorers
had learned how to deal with problems of
navigating through ice, compass variations
and the phenomenal rise and fall of the tides.
These skills would prove profitable in future
days, as the great trade of cod, whales and
furs developed in northern waters.

*Left: Munk's expedition at Churchill, where most of
his crew died of scurvy on board the ships. "As I could
not now any more stand the bad smell and stench from
the dead bodies," Munk wrote, "I spent that night on
deck, using the clothes of the dead." Woodcut taken
from Munk's 1624 account of his voyage.*

I n the evening, we were inclosed amongst
great pieces; as high as our Poope, and
some of the sharpe blue corners of them did
reach quite under us. All these great
pices...did heave and set, and so beat us
that it was wonderful how the ship could
indure one blow of it.

Thomas James, 1631

1616 *Midsummer Day*
Baffin/Bylot 1616 Baffin
and Bylot in lat. 74°30'N., -
"our shrowds roapes and sailes
were so frozen, that we could
scarce handle them"

1616
Baffin and Bylot in lat. 78°N.,
the farthest north attained by
any explorer until the 19th
century. Here "is the greatest
variation of the Compasse
of any part of the World known"

1616
Baffin/Bylot: "here our hope
of passage began to be lesse
every day ... for from this
Sound to the Southward wee
had a ledge of Ice between
the Shoare and us"

1631
Foxe at northernmost
point of his voyage

June 1610
Hudson enters strait

1615
"having dubbled the cape we
sawe the land trendinge round...
and very thick pestred with ice"

Aug 1610
Hudson at last reaches
"a spacious sea"

1612
Button first
explorer to traverse
this coast; names it
Hopes Checked

Hudson "made his course to
the south, thinking to cleere
himselfe of the ice that way:
but the more he strove the
worse he was, and the
more inclosed"

1619-20
Munk passes
the winter;
most of crew die

1612-13
Button takes
shelter for the
winter

1631
Foxe completes his exploration:
"now the further search of a
passage this way was
hopelesse"

June 23 1611
Crew mutinies and casts
Hudson and eight others
adrift

1631-32
James awaits thaw

Nov 1610 - *June* 1611
Hudson waits out the
winter; lone Indian
comes to trade furs

The Voyages of Hudson
and Baffin, 1610-16

- Known to Europeans, 1610
- Limit of spring ice
- Hudson, 1610
- Button, 1612-1613
- Baffin and Bylot, 1612-1616
- Munk, 1619
- Foxe, 1631
- James, 1631
- Winter camp
- Trading encounter
- Mutiny
- Deaths

Alone and Naked Among the Indians

THE WANDERINGS OF CABEZA DE VACA, 1528-36

Four survivors of a doomed army of conquistadors walk 1600 miles across North America and bring back reports of the land to the north of Spain's American possessions.

The conquest of Mexico by Hernan Cortés in 1519 had given the Spanish their first base on the American mainland. Cortés believed that the most promising area for expansion lay to the south and west; but rival conquistadors hoped to make their fortunes in the north. As early as 1519, Alonzo Alvaro de Pineda had coasted from Florida to Mexico, proving that they were parts of a continuous mainland. In 1528, Pánfilo de Narváez landed at Tampa Bay in Florida with an army of 400 men.

After allowing his ships to depart with only vague plans for a rendezvous, he led his army inland. They had brought little food, and as they ransacked the corn supplies of villages they found, the inhabitants became increasingly hostile. By the time the expedition reached the gulf, its numbers had been halved

> Throughout all this country we went naked, and as we were unaccustomed to being so, twice a year we cast our skins like serpents. The sun and air produced great sores on our breasts and shoulders, giving us sharp pain; and the large load we had... caused the cords to cut into our arms... The country is so broken and thickly set, that... thorns and shrubs tore our flesh wherever we went.
>
> Cabeza de Vaca, *La Relacion*, 1542

by illness and attack. The survivors built five ramshackle boats and tried to sail back along the coast to Mexico. Three of the boats sank, and two were driven ashore around Galveston Island, where the expedition disintegrated.

There were four survivors: Narváez's second-in-command, Alvar Núñez Cabeza de Vaca, a nobleman whose grandfather had conquered Gran Canaria; Captain Alfonso de Castillo; Andrés Dorantes; and Estevàn, a black slave from Morocco. In his account of his experiences, printed in 1542, Cabeza de Vaca recalled how "I was in this country nearly six years, alone among the Indians, and naked like them." The four were separated for a while, living among the tribes who eked out an existence in the harsh Texas coastlands. "The famine," de Vaca recalled, "is so great that they eat spiders and the eggs of ants, worms, lizards...the dung of deer...Were there stones in that land they would eat them."

In a state of semi-slavery, the three Spaniards and the Moroccan survived on their

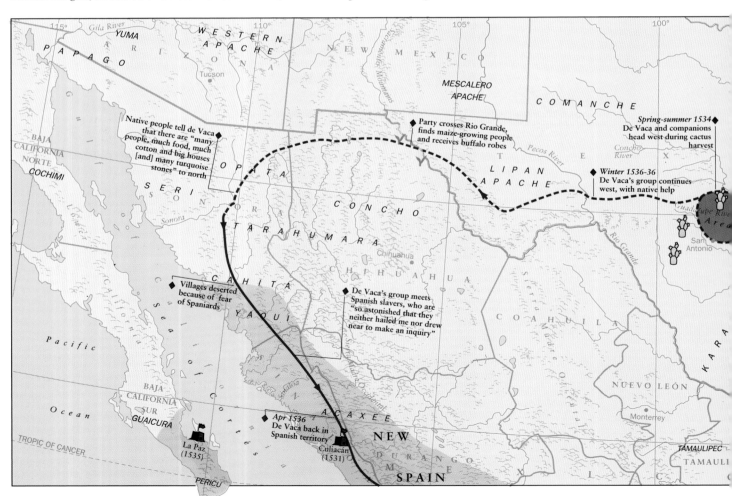

wits, their bartering skills and their willingness to learn. In 1534, they met up again, and decided to use the summer gathering of tribes at the annual cactus harvest to depart for Mexico. Their route was circuitous, and distances, directions and dates are understandably missing from de Vaca's account. But as they traveled across the (Texan) Colorado and Pecos rivers, the land became more fertile, and they found people living in "fixed dwellings." Using their rudimentary medical knowledge, they gained a reputation as faith-healers and were welcomed with great festivities wherever they went.

After crossing a "sterile and difficult" region to the Sonora valley, Cabeza de Vaca spotted an Indian wearing a Spanish horseshoe nail as an amulet. In the spring of 1536, the four travelers were picked up by Spanish slave raiders. By July they were in Mexico City, where they were questioned by Cortés and the viceroy, Antonio de Mendoza. Their reports stressed the factors that had dominated their eight years of survival: the country and its food supplies, the Indians, the hardships. They had seen the importance of cactus fruit and heard about buffalo herds

and "populous towns and very large houses." It was not much, but it encouraged the view that the next stage of expansion should be northward.

Cabeza de Vaca, meanwhile, went on to lead a 1000-mile walk across Brazil in 1540. His experiences had given him an understanding of the culture and values of the native people rare among his European contemporaries. The slave-raiders who found him told the Indians that "we were persons of mean condition and small force. The Indians... said [they] lied: that we healed the sick, they killed the sound; that we had come naked and barefoot, while they had arrived in clothing and on horses with lances; that we were not covetous of anything...[while] the others had the only purpose to rob whomsoever they found."

Right: The prickly pear (Opuntia ficus indica) was an essential source of food for the tribes of southern Texas. "The happiest part of the year," de Vaca wrote, "is the season of eating prickly pears; they have hunger then no longer, pass all the time in dancing, and eat day and night. While these last, they... set them to dry, and... put [them] in hampers like figs. These they kept to eat on the way back." An engraving of 1641 by J. T. de Bry.

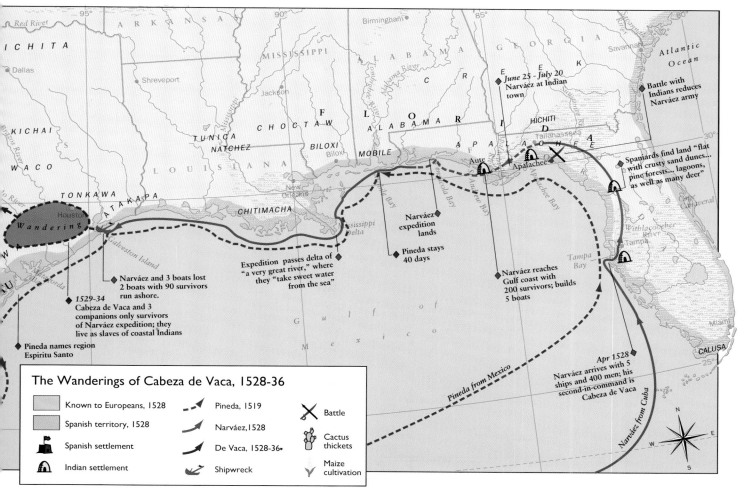

Narváez at Indian town — June 25 – July 20

Battle with Indians reduces Narváez army

Spaniards find land "flat with crusty sand dunes... pine forests... lagoons, as well as many deer"

Narváez expedition lands

Pineda stays 40 days

Narváez reaches Gulf coast with 200 survivors; builds 5 boats

Expedition passes delta of "a very great river," where they "take sweet water from the sea"

Narváez and 3 boats lost 2 boats with 90 survivors run ashore.

1529-34 Cabeza de Vaca and 3 companions only survivors of Narváez expedition; they live as slaves of coastal Indians

Pineda names region Espíritu Santo

Apr 1528 Narváez arrives with 5 ships and 400 men; his second-in-command is Cabeza de Vaca

Pineda from Mexico

Narváez from Cuba

The Wanderings of Cabeza de Vaca, 1528-36

- Known to Europeans, 1528
- Spanish territory, 1528
- Spanish settlement
- Indian settlement
- Pineda, 1519
- Narváez, 1528
- De Vaca, 1528-36
- Shipwreck
- Battle
- Cactus thickets
- Maize cultivation

Blade and Buckler

THE EXPEDITION OF HERNANDO DE SOTO, 1539-43

A Spanish conquistador leads and army of mailed soldiers across 3000 miles of what is now the southern United States.

When Cabeza de Vaca returned to Spain in 1537, he found an ambitious expedition being prepared for Florida. Its commander was Hernando de Soto. One of Pizarro's lieutenants in the conquest of Peru, he had gone there with "nothing more than blade and buckler" and come home a rich man. Now he was to lead his own expedition farther north than any Spaniard had ventured.

De Soto landed at Tampa Bay in May 1539 with a well-organized force of about 200 horsemen, 400 foot-soldiers, some fighting dogs and a small herd of hogs for food. Once away from the coast he hoped to find gold or other treasure, and his gubernatorial powers from the crown became in effect a licence to plunder the peoples of the interior. He soon revealed his methods: local chiefs were seized and held for a ransom of bearers, women and corn. Usually captives would be released once the next tribe was reached and the process would begin again. Inevitably, such tactics provoked resistance, and turned the expedition into a series of running skirmishes.

As de Soto marched westwards, the expedition's chroniclers noted many different peoples, from the warlike Timucua of Florida to the elaborate, temple-mound cultures of the Creek and Choctaw Indians. The Spanish

soldiers were the first Europeans to see the Mississippi. (At first, they called it "the great river," then Rio del Spirito Santo.) They crossed it in clumsy dugout canoes in June 1541 somewhere below present-day Memphis, where it was one-and-a-half miles wide. "A man standing on the shore could not be told, whether he were a man or something else from the other side." In eastern Arkansas, de Soto's outriders encountered Plains Indians, and heard reports of the great buffalo herds, and also of another sea. De Soto assumed this was the Pacific, and even considered trying to reach it.

No gold was found, though rumors of it explain many of the twists and turns of the expedition's route. One of the survivors recalled that "neither the governor nor anyone else knew where they were headed other than to find a land so rich as to satisfy their desires."

Depressed and repentant, de Soto died of a "flux of blood" in May 1542, and was buried in the Mississippi. After an abortive attempt

to reach Mexico overland, the survivors, led by Luis de Moscoso, headed back to the river. There they built crude boats which they sailed downstream, through the tangle of the delta channels, and along the coast to Mexico.

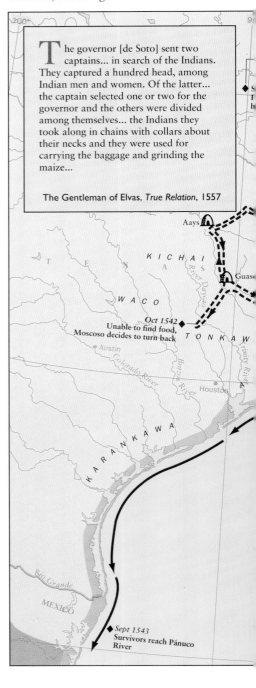

> The governor [de Soto] sent two captains... in search of the Indians. They captured a hundred head, among Indian men and women. Of the latter... the captain selected one or two for the governor and the others were divided among themselves... the Indians they took along in chains with collars about their necks and they were used for carrying the baggage and grinding the maize...
>
> **The Gentleman of Elvas,** *True Relation,* 1557

The Interior of Florida
REDRAWN FROM ABRAHAM ORTELIUS'S ATLAS, 1584

This map draws on de Soto's explorations in the vast region then known as Florida. It shows many native settlements, the southern Appalachians, and the Mississippi (*Rio del Spirito Santo*), incorrectly mapped as a short river flowing from inland mountains.

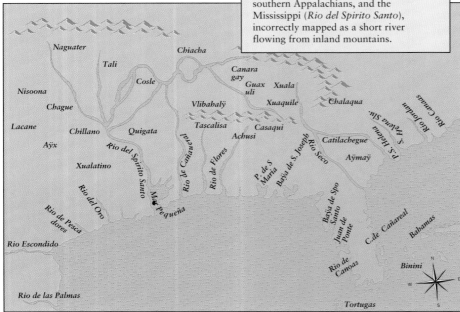

That 311 men survived says much for their fortitude, and for de Soto's qualities of leadership. But the cost of his methods was the mutilation, torture and killing of hundreds and thousands of native people. "Never resting anywhere," the historian Oviedo wrote, "they made neither settlement nor conquest, but caused desolation of the land and loss of liberty of the people."

In his History of the New World, *published 1565, Italian traveler Girolamo Benzoni, who had witnessed many such atrocities in the Americas, tells of de Soto's cruelties. De Soto seized a number of native people demanding that they lead him to gold. When they did not find any, "the governor becoming bitterly enraged, cut off their hands." From an engraving by Theodore de Bry.*

Oct 1541 to sends out scouting me time as Coronado aches upper Arkansas River, only 300 miles northwest

Coligua

Sept 1541 Expedition finds buffalo skins at this town

Pacaha
Casqui
Memphis

June 15 1541 First European sighting and crossing of Mississippi River

Quizquiz

Nov 1541–Mar 1542 Winter quarters. Interpreter Juan Ortiz dies Autiamque

QUAPAW

Anilco
Aminoya

Dec 1542–July 1543 Winter camp

Chicaza

Dec 1540–Apr1541 Winter quarters among Chickasaw

CHICASAW

Piachi

Nashville

May–June 1540 First European crossing of Appalachians

Chiaha
Coste
Xuala
Guaquili

Tali

May 1540 De Soto finds this major town depopulated by disease, and short of food

Cofitachequi

Apr 30 1540 De Soto's forces cross river

CATAWBA

Coosa

Aug 1540 De Soto takes Coosa chief and his sister hostage

YUCHI

TUSKEGEE

Ocute

Ichisi

Guachoya

July 2 1543 Survivors embark in 7 boats they have built

June 1542 Moscoso tries to return overland to Mexico

Naguatex
Shreveport

May 21 1542 After scouts report land to south impassable, De Soto dies; Luis de Moscoso takes command

CADDO

TUNICA

NATCHEZ

MISSISSIPPI

Jackson
Meridian

CHOCTAW

Atahachi

Oct 18 1540 Battle of Mabila – 2500 Choctaw killed; 20 Spaniards. De Soto hears that fleet is waiting at Achuse. Conceals news from his men and presses on

Mabila

ALABAMA

CREEK

FLORIDA

HICHITI

Tallahassee

Oct 1540 Maldonado's ships wait for de Soto at prearranged rendezvous

Achuse

Pensacola Bay

Mobile

BILOXI

Baton Rouge

Biloxi

New Orleans

LOUISIANA

CHITIMACHA

Luis de Moscoso, 1543

Gulf of Mexico

APALACHEE

Apalachee

Oct 1539–Mar 1540 Winter quarters

Sept 1539 Battle of the Lakes Spaniards take 300 Seminole prisoner

Ocale

Tampa

Tampa Bay

Ocale

TIMUCUA

GUALE

YAMASEE

Atlantic Ocean

Charlotte

Columbia

Augusta

Macon

Atlanta

Savannah

Charleston

Chattanooga

Birmingham

Montgomery

CHEROKEE

NORTH CAROLINA

SOUTH CAROLINA

GEORGIA

Ilapi

May 30 1539 De Soto lands; he remains in area until mid-July. Finds Juan Ortiz, survivor of Narváez expedition. He acts as interpreter.

Uzita

Charlotte Harbour

Miami

CALUSA

May 1539 De Soto leaves Havana with 9 ships and more than 600 men

The Expedition of Hernando de Soto, 1539–43

▨ Known to Europeans, 1539	⚓	Landing
▨ Spanish territory, 1539	⛺	Winter camp
➤ De Soto's expedition	✕	Battle
⛺ Indian settlement	✗	Skirmish
▨ Swamp	☠	Death of explorer

The Quest for Cibola
THE EXPEDITION OF VÁSQUEZ DE CORONADO, 1540-42

The Spanish expedition headed by Coronado fails in its quest for fabulous cities to rival Aztec Mexico; but it discovers a vast swathe of the North American interior.

By the late 1530s Antonio de Mendoza, recently appointed viceroy of New Spain, was ready to mount a full-scale expedition to explore the unknown lands to the north. Cabeza de Vaca's reports of populous towns to the north, rumors of precious metals, and fears that De Soto's planned expedition from Florida would stake out a rival claim, all lent urgency to the matter.

In 1539 a reconnaissance party, including Estevan (a north African slave who had been with Cabeza de Vaca), a Franciscan friar Marcos de Niza and several hundred native peoples followed the Indian road to Sinaloa. There Marcos heard tales of the "Seven Cities" further north in Cibola. Estevan crossed the desert with an advance party to reach the Cibola pueblos where he was killed by the apprehensive Zuñi inhabitants. Marcos almost certainly did not get even within distant sight of the place, which nevertheless he described as "a very beautiful city...bigger than the city of Mexico."

Encouraged by this report, the 30-year old governor of the frontier province of New Galicia, Francisco Vásquez de Coronado, left for the north in February 1540. He was accompanied by 330 Spaniards (two-thirds of them mounted), more than a thousand native allies and servants, and a baggage and provision train. So large a force was slow on the move, and difficult to feed; Coronado soon split the expedition into different groups. Hernando de Alarcón took three vessels along the coast with supplies, while the main force headed for the Seven Cities. These proved a sad disappointment. There were

Below: Pueblo Indians encountered by Coronado had inherited a long tradition of ceramic art. This storage jar from Arizona shows the design and spatter technique used in the 15th and 16th centuries.

Above: Indians defending their pueblo against Coronado's forces, drawn by a Spanish-Tlaxcalan mestizo, Diego Muñoz Camargo, within living memory of the event. Part of a manuscript presented to King Philip II of Spain by a Tlaxcalan embassy in 1585. The caption says that during Coronado's expedition "the Tlaxcalans were in the service of Your Majesty." This central Mexican people had also assisted Cortés in his conquest of the Aztecs.

only six (to which the collective name Cibola applied) and they were villages rather than cities.

Exploring parties sent out to east and west of the main force had varying fortunes. One led by López de Cárdenas in search of a river route to the Pacific, came to the Grand Canyon, the first Europeans to see it, and also the last for more than two hundred years. It was an awesome but frustrating sight, since for the Spaniards on its southern rim there was no way down or across the mighty chasm. Another group under Melchor Díaz reached the Lower Colorado River at Yuma, and crossed into California for a few days – pathfinders on the overland route from Mexico to Lower California. Yet another party under Hernando de Alvarado went east to the Upper Rio Grande, the Canadian River,

and the edge of the Great Plains. They brought back a Plains Indian, "the Turk," who described a country to the northeast, Quivira, rich in gold with lordly rulers. Excited by this news, Coronado, who had wintered among the pueblos of Tiguex on the Upper Rio Grande, set out for Quivira in 1541. After bridging the Pecos River he reached the plains: hundreds of miles of "land as level as the sea," where men became hopelessly lost, and the only trails were those made by the buffalo. It was on Coronado's expedition that Europeans for the first time saw the great buffalo herds, and the Plains Indians who lived off them.

On the plains Coronado headed north to the Arkansas River, and into the country of the Wichita Indians between the Arkansas and Kansas rivers. Meanwhile, 300 miles to the southeast, de Soto had crossed the Mississippi into eastern Arkansas – the nearest the two expeditions came to each other. Coronado had reached Quivira – a fertile land, but with no dwellings more impressive than thatched beehive-like huts, and no signs of great cities or great riches. Coronado decided to turn for home; it was a tattered and despondent party which reached Mexico City in the early fall of 1542.

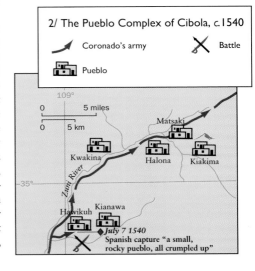

2/ The Pueblo Complex of Cibola, c.1540

Coronado's army — Battle ✗
Pueblo

0   5 miles
0   5 km

109°

Mátsaki
Kwakina   Halona   Kiakima
Zuñi River
35°
Hawikuh   Kianawa
Kianawa

July 7 1540
Spanish capture "a small, rocky pueblo, all crumpled up"

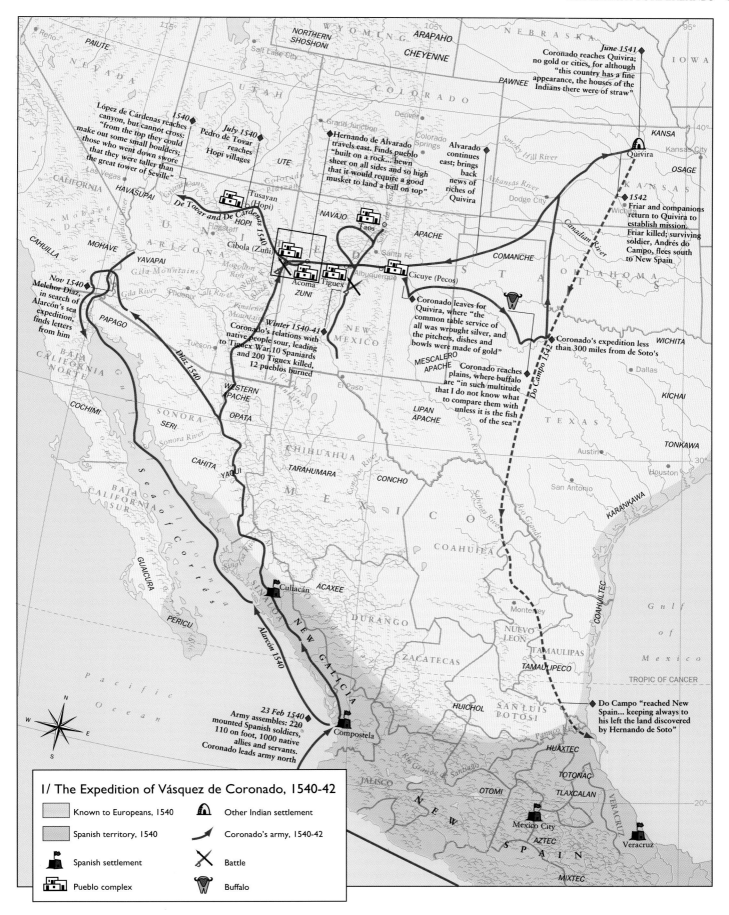

June 1541
Coronado reaches Quivira;
no gold or cities, for although
"this country has a fine
appearance, the houses of the
Indians there were of straw"

López de Cárdenas reaches
canyon, but cannot cross:
"from the top they could
make out some small boulders;
those who went down swore
that they were taller than
the great tower of Seville"

1540

July 1540
Pedro de Tovar
reaches
Hopi villages

Hernando de Alvarado
travels east. Finds pueblo
"built on a rock... hewn
sheer on all sides and so high
that it would require a good
musket to land a ball on top"

Alvarado
continues
east; brings
back
news of
riches of
Quivira

1542
Friar and companions
return to Quivira to
establish mission.
Friar killed; surviving
soldier, Andrés do
Campo, flees south
to New Spain

De Tovar and De Cárdenas 1540

Coronado leaves for
Quivira, where "the
common table service of
all was wrought silver, and
the pitchers, dishes and
bowls were made of gold"

Coronado's expedition less
than 300 miles from de Soto's

Nov 1540
Melchor Díaz
in search of
Alarcón's sea
expedition,
finds letters
from him

Winter 1540–41
Coronado's relations with
native people sour, leading
to Tiguex War. 10 Spaniards
and 200 Tiguex killed,
12 pueblos burned

Coronado reaches
plains, where buffalo
are "in such multitude
that I do not know what
to compare them with
unless it is the fish
of the sea"

23 Feb 1540
Army assembles: 220
mounted Spanish soldiers,
110 on foot, 1000 native
allies and servants.
Coronado leads army north

Do Campo "reached New
Spain... keeping always to
his left the land discovered
by Hernando de Soto"

1/ The Expedition of Vásquez de Coronado, 1540-42

Known to Europeans, 1540	Other Indian settlement
Spanish territory, 1540	Coronado's army, 1540-42
Spanish settlement	Battle
Pueblo complex	Buffalo

North to California

SPANISH COASTAL VOYAGES, 1539-43

The Spanish turn their ambitions northward.
They sail up the west coast in search of a
northeast strait through the continent to the
Atlantic Ocean.

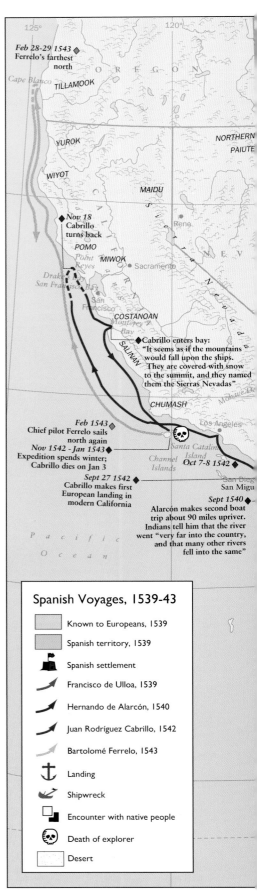

After conquering central Mexico, Hernando Cortés wanted to establish Spanish control to the north and find the rumored strait to the Atlantic, later known as the Strait of Anian. In 1524 he informed Charles V, "The voyage from the spice region to your kingdom would be very easy and very short...without any risk to the vessels... because they would always come and go through your dominions."

Progress was slow. In 1535 Cortés led an expedition which confused the "island of Santa Cruz" with the peninsula of Baja California and failed to colonize it. New reports then emerged, some from Cabeza de Vaca's travels (▶ *page 32*), of rich and populous regions to the north. In 1539 Cortés sent Francisco de Ulloa with three vessels northward to explore the coast beyond his own discovery of La Paz. Within a few months Ulloa reached the Gulf of California, naming it the Sea of Cortés, sensed the presence of the Colorado River and proved Baja California to be a peninsula. He then sailed north along its Pacific shore at least to the Isla de Cedros.

In 1540 the Spanish viceroy sent Alarcón on a voyage with supplies for Coronado (▶ *page 36*). Alarcón sailed into the Gulf of California and entered the Colorado River. By boat he followed it some 90 miles inland to its junction with the Gila. Yuma Indians told Alarcón of the death of a black man, Esteván, and Coronado's attack, on Cibola. Alarcón, deciding it was too far and too dangerous to reach Coronado, turned back.

In 1542 the viceroy sent further ships north, under Juan Rodríguez Cabrillo, who had heard that the Portuguese had discovered a northern strait between the two oceans. Cabrillo reached the harbor San Miguel, now San Diego, becoming the first European to land in Upper California. Sailing north, away from the coast because of winds, Cabrillo glimpsed neither Monterey nor San Francisco harbors. He turned back and probably did sight Drake's Bay but died in January 1543. Bartolomé Ferrelo, the chief pilot, courageously returned north along the coast.

The expedition explored 900 miles of unknown coast but found neither riches nor any great strait leading east. Further exploration north from New Spain had to wait to near the end of the century.

Below: Map by Juan de Martinez (1578) showing the seven cities of Cibola.

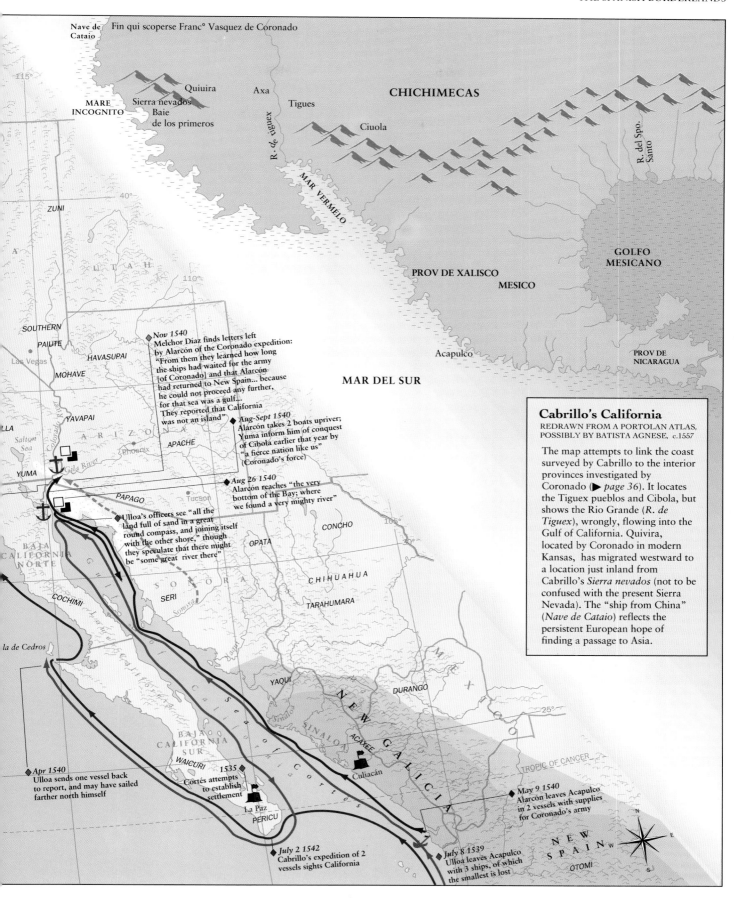

Nave de Cataio

Fin qui scoperse Franc° Vasquez de Coronado

Quiuira

Axa

CHICHIMECAS

MARE INCOGNITO

Sierra nevados
Baie
de los primeros

Tigues

Ciuola

R. de tiguex

MAR VERMELO

R. del Spo. Santo

ZUNI

40°

115°

110°

GOLFO MESICANO

PROV DE XALISCO

MESICO

SOUTHERN PAIUTE

HAVASUPAI

Las Vegas

MOHAVE

Acapulco

PROV DE NICARAGUA

MAR DEL SUR

Nov 1540
Melchor Díaz finds letters left
by Alarcón of the Coronado expedition:
"From them they learned how long
the ships had waited for the army
[of Coronado] and that Alarcón
had returned to New Spain... because
he could not proceed any further,
for that sea was a gulf...
They reported that California
was not an island"

YAVAPAI

Salton Sea

A R I Z O N A

APACHE

Phoenix

Aug-Sept 1540
Alarcón takes 2 boats upriver;
Yuma inform him of conquest
of Cibola earlier that year by
"a fierce nation like us"
(Coronado's force)

YUMA

Gila River

PAPAGO

Tucson

Aug 26 1540
Alarcón reaches "the very
bottom of the Bay; where
we found a very mighty river"

Ulloa's officers see "all the
land full of sand in a great
round compass, and joining itself
with the other shore," though
they speculate that there might
be "some great river there"

CONCHO

105°

30°

OPATA

BAJA CALIFORNIA NORTE

SONORA

SERI

CHIHUAHUA

TARAHUMARA

COCHIMI

la de Cedros

YAQUI

DURANGO

25°

BAJA CALIFORNIA SUR

WAICURI

1535
Cortés attempts
to establish
settlement

SINALOA

ACAXEE

Culiacán

N E W   G A L I C I A

TROPIC OF CANCER

Apr 1540
Ulloa sends one vessel back
to report, and may have sailed
farther north himself

La Paz
PERICU

July 2 1542
Cabrillo's expedition of 2
vessels sights California

May 9 1540
Alarcón leaves Acapulco
in 2 vessels with supplies
for Coronado's army

July 8 1539
Ulloa leaves Acapulco
with 3 ships, of which
the smallest is lost

N E W   S P A I N

OTOMI

M E X

Gulf of California

Mar de Cortés

Cabrillo's California

REDRAWN FROM A PORTOLAN ATLAS,
POSSIBLY BY BATISTA AGNESE, c.1557

The map attempts to link the coast
surveyed by Cabrillo to the interior
provinces investigated by
Coronado (▶ *page 36*). It locates
the Tiguex pueblos and Cibola, but
shows the Rio Grande (*R. de
Tiguex*), wrongly, flowing into the
Gulf of California. Quivira,
located by Coronado in modern
Kansas, has migrated westward to
a location just inland from
Cabrillo's *Sierra nevados* (not to be
confused with the present Sierra
Nevada). The "ship from China"
(*Nave de Cataio*) reflects the
persistent European hope of
finding a passage to Asia.

English Incursions, Spanish Responses

DRAKE, VIZCAÍNO AND OÑATE, 1579-1609

The English arrive unexpectedly on the Californian coast. Their activities prompt further Spanish ventures beyond the northern frontiers of New Spain.

After the disappointments of Coronado and Cabrillo (▶ *pages 36, 38*), official interest in New Spain's northern frontiers faded. The annual galleon from Manila to Acapulco might sight the northern Californian coast, but it rarely landed. It was the arrival of English seaman Francis Drake which jolted Spanish officialdom out of the assumption that the north Pacific was closed to foreigners.

In the spring of 1579, after raiding along the Pacific coasts of Spanish America, Drake approached the northwest coast somewhere near the present California-Oregon border. Turning south again he stayed at a bay for five weeks, though its identity remains the subject of controversy. Drake took possession of the land, allegedly invited by local Miwok Indians, and named it New Albion. In 1587 another English expedition, led by Thomas Cavendish, captured the Manila galleon off Cape San Lucas.

Spanish concern increased but reaction was leisurely. No Spanish ship reached Drake's area until one of the Manila galleons, commanded by Sebastián Rodriguez Cermeño, did so in 1595. He made a landfall near Cape Mendocino and sailed south of present-day Drake's Bay. But laden cargo vessels are unsuitable for coastal exploration and his galleon was wrecked.

Seven years later Sebastián Vizcaíno, in a more professional foray, sailed north from Acapulco, following Cabrillo's course of 60 years earlier. Beating against headwinds and with crews suffering from scurvy, Vizcaíno's ships reached Cape Mendocino after nine months. Vizcaíno himself turned back but one of his vessels reached Cape Blanco, from where "the coast ran northeast, and the cold was so great that they thought they should be frozen." Inland expeditions were even less successful. In 1582 Antonio de Espejo

Above: Oñate, governor of New Mexico, rode south along the Colorado River with 30 men in 1604. He reached the Gulf of California and inaccurately claimed to be the first Spaniard to do so. A translation of the inscription he made at El Morro reads: "Passed by here the Governor Don Juan de Oñate, from the discovery of the Sea of the South on the 16th of April, 1605."

journeyed along the Rio Grande as far as Zuñi and Hopi territory, reviving dreams of Coronado's day. In 1598, Juan de Oñate, governor of New Mexico, led 500 soldiers and settlers north to conquer and settle pueblo country. Oñate's grand design of a northern empire based on mines, ranches and missions was afflicted by desertions, sickness and Indian resistance. But he carried out useful exploration and established a mission settlement at Santa Fé in 1609. On paper a royal province, New Mexico was in fact a thinly-held salient, north of the main line of Spanish frontier posts.

Oñate's expeditions were the final stage of a northward ambition which had begun with Coronado. But apart from the pearl fisheries of the Gulf of California the Spanish had found little of immediate value. They were becoming convinced that if there were a Strait of Anian somewhere to the north it had better remain unfound. As one viceroy reflected, with backward glances at Drake and Cavendish, such a finding could "awaken someone who was asleep." New Spain's northern frontiers were protected by their inaccessibility.

Left: Since Coronado's day, the Spaniards had continued to speculate about fabulous kingdoms and a navigable strait through the North American landmass. Cornelius de Jode's 1593 map of "The Kingdom of Quivira" combines these fantasies with geographical knowledge of the day. The Californian coast is fairly accurately shown as far north as Cape Mendocino, where it takes an abrupt turn to the east into the mythical Strait of Anian, believed to lead to the Atlantic. The map shows the many buffalo seen by Coronado and Oñate.

Three hundred and sixty leagues from the city of Mexico towards the north pole... there are seven or eight provinces and nations of people all of different languages. The Spaniards generally call these provinces New Mexico. They must contain thirty thousand souls or more... The people of these provinces are very affable and docile. They all live in pueblos, which, for Indian dwellings, are very well arranged.

Francisco de Escobar *Relation*

Drake, Vizcaíno and Oñate, 1579-1609

- Known to Europeans, 1579
- Spanish territory, 1579
- Spanish territory, 1610

- Spanish settlement
- Mission
- Pueblo complex
- Francis Drake, 1579
- Sebastián Vizcaíno, 1602-03
- Juan de Oñate, 1598-1605
- Anchorage
- Shipwreck
- Indian uprising
- Buffalo

June 5 1579
Drake turns back because of "extreme and nipping cold... there followed most vile, thicke and stincking fogges"

Jan 1603
Expedition passes Cape Mendocino; smallest vessel, the pinnace *Tres Reyes*, reaches about lat.43°N, "where the coast turns to the northeast, and where the entrance to the Strait of Anian seems to begin"

June 17-July 23 1579
Drake spends 5 weeks; gets on well with Miwok "a people of a tractable, free and loving nature." Takes possession of country

Dec 16 1602
Vizcaíno reaches "a good harbor, well sheltered, and supplied with water, wood, and good timber"

1595
Cermeño's galleon shipwrecked while investigating coast

Nov 10 1602
Vizcaíno reaches "a port which must be the best to be found in all the South Sea"

1609-10
Town established; becomes capital of New Mexico

1601
Oñate leads expedition (with ox-drawn carts) in unsuccessful search for Quivira. It encounters Apache and great buffalo herds

1599
Acoma pueblo destroyed after native uprising

1598
Friars establish mission

1598
Oñate reaches pueblo country, accompanied by colonizing party of 500, mostly women and children

Jan 25 1605
Oñate reaches sea on St Paul's Day; hears reports of "yellow metal," silver and pearls

1604-05
Oñate leads expedition to the Colorado River ("as large as the Duero in Spain,)" the Gila River and the Gulf of California

Apr 16 1579
Drake sails north from Guatulco in *Golden Hind* and pinnace

Nov 4 1587
Cavendish captures Manila galleon

May 5 1602
Vizcaíno leaves Acapulco with 3 vessels

Seattle

WASHINGTON

Snake River

Portland

OREGON

CAYUSE

Cape Blanco

Boise

IDAHO

YUROK
ACHOMAWI
WIYOT

NORTHERN PAIUTE

WYOMING

CHEYENNE

NORTHERN SHOSHONI

Salt Lake City

COLORADO

Denver

MAIDU

Reno

NEVADA

ZUNI

UTAH

Las Vegas

SOUTHERN PAIUTE

UTE

Point Reyes
Drakes Bay
Monterey Bay

POMO
MIWOK
San Francisco
NEW ALBION

Santa Barbara Bay

CHUMASH

Los Angeles

CAHUILLA

San Diego Bay

Grand Canyon
Colorado River

Mohave Desert

HAVASUPAI

Tusayán
HOPI

NAVAJO

Taos
APACHE

Santa Fe
Cicuye
Albuquerque

KIOWA
KIOWA APACHE
OSAGE

COMANCHE
Oklahoma City

OKLAHOMA

Red River

YAVAPAI

ARIZONA

Gila River

Tucson

PAPAGO

WESTERN APACHE

Gila River

YUMA

San Jose River
Cibola

El Morro
Tiguex
ZUNI
Acoma

Rio Puerco
Rio Salado

Santo Domingo

MESCALERO APACHE

Pecos River

LIPAN APACHE

Abilene

TEXAS

PAPAGO

BAJA CALIFORNIA NORTE

SONORA

SERI

YAQUI

OPATA

TARAHUMARA

CONCHO

CHIHUAHUA

Rio Grande

COAHUILA

NUEVO LEON

Monterrey

Isla de Cedros

BAJA CALIFORNIA SUR

WAICURI

PERICU

Pacific Ocean

Cape San Lucas

ACAXEE

Culiacán

SINALOA

DURANGO

Saltillo

TROPIC OF CANCER

NEW GALICIA

NEW SPAIN

N S E W

Fantasies and Fabrications

THE APOCRYPHAL VOYAGES, 1592-1640

The imaginary discoveries of hoaxers, fantasists and charlatans find their way into the geography of northwest America.

Spanish expeditions had tracked the coast and penetrated inland far north from Mexico (▶ *pages 38-41*) but they did not find what they expected: the Strait of Anian, gold and silver mines, or populous towns and cities. Such were ambitions, however, that fact sometimes became confused with fiction.

Lorenzo Ferrer Maldonado alleged that in 1588 he sailed from the Atlantic across the top of North America to the Strait of Anian and then into the Pacific. He claimed to achieve this, and back again, in a single summer. By the time his account was published in the late 18th century it was clear that the Strait of Anian did not exist.

More puzzling was Juan de Fuca's voyage in command of a Spanish expedition of 1592. Greek-born pilot Fuca claimed that the land north of the California coast turned north-east, where he discovered a great inlet whose entrance was marked by an "exceeding high Pinacle" on its northern side. Through the inlet they came to the "North Sea," and countries rich in gold.

Fuca's story, related to English promoter Michael Lok in 1596, has been surrounded by controversy ever since. There was indeed a Greek pilot in Spanish service on the northwest coast between 1588 and 1594. And there is a strait at a similar latitude (now named after Juan de Fuca) with a pillar of rock at its *southern* entrance. Fuca or Lok may have embellished the account to sustain interest in the Northwest Passage.

A more preposterous story was published in 1708, and reprinted in England and France in the mid-18th century, of a supposed voyage by Admiral Bartholomew de Fonte. He was said to have sailed north from Lima in 1640, in search of a Northwest Passage. On the northwest coast, Fonte claimed to have explored an extensive network of straits and rivers, and met a Boston ship trading furs. This supposedly proved that a Northwest Passage must exist. The Spanish archives contained no reference to Fonte, but this was ignored. Even so judicious a reader as Benjamin Franklin thought Fonte's account was genuine. The narratives of Fuca and Fonte, however spurious, were to influence the course of later exploration as much as many genuine expeditions.

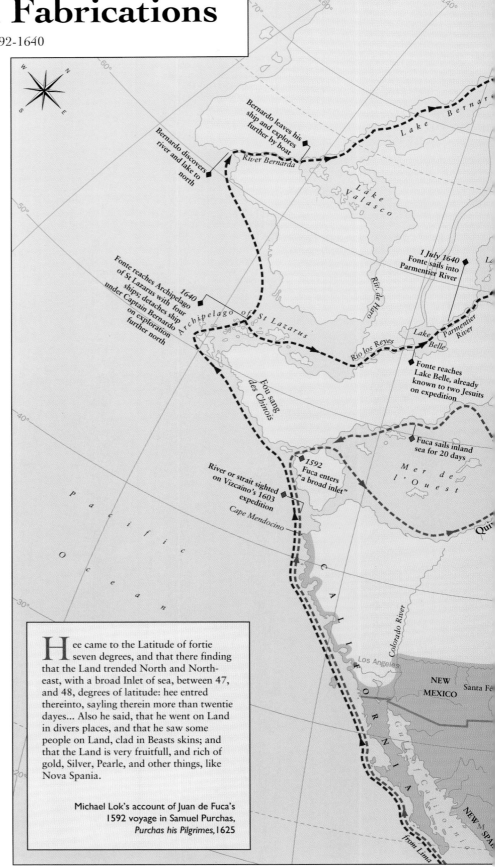

> Hee came to the Latitude of fortie seven degrees, and that there finding that the Land trended North and North-east, with a broad Inlet of sea, between 47, and 48, degrees of latitude: hee entred thereinto, sayling therein more than twentie dayes... Also he said, that he went on Land in divers places, and that he saw some people on Land, clad in Beasts skins; and that the Land is very fruitfull, and rich of gold, Silver, Pearle, and other things, like Nova Spania.
>
> Michael Lok's account of Juan de Fuca's 1592 voyage in Samuel Purchas, *Purchas his Pilgrimes,* 1625

One of Bernardo's crew accompanies Indians to head of Davis Strait in latitude 80° N

Strait of Ronquillo
Lake Ronquillo

17 July 1640 Fonte meets Boston ship commanded by Captain Shapley in search of Northwest Passage

14 July 1640 Fonte sails out of Lake Fonte into Strait of Ronquillo

GREENLAND

Baffin Bay

Davis Strait

Hudson Strait

Cape Walsinghant

Hudson Bay

LABRADOR

NEWFOUNDLAND

NEW FRANCE

CANADA

C A N A D A

Gulf of St Lawrence

Québec

River of Canada

Montreal

Lake Superior

Minneapolis

Lake Michigan

Lake Huron

Toronto

Lake Ontario

Lake Erie

Boston

Detroit

Cleveland

New York

Chicago

Philadelphia

U N I T E D S T A T E S

Washington DC

Indianapolis

Missouri River

Mississippi River

Kansas City

St Louis

Ohio River

O F A M E R I C A

Arkansas River

Charleston

Atlantic Ocean

LOUISIANA

Memphis

Mississippi River

Dallas

FLORIDA

New Orleans

Bahamas

TROPIC OF CANCER

Rio del Norte

Rio Grande

Monterrey

G u l f o f M e x i c o

CUBA

ARCTIC CIRCLE

> The 17th (July) we came to an Indian Town, and the Indians told our Interpreter Mr Parmentiers, that a little way from us lay a great ship where there had never been one before... my second Mate was an English man, an excellent Seaman, as was my Gunner, who had been taken prisoner at Campechy, as well as the Master's Son; they told me the Ship was of New England, from a Town called Boston...I received (the Owner) like a Gentleman, and told him, my commission was to make Prize of any people seeking a North West or West Passage into the South Sea, but I would look upon them as Merchants trading with the Natives for Bevers, Otters, and other Furs and Skins.
>
> The Fonte Letter, 1708

Apocryphal Voyages, 1592-1640

The "discoveries" of Juan de Fuca and Bartholomew de Fonte found their way onto the maps of the 18th-century French cartographers Philippe Buache and J. N. de L'Isle, together with other fictitious explorations including the land of Fou sang, allegedly discovered by the Chinese in the 5th century AD.

Here, the French cartographers' version of these apocryphal voyages has been combined with a modern map showing what was actually known to Europeans in 1640.

Known to Europeans, 1640

Juan de Fuca, 1592

Bartholomew de Fonte, 1640

Part II : The Opening of a Continent

The early decades of the 17th century saw the first sustained European effort to colonize North America. With settlement came more detailed local exploration of the eastern coastal regions, a better understanding of the land, and more precise maps. But while tiny Spanish garrisons guarded the northern outposts of their vast American empire and the English clung to their precarious coastal settlements, French fur traders and missionaries pushed deep into the heart of the continent and down the Mississippi to the Gulf of Mexico.

In 1600, there was little to mark the European presence in North America: a handful of Spaniards in Florida, and a few summer fishing camps in the north. But in the decades that followed, settlements – mostly English – were established along the coast from Newfoundland to Virginia. The initial cost was high in terms of people and money, but by the third decade of the century the little clusters of European occupation were taking on a more permanent appearance.

There was some exploration inland, although acquired knowledge was mainly local. Exploration was secondary to the need to plant, to grow and to survive. Behind the coast the terrain was often rugged and unpromising, with no easy routes into the interior, and an array of Indian peoples to bar the way.

The pioneer French settlements on the St Lawrence served as a springboard for a different kind of expansion. The succession of rivers and lakes drew the French westward. They had three main motives: the quest for a route to the Pacific; the search for furs; and the missionary impulse to convert the Indians. The traders, or *coureurs du bois* as they were called, pushed deep into the interior in their never-ending quest for beaver skins. Although the English tried to outflank them in the north by setting up trading posts on Hudson Bay, the French set the pace. The *coureurs du bois* came nearer to living on easy terms with the Indians than any other group of Europeans. They were quick to pick up Indian wilderness skills, and the birchbark canoe in summer and the snowshoe in winter became indispensable to Europeans traveling across the roadless terrain of Canada.

If the rough, often illiterate *coureurs du bois* were the outriders of European discovery in the north, it is to the missionaries that we owe reliable narratives of the course of exploration. Their writings give a detailed picture of the land and its inhabitants, with the Indian far removed from the crude stereotype which often appeared in other accounts.

As the French pushed westward, opening to view the immense inland waters of the Great Lakes, they heard Indian reports of a great river, the Mississippi. By the 1680s they had reached its outlet to the sea. At first, the French were disappointed that this was not the western or Pacific Ocean but the Gulf of Mexico; but they soon realized that from this vantage point they could dominate the North American heartland, threatening the silver mines of New Spain in one direction and the cramped coastal colonies of the English in another.

At the end of the 17th century, however, the French empire in North America was an outline rather than a reality. Impressive though the French advance had been, it was buttressed by little in the way of settlement – no more than a scattering of trading posts, mission stations and military forts. In both exploring and trading the French depended on Indian help, and the necessities of the fur trade required the preservation rather than the elimination of wilderness. The fine thread of the explorers' tracks on the map tells its own story.

The Beginnings of Spanish Florida

FRANCO-SPANISH RIVALRY,1562-74

In the second half of the 16th century the murderous national and religious antagonisms of contemporary Europe reach North America.

By the mid-16th century the Spanish recognized that Florida, lying close to the homeward route of the treasure fleets, had become strategically very important. One plan was for a base on the roadstead of Port Royal (Santa Elena), just north of Ayllón's short-lived settlement of 1526 on the Savannah River (▶ *page 22*). Such projects were thrown into disarray, however, by the unexpected arrival of the French.

In 1562 three French ships took possession of St Johns River before sailing on to establish the settlement of Charlesfort at Port Royal. This fort was soon abandoned but two years later a larger French force built another fort on St Johns River, Fort Caroline, in alliance with local Indians, the Timucua. Exploring parties were sent into the interior, both along the river and more directly west, in search of the preciousmetals reported inthe "Apalatci" mountain. Cibola (▶ *page 36*) was thought to be "towardes the southe sea" and an oddly precise Indian report claimed it was only 22 days' paddling distance away. But weak leadership, internal quarrels and disputes with the Indians meant that this French venture was also abandoned, and when a rescue expedition of seven ships arrived in August 1565 it was the prelude to a bloodbath.

Spanish anxieties had been roused by reports of these French settlements, and close behind the French force came a Spanish armada under Pedro Menéndez de Avilés. Within a few weeks it had wiped out the settlers. They were killed, Menéndez explained, not merely as Frenchmen but as heretics.

As Governor of Florida, Menéndez pursued an energetic policy of exploration, conquest and settlement. In the tradition of Cortés and de Soto, he conjured up a grand design of an empire based on peninsular Florida which would extend west to Mexico and north along the coast as far as he could reach. Along Florida's Atlantic coast he set up a string of forts, while on its Gulf coast he established posts at Tampa Bay and Charlotte Harbor.

To the north, Menéndez encouraged a Jesuit mission to Chesapeake Bay in 1570 and significantly expanded his empire through the inland expeditions of Captain Juan Pardo from Santa Elena. In 1566 Pardo and 125 men followed the Savannah River for 250 miles northwest. They established the small fort of San Juan in Cheraw country, near what is now the border between South Carolina and Georgia. The following year Pardo returned to San Juan, following Indian roads west over the Appalachians and into the Tennessee Valley, and approaching de Soto's path of more than a quarter-century earlier.

The way seemed open for a direct if distant land route to Mexico; but men at the small posts Pardo left behind were either attacked by Indians or died of starvation. In the north, the few Jesuits at Chesapeake Bay had already died by 1571, presumably at the hands of the Indians. From Santa Elena to the south, settlements faltered, from disillusionment, Indian suspicion and European hostility.

Soon the only Spanish garrisons left were those at San Pedro and San Agustín, the latter being *presidio* of the colony. The northern areas were left to the missionaries, whose efforts to change indigenous customs led to unrest among the Guale and Cusabo Indians. San Agustín was subject to much rebuilding and resiting, and was destroyed by an English expedition under Francis Drake in 1586. Nevertheless it showed the tenacity of the Spanish presence in Florida and it was the first permanent European colonial settlement in what was to become the United States. Today it is St Augustine, with a history of continuous occupation of well over 400 years. In the late 16th century it was a reminder to other European nations that Spain's claims of imperial dominion extended to North America.

> The two promontories of Florida and Yucatan form the Gulf of Mexico, or Gulf of Florida. A great current pours without ebb between Cuba and Yucatan into this gulf, to emerge between Cuba and Florida. This is one of the reasons that ships going to the Indies cannot go back as they have come, for the current is constant and there is no wind blowing along the route of entrance, so that the mariners go north to search for one. Thus it is a matter of great moment in the preservation of the Indies, and for its trade and commerce, that Florida remain Spanish and be strongly guarded.
>
> **Report by Bartolomé Barrientos, 1565**

Below: "The French select a place for building a fort." This engraving of either Fort Caroline or Fort Charles was done by the artist Jacques Le Moyne de Morgues when he accompanied Laudonnière's expedition to Florida in 1564. Although built of wood, its outline is that of a typical European fort of the period.

Jesuit mission (1570)

Pardo follows native roads across Appalachians *1567*

1566 Juan Pardo and 125 men set out "to discover and conquer the interior of the country." Establishes fort of San Juan

San Juan

CHERAW

Cheraw

COOSA

May 17 1562 Ribaut finds "one of the greatest and fairest havens." Builds fortress and leaves garrison of 30 before returning to France

1563 Settlement abandoned

Charlesfort / San Felipe (Fr.1562)   (Sp.1566)

May 3 1562 Ribaut enters mouth of a "fair river." Received "very gently" by native people

San Pedro (1566)

Fort Caroline (Fr.1564) / San Mateo (Sp.1565)

Apr 30 1562 Jean Ribaut's expedition of 150 French Huguenots in 3 ships sights land

May 1 1562 Ribaut lands. Sets up pillar with arms of France. Asks inhabitants about Cibola. They tell him it is 22 days' journey by canoe

Jun 22 1564 Laudonnière's expedition of 300 French in 3 ships lands. Greeted ceremonially by 400 people, who show them pillar left by Ribaut. French build Fort Caroline

Aug 1565 Food and discipline problems at settlement. Ribaut arrives with rescue fleet of 7 ships

1564-65 French exploring parties search for precious metals

Sept 1565 Spanish fleet under Pedro Menéndez wipes out French settlers: "I had Juan Ribao, with all the rest, put to the knife..." Menéndez founds San Agustín

San Agustín (1565)

Tocabaga (1567)

Santa Lucia (1566)

San Antonio (1567)

Tegasta (1567)

Havana

CUBA

Gulf of Mexico

Franco-Spanish Rivalry, 1562-74

Known to Europeans, 1562

Spanish territory, 1562

Route of Spanish treasure fleets

French expeditions

Ribaut, 1562

Exploring parties, 1564-65

Spanish expeditions

Menéndez, 1565

Pardo, 1566

Pardo, 1567

Indian trail

French settlement

Spanish settlement

Spanish mission

Indian settlement

Massacre

The Lost Colony of Roanoke

ENGLISH COLONIZING ATTEMPTS IN "VIRGINIA," 1584-90

The first serious English effort to establish a colony in North America brings first-hand knowledge of New World conditions, but ends in tragedy.

By the 1580s, the English court was becoming interested in establishing settlements in North America. The region soon to be called Virginia had the advantage of a temperate climate, which could produce a whole range of "Mediterranean" products, and was a safe distance from the Spanish bases. The fate of the French colony in Florida (▶ *page 46*) was a grim reminder of the risks, but worsening relations between England and Spain strengthened the argument for a base from which to attack the Spanish Indies.

In 1584 Walter Raleigh obtained a royal grant to settle "lands and territories not actually possessed by any Christian prince," and sent out two ships under Philip Amadas and Arthur Barlowe. They entered an inlet on the Outer Banks (of modern North Carolina) which the Indians called Hatarask, and which the explorers renamed Port Ferdinando after their Portuguese pilot; they established good

Above: This watercolor of a Virginia Indian in body paint is the work of John White, official artist on Grenville's 1585 expedition, and governor of the 1587 colony at Roanoke. White had accompanied Frobisher on his 1577 voyage to Baffin Island (▶ page 28). His paintings of the people, plants and animals of North America, helped to shape European images of the new continent.

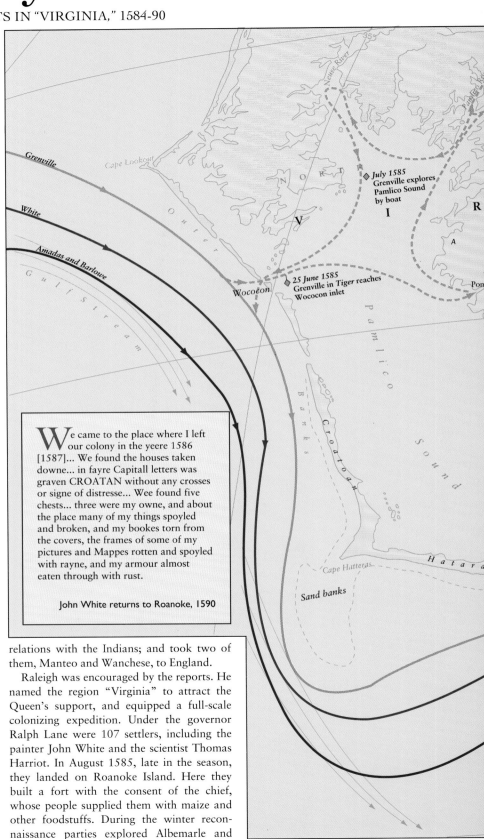

> We came to the place where I left our colony in the yeere 1586 [1587]... We found the houses taken downe... in fayre Capitall letters was graven CROATAN without any crosses or signe of distresse... Wee found five chests... three were my owne, and about the place many of my things spoyled and broken, and my bookes torn from the covers, the frames of some of my pictures and Mappes rotten and spoyled with rayne, and my armour almost eaten through with rust.
>
> **John White returns to Roanoke, 1590**

relations with the Indians; and took two of them, Manteo and Wanchese, to England.

Raleigh was encouraged by the reports. He named the region "Virginia" to attract the Queen's support, and equipped a full-scale colonizing expedition. Under the governor Ralph Lane were 107 settlers, including the painter John White and the scientist Thomas Harriot. In August 1585, late in the season, they landed on Roanoke Island. Here they built a fort with the consent of the chief, whose people supplied them with maize and other foodstuffs. During the winter reconnaissance parties explored Albemarle and

Mar-Apr 1586
Lane follows river west in search of "a good mine, or a passage to Southsea"

Moratuc

Chawanoac

Mar 1586
Lane expedition, probably with Manteo as interpreter, searches for overland route to Chesapeake Bay

Weapemeoc

C A R O L I N A

cotan

scogoc

G I N I A

Masequetuc

Skicóak

Norfolk

Chesepiuc

Chesapeake Bay

Winter 1585-86
Lane sends exploring party north, which reaches Chesapeake Bay

Cape Henry

Alligator River

O N Q U I A N

Dasemunkapeuc

July 1587
e arrives with colonizing party of men, 17 women and 11 children; nd Manteo, who he baptizes and appoints "Lord of Roanoke"

27 July 1585
Grenville's fleet of five ships arrives at Roanoke; leaves 7 settlers under Governor Lane

Port Ferdinando

June 1586
Fighting with Indians, after which Drake evacuates settlement; Grenville arrives with supplies to find settlers gone, but leaves garrison of 15

Outer

Banks

July 1584
2 ships under Amadas and Barlowe reach Port Ferdinando; Barlowe explores Roanoke Sound; takes 2 Indians, Manteo (Croatan) and Wanchese (Roanoke) back to England

Aug 1587
White sails for England to procure supplies. On his return in 1590, finds colony abandoned

The English in "Virginia," 1584-90

Known to Europeans, 1584	Swamp
Amadas and Barlowe, 1584	English settlement
Grenville, 1585	Indian settlement
Lane's expeditions, 1585-86	Skirmish
White, 1587	

Pamlico sounds, pushed along the Roanoke, Chowan and Pamlico rivers, surveyed the Outer Banks from Cape Lookout to Cape Henry, and reached Chesapeake Bay. But the settlement was racked by quarrels, and relations with the Indians worsened, probably over its dependence on them for food. When Drake's fleet called by in June 1586, the demoralized settlers accepted his offer of a return home.

A fresh attempt to settle was made in 1587, when John White returned with more than a hundred people, including several families. After appointing Manteo "Lord of Roanoke," White returned to England to arrange for further supplies. At this point, the indecision and ineptitude which had marked the Roanoke ventures turned to tragedy. With the Spanish Armada looming, White was unable to organize a relief expedition. By the time he got back to Roanoke in 1590, the settlers had all disappeared. Among them were his own daughter, together with her husband and baby daughter Virginia. The fate of the colonists remains a mystery: they may have moved to Croatan Island or Chesapeake Bay, been killed by Indians or assimilated into the local tribes. Tantalizing reports of whites among the Indians continued to circulate as late as the 18th century.

The Golden Fleece

NEWFOUNDLAND FISHERY AND SETTLEMENT, 1500-1763

Newfoundland's fisheries yield great wealth and in the 16th century attract more Europeans than any other part of North America.

From the time of Cabot and the Corte-Réals (▶ *page 20*) the shores of Newfoundland were a familiar landfall for European seamen. Each year the island's coasts and offshore fishing banks provided cargoes for hundreds of vessels from Portugal, Spain, France and England. Newfoundland cod, a limitless source of cheap protein, became a staple of the European diet. Yet the growth of fisheries excited little interest in the geography of the region. Throughout the 16th century it was assumed that Newfoundland was at least two islands, perhaps even a group.

The English concentrated on inshore fishing, involving only the light salting of the fish before laying it out to dry on "flakes" or stages. The French and others fished further out on the banks and carried the fish back to Europe after heavily salting it at sea.

The English, with their presence onshore, made the decisive move towards settlement and claiming possession. The Newfoundland Company was founded in 1610, with a charter claiming rights over the southeast coast from Cape Bonavista to Cape St Mary's. It immediately sent out a small colonizing venture under John Guy, who established the first permanent settlement at Cuperts (or Cupids) Cove. Settlers ashore helped to supply and repair the fishing fleets and in winter they would protect the fishermen's flimsy buildings, stages and boats from the Beothuk Indians, their rivals, or the ravages of the elements.

By the latter half of the 17th century there were 30 or so establishments along the "English Shore" between Cape Bonavista and Cape Race, though most had only a dozen residents, not all of them permanent. The French also set up small settlements along the "South Shore" from Plaisance westward. The English still concentrated on inshore fishery, while the French fished along the Gulf. But in 1713 the Treaty of Utrecht recognized British sovereignty over Newfoundland and the French withdrew.

A prominent English settler of the 17th century, William Vaughan, claimed that the Newfoundland fisheries, together with their trading and shipping activities, were a Golden Fleece yielding more wealth to England than the treasure of the Indies to Spain.

Left: This illustration from the original manuscript of Herman Moll's 1720 map of North America shows the inshore dressing and drying of cod, as practised by the English in Newfoundland. The stages were for curing the fish, and the casks were used to catch the cod-liver oil.

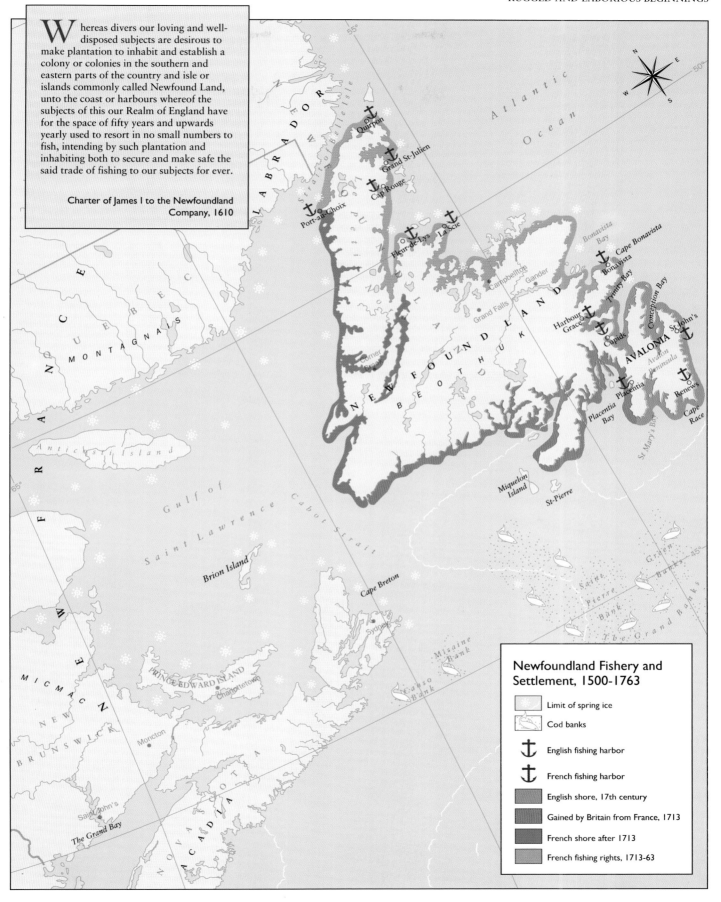

Whereas divers our loving and well-disposed subjects are desirous to make plantation to inhabit and establish a colony or colonies in the southern and eastern parts of the country and isle or islands commonly called Newfound Land, unto the coast or harbours whereof the subjects of this our Realm of England have for the space of fifty years and upwards yearly used to resort in no small numbers to fish, intending by such plantation and inhabiting both to secure and make safe the said trade of fishing to our subjects for ever.

Charter of James I to the Newfoundland Company, 1610

Newfoundland Fishery and Settlement, 1500-1763

✳	Limit of spring ice
	Cod banks
⚓	English fishing harbor
⚓	French fishing harbor
	English shore, 17th century
	Gained by Britain from France, 1713
	French shore after 1713
	French fishing rights, 1713-63

The Founding of New France

FRENCH SETTLEMENT IN CANADA, 1600-08

Champlain explores the St Lawrence and the Atlantic coast. The French begin to develop two areas of trade and settlement, one on the St Lawrence, the other in Acadia.

After the failure of the Québec colony of 1541-43 (▶ *page 26*) Breton and Basque vessels continued to visit the Gulf of St Lawrence for fishing and trading. But it was not until the 1580s that the French again reached Cartier's great "River of Canada." Tadoussac, at the junction of the St Lawrence and Saguenay rivers, then became a regular summer rendezvous for French ships and the Montagnais Indians of the interior.

In 1600, an all-year trading post was built there, but because of severe weather it was abandoned before the winter was out, leaving two-thirds of the small garrison dead from scurvy. The French complained that winter lasted more than six months there and they again questioned whether Europeans could survive such hostile conditions.

Samuel de Champlain took a different view. The French explorer had already accompanied a Spanish expedition to their American dominions. Appointed royal geographer by Henri IV on his return, he went on to lay the foundation for France's own empire on the continent. But royal backing for

> Snow fell first on the sixth of October... This we had to a depth of three or four feet up to the end of the month of April... Our beverages all froze except the Spanish wine. Cider was given out by the pound... It was difficult to know this country without having wintered there; for on arriving in summer everything is very pleasant on account of the woods, the beautiful landscapes, and the fine fishing.
>
> **Champlain describes the winter at Sainte-Croix, 1604-05**

Champlain did not extend to the provision of ships, and when he first visited the northeast in 1603, it was as an observer aboard a fur-trading ship, the *Bonne-Renommée*, commanded by François Gravé.

Champlain was the first European to venture up the Saguenay River, forty or fifty miles from Tadoussac. Indians told him about a salt sea to the north and, six years before the English reached Hudson Bay, Champlain

argued that this must be a gulf of the Atlantic. He then journeyed with Gravé to Hochelaga where they were stopped, as Cartier had been, by the Lachine Rapids. Unlike Cartier, they had Indian interpreters with them who knew of three huge lakes to the west. These were presumably Lakes Ontario, Erie and Huron and Champlain considered the latter to be the western ocean.

After they detoured a few miles into the Richelieu River, the Indians told them about a waterway, eventually known as the Hudson, which flowed down to the Atlantic coast. In his first few months of exploration, Champlain had gained an extensive if still sketchy knowledge of the lands bordering the St Lawrence.

In 1604 Champlain switched his attention to the Atlantic coast, where he accompanied the colonizing expedition led by Sieur de Monts to explore the Bay of Fundy and to set up a post on the Maine coast at the Sainte-Croix River. After a miserable winter in which the garrison suffered from cold and scurvy, the little settlement was moved to Port

Left: Champlain's first fort at Québec, the Habitation, *resembled a late medieval European Castle and was clearly built with defense in mind. The engraving was first published in the* Voyage due Sieur de Champlain *(1613).*

Above: In 1623 Champlain replaced his original fort with a larger, stronger building. The clay pipe (left) and lead inkwell (right) were found in the surrounding ditches, and are believed to date from this second period of occupation.

French Settlement, 1600-08

	Limit of spring ice
	Known to Europeans, 1603
	French settlement
	Gravé and Champlain, 1603
	De Monts and Champlain, 1604-05
	Champlain, 1606
	Champlain, 1607
	Trading encounter
	Death of settlers
	Rapids

Royal in the Bay of Fundy. It survived there until 1607. These faltering ventures at settlement were accompanied by alliances with the Micmac and Etchemin Indians and further exploration. Champlain and de Monts coasted the shores of Maine, entered the Penobscot River and sailed south along the New England coast as far as Cape Cod. The great peninsula of Acadia and the Bay of Fundy would soon appear on the maps for the first time.

Disappointments at Sainte-Croix and Port Royal turned the French back to the St Lawrence, and in 1608 Champlain established a settlement at Québec, near the deserted Indian site of Stadacona. Here,

where the river narrowed, the French built a small, fortress-like establishment, complete with moat and drawbridge. Only eight out of the garrison of 28 survived the first winter, but the French were slowly learning the techniques of cold-weather survival.

It would be long before this and other tiny French settlements could in any sense be regarded as permanent. Even so, the shape of 17th-century New France could now be glimpsed in embryo.

Norembèque Becomes New England

EXPLORATIONS ON THE NORTHEAST COAST, 1602-16

The English explore the little-known coast
from New York to Maine, with a view to
settlement as well as trade.

After the voyages of Verrazano in 1524 and Gomes in 1525, along the shores of what Verrazano called "Norembèque" (▶ *page 24*), there was little further exploration of the region for the rest of the century. It could be hazardous, for along the coast there were reefs and shoals and the area was subject to summer storms. However there was some European fishing and trading, an overspill from further north, and occasionally Europeans landed and made contact with the Indians who were living there.

It was not until the early 17th century that sporadic interest in the region became more

Gosnold meets Micmac Indians off the Maine coast, May 1602:
They came boldly aboord us being all naked, saving about their shoulders certaine loose Deere-skinnes, and neere their wastes Seale-skinnes [but] one that seemed to be their Commander wore a Wastecoate of blacke worke, a paire of Breeches, cloth Stockings, Shooes, Hat, and Band, one or two more had also a few things made by some Christians, these with a piece of Chalke described the Coast thereabouts, and could name Placentia of the New-found-land, they spake divers Christian words, and seemed to understand much more than we.

Samuel Purchas, *Pilgrimes*, 1625

systematic. The French looked to the coast between the Penobscot River and Cape Breton, now becoming known as Acadie or Acadia. The English were more active along the coast running south from the Penobscot to about latitude 40°N, an area which they called North Virginia. English reconnaissance voyages surveyed much of this coastline, looking for possible areas for settlement as well as trade; for somewhere along that coast was Verrazano's "Refugio," with its good harbor, friendly Indians and fertile soil.

In 1602 an expedition under Bartholomew Gosnold reached and named such features of the coast as Cape Cod and Martha's Vineyard. Three years later George Waymouth sailed up the St George River, where he was impressed, perhaps over-impressed, by the fertility of the region. He seized five Indians

(probably Eastern Abenaki of the Etchemin tribe) and took them back to England. One of them returned to his own country in 1607, with a hundred English colonists sent out by the Virginia Company. They established a settlement, Fort St George, near the mouth of Sagadahoc, now the Kennebec River. After suffering the same severe winter conditions and casualties that were experienced by the French further north at Sainte-Croix and Port Royal (▶ *page 52*), the settlement was abandoned. Summer landings, mistaken assumptions about a Mediterranean-style climate, and the sight of land cleared and

planted by Indians, meant that the European settlers were surprised by the harsh winter of the "Little Ice Age."

The most important exploration was made by an English navigator leading a Dutch expedition. The initial objective was to search for a polar passage to the Pacific. Sailing in the *Half Moon*, thwarted by early summer ice in the Barents Sea, Henry Hudson turned west across the Atlantic to the American coast. He was probably prompted by information from John Smith in Virginia (▶ *page 56*). In September 1609 Hudson sailed, as Verrazano had already done, through the narrows and

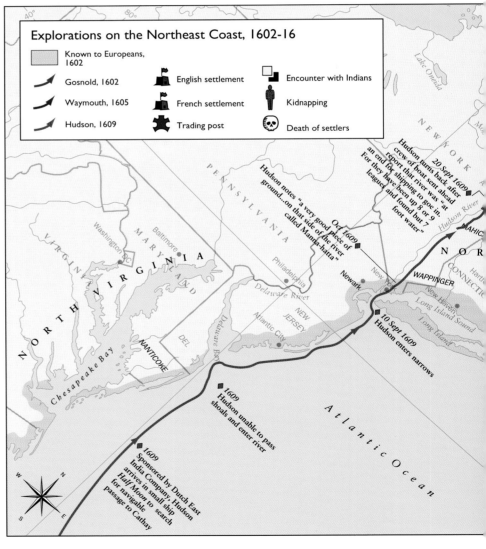

Explorations on the Northeast Coast, 1602-16

- Known to Europeans, 1602
- Gosnold, 1602
- Waymouth, 1605
- Hudson, 1609
- English settlement
- French settlement
- Trading post
- Encounter with Indians
- Kidnapping
- Death of settlers

into New York Harbor. He then entered the river now known as the Hudson and sailed up it as far as present-day Albany. As the water shoaled it was soon realized that he had not found a strait to the Pacific. Nevertheless, Hudson had confirmed the existence of a great harbor and had journeyed up the most important waterway on the east coast. When he turned back, somewhere near the Mohawk River, he was less than a hundred miles from the spot reached a few weeks earlier by Samuel de Champlain, pushing south from the St Lawrence (▶ page 58).

Hudson's explorations formed the basis for a Dutch claim to an area soon to be known as New Netherland. To the north John Smith, who in 1614 mapped the coast from Cape Cod to the Penobscot, gave a new and prophetic name to the region where English settlers would soon arrive: New England.

Right: Part of the "Velasco map" c.1610, sent to Spain in 1611 by the Spanish ambassador in London, Don Alonso de Velasco. This English manuscript map, which stretches from Cape Fear to Newfoundland, shows a surprisingly full knowledge of the recent exploration of the English, French and Dutch. Probably put together from a number of separate surveys, it includes Hudson's explorations of the Hudson River in 1609, and good representations of the Kennebec and Penobscot rivers. Some of the inland detail "is done by the relation of Indians."

The First English Colony

CAPTAIN JOHN SMITH AND THE SETTLING OF VIRGINIA, 1607-12

English settlers establish their first permanent colony in North America and explore the tidal rivers of Virginia.

After Raleigh's settlers disappeared in the 1580s (▶ *page 48*), occasional, ill-documented voyages kept the memory of the lost colony alive and maintained a tenuous legal claim to the region. In 1606 the Virginia Company was founded to promote settlement and trade. It attempted to colonize "North Virginia" (later New England) but its settlement on the Sagadahoc River failed in 1607-08 (▶ *page 54*). Meanwhile better-capitalized shareholders were organizing another venture further south.

In April 1607 three ships carried 120 settlers into Chesapeake Bay. They settled 60 miles upriver at Jamestown, and the tiny colony survived dissension and hardship to become the first permanent English settlement in America. Captain John Smith soon emerged both as its political strong man and the most prominent of its early explorers. In May 1607 he traveled upriver from Jamestown with Christopher Newport, past Arrohattoc and as far as the falls of the James River. Newport, reported Smith, had secret instructions "not to returne without a lumpe of gold, a certainty of the south-sea or one of the lost colony of Sir Walter Rawley." But he did bring back a map, drawn for him by an Indian, showing that far upriver were "certaine huge mountaines called Quirank." This was perhaps the first the Europeans heard of the Blue Ridge mountains.

In December 1607 Smith led a small party up the Chickahominy River, where he was captured by Indians and taken before the dominant chief, Powhatan. Smith's captivity, his dealings with Powhatan and his sub-chiefs, and the well-known part played in his release by Pocahontas, demonstrate the colony's early relations with the Indian inhabitants of the area: at times, help and co-operation, at others, ambushes and reprisals. In 1610 Powhatan delivered an ultimatum to the settlers to "depart his Country, or confine ourselves to James Towne only, without searching further up into his Land or Rivers."

Smith had already journeyed well beyond Powhatan's boundaries. In two expeditions in summer 1608 he explored Chesapeake Bay and the main rivers running into it, hoping to find a route to the Pacific. But after his second venture he became convinced that the stretches of salt water reported by the Indians lay to the north in Canada.

Above: Powhatan's deerhide mantle, decorated with shells, was brought to England before 1656, when it was mentioned in the inventory of the Tradescants, who owned land in Virginia. The circles are believed to represent the many tribal groups under Powhatan's domination.

> Their chiefe is called Powhatan... Some countries he hath which have been his ancestors, and came unto him by inheritance... All the rest of his Territories... have been his severall conquests... At Werewcomoco, he was seated on the river Pamauke, some 14 miles from James Towne, but he took so little pleasure in our nearer neighbourhood...that he retired himself to a place in the deserts at the top of the river Chickahamania
>
> John Smith, A Map of Virginia, 1612

Left: John Smith's A Map of Virginia (1612) outlined the main features of tidewater Virginia, with a mass of information about its Indian inhabitants. The crosses mark the limits of Smith's own explorations; everything beyond them he based on Indian information.

Smith meets Iroquoian-speaking
Indians(the Susquehannock),
who have European metal goods

Sasquesahannock

Tockwough

Smith passes site of
modern Washington DC in
search of the "big sea water"
of the Indians

Washington D.C.

Baltimore

Smith meets Nanticoke Indians,
outside Powhatan's terrieries

Smith explores
Rappahannock River until
he encounters Manahoac
Indians

Smith has Indian guide,
Mosco, up Potomac River
in search of the "glistering
metal" reported by Indians

May 1607
Powhatan Indians prevent
Newport going beyond the
falls towards land of the
Monacan Indians

Toppahannock

Wighcocomoco

Chesapeake
Bay

Powhatan

Falls

Chickahominy

Richmond

Werowocomo

Smith taken
before Powhatan

A t l a n t i c

O c e a n

Arrohatoc

Waenoc

Accomac

Dec 1607
Smith captured by
Powhatan's half-brother

Jamestown

James River

Cape Charles

VIRGINIA

Apr 1607
120 English colonists
found settlement

Nansemond

Cape Henry

Sept 1608
Smith elected
president of colony

Albemarle Sound

Roanoke
Island

NORTH CAROLINA

Pamlico
Sound

Captain John Smith and the
Settling of Virginia, 1607-12

	Powhatan's territory
	Indian settlement
	English settlement
	Newport and Smith, May 1607
	Smith, Dec 1607-Jan 1608
	Smith, Jan-July 1608
	Smith, July-Sept 1608
	Falls

WEST
VIRGINIA

Shenandoah Mountains

Shenandoah River

MARYLAND

NEW JERSEY

Atlantic City

Delaware Bay

NANTICOKE

DEL

SUSQUEHANNOCK

MANAHOAC

Rappahannock River

VIRGINIA

MONACAN

MANGOAK

Roanoke River

To the Great Lakes

THE TRAVELS OF SAMUEL DE CHAMPLAIN, 1609-16

Explorer, trader and empire-builder Samuel de Champlain secures Acadia and the St Lawrence for France. He pushes west, where Indians tell him of the Great Lakes.

By 1603 Champlain had made short excursions along the Saguenay and Richelieu rivers and had sailed up the St Lawrence as far as the Lachine Rapids. His next six years were to be occupied with the foundling French settlement in Acadia and at Québec (▶ *page 52*).

In 1609 he returned to exploration. Entering the Richelieu River again, Champlain this time reached the lake soon to be named after him. Coming down from the north, Champlain and his two French companions set foot in what is now New York state a few months before Hudson arrived on its Atlantic coast (▶ *page 54*). This was the country of the Iroquois, that formidable group of tribes based on the Hudson and Mohawk rivers. At Ticonderoga, Champlain used his arquebus to help the Montagnais, Ottawa Algonquins and Hurons defeat the Iroquois.

In years to come Champlain used his relationships with the Ottawa and Huron

> I had much conversation with them [the Huron] regarding the source of the great river and regarding their country, about which they told me many things, both of the river, falls, lakes and of the tribes living there... They spoke to me of these things in great detail, showing me by drawings all the places they had visted.
>
> Champlain, *Voyages*, 1613

Indians, middlemen of the fur trade, to penetrate westward. It was no easy task, though, to persuade Indians to let Frenchmen through to the fur-trapping areas. In 1613 Champlain went by canoe along the Indian trade route of the Ottawa River as far as Allumette Lake, following the path of a young Frenchman, Nicolas de Vignau, whom he had left among the Indians two years earlier.

In 1615 Champlain made his most

A Montagnais woman and man. A contemporary engraving from Champlain's own drawing.

Below: Confrontation at Ticonderoga, 1609. Champlain, alongside his Montagnais, Algonquin and Huron allies, faces the Iroquois. From Champlain's Voyages.

Map labels:
- **MONTAGNAIS** *1608* — Champlain founds settlement
- **QUEBEC**
- *Aug 1615* Champlain reaches Lake Huron, his *Mer Douce* or Freshwater Sea
- **NIPISSING** — Lake Nipissing
- *June 1613* Champlain goes 175 miles along Indian trade route before Algonquin bar his way
- **ALGONQUIN**
- Ottawa
- **MER Douce** — Lake Huron
- **HURON**
- **PETUN**
- **OTTAWA** — Toronto
- *Jan 1616* Champlain, at his farthest west, visits Petun and Ottawa
- **NEUTRAL**
- Niagara Falls
- *Sept 1615* Champlain accompanies Huron and Algonquin war party
- *Oct 1615* War party fails to take Iroquois fortified "town" of Oneida or Onondaga. Champlain is wounded, and is carried away in a basket "pinioned on the back of one of our Savages"
- **Lac St Louis** — Lake Ontario
- **IROQUOIS**
- **UNITED STATES**
- Lake Erie
- **MOHAWK**
- Montréal
- Richlieu River
- Lake Champlain
- **VT.**
- **N.H.**
- Ticonderoga 1609
- *Sept 1609* Hudson's farthest north
- **MASS.**
- Lake Winnipesaukee
- Portland
- Bangor
- **MAINE**
- **N.B.**
- Fredericton
- Saint John
- Chesuncook Lake
- Moosehead Lake
- Penobscot River
- Bay of Fundy
- *July 1609* Champlain assists his Indian allies to defeat Mohawk (Iroquois). Indians tell him of a river not far to the south (the Hudson) "flowing into the sea on the Norumbeague (Atlantic) coast"
- **CANADA**
- **NEW FRANCE**
- **ONTARIO**
- St Lawrence River
- River of Canada
- Île d'Orléans

The Travels of Samuel de Champlain, 1609-16

- Known to Europeans, 1609
- French settlement
- Indian settlement
- Indian trade route
- Hudson, 1609

Champlain
- 1609
- 1613
- 1615
- 1616
- Battle

celebrated journey, 700 miles west from the Lachine Rapids to the land of the Huron. He traveled along the Ottawa River again, which was to become the main French route to the interior, and arrived at Lake Huron. After noting the fertility of the land under its Huron cultivators, Champlain accompanied a Huron band across the eastern tip of Lake Ontario on an unsuccessful campaign against the Iroquois. Before returning to Québec, Champlain explored in 1616 the eastern shores of Lake Huron to the land of the Petun or Tobacco Indians.

This was Champlain's last major expedition. His great concern was to persuade the home government to give more attention and more resources to Canada. He saw the trading and agricultural potential of "a country nearly 1800 leagues in length, watered by the fairest rivers in the world and by the greatest and most numerous lakes," from which might be found "the South Sea passage to China and the East Indies."

In 1610, Champlain sent a young Frenchman, Etienne Brulé, to live with an Indian chief and learn the Iroquois language. Brulé became the first of a new kind of explorer: the *coureurs de bois*. These fur traders lived among the Indians, learned Indian survival skills and traveled by Indian means, canoeing the rivers and portaging the falls. They became the outriders of French exploration in North America in the 17th and 18th centuries.

Brulé himself reached lakes Huron and Ontario before his mentor Champlain, and was probably the first white man to see lakes Erie and Superior. But he kept no written records. Champlain, by contrast, was a keen publicist. He described his travels in his *Voyages*, illustrated with drawings and maps, and published in successively larger editions in 1613, 1619 and 1632. These reveal greatly improved knowledge of northeast America, for much of which Champlain should be given credit. Champlain found no route to the western ocean but he established, through alliances with the Indian nations, a fur-trade network stretching from the Gulf of St Lawrence to Lake Huron and beyond.

Inset map labels:
- **MER DU NORT GLACIALLE**
- C. Worsnam
- **NOUVELLE FRANCE**
- La nation des Puans
- Isle où il y a une mine de cuivre
- Lac des Biserznis
- Petite nation des Algommequins
- Algommequins
- Grand lac
- Mer douce
- Gens de petun
- Hurons
- Lac St Louis
- Ch...nplain
- Hirocois
- La nation neutre
- Nation ou il y a quantité de boufles Virginia
- Riviere de Champlain
- Isle de l'Ascension

New France
REDRAWN FROM SAMUEL DE CHAMPLAIN'S CARTE DE LA NOUVELLE FRANCE, 1632

This was the last of several maps made by Champlain of eastern Canada. It draws on his explorations in the St Lawrence valley and along the shores of lakes Huron (*Mer douce*) and Ontario (*Lac St Louis*). Champlain was able to use information given to him by Indians, and by his associates such as Etienne Brulé, about lakes Erie and Superior (*Grand Lac*). Only Lake Michigan is missing.

The Great Lakes and Beyond

THE JESUIT MISSIONARIES, 1630-1670

Black-robed Jesuit missionaries probe the series of mighty lakes west of the St Lawrence. By the end of the 1640s all five Great Lakes begin to take shape on the maps.

Champlain's successors around the Great Lakes were mainly Jesuits. Each year they sent reports back to France from their mission stations among the Indians. They gave a vivid picture of the various tribes at the moment they first met the material culture, aggressive religion and deadly diseases of Europe. They also reported the activities of the *coureurs de bois*. These French traders and adventurers, often the true European pathfinders, rarely left any written record of their travels.

In 1634 Champlain sent Jean Nicollet, an experienced trader with Indians, to the west. With help from Huron guides, Nicollet became the first European to see Lake Michigan, meet the Siouan-speaking Winnibago Indians, and hear of the mighty Sioux nation still farther west. Nicollet journeyed from Green Bay to the Fox River, only three days from the Wisconsin River, a tributary of the Mississippi – as yet unknown to the French but taking misty shape in Jesuit reports as a great river that might lead to China.

French traders and missionaries persistently speculated about a way to the western ocean but their immediate aim was to explore and exploit the area of the Great Lakes. The Jesuits followed Indian trails out of Huronia. They reached the strategic and commercial "hinge" of Sault Sainte-Marie, an area between lakes Huron and Superior where Indian tribes came from all sides to trade. In another direction they reached the northern shores of Lake Erie. In 1642, they founded Montréal at a site on the St Lawrence where the Ottawa River led west, providing a safe route some distance from the Iroquois.

The expansion of French knowledge and influence was interrupted in the late 1640s and 1650s by the long-threatened Iroquois war over Huronia. Warriors from the Iroquois Confederacy wiped out most Huron villages, sent several Jesuits to a fiery death and wrecked the fur trade. The old Huron-dominated organization was broken and the French were forced west for furs. As the Iroquois raids died down in the mid-1650s dozens of *coureurs de bois* ventured westward to keep the faltering supply of furs on the move. During a lull in the fighting Jesuit fathers visited the Iroquois homeland and brought back first-hand accounts of a large area from Lake Ontario to the center of modern New York state. In the late 1650s the Iroquois returned to the attack. Regular French troops were brought in to defeat them finally in 1667.

Settlement and trade revived. Lake Superior, still only known by Indian report, was a particular focus for the French. Father Jérôme Lalemant saw it as a nodal point providing waterways to the Hudson Bay, the Gulf of Mexico and the Gulf of California. The Jesuits, joined now by other missionaries, the Sulpicians and the Recollets, would soon determine the outline of the Great Lakes.

From Lake Michigan Father Allouez followed Nicollet's old route to Green Bay to establish a mission among the Siouan-

Indians wearing snow shoes visit the mission at Sault Saint-Louis. This pen and wash drawing was made by Father Claude Chauchetier.

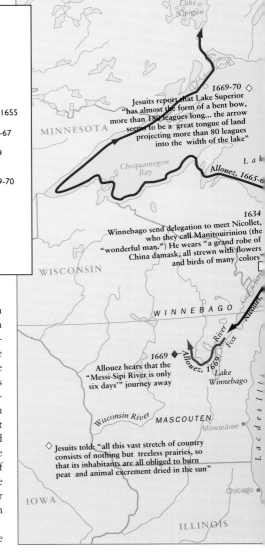

The Jesuit Missionaries, 1630-70

- Known to Europeans, 1630
- French settlement
- Dutch settlement
- Nicollet, 1634
- Brébeuf and Chaumonot, 1640-41
- Jogues and Raymbaut, 1641
- Le Moyne, 1654
- Chaumonot, 1655
- Allouez, 1665-67
- Allouez, 1669
- Dollier and Galinée, 1669-70
- Iroquois advance
- Jesuit mission
- Trading center
- Ceremonial encounter

1669-70
Jesuits report that Lake Superior "has almost the form of a bent bow, more than 180 leagues long... the arrow seems to be a great tongue of land projecting more than 80 leagues into the width of the lake"

Allouez, 1665-6

1634
Winnebago send delegation to meet Nicollet, who they call Manitouiriniou (the "wonderful man.") He wears "a grand robe of China damask, all strewn with flowers and birds of many colors"

1669
Allouez hears that the "Messi-Sipi River is only six days'" journey away

Allouez, 1669

Jesuits told: "all this vast stretch of country consists of nothing but treeless prairies, so that its inhabitants are all obliged to burn peat and animal excrement dried in the sun"

MINNESOTA
Chequamegon Bay
WISCONSIN
WINNEBAGO
Lake Winnebago
Wisconsin River   MASCOUTEN
Milwaukee
IOWA
Chicago
ILLINOIS

speaking Indians of Wisconsin. Pointing to the next phase of French expansion he described the land of the Mascouten Indians on the upper Fox River as "a very attractive place, where beautiful Plains and Fields meet the eye as far as one can see" – and only six days from the great river named "Messi-Sipi."

Mapping the Lakes
REDRAWN FROM A JESUIT MAP OF THE GREAT LAKES, 1672

The Jesuit Fathers Dablon and Allouez produced this map to show the French missions in relation to "the tribes of these regions." It was the most accurate representation of Lake Superior until the 19th century, and the connection between Lake Illinois and Green Bay (*Baye des Puans*) is clearly marked.

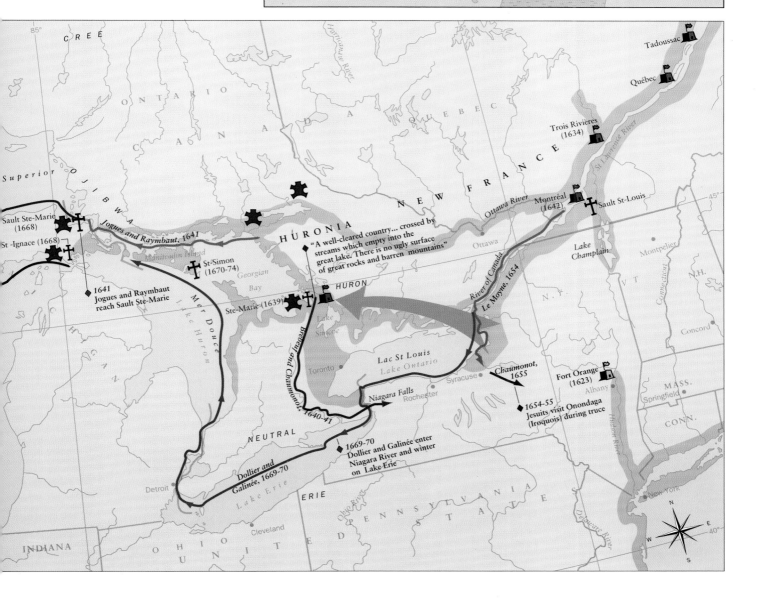

Down the Mississippi

THE JOURNEY OF JOLLIET AND MARQUETTE, 1673

The French reach the great river of the interior and follow it towards the sea – not the western ocean as they had hoped, but the Gulf of Mexico.

This map was probably drawn by Father Marquette himself during the winter following his Mississippi expedition with Jolliet. Although the latitudes are one degree too far south, it is surprisingly accurate, and shows for the first time the mouths of the Missouri (Pekittan8i) and Ohio (Ouabougkigou).

After the end of the Iroquois wars, at a ceremony at Sault Sainte-Marie in 1671, French officials told delegates from 17 Indian nations that the king of France was taking possession "of the territories from Montréal as far as the South Sea, covering the utmost extent and range possible." In May 1673 fur trader Louis Jolliet, with Father Jacques Marquette and five *voyageurs*, left to follow the great river to the south and find its outlet. Called the "Michissipi" by the Indians, the French believed it flowed into "the Sea of California."

Jolliet and Marquette canoed to the Fox River, crossed the Fox-Wisconsin portage and went on to the Mississippi. Paddling downstream, they saw fertile land on both banks, strange birds and plants and large herds of bison. It was 200 miles before they saw any Indians, poor though friendly Illinois displaced by the Iroquois wars. Further down, the placid waters of the Mississippi were disturbed by a large river thundering in from the west, the Missouri in full flood. Past the ox-bow bend of the Mississippi, they came to another great river, the "Ouabouskigan" or "Ohio." Jolliet and Marquette followed the Mississippi another 450 miles, but then, about 700 miles from the sea, fear of the Spaniards turned them back. Returning, they discovered an important short-cut to the Chicago Portage and Lake Michigan.

The explorers had found no precious metals, no furs, no wealthy Indian nations. Nor had they discovered a route to the Pacific, for clearly the Mississippi flowed into the Gulf of Mexico. But Indians reported that the Missouri led to the Western Ocean, and on the east bank the Ohio and Illinois rivers offered good commercial and strategic prospects. The Ohio provided a route into the backcountry behind the English seaboard settlements. Marquette wrote of the fertility of the Illinois valley, and their return route, modified, might take European boats all the way from the Great Lakes to the Gulf of Mexico. Lastly, they had made the link with the Great River – Espiritu Santo to the Spaniards – crossed by de Soto in 1541 (▶ *pages 34-35*). According to Father Dablon, Jesuit superior at Sault Ste-Marie: "It is certainly most probable that the river which geographers trace and call Saint Esprit is the Mississippi."

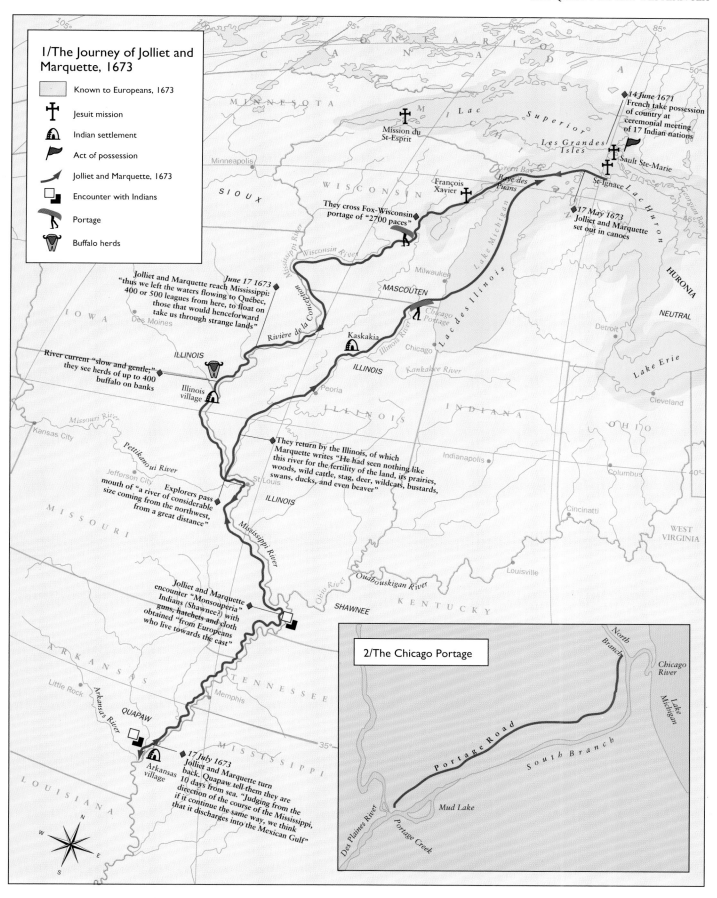

1/The Journey of Jolliet and Marquette, 1673

Known to Europeans, 1673
Jesuit mission
Indian settlement
Act of possession
Jolliet and Marquette, 1673
Encounter with Indians
Portage
Buffalo herds

14 June 1671 French take possession of country at ceremonial meeting of 17 Indian nations

17 May 1673 Jolliet and Marquette set out in canoes

They cross Fox-Wisconsin portage of "2700 paces"

Mission du St-Esprit

François Xavier

Les Grandes Isles

Sault Ste-Marie

St-Ignace

June 17 1673 Jolliet and Marquette reach Mississippi: "thus we left the waters flowing to Québec, 400 or 500 leagues from here, to float on those that would henceforward take us through strange lands"

Kaskakia

Chicago Portage

River current "slow and gentle;" they see herds of up to 400 buffalo on banks

Illinois village

They return by the Illinois, of which Marquette writes "He had seen nothing like this river for the fertility of the land, its prairies, woods, wild cattle, stag, deer, wildcats, bustards, swans, ducks, and even beaver"

Explorers pass mouth of "a river of considerable size coming from the northwest, from a great distance"

Jolliet and Marquette encounter "Monsouperia" Indians (Shawnee?) with guns, hatchets and cloth obtained "from Europeans who live towards the east"

QUAPAW

Arkansas village

17 July 1673 Jolliet and Marquette turn back. Quapaw tell them they are 10 days from sea. "Judging from the direction of the course of the Mississippi, if it continue the same way, we think that it discharges into the Mexican Gulf"

2/The Chicago Portage

North Branch
Chicago River
Lake Michigan
South Branch
Portage Road
Mud Lake
Des Plaines River
Portage Creek

The French Reach the Sea

THE JOURNEY OF LA SALLE, 1682

La Salle's canoe journey down the Mississippi to the sea opens the way to a French empire stretching from the St Lawrence to the Gulf of Mexico.

When Jolliet and Marquette discovered the Mississippi River it seemed to hold out glittering prospects (▶ *page 62*), but the area was not explored any further for nine years. Although French fur traders were keen to expand their activities, the French government wanted to pursue a more cautious policy, preferring to develop a close-knit colony on the St Lawrence rather than far-flung trade with Indians.

The explorer who closed the gap between the sea and the farthest south point reached by Jolliet was the controversial French explorer, René-Robert, Cavalier de La Salle. La Salle spent much of the 1670s in arduous travels between Québec, the Great Lakes, and the country around the Illinois River. He was joined by his lieutenant, Henri de Tonty, and the Recollet order missionary, Louis Hennepin. In 1680, Hennepin and two companions went ahead to prepare the way for La Salle's Mississippi expedition. Traveling west, they were captured by the Sioux and carried off into captivity, before being rescued by the French explorer Dulhut (▶ *page 68*). Hennepin's account of his adventures, first published in France in 1697 and in an English translation the following year, became one of the most widely-read narratives of French exploration in North America. Yet it was scarcely a reliable source: Hennepin had much to say about his own exploits and his extravagant claims were part of the fabrications, intrigues and visionary plans which surrounded La Salle's career.

La Salle's Mississippi expedition of 1681-82 was part of the French attempt to dominate the western fur trade. It was also part of a grandiose project for a huge French commercial empire stretching from the St Lawrence to the ice-free ports of the Gulf of Mexico. The French commanded both the middle stretches of the continent and its strategic waterways. The way was open for the next great thrust westward.

Like most of La Salle's ventures, the expedition was much more modest than originally envisaged. He abandoned plans to sail downriver to the Gulf of Mexico in an armed sailing vessel. La Salle's party of about 40 French and Indians made the journey in less imposing fashion, by canoe. For much of the time they followed the route of Jolliet and Marquette, paddling past the mouths of the Missouri and Ohio rivers, and like them impressed by the fertility of the region and its abundant wildlife. As La Salle passed the furthest point of the earlier expedition they began to encounter Indians as yet unfamiliar to Europeans, people of the Taensa, Natchez and Choctaw tribes. Although La Salle assumed that he was the first European on these waters in fact he was following the track of the survivors of de Soto's expedition 140 years earlier, as they made their last bid to escape to the sea after de Soto's death (▶ *page 34*).

In April 1682 La Salle's expedition sighted the sea. Despite straightened circumstances he arranged as ambitious a ceremony as he could muster. He raised a cross and the arms of France and against a background of hymns and a fusillade of musket-fire declared that he "took possession of that river, of all rivers that enter it and of all the country watered by them." His exploration represented an expansionism in which commercial, spiritual and military motives were all present.

Left: Louis Hennepin's 1697 engraving of a "vast and prodigious Cadence of Water" was the first printed illustration of the Niagara Falls. Hennepin, a relentless self-publicist, claimed that the falls were 600 feet high; they are actually only 193 feet.

Fort Ste-Croix
(1683)

St-Antoine
(1686)

Hennepin
freed by
Dulhut

IOWA
1680
Hennepin travels
west; captured
by Sioux

Fort
Crèvecoeur
(1680)

Fort St-Louis
(1682)

Fort St-Joseph
(1679)

Sault Ste-Marie

Fort
Michilimackinac

Fort Frontenac (1673)
(Cataraqui)

Fort Niagara
(1668)

Montréal

Mar-Apr 1680
La Salle travels overland
from Fort Crèvecoeur to
Fort Niagara

Feb 1682
La Salle party enters
Mississippi River from
Illinois River

Tonty notes that Ohio River
is 500 leagues long, and
that along it "the Iroquois
advance to make war
against the nations
of the south"

La Salle encounters Chickasaw,
called *Têtes Plats* by French because
of their habit of flattening heads of
their children

French reach Arkansas River,
farthest south of Jolliet and
Marquette in 1673. La Salle
sets up arms of France

French begin to see large
numbers of alligators

French reach Taensa, sunworshippers
like the Natchez and other tribes
of the region

French pass mouth
of Red River

April 1682
"We discovered the open sea, so that on
9 April, with all possible solemnity, we
performed the ceremony of planting the cross
and raising the arms of France. The Sieur de
La Salle,in the name of His Majesty (Louis XIV),
took possession of that river, of all rivers that enter
it and of all the country watered by them"

The river Mississippi is 800 leagues
long, without rapids, to wit 400 from
the country of the Sioux, and 400 from the
mouth of the Islinois River to the sea. The
banks are almost uninhabitable, on account
of the spring floods.The woods are chiefly
poplar, the country one of canes and briars
and of trees torn up by the roots; but a
league or two from the river, is the most
beautiful country in the world, prairies,
open woods of mulberry trees, vines, and
fruits that we are not acquainted with. The
savages gather the Indian corn twice in the
year.

Henri de Tonty, *Memoir*, 1693

The French on the Mississippi, 1678-82

Known to Europeans, 1678	
French post	
La Salle, 1678	Tonty, 1679
La Salle, 1680	Hennepin, 1680
La Salle, 1682	Capture
Act of possession	

The Northern Approach

TRADE AND EXPLORATION IN HUDSON BAY, 1659-90

Rivalry between French and English fur traders fuels the exploration of the far north, and leads to armed conflict.

In 1631-32 Foxe and James had failed to find a Northwest Passage through Hudson Bay (▶ *page 30*) and no European vessel entered the bay for almost 40 years. The French in Canada, after discovering that the Indians beyond the St Lawrence acquired beaver furs from the Cree Indians or "Christinos," revived interest in the far north. A Frenchman described these Algonquian-speaking Indians as "the best huntsmen of all America" at a time when they were

Below: The beaver was the staple of the Canadian fur trade. This pen and ink drawing is believed to be the work of the Jesuit Louis Nicolas, c.1700.

expanding along the southwest shores of Hudson Bay and past onto the plains.

Groseilliers and Radisson, two of the most enterprising *coureurs de bois*, reached the Lake Superior area in 1659-60, almost certainly not the coast of Hudson Bay as they claimed. They realized that the centre of Indian trade lay beyond Lake Superior and were convinced that the best way to bring back the furs of the Cree was not by the tortuous canoe route to the St Lawrence, but by the shorter carrydown to the shores of Hudson Bay, and then out by ship.

Officials in Québec were not impressed, but in England Groseilliers and Radisson gained the support of a consortium of businessmen and courtiers. In 1668 Groseilliers reached Hudson Bay in the 40-ton *Nonsuch*, wintered at Rupert River and returned with a cargo of furs. This was a decisive moment in the history of the Canadian fur trade. In 1670 some original subscribers, with other investors, were granted a royal charter incorporating the

Rival Claims

REDRAWN FROM SAMUEL THORNTON'S MAP, 1709

Thornton's map, prepared for the Hudson's Bay Company, shows the two rival routes to the fur-trading country of the Canadian interior: the English approach through Hudson Strait and Hudson Bay; and the French along the St Lawrence. The boundary between English and French territory in Labrador represents the English claim at the time.

Hudson's Bay Company. "Factories" or "forts" were soon established at Moose and Albany rivers. In 1684 the Company moved out of the James Bay area and built York Fort at Port Nelson, near the mouths of the Nelson and Hayes rivers, from where it could tap the rich fur trade of the far interior.

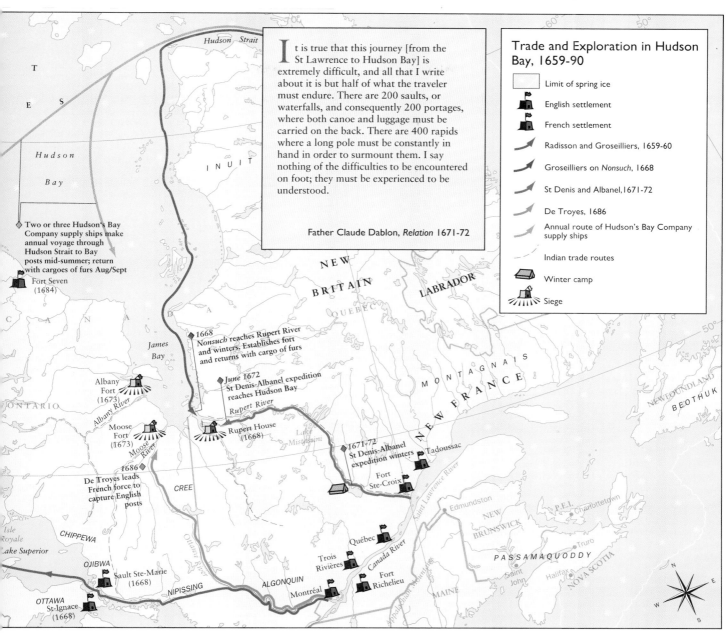

It is true that this journey [from the St Lawrence to Hudson Bay] is extremely difficult, and all that I write about it is but half of what the traveler must endure. There are 200 saults, or waterfalls, and consequently 200 portages, where both canoe and luggage must be carried on the back. There are 400 rapids where a long pole must be constantly in hand in order to surmount them. I say nothing of the difficulties to be encountered on foot; they must be experienced to be understood.

Father Claude Dablon, *Relation* 1671-72

Trade and Exploration in Hudson Bay, 1659-90

- Limit of spring ice
- English settlement
- French settlement
- Radisson and Groseilliers, 1659-60
- Groseilliers on *Nonsuch*, 1668
- St Denis and Albanel, 1671-72
- De Troyes, 1686
- Annual route of Hudson's Bay Company supply ships
- Indian trade routes
- Winter camp
- Siege

Two or three Hudson's Bay Company supply ships make annual voyage through Hudson Strait to Bay posts mid-summer; return with cargoes of furs Aug/Sept

In Canada the French were concerned. Their earlier attempts to reach Hudson Bay overland from the St Lawrence had failed because of rough terrain. The Jesuits reached Lake Necouba in 1661 but this was only half way between Tadoussac and James Bay. In 1671-72, prompted by the news of the English arrival, another French group, including Jesuit Father Albanel, made the journey overland. Over two seasons they crossed 200 portages and 400 rapids. In 1674 and 1679 two more reconnaissance probes followed, prompted by a growing fear that the Bay posts were threatening the French hold on the northern fur trade.

In the 1680s, as the French and English governments drifted into war in Europe, hostilities broke out in Hudson Bay. In 1686 Pierre de Troyes led an armed force overland from Montréal, capturing all the Hudson's Bay Company posts except York. Open hostilities continued in a sporadic way for almost 30 years, with raids, counter-raids and seizures of posts and furs.

The rivalry between the traders of the St Lawrence and those of Hudson Bay was to last 150 years, and before it ended the fur trade had reached across the continent to the Pacific.

Right: In 1670, two years after the Nonsuch *arrived at Rupert River, a group of its original shareholders joined with other investors to form the Hudson's Bay Company. The Company's charter was granted by Charles II, whose portrait appears in the document's illuminated initial.*

Towards the Prairies

THE JOURNEYS OF DULHUT, NOYON AND KELSEY, 1678-92

As the French push west towards the Winnipeg basin, they are outdistanced by a young English fur-trader from Hudson Bay.

Despite the well-publicized exploits of La Salle in the Mississippi valley (▶ *page 64*), most of the furs traded by the French came from the upper country. Here, in the *pays en haut* beyond Lakes Michigan and Superior the *coureurs de bois* had traveled ever farther west since the mid-17th century, their search for furs often co-existing rather awkwardly with the missionaries' concern with souls.

Daniel Greysolon Dulhut (Duluth in modern usage) was one of the most important French agents in this region. He left Sault Sainte-Marie in 1679 on a peace-making mission among the Sioux and their neighbors the Cree, Assiniboin and Chippewa. These Indians lived west and north of Lake Superior, where river access to the English posts on Hudson Bay was a possibility which alarmed the French. Dulhut's farthest west point was Lake Mille Lacs in modern Minnesota, but during his winter stay at the western end of Lake Superior (on the site of modern Duluth) he sent three men to explore even farther west. Where they traveled is not clear, but they picked up reports from the Sioux of a "great lake" 20 days' journey away "whose water is not good to drink." The European preoccupation with finding a way through the

continent to the Pacific was as strong as ever, and Dulhut took this as a reference to the Western Ocean.

By the mid-1680s the French presence in the area had been strengthened by the setting up of two posts, at Kaministiquia on the northwest shore of Lake Superior and at Lake Nipigon. In the late 1680s Jacques de Noyon canoed up the Kaministiquia River, perhaps as far as Lake of the Woods. Indians told him that from the lake a river flowed into the western ocean, presumably refering to the Winnipeg River and Lake Winnipeg. Noyon also thought he heard reports of bearded white men on horseback and stone cities. The French would not have an immediate opportunity to investigate these intriguing reports, for the tide of French westward expansion was interrupted by the Anglo-French wars of 1689-1713.

During these wars the Hudson's Bay Company maintained its cautious policy of waiting at its bayside posts for the Indians to come down to trade. Against this background in 1690-92, Henry Kelsey, "a very active Lad, delighting much in Indian Company," left York with a party of Cree. He was given instructions "to call, encourage, and invite,

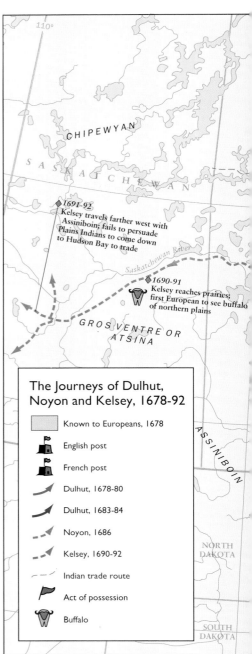

The Journeys of Dulhut, Noyon and Kelsey, 1678-92

	Known to Europeans, 1678
	English post
	French post
	Dulhut, 1678-80
	Dulhut, 1683-84
	Noyon, 1686
	Kelsey, 1690-92
	Indian trade route
	Act of possession
	Buffalo

1691-92
Kelsey travels farther west with Assiniboin; fails to persuade Plains Indians to come down to Hudson Bay to trade

1690-91
Kelsey reaches prairies; first European to see buffalo of northern plains

Left: A buffalo, from the first English edition of Father Hennepin's A New Discovery of a Vast Country in America *(1698). "Those Bulls ," Hennepin wrote, "have a very fine coat, more like wool than hair... Their Head is of a prodigious bigness... and they have between their two Horns an ugly Bush of Hair, which falls upon their Eyes, and makes them look horrid."*

◆ *1690*
Kelsey and Cree follow Indian trade route

Cape Churchill

H u d s o n
B a y

York Fort
(1684)

Fort Severn
(1685)

James Bay

Rupert River

Fort Albany
(1679)

Rupert House
(1668)

Lake Mistassini

Témiscaningue
(Moose Fort)
1673

Albany River

Moose River

Fort La Tourette
(1684)

◆ *1686*
Noyon reaches further west in Canada than any other Frenchman in 17th century

Fort Népigon
(1679)

CHIPPEWA

Winnipeg

Lake of the Woods

Rainy Lake

Fort Kaministiquia
(1678)

Isle Royale

Lake Superior

OJIBWA

Sault Ste-Marie (1668)

◆ *July 1679*
Dulhut raises French standard in Sioux settlement

Chaquamegon Bay

MINNESOTA

Three of his men go west with Sioux war party for unknown distance

SIOUX

Lake Mille Lacs

Fort La Pointe
(1693)

Duluth

OTTAWA

St-Ignace
(1668)

Georgian Bay

Lake Huron

Canada River

U N I T E D   S T A T E S

◆ *1680*
Dulhut rescues Hennepin group from Sioux

Minneapolis

Lake Erie

the remoter Indians to a trade with us." Traveling always with Indians, Kelsey seems first to have paddled along the Hayes or Nelson rivers to the Lake Winnipeg region, and then on to the Saskatchewan River, that great highway of the Indian trade. The next summer he followed the Cree on the track of the Assiniboin Indians southwest across the Saskatchewan River, and onto the great plains of western Canada. Here Kelsey saw buffalo herds, encountered grizzly bears and visited the Indians of the prairies, not just Assiniboin but also the mysterious "Naywatamee Poets" (probably Blackfoot Atsina).

The culture of the Plains Indians was based on the buffalo hunt and they declared themselves too fearful of the Cree and too unfamiliar with canoes to accept Kelsey's invitation to open trade with the distant Hudson's Bay posts. What the Company made of Kelsey's wanderings is not known. It neither used nor published his journal, the main part of which, with its curious rhyming prologue, was only discovered in the 20th century (*right*). No evidence of Kelsey's journey appeared on contemporary maps and in an era when Company servants were reluctant to leave the security of their bayside posts, his was undoubtedly a lone and adventurous undertaking.

I n sixteen hundred & ninety'th year
I set forth as plainly may appear
Through Gods assistance for to understand
The natives language & to see their land
And for my masters interest I did soon
Sett from ye house ye twealth of June
Then up ye River I with heavy heart
Did take my way & from all English part
To live amongst ye Natives of this place
If God permits me for one two years space
The Inland Country of Good report hath been
By Indians but by English not yet seen.

From Henry Kelsey his Book, *1690-91*

Part III : Expanding Frontiers

As the English settlements on the east coast became more numerous and more secure, their traders pushed deeper into the interior, where they came into conflict with the French.

The rivalry which ensued was to dominate North American exploration in the first half of the 18th century, exploding into war in the 1750s. The British emerged the victors, but the new breed of colonists who had sprung up on the frontier would soon seize control of their own destiny. By the time traders and trappers had crossed the Mississippi to the foothills of the Rockies, the United States had declared independence, and was ready to explore its western lands.

During the 17th century English settlers established colonies along the Atlantic seaboard from New England to the Carolinas. There was some inland expansion along Indian trails with the help of Indian guides, but until the middle of the century, the tracks of the trader-explorers stopped short as they approached the Appalachian Mountains.

The deepest thrusts inland came in the south, where the mountain barrier fell away, allowing easier access to the interior. Deer skins rather than beaver furs were the main attraction here, but in many other ways the English traders of the region were the counterparts of the Canadian *coureurs du bois*. Much of their exploration was poorly recorded, but they reached far into the southern interior, towards the Mississippi. By the end of the century the English were challenging the long-established but weak Spanish grasp on Florida and the new French sphere of influence in Louisiana.

The first half of the 18th century saw exploration taking place in the context of fierce international rivalry as France, Spain and Britain struggled for control of the North American interior. A premature French attempt under La Salle to settle the Gulf coast of present-day Texas failed, but from their posts in the Mississippi valley the French edged westwards along the rivers towards New Spain. By the 1730s and 1740s the French seemed about to take control of the entire interior of the continent.

West of the Mississippi the Mallet brothers prospected the route to Santa Fé, while La Vérendrye reached the Upper Missouri from Canada. East of the great waterway the French pushed up the Ohio to confront the British traders who had filtered across the Appalachians. Despite the spider's web of their routes on the maps, French dominance was fleeting and illusory, and disappeared in the cannon-blasts of the Seven Years' War. The peace of 1763 gave the British sovereignty over Canada and all lands east of the Mississippi.

The remaining decades of the century saw the expansion of British settlement across the Appalachians. The American Revolutionary War checked this movement for a few years, but after the fighting ended American settlers flooded across the mountains into the fertile lowlands of Kentucky. A new type of American folk-hero emerged in the person of Daniel Boone – hunter, trailblazer and Indian fighter. Farther west, across the Mississippi, traders and explorers of several nations were active in the Missouri country. By the end of the century they were poised to cross the Rockies and fulfil the age-old dream of opening a trans-continental route to the Pacific.

Inland from the Northeast Seaboard

THE EXPANSION OF THE NORTHERN COLONIES, 1630-1700

As European settlements spring up along the northeast coast, fur traders push inland along the river valleys.

The settlement of New England, which began with the arrival of the Pilgrim Fathers at Plymouth in 1620, reached impressive proportions with the "Great Migration" to Massachusetts in the 1630s. But it was not accompanied by any immediate exploration of the interior. Although fur-traders soon pushed inland along the river valleys, their journeys were limited by the Indians. Only after disease and war had weakened the Pequot, Wampanoag and Narragansett was deep penetration of the interior possible. Even then the way was barred by the parallel ridges of the Appalachians.

In 1633 John Oldham opened up the overland trail from Boston to Connecticut,

Right: Knives were among the goods most commonly exchanged with the Indians for furs. This mid-17th century Flemish knife has a brass handle in the shape of a hunter with gun and dog. It was found on the site of a Susquehannock village in Pennsylvania.

and found fertile soil and plentiful supplies of beaver. He was followed by Edward Winslow, and William Pynchon, who traded and explored along the Connecticut River. Simon Willard in the 1640s pushed up the Merrimack River, and in 1652 John Sherman and Jonathan Ince reached its source at Lake Winnipesaukee. Further north Darby Field followed the Saco River to the White Mountains, and looked across to the Gulf of St Lawrence and into the region of French dominance. Boundary disputes between the separate colonies, wars with the Indians, and the traders' continuing search for furs, opened up more of the interior, but exploration remained mainly local.

To the south, Hudson's voyage of 1609

Left: A 17th-century chevron bead, one and a half inches long, found at an Iroquois village site, probably Oneida.

(▶ *page 54*) was followed by the arrival of Dutch traders and settlers. From Fort Orange, more than a hundred miles up the Hudson, the Dutch traded with the dominant Iroquois or Five Nations. The Iroquois were the middlemen in the fur trade; to preserve this position they discouraged exploration through their territory. In the winter of 1634-35, however, they allowed three Dutchmen to visit the chief fortified settlement or "castle"of the Oneida Indians. The Dutch saw French goods there, and were told how favorable the French trade terms were compared to their own.

Rivalry between the Hudson and Great Lakes trading areas became fiercer after the English annexed the Dutch settlements in 1664. Traders and interpreters from what was now the English colony of New York (formerly New Amsterdam) thrust deep. into Indian country. In 1685 an Albany trader, James Roseboom, was guided by French deserters into the heart of the French trading empire at Michilimackinac, where he traded furs with the Ottawa. Even more enterprising was the journey of Arnout Viele, a Dutch trader and Indian interpreter working for the English. In 1692-94 he traveled from Albany at least as far southwest as the almost unknown Ohio valley to open trade with the Shawnees. Far-ranging though these journeys were, they were isolated forays rather than precursors of any systematic program of exploration and exploitation.

Above: A Dutch flint-lock trade gun made around 1660. Such guns were often sold in the North American beaver trade.

This castle likewise is situated on a very high hill, and was surrounded by two rows of palisades. It was 767 paces in circumference. There are 66 houses, but much better, higher, and more finished than all the others we saw... In the afternoon one of the council came to me... He told us that we were not worth anything, because we did not bring him a present. Then he told us how the Frenchmen had come thither to trade with six men, and had given them good gifts.

The Dutch reach Oneida Castle , 1634-35.
From the narrative of H.M. van den Bogeart

1642
Field, with two Indians, reaches edge of French domain and sees "a sea to the westward, which he judged to be the Gulf of Canada"

1652
Sherman and Ince find source of Merrimack River

1640s
Willard explores Merrimack

1635
Pynchon follows Oldham's trail and trades in region

1631
Visit of Mahican chief kindles interest in trade

Boston (1630)

1620
Pilgrim Fathers arrive

Plymouth (1620)

1633
Oldham opens overland trail from Boston to Hartford

Winter 1634-35 Van den Bogaert visits fortified settlement of Oneida; finds French trade goods there

Oneida Castle

Fort Orange (1623)

Albany (1664)

Fort Nassau (1614)

MAHICAN

Providence (1636)

Newport (1639)

NEW NETHERLANDS

Hartford (1637)

NARRAGANSETT

1632
Winslow and Holmes establish trading post

New Amsterdam (1623)

New York City

Breukelen (1646)

Fort Christina (1638)

Philadelphia

NEW SWEDEN

DELAWARE

Providence (1649)

St Mary's (1634)

NANTICOKE

Jamestown (1607)

Fort Richelieu (1642)

Montreal (1642)

Quebec City

EASTERN ABENAKI

MALISEET

PASSAMAQUODDY

Penobscot River

PENACOOK

The Expansion of the Northern Colonies, 1630-1700

▢	English territory, 1630
▢	Dutch territory, 1630
▢	Swedish territory, 1630
▢	French territory, 1630

English	Dutch	Swedish	French	
🏰	🏰	🏰	🏰	settlement

→ Winslow, 1632/ Pynchon, 1635

→ Oldham,1633

→ Van den Bogaert, 1634-35

→ Field, 1642

→ Willard, 1640s/Sherman and Ince, 1652

→ Roseboom, 1685-86 (route uncertain)

→ Viele, 1692-94 (route uncertain)

✦ Trade with Indians

From Tidewater to Mountains

EXPLORERS FROM VIRGINIA, 1670-1750

Explorers and traders move inland from Virginia. They investigate the Appalachians and the fringes of the Mississippi river system.

In the early years the settlers in Virginia, like those in New England, concentrated on survival and explored little inland. Settler knowledge stopped at the line of falls, and not until the 1640s were forts established upstream on the main rivers.

In 1650 Edward Bland and Abraham Wood led an expedition to the Roanoke River from the most important of these forts, Fort Henry on the Appomattox. William Berkeley, the Governor of Virginia during 1642-52 and 1660-77, believed that the Pacific Ocean lay in the near west (as shown in John Farrer's map of 1651) and encouraged the venture.

Rich Adjacent Vallyes

REDRAWN FROM JOHN FARRER'S
MAPP OF VIRGINIA, 1651

Farrer was an official of the Virginia Company. His map, made in London, embodies the still-popular belief that the Pacific lay just beyond the Appalachians, not far from the English plantations. The reference to Francis Drake's Californian landing (▶ *page 40*) reinforces the English claim to the Pacific coast, "whose happy shores, (in ten dayes march... from the head of James River, over those hills and through the rich adjacent Vallyes...) may be discovered to the exceeding benefit of Great Brittain, and joye of all true English."

Berkeley's second term of office was marked by more serious exploration. In 1670 John Lederer, a young German doctor, made three journeys inland. His precise routes are far from certain, but he did climb the eastern slopes of the Blue Ridge mountains. Across the Shenandoah valley he saw in the distance, not the South Sea as some had hoped, but the looming peaks of the Appalachians. Lederer was thus able to correct the "great errour" of imagining the North American continent as being only 8 or 10 days' journey across. Lederer made his own errors however. Meeting strange Indians on his second journey, probably fugitive Erie from the northwest, Lederer suspected they had traveled from California "from whence we may imagine some great arm of the Indian Ocean or Bay streches into the Continent towards the *Apalataen* Mountains into the nature of a mid-land Sea."

After Lederer there began a more purposeful phase of exploration, much of it organized by Abraham Wood at Fort Henry. In 1671 Wood sent Thomas Batts and Robert Fallam inland with Indians who took them into the Appalachians, to a tributary of the Kanawha River. Predisposed to find oceans or seas to the west, they checked to see if the stream was tidal. But since the Kanawha

I would not advise above half a dozen, or ten at the most, to travel together; and of these, the major part Indians: for the Nations in your way are prone to jealousies and mischief towards Christians in a considerable Body.

John Lederer, *Discoveries,* 1672

flowed into the Ohio they were in fact on the eastern edge of the Mississippi system, two years before Jolliet and Marquette (▶ *page 62*) reached the great river from the north.

In 1673 Wood sent out James Needham and a youth, Gabriel Arthur. They were led along the well-worn Indian trade route of the Occaneechee Path, across Cherokee territory and probably as far as the Little Tennessee River. Needham was killed by an Occaneechee, but Arthur spent a terrified year with a band of Tomahitan Indians, "in a strange land, where never English man before had set foote, in all likelihood either slaine, or att least never likely to return to see the face of an English man." The Tomahitan took Arthur on their raids towards the Ohio and then south towards the Gulf coast, before he escaped.

By 1699 the Virginians knew enough about the land beyond the Appalachian mountains to realize how close they were to the French. The planter and explorer, Cadwallader Jones, proclaimed to the Governor of Virginia, Francis Nicholson, that it "cannot rationally be above one hundred miles into Louisiana Country." This was the year of the first French settlements in Louisiana, and Nicholson warned that if the French "settle that River [the Mississippi] that and the River of Canada will encompass all the English Dominions her." It was not from Virginia but from further south that the main English response would come.

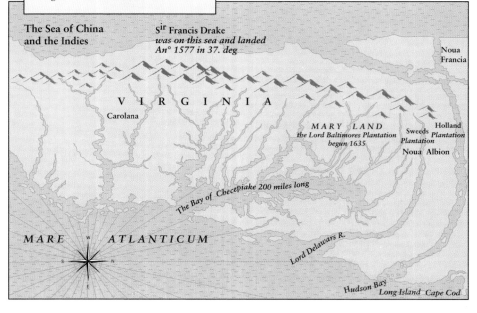

The Sea of China and the Indies

S^{ir} Francis Drake *was on this sea and landed An° 1577 in 37. deg*

Noua Francia

V I R G I N I A

Carolana

M A R Y L A N D *the Lord Baltimores Plantation begun 1635*

Sweeds Plantation

Holland Plantation

Noua Albion

The Bay of Checepiake 200 miles long

M A R E   A T L A N T I C U M

Lord Delawars R.

Hudson Bay   Long Island   Cape Cod

Aug 1670
Lederer sights Appalachians, but fails to find Indian pass "Zynodoa" (Shenandoah?)

Sept 1671
Indians guide Batts and Fallam along Roanoke valley and through mountains; first Europeans to cross Appalachians

14 March 1670
Lederer from an "Eminent Hill" sees Blue Ridge ahead

Sept 1671
Batts and Fallam reach edge of Mississippi watershed

1673-74
Arthur spends year travelling with Tomahitan war parties

May 1673
Needham and Arthur follow Occaneechi Path southwest

Needham killed by Occaneechi

Lederer meets Indians, who he believes have come from California

26 June 1670
Lederer describes a large, imaginary lake which remains on maps for many years

Explorers from Virginia, 1650-1700

Known to Europeans, 1650

English settlement

Spanish settlement

Bland-Wood, 1650

Lederer, March 1670

Lederer, May-July 1670

Lederer, August 1670

Batts-Fallam, 1671

Needham-Arthur, 1673-74

Indian path

Encounter with Indians

Death of explorer

Falls

A Prospect into Unlimited Empires

EXPLORATION AND TRADE FROM SOUTH CAROLINA, 1670-1715

*Traders from the new English colony of
South Carolina follow Indian paths towards
Florida and the Mississippi, challenging both
the Spanish and the French.*

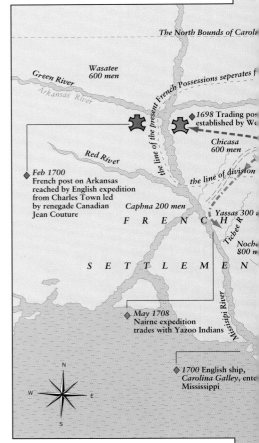

The founding of the colony of South Carolina in 1670 extended the southern frontier of English settlement and trade to within striking distance of the Spanish missions and garrisons in Florida. Inland, the southern ranges of the Appalachians were lower than those which hemmed in the Virginia settlements, and a network of Indian trails promised easier routes across them. Lederer (▶ *page 74*) dedicated his *Discoveries* (1672) to Lord Ashley, the proprietor of South Carolina. The preface pointed out that though the Appalachians "deny Virginia passage into the West Continent" they "stoop to your Lordships Dominions, and lay open a Prospect into unlimited Empires."

Among the first settlers at Charles Town (later Charleston) was Dr Henry Woodward. He made a series of probes deep into the back country: northwest to Catawba territory; west to open up trade with the warlike Westo on the Savannah River; and southwest to the lands of the powerful Creek confederacy. Woodward was followed by numerous Indian traders operating out of Charles Town, and later from Savannah, trading for deer skins, exploring and slave-raiding. Much of what they accomplished and where they went is unrecorded.

By the end of the century individual exploits emerge more clearly. In 1698 Thomas Welch followed the Indian paths all the way to the Mississippi to open trade contacts with the Chickasaw and Quapaw. The next year a Charles Town ship sailed a hundred miles up the Mississippi before being turned away by the French; but the main threat to France's planned empire in Louisiana came overland. In 1699 a renegade Canadian, Jean Couture, who had been with La Salle and Tonty (▶ *page 64*), led a trading party from Charles Town to the Mississippi. By February 1700 Couture, who was reputed to know eight or nine Indian languages, and to be "the Greatest Trader and Traveller amongst the Indians for more than Twenty years," had reached the mouth of the Arkansas, where he had commanded a French post in the 1680s.

Usually on foot, with a trail of pack-horses, the traders from Charles Town were spreading across the Southeast. By 1707 the Governor of South Carolina could claim that

"Charles Town trades near 1000 miles into the Continent." This expansion had a devastating impact on the Spaniards in Florida, where their missions among the Guale collapsed in the face of the English advance. The first Englishman to reach the Everglades was the trader Thomas Nairne. He accompanied a party of Yamasee Indians on a slave-raid in the region in 1702, and in 1705 boasted that "we have these past two years been intirely kniving all the Indian towns in Florida." In 1708 Nairne led a trading expedition into the Mississippi valley, and on his return drew up maps and proposals pleading for British government support for an aggressive trading policy based on alliances with the southern Indians.

Rather different in attitude and interest was John Lawson. A surveyor-explorer rather than a trader-explorer, he followed 600 miles of Indian paths to survey the interior of the Carolinas in 1700-01. But while their callings were different, the risks were the same: both Lawson and Nairne were killed by Indians, Lawson by Tuscarora in 1711, and Nairne at the outset of the Yamasee-Creek war of 1715.

Above: Surveying with the Swiss colonist Baron von Graffenried in 1711, Lawson was captured by Tuscarora Indians. This pen and wash drawing by Graffenried's colleague Franz Louis Michel shows them, with their black servant, seated before the Indian tribunal which sentenced them to death. Graffenried secured his release, but Lawson was burned soon afterwards. The servant's fate is not known.

Illinoy River

Illinois Lake
Lake Michigan

N O R T H

Weachthenocs 800 men

1711
Lawson killed by
Tuscarora Indians

◆ *Feb 1701*
Lawson reaches Occaneechee Town

English of South Carolina

L E V E L   C O U N T R Y   C A R O L I N A

Cussate alias Hockelegie River

Tennessee River

Cherecie 3000 men

Neus R

◆ 1670 Woodward reaches Catawba territory
- "a Country soe delitious, pleasant and fruitfull,
that were it cultivated doubtless it would prove
a second Paradise"

F R E N C H   R E F U G E S

Pedegoe R
Cabot creek
Cusa R

◆ Noted on later English map:
"Coll.Welch to the Mississippi in 1698
- since followed by our Traders"

Road to Virginia

E N G L I S H

S E T T L E M E N T

Ashly R
Cooper R
Santee R

*w Riff of Rocks
tt place to Settle
English Factory*

*Cussate
100 men*

S O U T H

Chattahuche R

Flint R

*Apalachi
Indians 200 men*

Savanna 150 men

Savanna R

■ Charles Town

*Chatahuches
80 men*

*Okesee Nation
700 men*

*Yamasee
350 men*

◆ 1674
Woodward reaches
Westo Indians on
Savannah River

▣ Port Royall

*ench
Chacta R
0 men*

*actas
0 men*

Moutila R

🛖 Talapoosie
Indians
3200 men

🛖

◆ 1685 Woodward reaches Lower Creeks
at Coweta. Despite Spanish opposition
opens trade in deerskins

C A R O L I N A

no Inhabitants from hence to the Point of Florida

the Road of the Ochese going to War with the Florideans

◆ 1715 Nairne killed
by warring Yamassee

☠

*Pancicolas
150 men*

▣ Pancicola Fort
80 Spaniarts

*rt Louis
Louisiana
) French*

◆ Jan 1708
Nairne expedition reaches
chief town of Talapoosa Indians

S Juans R

▣ S Augustin

P A R T

O F   T H E

W E S T E R N

O C E A N

The South Bounds of Carolina

*Old
Apalachia*

*Bay of
Apalachia*

Here the Carlina
Indians leave ther
Canoes when they goe
to War against the Florideans
F L O R I D A

◆ 1702
Nairne and 33 Yamassee go "slave hunting"
in a region of "Large inland Lakes,
some of them joyned together"

Villages of yᵉ Florideans

Gulf of Florida

P A R T   O F   T H E

B A Y   O F

M E X I C O

Exploration and Trade from South Carolina, 1670-1715

REDRAWN FROM THOMAS NAIRNE'S MAP OF 1711

Nairne's map of South Carolina showed "the settlements of the English,
French and Indian Nations from Charles town to the River Missisipi."
It also marked the Indian pathways used by the European traders.

Additions to Nairne's original map:

English French Spanish

■ ◆ ■   settlement

✦ ✦   trading post

🛖 Native settlement

☠ Death of explorer

➤ Henry Woodward, 1670s-80s

➤ Thomas Welch, 1698

➤ John Lawson, 1700-01

➤ Thomas Nairne, 1702

➤ Thomas Nairne, 1708

The Country, thro' which we pass'd...
gave us a great deal of Satisfaction.
About Three a Clock, we reach'd the Town,
and the *Indians* presently brought us good
fat Bear, and venison... Their cabins were
hung with... fat Bear, and barbakued or
dried Venison; no *Indians* having greater
Plenty of Provisions than these. The Savages
do, indeed, still possess the Flower of
Carolina, the *English* only enjoying the Fag-
end of that fine Country.

John Lawson reaches Occaneechee Town.
From his *New Voyage to Carolina*, 1709

Naturalists, Artists and Surveyors

THE EXTENSION OF KNOWLEDGE IN THE SOUTHERN COLONIES, 1712-30

In the wake of the explorers a new type of visitor arrived at the frontier: the naturalists and surveyors who set about recording the area and its wildlife.

As fear of French expansion from Louisiana came to dominate official thinking in England's southern colonies in the early 18th century, the attitude of the Cherokee, Creek and Choctaw along the southern flanks of the Appalachians became crucial. "While they are our friends," a British official pointed out, "they are the cheapest and strongest barrier for the protection of our settlements." In the struggle for the allegiance of the southern Indian nations an unexpected part was played by an eccentric Scottish baronet, Sir

Alexander Cuming. His scientific interests had brought him membership of the Royal Society. In 1730, during a specimen-collecting journey from Charles Town westward into the mountains, Cuming persuaded the Cherokee to accept an alliance with the British. He confirmed the treaty arrangements by taking a delegation of Cherokee chiefs back with him to London, where they received a ceremonial welcome from the British government.

Cuming's interest in natural history, if not his political activities, indicated a new type of visitor to the frontier. He had been preceded some years earlier by Mark Catesby, "the founder of American ornithology" as one authority has described him. Between 1712 and 1725 Catesby traveled across the southern colonies observing the natural history of the region, collecting specimens, and later painting them. Observers such as Catesby, Lawson and Cuming were a

> However small this distance may seem to such as are us'd to travel at their Ease, yet our Poor Men, who were oblig'd to work with an unwieldy Load at their Backs, had reason to think it a long way; Especially in a Bogg where they had no firm footing, but every step made a deep Impression which was instantly fill'd with Water. At the same time they were labouring with their Hands to cut down the Reeds, which were Ten-feet high, Their Legs were hampered with the Bryars.
>
> William Byrd's surveyors advance half a mile through the Great Dismal Swamp, from *History of the Dividing Line betwixt Virginia and North Carolina, 1841*

Below: This map by William Byrd shows the 1728 Dividing Line between Virginia and North Carolina. To survey the line, Byrd and his fellow commissioners would have used equipment like the theodolite (above right) and level (opposite), illustrated in William Gardiner's 1737 book Practical Surveying.

different sort of explorer from those who had gone before them, but they were representative of many who were to follow. John and William Bartram, the Swede Peter Kalm, the Frenchman André Michaux, found a new world of nature in North America which caught both the imagination and scientific curiosity of their contemporaries. Their interests were wide and varied: a careful listing and drawing of a plant or bird one moment, a description of Indian customs or some spectacular landscape scene the next. The title of Mark Catesby's two-volume work indicated the range both of area and subject which might be covered by these polymaths: *The Natural History of Carolina, Florida, and the Bahama Islands; Containing the Figures of Birds, Beasts, Fishes, Serpents, Insects, and Plants: Particularly the Forest-Trees, Shrubs, and Other Plants... To Which are added Observations on the Air, Soil and Waters; with Remarks upon Agriculture, Grain, Pulse,*

Psittacus Carolinensis Linnai.
The Parrot of Carolina.

Roots, Etc. To the Whole is prefixed a New and Correct Map of the Countries Treated of.

While the naturalists roamed at will along the frontier, those who labored behind them had a narrower but no less dedicated intent; for as settlement moved into the interior, so the land had to be surveyed, and boundaries established. One of the best-known examples of this activity was the survey of 1728 which laid down the boundary between Virginia and North Carolina. This drove a line 240 miles west from the coast through forests, across rivers and swamps, to the Blue Ridge Mountains. One of the Virginia commissioners was William Byrd, whose account of the survey, *History of the Dividing Line*, was a graphic description of the back country in this period, its terrain, wild life, and human inhabitants, both European and Indian. The survey, like others of its kind, formed an intermediate stage between primary exploration and settlement. It marked the beginning of a process of recording the main features of a region after the first wave of European intruders had passed across it.

Above: The Parrot of Carolina and the Cypress of America, from Mark Catesby's The Natural History of Carolina, Florida and the Bahama Islands *(1731).*
"This Bird," Catesby wrote, "is of the bigness, or rather less than a Black-bird weighing three ounces and a half: The fore-part of the Head Orange-Colour, the hind-part of the Head and Neck yellow. All the rest of the Bird appears green; but upon nearer scrutiny the interior vanes of most of the wing-feathers are dark-brown... The Legs and Feet are white: the small Feathers covering the Thighs, are green, ending at the Knees with a verge of Orange-colour. They feed on Seeds and Kernels of Fruit, particularly those of Cypress and Apples. The Orchards in Autumn are visited by numerous flights of them; where they make great destruction... Their Guts is certain and speedy poison to Cats. This is the only one of the Parrot kind in Carolina; some of them breed in the Country; but most of them retire more South..."
"The Cypress (except the Tulip-tree) is the tallest and largest in these parts of the world. Near the Ground some of 'em measure 30 foot in circumference... the tree increases only by seed- which in form are like the common Cypress, and contain a balsamic consistance of a fragrant smell. The Timber this Tree Affords, is excellent, particularly for covering Houses with, it being light, of a free Grain, and resisting the injuries of the weather better than any other here. It is Aquatic, and usually grows from one, five or six foot deep in water; which secure situation seems to invite a great number of different Birds to breed in its lofty branches; amongst which these Parrots delight to make their Nests..."

Mathematical Instruments
Contrived & Made in Metals, Ivory, or Wood, according to the latest
Observations of Philosophers and Practitioners of Mathematical
Arts, by Thos. Heath at the Hercules next the Fountain in y.e Strand. London.
With Books of their Use.   Thos. Heath sculp.

The Race for the Ohio

TRADE AND DIPLOMACY IN THE OHIO COUNTRY, 1729-54

Traders from the English colonies follow migrating Indians into the Ohio valley, bringing them into direct conflict with the French.

Since La Salle's time, the French trade routes from the Great Lakes to the Upper Mississippi had hinged on the Wisconsin and Illinois portages, well to the northwest of the Ohio; and apart from Arnout Viele's journey of 1692-94 (▶ *page 72*), the English had made little attempt to exploit the little-known country west of the Pennsylvanian settlements. But a war with the Fox Indians during the early 1700s forced the French to re-route their trade along the Wabash and Maumee rivers. In 1729 Chaussegros de Léry, Chief Engineer of Canada, made the first proper survey of the Allegheny and Upper Ohio rivers; and by the 1730s the French were building posts at Fort Vincennes, Fort Oniatenon and Fort Miami.

But as the Delaware and Shawnee Indians migrated west from the Pennsylvania backcountry across the Alleghenies towards the Forks of the Ohio, English traders worked their way along the Susquehanna, West Branch and Juanita rivers in an effort to keep in touch with the retreating Indian groups.

These sporadic ventures turned into more purposeful expansion in the mid-1740s, as war in Europe prevented goods reaching the French merchants in North America. The Pennsylvania trader George Croghan took advantage of the lessening of French activity to build advanced posts at Logstown on the Monongahela, where there was an important Indian trading village, and at other locations on the Upper Ohio. In 1748 he set up a post at Pickawillany, deep in the French trading area among the Miami Indians. Helped by the German, Conrad Weiser, who had traveled widely among the Indians, Croghan negotiated in 1751 and 1752 treaties with the Six Nations and with the Miami, Shawnee and Delaware tribes. With perhaps as many as 300 English traders on or near the Ohio, the whole region seemed about to fall British.

The French response, as war clouds gathered again in Europe, was a military one, a devastating attack on Croghan's post at Pickawillany in 1752, followed the next year by an ambitious fort-building program farther east along a line stretching from Lake Erie to the Forks of the Ohio. It was at the last of these establishments, Fort Duquesne, that fighting broke out in 1754 between French troops and Virginian militia under George Washington. The clash marked the beginning of large-scale hostilities between Britain and France in America which continued until the final French defeat in 1760. Three years later the Treaty of Paris confirmed that North America east of the Mississippi was to be British, and the way seemed open for the next phase of frontier expansion.

> **B**rethren: it is a great while since we, your Brothers the English, first came over the Great Water; as soon as our ships struck the Land you the Six Nations took hold of her and tyed her to the Bushes, and for fear the Bushes would not be strong enough to hold her you removed the Rope and tyed it about a great Tree; then fearing the winds would blow the Tree down, you removed the Rope, and tyed it about a great Mountain in the Country (meaning the Onondaga), and since that time we have lived in true brotherly Love and Friendship together.
>
> George Croghan's speech to the Six Nations, 28 May 1751

Trade and Diplomacy in the Ohio Country, 1729-54

English   French

post or settlement

De Léry, 1729

Croghan, 1740s

Indian path

Other Pennsylvania traders

Indian migration

Battle

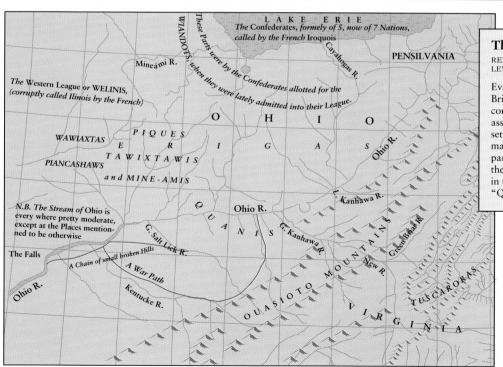

The Colonial Frontier

REDRAWN FROM A MAP BY
LEWIS EVANS, 1755

Evans's "general map of the Middle
British Colonies, in America" was
commissioned by the Pennsylvania
assembly to encourage permanant
settlement in the frontier areas. The
mapping of the Ohio region is
particularly accurate, and draws upon
the knowledge George Croghan gained
in the course of his journeys. Evans's
"Quani" Indians are Shawnee.

From the Blue Ridge to Cumberland Gap

THE EXPLORATIONS OF SALLEY, WALKER AND GIST, 1742-52

The English settlements expand westwards.
Along the frontiers routes are found through
the Appalachians into the bluegrass country
of the Kentucky valley.

By the 1740s the Indian traders pushing west across the Appalachians from the English middle colonies were being joined by frontiersmen with different objectives. They were looking for land suitable for settlement. In Virginia, particularly, land speculators and land companies found a favorable environment, for the colony's founding charter gave it claims stretching far to the west from the Atlantic seaboard. Some indication of Virginian ambitions was given as early as 1716. The governor, Alexander Spottswood, led his gentlemen companions, the Knights of the Golden Horseshoe, through the James River gap in the Blue Ridge, and on to the Shenandoah valley. One aim of this ceremonial procession, he explained, was "to satisfy myself whether it was practicable to come at the [Great] Lakes."

As passes through the Blue Ridge were discovered and negotiated, so land grants were assigned west of the mountains. In 1737 the Virginia Council allocated 10,000 acres of land to John Howard on the understanding that he carried out exploration west to the Mississippi. In 1742, joined by the experienced traveler John Peter Salley, Howard led a small group out of the Valley of Virginia at the James River, down the New and Kanawha rivers, onto the Ohio, and so down the Mississippi. There the venture came to an abrupt end as the group were "suddenly surprised by a Company of Men, Viz. to the Number of Ninety, consisting of French men Negroes, & Indians, who took us prisoners and carried us to the Town of New Orleans."

In 1749 the Loyal Land Company received a huge grant of 800,000 acres west of the Alleghenies, and the next year sent Dr Thomas Walker from Virginia to investigate settlement sites and routes. Walker crossed the Blue Ridge and the Holston valley, and reached Cumberland Gap – the gateway through which thousands of settlers were later to flood into the bluegrass country of Kentucky. Walker never reached the fertile lowlands himself, for he worked along the Indian trail, the Warriors' Path (used by the Cherokee in their incursions into Shawnee territory), to the north, before turning east along the Big Sandy River, across the Cumberland Mountains, and back to the Staunton River.

> We killed in the Journey [of four months] 13 Buffaloes, 8 Elks, 53 Bears, 20 Deer, 4 Wild Geese, about 150 Turkeys, besides small Game. We might have killed three times as much meat, if we had wanted it.
>
> Thomas Walker's *Journal*, 1750

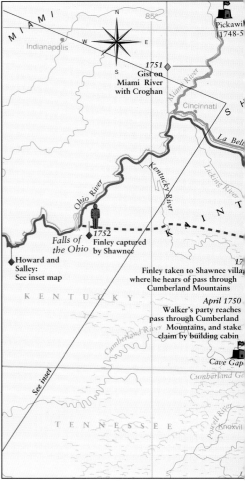

The next year Christopher Gist of Maryland reached the bluegrass country from the north. An associate of George Croghan (▶ *page 80*), and recently appointed agent of the Ohio Company, Gist crossed the Ohio, and in a huge sweep struck into Kentucky, crossing the upper reaches of the Kentucky River before bearing away east. It was left to a Pennsylvania trader, John Finley, to discover the connection between Cumberland Gap and the fertile Kentucky lowlands. Finley was captured on the Ohio by the Shawnee in 1752, and taken to their village near the Upper Kentucky River. There he learned of a pass through the mountains, clearly the one found by Walker, and soon to be known as the Cumberland Gap. Finley returned to Pennsylvania with the news, and although the looming hostilities with the French prevented any immediate response, his knowledge was to play an important part in the opening up of the region after the war.

Croghan's Post (Conchake, 1750-53)

DELAWARE

Great Trail

Logstown (Chiningué, c. 1743-53)

Forks of the Ohio

80°

Ohio River

Tuscarawas River

Muskingum River

Columbus

Scioto River

SHAWNEE

Raystown Path

Raystown (Bedford)

Shippensburg

PENNSYLVANIA

Juniata River

Lancaster

Philadelphia

MARYLAND

N. J.

40°

75°

DELAWARE

Delaware Bay

Baltimore

Potomac River

Frederick

Washington DC

Winchester

VIRGINIA

Chesapeake Bay

WEST VIRGINIA

Kanawha River

Appalachian Mountains

Monongahela River

Charleston

New River

Greenbrier River

March 1742
Howard and Salley set out, with three others, traveling overland and by canoe

Staunton

Shenandoah River

March 1750
Walker, "employed for a certain consideration to go to the Westward to discover a proper Place for Settlement," sets out from his house with five companions

1751
Gist reaches lowlands of eastern Kentucky

Great Trading Path

Castle Hill

James River

Richmond

1716
Alexander Spottswood leads Knights of the Golden Horseshoe across Blue Ridge

Warriors Path

Big Sandy River

Cumberland Mountains

Drapers Meadows

Chiswells

Wolf Hills

Stalnakers

Big Lick

Staunton River

Blue Ridge

VIRGINIA

Petersburg

Occaneechi Path

Roanoke River

Atlantic Ocean

Moccasin Gap

Watauga River

NORTH CAROLINA

Dan River

Holston River

Warriors Path

CHEROKEE

Great Trading and Warrior Path

Yadkin River

Betharaba

Winston-Salem

Salisbury

CATAWBA

TUSCARORA

Below: Wampum belts served as a gift and token of agreement among the tribes of the northeast. This example, with two equally-sized figures picked out in beads, is traditionally associated with the treaty between the Quaker followers of William Penn and the Delaware Indians on the founding of Pennsylvania in 1681.

The Explorations of Salley, Walker and Gist, 1742-52

Indian	English	Dutch	French	
				settlement

- - - - Indian trail

Spottswood, 1716

Howard and Salley, 1742

Walker, 1750

Gist, 1751

Finley, 1752

Capture

Pass

Falls

Lands Further Off

DANIEL BOONE AND THE OPENING OF THE TRANS-APPALACHIAN WEST, 1763-76

As the French and Indian War dies away, Daniel Boone and others on the frontier scout paths across the Appalachians for settlers to follow.

The influx of traders and land scouts did little to reassure the Indian nations, already nervous after the ponderous exercise of British military power that had crushed the French. In 1763 Indian resentments and fears exploded: an Ottawa chief, Pontiac, led an uprising of Shawnee, Delaware, Ojibwa and other western tribes. It was only suppressed at a fearful cost in lives to both sides.

The British government tried to stabilize the situation with the Proclamation of 1763,

Daniel Boone's, adventures in the fertile valleys west of the Appalachians made him a legendary figure. A colonel in the 1763 war against France, Boone went west when victory gave Britain a claim to the Mississippi. The defeat of the Shawnee in 1774 made a major expansion west feasible, and Boone helped drive a road across to the new frontier settlements.

which virtually banned settlement west of the Appalachians. But this was only, in George Washington's words, "a temporary expedient to quiet the minds of the Indians," and successive revisions changed both the boundary lines and the conditions under which settlement and trade were allowed. Land-hungry colonists in Pennsylvania, Virginia and North Carolina pressed on the central Appalachian frontier, where military

roads cut by the British during the war afforded settlers easy access. One official noted that the eager groups which pressed against the frontier always thought that "the lands further off, are still better than those upon which they are already settled."

The Forks of the Ohio, the Kanawha valley and the Tennessee River all attracted settlers, but most alluring were the hills and blue-grass meadows of "Kaintuck" or Kentucky. Gist and Finley (▶ *page 82*) had brought back reports of a lush and bountiful land, with fertile soil and plentiful game. It was here that the most spectacular expansion was to occur, but first routes suitable for settlers had to be found. While military surveyors mapped the former French territory along the Ohio, Illinois and Mississippi rivers, hunters and landscouts fanned out across the intervening country. In 1766 separate parties led by James Smith and Isaac Lindsey passed through Cumberland Gap, and news of their travels attracted the attention of the man who was to become the most celebrated "frontiersman" of the period, Daniel Boone.

While serving with the British army during the war, Boone had met Gist and Finley, and heard details from them about the bluegrass country. Working for a North Carolina land speculator, Judge Richard Henderson, and also trapping on his own account, Boone made his first attempt to reach Kentucky in 1767-68, but fell short of the Cumberland Gap as he hunted in the hill country around the Big Sandy River. In 1769, with Finley as guide, Boone's party reached Cumberland Gap, and followed the Warrior's Path into eastern Kentucky. Two years of wandering, exploring and fighting gave Boone a unique knowledge of the country between the Cumberland and Ohio rivers, where his

> S ometimes I feel like a leaf carried on a stream. It may whirl about and turn and twist, but it is always carried forward.
>
> Daniel Boone, after the death of his son at the hands of Indians in 1773

adventurous exploits made him the embodiment of the American "frontiersman."

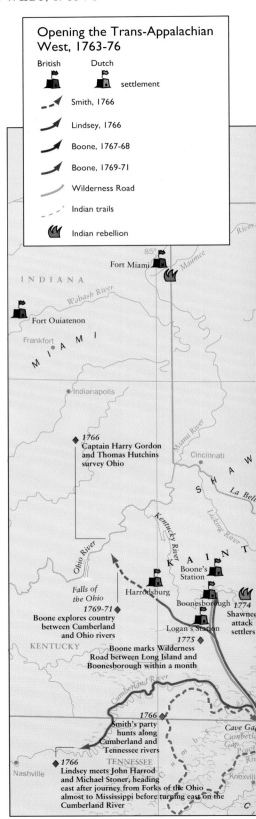

Opening the Trans-Appalachian West, 1763-76

British   Dutch

🏰   🏰   settlement

⇢ – ⇢ Smith, 1766

⇗ Lindsey, 1766

⇗ Boone, 1767-68

⇗ Boone, 1769-71

━━━ Wilderness Road

– – – Indian trails

🔥 Indian rebellion

INDIANA

Wabash River

Fort Miami 🏰 🔥   Maumee River

🏰 Fort Ouiatenon

Frankfort

M I A M I

•Indianapolis

1766
Captain Harry Gordon and Thomas Hutchins survey Ohio

Cincinnati

S H A W

La Bell

Ohio River

Kentucky River

Licking River

K A I N T

Falls of the Ohio

Boone's Station

🏰 Harrodsburg

Boonesborough 🏰 1775

🔥 Shawnee attack settlers

1769-71 ◆
Boone explores country between Cumberland and Ohio rivers

KENTUCKY

Logan's Station

1775 ◆
Boone marks Wilderness Road between Long Island and Boonesborough within a month

Cumberland River

◆ *1766*
Smith's party hunts along Cumberland and Tennessee rivers

Nashville

◆ *1766*
Lindsey meets John Harrod and Michael Stoner, heading east after journey from Forks of the Ohio almost to Mississippi before turning east on the Cumberland River

TENNESSEE

Cave Ga Cumberl Gap

Knoxvill

By 1774 there was settlement as far west as Harrodsburg, though in that year Indian war broke out as the Shawnees tried desperately to retain their hunting grounds in the face of settler encroachment. Their defeat cleared the way for the settlement of Kentucky. Boone helped to mark and clear the Wilderness Road between the Holston River and the new settlements. By the outbreak of the Revolution in 1776, the western frontier had moved forward massively, and by 1790 Kentucky had a population of 70,000 settlers.

Right: One of Daniel Boone's beaver traps. Boone, who spent over thirty years trapping and hunting buffalo and game in the trans-Appalachian West, used this trap on his journey along the Kanawha River with Paddy Huddleston in 1789

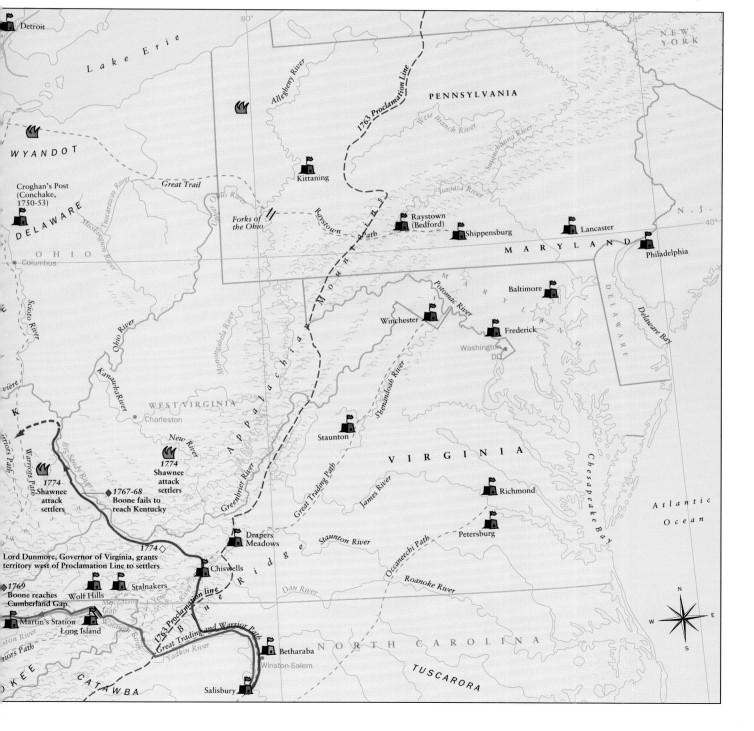

Detroit

LAKE ERIE

WYANDOT

Croghan's Post (Conchake, 1750-53)

DELAWARE

OHIO

Columbus

Great Trail

Forks of the Ohio

Kittaning

PENNSYLVANIA

West Branch River

Susquehanna River

Raystown (Bedford)

Shippensburg

Lancaster

N. J.

Philadelphia

MARYLAND

Baltimore

Delaware Bay

DELAWARE

Winchester

Frederick

Washington DC

Scioto River

Kanawha River

WEST VIRGINIA

Charleston

New River

1774 Shawnee attack settlers

1774 Shawnee attack settlers

1767-68 Boone fails to reach Kentucky

Warriors Path

Big Sandy River

Greenbrier River

Monongahela River

Appalachian Mountains

Potomac River

Shenandoah River

Staunton

VIRGINIA

James River

Great Trading Path

Richmond

Atlantic Ocean

Chesapeake Bay

Drapers Meadows

1774

Lord Dunmore, Governor of Virginia, grants territory west of Proclamation Line to settlers

Chiswells

1769 Boone reaches Cumberland Gap

Wolf Hills

Stalnakers

Moccasin Gap

Martin's Station

Long Island

1763 Proclamation line

Great Trading and Warrior Path

Yadkin River

Dan River

Roanoke River

Staunton River

Petersburg

Occaneechi Path

Betharaba

Winston-Salem

NORTH CAROLINA

TUSCARORA

Salisbury

CATAWBA

KEE

N
S
W
E

To Explore the Most Unknown Parts

THE TRAVELS AND WRITINGS OF JONATHAN CARVER, 1766-78

The war with France finally over, gradually the British explore their new territory. Jonathan Carver winters with Plains Sioux and keeps a record of his experiences.

The French had been defeated in North America by 1760, but it was three years before Britain and France reached a negotiated settlement. This, plus the disruption of Pontiac's Rebellion (▶ *page 84*), delayed British activity beyond the Great Lakes for a few years.

> N ear this nation [Cheyenne] I learned is a river rising from mountains in their neighbourhood and running north of the west till it falls into salt water, enlarging much in its course. On enquiring after a passage from the Indians they wou'd speak and make signs of great waters to the north west but whether salt or fresh, straits, rivers, seas, or inland lakes is hardly to be gathered from people whose way of life leads them into no such researches.
>
> **From Jonathan Carver's manuscript journal**

In October 1765 Ranger leader, Major Robert Rogers, was put in command of the strategic post at Michilimackinac. He made plans for moving westward on the upper Mississippi, hoping to find goods to trade and new areas to explore. Although the French had lost their territorial rights there were still French traders on the Mississippi. And although part of the treaty meant that New Orleans was now under Spanish control it still continued as a French trading entrepôt. In 1766 Rogers sent out some small-scale expeditions, not just to divert trade towards the Great Lakes, but also to undertake some exploration.

In 1764 Rogers had informed the British government that beyond "the Head of the Mississippi" lay a river "called by the Indians

Below: This engraving, from the 1778 edition of Carver's Travels, *shows the portage around the Falls of St Anthony. Situated on the Mississippi at modern Minneapolis, they were named by Louis Hennepin (▶ page 64) in 1680-81. "This amazing*

Ouragan" which flowed to the Pacific. This reincarnation of the French "River of the West" caught the imagination of at least one of the men sent out by Rogers, Jonathan Carver. Carver had been a captain in the colonial forces during the recent war with France. After leaving the army he taught himself map-making and surveying in Boston since, as he put it, he was determined "to explore the most unknown parts" of the "vast acquisition of territory" that Britain had gained as a result of the war.

Rogers employed Carver to explore west of Michilimackinac. Accompanied by traders and Indians, Carver left Michilimackinac in September 1766, taking the old French route first prospected by Jolliet and Marquette (▶ *page 62*). He journeyed through Lake

body of waters," wrote Carver, "which are above 250 yards over, form a most pleasing cataract; they fall perpendicularly about 30 feet, and the rapids below... render the descent considerably greater."

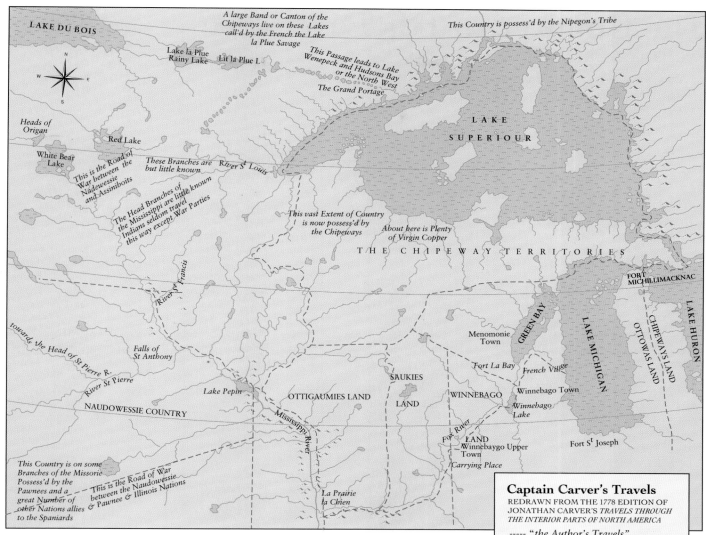

The map carries the following annotations:

LAKE DU BOIS

A large Band or Canton of the Chipeways live on these Lakes call'd by the French the Lake la Plue Savage

This Country is possess'd by the Nipegon's Tribe

Lake la Plue Rainy Lake

Lit la Plue L

This Passage leads to Lake Wenepeck and Hudsons Bay or the North West

The Grand Portage

Heads of Origan

Red Lake

White Bear Lake

This is the Road of War between the Nadewessie and Assiniboits

These Branches are but little known

River St Louis

The Head Branches of the Mississippi are little known Indians seldom travel this way except War Parties

LAKE SUPERIOUR

This vast Extent of Country is now possess'd by the Chipeways

About here is Plenty of Virgin Copper

THE CHIPEWAY TERRITORIES

FORT MICHILLIMACKNAC

River Francis

towards the Head of St Pierre R.

Falls of St Anthony

River St Pierre

Lake Pepin

NAUDOWESSIE COUNTRY

OTTIGAUMIES LAND

SAUKIES LAND

Menomonie Town

Fort La Bay

French Villge

GREEN BAY

LAKE MICHIGAN

OTTOWAS LAND

CHIPEWAYS LAND

LAKE HURON

WINNEBAGO LAND

Winnebago Town

Winnebago Lake

Mississippi River

Fox River

LAND

Winnebaygo Upper Town

Carrying Place

Fort St Joseph

This Country is on some Branches of the Missorie Possess'd by the Pawnees and a great Number of other Nations allies to the Spaniards

This is the Road of War between the Naudowessie & Pawnee & Illinois Nations

La Prairie la Chien

Captain Carver's Travels

REDRAWN FROM THE 1778 EDITION OF JONATHAN CARVER'S *TRAVELS THROUGH THE INTERIOR PARTS OF NORTH AMERICA*

----- "*the Author's Travels*"

Michigan, Green Bay, and Fox River to the upper Mississippi. Once on the Mississippi, Carver followed a route taken by Hennepin while he was a prisoner of the Sioux, the Falls of St Anthony and Lake Pepin (▶ *page 64*). He described a cave 30 miles below the Falls. "The Indians term it Wakon-teebe, that is the Dwelling of the Great Spirit... I found in this cave many Indian hieroglyphicks, which appeared very ancient."

In November Carver encountered Sioux for the first time. They were Dakota or Plains Sioux, Naudouwessie, as Carver called them. He then followed the Minnesota River about 200 miles to the main Sioux encampment, where he spent the winter. The Sioux told him of further Indian nations to the west: the Mandan and, beyond them, the Cheyenne. In April 1767 he left for Michilimackinac following a more northerly return route.

Carver's journey was longer than any other made between 1763 and 1775, but he was handicapped by the lack of trade goods that

had been promised by Rogers. In practical terms Carver achieved little and as the threat of revolution in America grew, both Rogers and Carver were unable to persuade the British government to mount further western expeditions. Both men fell on hard times.

Carver's account of his exploits, heavily re-written, was republished in 1778 as *Travels through the Interior Parts of North America*. A bestseller, it was translated into several European languages. But it was too late to be of help and in 1780 Carver died in a state of abject poverty. Despite an element of plagiarism and tall stories, Carver's account remains more than an engaging travel narrative. It is one of the first detailed accounts of the Plains Sioux and makes some perceptive comments on North American geography.

Carver's map shows his routes between the Great Lakes and the Upper Mississippi, and is extensively annotated. In print, though not on this map, he was one of the first to sense the existence of a great range of mountains running from north to south down the centre of the continent, forming a barrier to explorers trying to reach the Pacific from the east.

The Shining Mountains, as he called them, formed a true continental divide, with rivers flowing to all points of the compass – and that to the west was the River "Oregon." Although Carver sited the range too far east, in all except location his remarks conjured up the mighty spectacle of the Rockies:

"This extraordinary range of mountains is calculated to be more than three thousand miles in length, without any very considerable intervals, which I believe surpasses anything of the kind in other quarters of the globe."

The Country of His Discovery

LA SALLE IN THE GULF OF MEXICO, 1684-86

*La Salle tries to return to the Mississippi to
found a French colony, but the attempt ends
in confusion and tragedy.*

In 1682 La Salle's journey down the Mississippi (▶ *page 64*) opened vistas of a French empire commanding the heartland of the North American continent from Louisiana to the Great Lakes. After failing to win support in Québec for his plan to establish a chain of forts stretching from his new post (Fort St-Louis) on the Illinois River to the mouth of the Mississippi, La Salle returned to France at the end of 1683. There, Diego Dionisio de Peñalosa, the exiled former Spanish governor of New Mexico, had approached French ministers with plans for seizing the allegedly silver-rich territories of Gran Quivira and Teguayo which he said lay on New Mexico's eastern frontier. It was supported by La Salle's first-hand knowledge of the Mississippi valley. With France and Spain at war his proposal was approved and although the two countries signed a truce in August 1684, by then La Salle's expedition of four ships and 300 settlers was already at sea.

The expedition has been surrounded by controversy. La Salle missed the Mississippi delta completely, landing some 400 miles to the west at present-day Matagorda Bay. Here he founded his settlement, naming it Fort St-Louis.

Some historians have accused La Salle of deliberate deception, claiming that he knew where he was all along but placed the mouth of the Mississippi far to the west in order to increase French territorial claims at the expense of the Spanish. As a result, some cartographers even showed it as a branch of the Rio Grande. But it now seems that La Salle was genuinely mistaken. When he had journeyed down the Mississippi in 1682, he had tried to determine the longitude of the delta, but a broken compass and an "unsuitable" astrolabe led him to calculate it inaccurately. He appears not to have realized his error and was baffled to find that the dry coastal plains around his little outpost bore no resemblance to the silt-filled channels of the Mississippi he had negotiated three years earlier.

La Salle's forays from Matagorda Bay are as obscure as much else in these years. In the winter of 1685-86, if Indian reports are accurate, he seems to have reached as far west as the Rio Grande, possibly in search of Gran Quivira and its silver. In the summer of 1686, with the settlement marooned after the shipwreck or departure of its vessels, La Salle made an unsuccessful attempt to find the Mississippi, and follow it to the other Fort St-Louis on the Illinois River, where his trusted lieutenant, Tonty, was in command. Deaths, desertions and disputes weakened the little colony and led to a final desperate attempt by La Salle in 1687. Somewhere near the Brazos River violent quarrels resulted in the deaths of La Salle and six other members of the party.

The survivors, under Henri Joutel, eventually reached Fort St-Louis (Illinois) in September 1687, but Tonty had already launched a relief expedition in which he reached the mouth of the Mississippi and founded a French post on the Arkansas River. In 1689 he tried again by way of the Red River, but fell short of Matagorda Bay. It was left to Spanish search parties to piece together the story of the settlement's final days (▶ *page 90*). At the end of 1688, most of the few remaining colonists had been wiped out by the Karankawa Indians and the fort pillaged. They were still incensed, a young survivor later reported, by La Salle's behavior when he, "on coming, arbitrarily took their canoes for ascending the river to establish a settlement."

A Very Great Country

REDRAWN FROM LOUIS HENNEPIN'S MAP, 1697

This influential map of "a very great country discovered in America" draws on both La Salle's and Hennepin's own explorations down the Mississippi. Its one major error reflects the territorial rivalries of the period: the great river has been pushed westward, extending the French claim at the expense of the Spanish.

Left: One of the earliest known drawings of a calumet, or peace pipe, widely used in Indian ceremonial and peace-making occasions, from Minet's account of La Salle's 1682 expedition. Minet, an engineer and map-maker who was on the expedition, describes a meeting with the Chickasaw in which "six of them came back without arms with the peace pipe... the next day they danced the calumet... They brought two large calumets decorated with feathers of all colors and a large quantity of the hair of their enemies."

He proposes to return "to the country of his discovery by the mouth of the river in the Gulf of Mexico...we can effect there for the glory of our King very important conquests, both by land and sea...the provinces which may be seized are very rich in silver mines - they adjourn the River Colbert [Mississippi] - they are far removed from succor - they are open everywhere on the side on which we should attack them, and are defended only by a small number of persons."

La Salle to the Marquis de Seignelay,
French Minister of the Marine, 1684

La Salle in the Gulf of Mexico, 1684

- New Spain, 1684
- French trading post
- Indian settlement
- La Salle, 1684-86
- La Salle and Joutel, 1687
- Tonty, 1686
- Tonty, 1689
- Shipwreck
- Massacre
- Death of explorer

Fort St-Louis (1682)

Chicago

1686 Tonty sets out in search of La Salle

14 Sept 1687 Joutel and survivors reach Fort St-Louis

1689 Tonty sets out on second search

Fort Crèvecoeur (1680)

St Louis

1686 Tonty establishes post on Arkansas River

Arkansas Post
QUAPAW

1687 Survivors under Joutel reach Arkansas Post, commanded by Jean Couture

Memphis

1689 Tonty, deserted by his men, and with Spaniards nearby, turns back

CADDO

Shreveport

Jackson

NATCHEZ

1686 La Salle reaches Cenis [Tejas] Indians

New Orleans

1686 Tonty sends canoes east and west along coast in search of La Salle

19 Mar 1687 La Salle and 6 others killed in quarrels

APACHE

JUMANO

GRAN QUIVIRA

T E G U A Y O

San Antonio

Dallas

Houston

Fort St-Louis (1685-88)

KARANKAWA

Summer 1686 La Salle's ships wrecked

Galveston Bay

Matagorda Bay

Feb 1685 La Salle arrives with 4 ships and 300 settlers. Establishes French settlement

Cabo de Lodo

1686

Late 1688 Surviving colonists wiped out by Karankawa

Oct 1685-Mar 1686 La Salle takes party northwest towards Rio Grande

M E X I C O

Rio Escondido

N E W   S P A I N

Monclova

NUEVO LEÓN

Monterrey

Rio del Norte

TAMAULIPAS

Tampico

G u l f   o f   M e x i c o

A Thorn in the Heart of America

LAND AND SEA SEARCHES FOR LA SALLE, 1686-90

The Spanish hear of La Salle's colony and send out expeditions to "pluck out the thorn which has been thrust into the heart of America."

Since the collapse of Oñate's high-flown schemes (▶ *page 40*) the frontier province of New Mexico had settled into a humdrum existence. Less than 3,000 Spanish settlers were scattered along the upper valley of the Rio Grande from Socorro to Santa Fé, and only occasional missionaries, traders or punitive parties pushed east into the country of the Jumano Indians. The Pueblo Uprising of 1680, which drove Spanish settlers from Santa Fé and back to El Paso, stifled thoughts of expansion in the upper valley.

To the south, Bosque and Larios crossed the lower Rio Grande in 1675. And Mendoza

responded in 1684 to Jumano appeals for help against the Apache. In 1685 a more immediate threat than the Apache emerged. A French deserter from La Salle's expedition (▶ *page 88*) reported that the French had arrived on the Gulf coast.

During the next five years, five sea and six land expeditions were sent out to find the French intruders, who threatened to push a wedge between the Spanish settlements in Mexico and Florida. As the Council of the Indies put it in 1686, "prompt action is necessary to pluck out the thorn which has been thrust into the heart of America."

The settlement proved difficult to find. The knowledge that 16th century Spanish explorers had gained of the Gulf area had been mostly forgotten. Spanish expeditions deciphered the complex maze of the Mississippi delta. In 1687 and 1688 they entered San Bernardo (now Matagorda) Bay and saw the wrecks of La Salle's ships, but they missed the settlement on the bay's northwest arm. Land searches fared no better. A lone Frenchman was found living among the Indians. There were doubts that this French colony existed.

Then, in April 1689, Indians handed papers obtained from Tejas (Texas) Indians to the

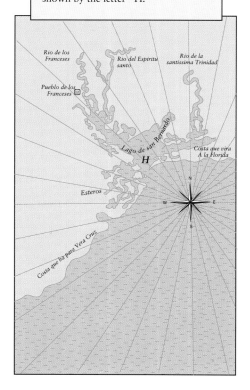

San Bernardo Bay

REDRAWN FROM CARDENAS'S MAP OF SAN BERNARDO BAY, 1691

De Cárdenas's map, the first detailed survey of "San Bernardo" (now Matagorda) Bay, showing the route explored in 1690 by Francisco de Llanos in a Spanish frigate. La Salle's Fort St-Louis is shown here as "Pueblo de los Franceses" and the wreck of one of his ships, *Aimable*, is shown by the letter "H."

east, to officials in New Mexico. Among them was a parchment painting of a frigate, with a handwritten plea for help from two Frenchmen living among the Tejas. In the same month, the most persistent Spanish searcher, Alfonso de León, found the ruins of Fort St-Louis. De León rescued the two Frenchmen and the following year a few more survivors were found living among the Tejas, mostly children. Father Damián Massenet founded two missions and in 1691 Domingo de Terán, governor of the new province of Texas, led an expedition as far as the Red River. But the dispersal of the La Salle colony, problems with the Tejas and other calls on resources led the Spanish to abandon the new missions in 1693 and withdraw to the Rio Grande.

Right: Two of La Salle's men, Jean l'Archevêque and Jacques Grollet, scrawled a desperate rescue plea on this parchment painting of a frigate. The Tejas Indians passed it to Jumano and Cíbolo Indians, who passed it to the Spanish governor of New Vizcaya at El Parral in 1689. The message reads: "We are sorely grieved to be among beasts like these who believe neither in God nor in anything. Gentlemen, if you are willing to take us away, you have only to send a message."

Spanish Searches for La Salle, 1686-90

- Spanish territory, 1686
- Spanish settlement
- Spanish mission
- French settlement
- Bosque and Larios, 1675
- Mendoza, 1684
- Barroto and Romero, 1686
- Rivas and Irarte, 1687
- Pez and Gamarra, 1687
- Pez and Rivas, 1688
- León, 1689
- Terán, 1691
- Indian uprising
- Skirmish
- Shipwreck

◇1689
De Léon finds two survivors from La Salle's expedition, naked "except for an antelope's skin, and with their faces, breasts arms painted like the Indians"

◇1690
Fr Massenet, de Leon's missionary chaplain, founds missions

◇1687
Rivas/Irarte expedition sees wreck of one of La Salle's ships, *Belle*, but fails to find his fort

◇1688
Pez/Rivas expedition sees wreck of another of La Salle's ships, *Aimable*, but again fails to find his fort

◆1686
Expedition off Mississippi Delta, which they fail to identify but name Cabo de Lodo (Cape of Mud)

◇1687
Pez/Gamarra expedition skirts Mississippi Delta, and identifies its four channels

◆1686
Officer of expedition describes Pensacola Bay as "the best bay I had ever seen in my life"

◆1686
Barroto/Romero expedition finds Spanish garrison struggling against English traders inland

Three leagues down the creek we found it [Fort St Louis]... and found all the houses sacked, all the chests, bottle-cases, and all the rest of the settlers' furniture broken... We found three dead bodies scattered over the plain. One of these, from the dress that still clung to the bones, appeared to be that of a woman... The principal house of this settlement is in the form of a fort, made of ship's timber, and with a slope to turn off water. Next to it, without any partition, is another apartment, not so strong, which must have served as a chapel where mass was said. The other five houses are of stakes, covered with mud inside and out; their roofs are covered with buffalo-hides.

De León's expedition reaches Fort St-Louis, 22 April 1689

New Frontiers

EUROPEAN BEGINNINGS IN LOUISIANA AND TEXAS, 1698-1722

Amid tense rivalry, the Spaniards and French explore inland from the coast of the Gulf of Mexico. The French found a settlement at present-day New Orleans.

There had been a flurry of activity along the Gulf coast, prompted by La Salle's arrival at present-day Matagorda Bay, which lasted only until Spanish search parties revealed the expedition's fate. There was then a short-lived lull. But by the late 1690s rumors and counter-rumors of French, Spanish and English activities heightened the tension around these early European ventures into Louisiana and Texas.

In 1698 the Spaniards established a fort at Pensacola Bay. The following year a French expedition, commanded by Sieur d'Iberville, arrived on the coast but after the Spaniards turned them away from Pensacola, Iberville sailed on to the Mississippi delta. As La Salle had foreseen, a French base at the mouth of the Mississippi would be safely distant from the Spanish bases in Florida. Meanwhile English overseas expansion towards the Mississippi valley from the Carolinas posed a commercial rather than a military challenge.

Under Iberville and his brother Sieur de Bienville the French built forts at Biloxi and Mobile and on the Mississippi. They also negotiated alliances with the Natchez, Choctaw and other Indian tribes, and sent out exploring expeditions. Iberville himself investigated the maze of the delta and Bienville reached the Red River. The new settlements were a magnet for explorers. In 1700 Tonty came down the Mississippi from Illinois and the mining prospector Pierre Le Sueur made them his base for a remarkable upriver journey to the Sioux country of Minnesota, returning with samples of lead and copper in 1702.

The French traveled in heavy dugout boats, for the bark canoes of the north were unsuited to the sluggish, snag-ridden waterways of Louisiana. La Salle's plan of shipping out the furs of the north from a warm-water port on the Gulf still had appeal, but they were equally beguiled by prospects to the west – the trade and silver of New Spain. In 1714 Louis de St Denis journeyed from his new post at Natchitoches to the presidio of San Juan Bautista on the lower Rio Grande. When St Denis surprised the Spaniards by arriving on the Rio Grande this led to some uneasy collaboration between the Spaniards and French.

This was brought to an end as war broke out between the two nations in Europe and as Spanish expeditions drove deep into Texas. The French from the Mississippi and the Spanish from New Mexico approached each other, in places crossing and touching, in the vast new frontier area of eastern Texas.

For the French, Bénard de La Harpe broke new ground in 1719 when he reached the plains between the Red and Arkansas rivers looking for Indian trade and for a route to New Mexico. Yet it was the Spanish thrusts which were the more purposeful, showing the distinctive characteristics of Spanish expansion elsewhere in the Americas. Expeditions of Ramón and St Denis in 1716, of Alarcón in 1718, and Aguayo in 1721-22, the last two including settlers and stock, left in their wake a chain of Franciscan missions and fortified presidios. The farthest east, at Los Adaes, was only a dozen miles from the French fortified post at Natchitoches.

For their part the French tightened their grip on the lower Mississippi. In 1718 they founded a settlement at New Orleans as well as other settlements among the Natchez, on the east bank of the Mississippi, above its confluence with the Red River. Since the new Spanish establishments in eastern Texas blocked any southerly route westward, the French began to look farther north for a way through. In that direction would lie "a great river, which comes from the west, on which there are numerous nations." The words were Tonty's; the river was the Missouri.

Right: The French frontier post at New Biloxi, Louisiana, was sited across the bay from Fort Maurepas (Old Biloxi). This drawing, by Jean Baptiste Le Buteaux, shows the post in December 1720. Buildings are still going up, and already the camp is bustling with boat-construction and other activity. A flat-bottomed boat typical of the Mississippi region, lies near its moorings. Within two years, however, the settlement was transfered to New Orleans.

1718
Alarcón expedition lays foundations of mission and fort

Indians inform La Harpe that to the northwest "a white people traded for metal with the Padouca, 15 days' journey off"

La Harpe notes that "the Indians build their huts dune-fashion out of clay and reeds, and paint their coat of arms on a hide of leather, which they thrust over the door"

1721-22
Marquis of Aguayo leads 500 soldiers and settlers across country to strenghen missions

1713
St Denis establishes French Post

1722
Aguayo expedition builds fort and leaves settlers

1719
La Harpe heads northwest "to effect an entrance, by treating with the Indians, into New Mexico"

1721
Party from Aguayo expedition establish fort

1700
Iberville encounters Natchez, last survivors of Mississippi temple mound culture

1714
St Denis party arrives on foot from Natchitoches

1721
Aguayo expedition builds fort

Fort St Louis (1702)

Pensacola (1698)

1716
St Denis (in Spanish service) and Ramón found missions

1718
Governor Alarcón of Texas and Father Olivares set out with 72 settlers, 548 horses, and other livestock. They cross prairies during unusually hard rainy season

1699
Iberville and Bienville explore delta

Fort de la Boulage (1700)

1699
Iberville turned away by Spanish

1699
Bienville turns back *Carolina Galley* at English Turn

1718
Alarcón inspects the new missions

European Beginnings in Louisiana and Texas, 1698-1722

Spanish territory, 1698

Area of Iberville's explorations

Alarcón, 1718

French Spanish Indian

Iberville, 1699-1700

La Harpe, 1719

settlement

St Denis, 1714

Aguayo, 1721-22

Spanish mission

Ramón and St Denis, 1716

The Spaniards trade with the Kansas and give them sabres for horses, but never any firearms. It would have been well if the English and French had followed this rule with other nations.

Bénard de La Harpe, 1719

The Mouth of the Mississippi

REDRAWN FROM GUILLAUME DE L'ISLE'S 1718 MAP OF LOUISIANA

Drawing from d'Iberville, St Denis and others, de L'Isle's map was the major authority on the Mississippi valley and delta for travelers and cartographers for over 50 years to come. This inset map of the "Embouchure du Mississippi" shows the delta in detail, including Lakes Maurepas and Ponchartrain, and the newly-established French settlements. New Orleans, founded in 1718, was not on de L'Isle's original map, although it was added to later editions.

The Muddy River

BOURGMONT'S EXPLORATIONS ALONG THE MISSOURI, 1712-24

*The French attempt to expand their trading
empire along the Missouri in a search for
silver and a river route to the Pacific.*

After Jolliet and Marquette sighted the mouth of the Missouri in 1673 (▶ *page 62*) there began a new phase of speculation and exploration. That the "Pekitanoui" or Muddy River was a major waterway was not in doubt, but its length, direction and source were all unknown. First reports placed the upper Missouri far south of its true location, and consequently much nearer Spanish settlements than was actually the case. Indian reports of other waterways to the west – the Osage, Kansas and Platte rivers – added to the confusion.

At the turn of the century the French had begun to establish posts on the Mississippi near its juncture with the Missouri. But it was some ten to twenty years before reliable first-hand reports of the Missouri country became available. The most important of these came from the French soldier and trader, Etienne Veniard de Bourgmont. In 1712 Bourgmont, who had been commander at Fort Detroit, returned with the Missouri Indians to their homeland after they had fought as allies of the French against the Fox Indians. He lived among them for the next five or six years, had

a child by a Missouri woman, and traveled widely. In 1714 he journeyed about 600 miles up the Missouri to the mouth of the Platte, persuading successive Indian tribes, jealous of their privileges as trading middlemen, to let him pass through their territory. From the Missouri Indians he reached the Osage, and from there he moved on to the Pawnee. The Pawnee, however, refused to let him through to the territory of the "Padouca," the fearsome Comanche of the plains.

A more official French initiative was made in 1719, when du Tisné, one of Bienville's

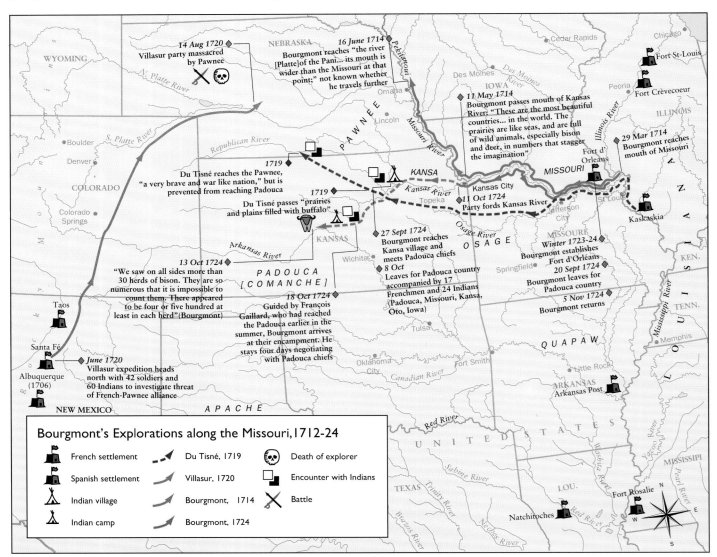

Bourgmont's Explorations along the Missouri, 1712-24

- French settlement
- Spanish settlement
- Indian village
- Indian camp
- Du Tisné, 1719
- Villasur, 1720
- Bourgmont, 1714
- Bourgmont, 1724
- Death of explorer
- Encounter with Indians
- Battle

Map labels:
- **14 Aug 1720** Villasur party massacred by Pawnee
- **16 June 1714** Bourgmont reaches "the river [Platte] of the Pani... its mouth is wider than the Missouri at that point;" not known whether he travels further
- **11 May 1714** Bourgmont passes mouth of Kansas River: "These are the most beautiful countries... in the world. The prairies are like seas, especially bison and deer, in numbers that stagger the imagination"
- **29 Mar 1714** Bourgmont reaches mouth of Missouri
- **1719** Du Tisné reaches the Pawnee, "a very brave and war like nation," but is prevented from reaching Padouca
- **1719** Du Tisné passes "prairies and plains filled with buffalo"
- **11 Oct 1724** Party fords Kansas River
- **27 Sept 1724** Bourgmont reaches Kansa village and meets Padouca chiefs
- **8 Oct** Leaves for Padouca country accompanied by 17 Frenchmen and 24 Indians (Padouca, Missouri, Kansa, Oto, Iowa)
- **Winter 1723-24** Bourgmont establishes Fort d'Orléans
- **20 Sept 1724** Bourgmont leaves for Padouca country
- **5 Nov 1724** Bourgmont returns
- **13 Oct 1724** "We saw on all sides more than 30 herds of bison. They are so numerous that it is impossible to count them. There appeared to be four or five hundred at least in each herd" (Bourgmont)
- **18 Oct 1724** Guided by François Gaillard, who had reached the Padouca earlier in the summer, Bourgmont arrives at their encampment. He stays four days negotiating with Padouca chiefs
- **June 1720** Villasur expedition heads north with 42 soldiers and 60 Indians to investigate threat of French-Pawnee alliance

Place names: WYOMING, NEBRASKA, Cedar Rapids, Chicago, Fort St-Louis, Des Moines, IOWA, Peoria, Fort Crèvecoeur, Omaha, Lincoln, ILLINOIS, N. Platte River, S. Platte River, Boulder, Denver, Republican River, COLORADO, Colorado Springs, Kansas City, Topeka, MISSOURI, Fort d'Orléans, St Louis, Kaskaskia, PAWNEE, KANSA, Kansas River, Jefferson City, Osage River, OSAGE, Arkansas River, KANSAS, Wichita, Springfield, PADOUCA [COMANCHE], Tulsa, Oklahoma City, Canadian River, Fort Smith, QUAPAW, Little Rock, Memphis, TENN., KEN., ARKANSAS, Arkansas Post, Taos, Santa Fé, Albuquerque (1706), NEW MEXICO, APACHE, Red River, UNITED STATES, TEXAS, Trinity River, Brazos River, Nueces River, Sabine River, LOU., Washita River, MISSISSIPPI, Natchitoches, Fort Rosalie, Pearl River, Mississippi River, LOUISIANA

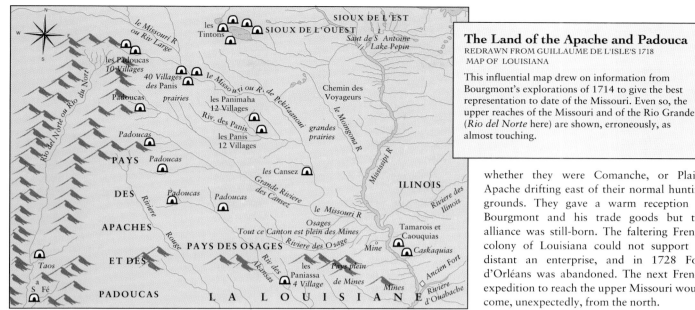

This influential map drew on information from Bourgmont's explorations of 1714 to give the best representation to date of the Missouri. Even so, the upper reaches of the Missouri and of the Rio Grande (*Rio del Norte* here) are shown, erroneously, as almost touching.

officers, tried to follow Bourgmont's steps with a treaty-making expedition. From the French post at Kaskaskia he entered Osage territory and, with difficulty, Pawnee country, but he, also, was prevented from reaching the Padouca. Exaggerated reports of du Tisné's exploits reached the Spanish authorities, who were already worried that Plains Indians on New Mexico's eastern borders would obtain guns. By this time most southern Plains Indians had acquired horses, originally traded or stolen from Spanish ranches in New Mexico. This had already increased their mobility and the range of their buffalo hunts and war parties. If they were to acquire guns this would give them a formidable increase in firepower.

The Spaniards were further alarmed by the prospect of a French-Pawnee alliance. In 1720 they sent Don Pedro de Villasur north to investigate, with nearly a hundred soldiers and Indians. The expedition reached the Platte River, where it was attacked by Pawnee. Most of the party was massacred.

Since both the French and Spanish persistently underestimated the distance between them, Indian reports of strange white men in the interior kept nerves on edge in both Louisiana and Mexico. In response to the Villasur expedition the French entrusted Bourgmont with a mission to find the mysterious Padouca. In doing so Bourgmont might open up a way to the silver mines, and beyond them, the *Mer de l'Ouest*.

Bearing the grand title of "Commandant of the Missouri River," Bourgmont established Fort d'Orléans on the north bank of the Missouri. In 1724 he left on his best-known exploring venture. With a few Frenchmen, his young mixed-blood son and large numbers of Indians, he journeyed westward. In October he finally reached the Padouca, in an encampment on the prairies east of the Big Bend of the Arkansas. Scholars are divided as to whether they were Comanche, or Plains Apache drifting east of their normal hunting grounds. They gave a warm reception to Bourgmont and his trade goods but the alliance was still-born. The faltering French colony of Louisiana could not support so distant an enterprise, and in 1728 Fort d'Orléans was abandoned. The next French expedition to reach the upper Missouri would come, unexpectedly, from the north.

Below: Kansa on the move. Bourgmont wrote that women and dogs carried skins for shelters and other utensils in bundles weighing 300 lbs. This engraving is from Histoire de la Louisiane *by Le Page du Pratz, who described how Bourgmont traveled through the territory of these "naturels du nord" on his 1724 mission to make peace with the Padouca. Settled in Natchez, du Pratz later lived amongst Natchez Indians and described the tragic deportation by the French of a tribe he saw as most civilized.*

> I t is true that we go to the home of the Spaniards, but they trade to us only some horses, a few knives, and some inferior axes; they do not trade in fusils, or lead, or gunpowder, or kettles, or blankets, or any of the goods that the great French chief has given us. Thus, the French are our true friends.
>
> Speech of the Padouca chief to Bourgmont,
> October 1724

Naturels du Nord qui vont en chasse d'hyver avec leur Famille

The Land of the Mandan

THE EXPLORATIONS OF THE VÉRENDRYES, 1738-43

La Vérendrye was the last great French explorer of North America. He and his sons reveal the geography of an immense area stretching from the Saskatchewan to the Missouri.

"After sailing up the Missouri as far as it is navigable," the Jesuit geographer and traveler Father Charlevoix had written, "you come to a great river which runs westward and discharges into the sea." There were also numerous Indian reports which told of a light-skinned, bearded people of advanced civilization, called "Mantannes," who lived on the banks of "a great river which flowed west."

These reports prompted Sieur de La

> On the morning of the 28th we arrived at the place indicated as a rendezvous for the Mandan, who arrived in the evening, one chief with thirty men and four Assiniboin... I confess I was greatly surprised, as I expected to see people quite different from the other savages according to the stories that had been told us. They did not differ from the Assiniboin, being naked except for a garment of buffalo skin carelessly worn without any breechcloth. I knew then that there was a large discount to be taken off all that had been told me.
>
> **La Vérendrye reaches the Mandan, November 1738**

Vérendrye's expedition of 1738. A French fur trader from Canada, he had outflanked the troublesome Sioux with a chain of posts from Lake Superior to Fort La Reine on the Assiniboine River (▶ *page 104);* now he was in a position to expand his trading empire south westward.

In October they left the woods, waters and their bark canoes, striking across the prairies on foot. They followed Indian trails and were accompanied by Assiniboin, plains Indians who hunted buffalo for the expedition as it marched southwest. Early in December they reached the first Mandan village, 150 cabins surrounded by fortifications. The inhabitants were neat, industrious, well-provided, and if lighter-skinned than most, unmistakably Indian. Other Mandan villages lay further along the banks of a wide, muddy river flowing southwest – a local, reverse twist of the Missouri. Here La Vérendrye left two of his men. The following summer they would meet Indians from further west who not only had horses but also oddments of Spanish manufacture. In 1741 La Vérendrye's eldest son, Pierre, brought back two horses from the Mandan villages to Fort La Reine.

In 1742 La Vérendrye sent two of his sons, Louis-Joseph (the

Above: La Vérendrye's sons buried this lead plate at an Indian village on the Missouri River, nearby present-day Pierre, South Dakota. It was not discovered until 1913. Stamped on the front is a formal act of possession on behalf of the French crown. On the back, the Vérendryes scratched their own message: "Deposited by the Chevalier and de La Vérendrye witnesses – St. Louy de Londette A. Miotte, the 30th March 1743."

Chevalier) and François, on a renewed search for the western sea. They reached the Mandan villages again, crossed the Missouri and traveled with "Bow" Indians across the Badlands of North Dakota. Their precise journey is unknown but early in 1743 their apprehensive Indian companions forced them to turn back from the mountains – probably the Black Hills of Dakota – from whose summit they hoped to see the sea. In reality they were not only more than a thousand miles from the Pacific, but in between lay the massive barrier of the Rocky Mountains.

Some of the information the Vérendryes received from Indians was either fanciful to begin with, or seriously misinterpreted by the explorers, but it provided glimpses of Spaniards in distant New Mexico or Frenchmen in Illinois. They now knew about the Mandan, although the plains Indians remained mysterious. Contemporary French maps hint that La Vérendrye had come close to both the western sea and the River of the West, but in reality he found neither. His sons revealed that the river of the Mandan flowed southeast, and that it must be the Missouri. But the link between the northern and southern approaches to the upper Missouri had still not been made.

Fact and Fantasy

REDRAWN FROM PHILIPPE BUACHE'S 1754 MAP

Buache's map intended to show the "discoveries of French officers to the west of Lake Superior." La Vérendrye's explorations are set in the context of the theoretical geography of the period: the 1738 route to the Mandan or the "Ouachipouanes," for example, is shown ending on a River of the West, which flows into a gigantic Sea of the West (▶ *page 42).*

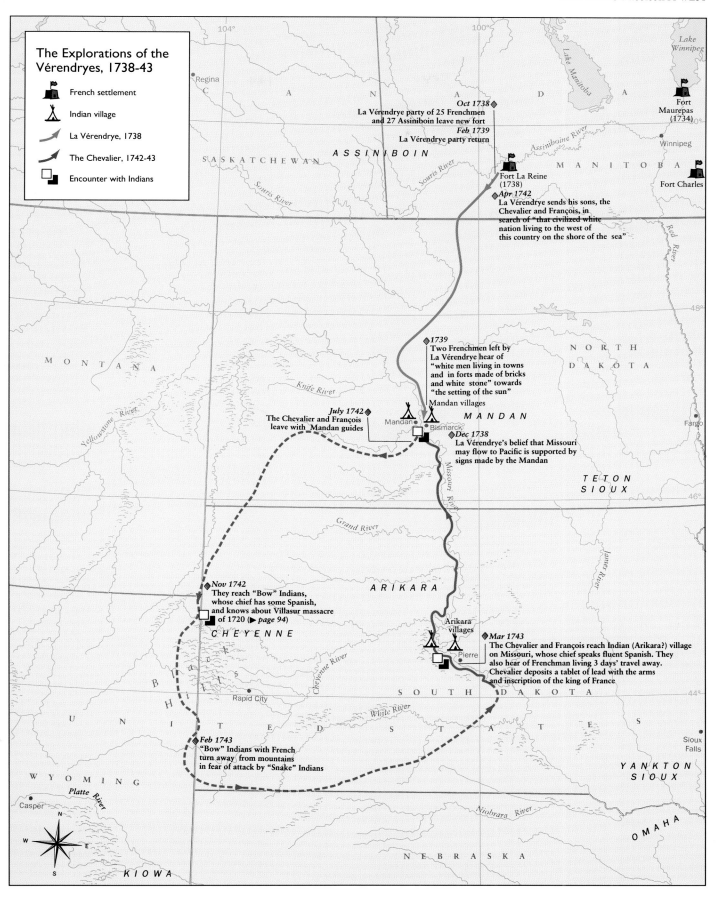

The Explorations of the Vérendryes, 1738-43

French settlement

Indian village

La Vérendrye, 1738

The Chevalier, 1742-43

Encounter with Indians

Oct 1738 La Vérendrye party of 25 Frenchmen and 27 Assiniboin leave new fort

Feb 1739 La Vérendrye party return

Fort Maurepas (1734)

Winnipeg

Fort La Reine (1738)

Fort Charles

Apr 1742 La Vérendrye sends his sons, the Chevalier and François, in search of "that civilized white nation living to the west of this country on the shore of the sea"

1739 Two Frenchmen left by La Vérendrye hear of "white men living in towns and in forts made of bricks and white stone" towards "the setting of the sun"

Mandan villages

July 1742 The Chevalier and François leave with Mandan guides

Mandan

Bismarck

Dec 1738 La Vérendrye's belief that Missouri may flow to Pacific is supported by signs made by the Mandan

M A N D A N

N O R T H   D A K O T A

Fargo

T E T O N   S I O U X

Grand River

A R I K A R A

Arikara villages

Pierre

Mar 1743 The Chevalier and François reach Indian (Arikara?) village on Missouri, whose chief speaks fluent Spanish. They also hear of Frenchman living 3 days' travel away. Chevalier deposits a tablet of lead with the arms and inscription of the king of France

Nov 1742 They reach "Bow" Indians, whose chief has some Spanish, and knows about Villasur massacre of 1720 (▶ page 94)

C H E Y E N N E

Rapid City

White River

S O U T H   D A K O T A

Sioux Falls

Feb 1743 "Bow" Indians with French turn away from mountains in fear of attack by "Snake" Indians

Y A N K T O N   S I O U X

W Y O M I N G

Casper

Platte River

N   E   B   R   A   S   K   A

Niobrara River

O M A H A

K I O W A

Regina

S A S K A T C H E W A N

C   A   N   A   D   A

A S S I N I B O I N

Souris River

Assiniboine River

M A N I T O B A

Red River

Lake Winnipeg

Lake Manitoba

M O N T A N A

Yellowstone River

Knife River

Missouri River

James River

Cheyenne River

B   l   a   c   k   H   i   l   l   s

U N I T E D   S T A T E S

N
W   E
S

104° 100° 48° 46° 44°

To Santa Fé from the East

THE EXPLORATIONS OF PIERRE AND PAUL MALLET, 1739-40

In their quest for trade with the silver-rich provinces of New Spain, the Mallet brothers are the first French traders to reach the frontier town of Santa Fé from the east.

Throughout the 18th century the French hoped to find a practicable route between the Mississippi valley and New Mexico which would lead them to Spain's rich sources of silver. Initially it was French traders from Illinois and Louisiana who were most active in their attempts to reach New Spain for trade and possibly conquest.

The French were mistaken, however, for the silver provinces of northern Mexico – New Galicia, New Vizcaya and New León – did not stretch up the Rio Grande as far as New Mexico and Santa Fé. It was a triumph of illusion over reality that a sleepy little town of adobe huts should take on the semblance of an El Dorado.

In 1739 the first French trading party, nine Canadians led by Pierre and Paul Mallet, arrived in Santa Fé from New Orleans. They had successfully crossed what was thought to be unpassable wilderness inhabited by hostile Jumano, Apache and Comanche. Their circuitous route had been based on another common misconception of the French, that the best way to New Mexico lay along the Missouri River. When the Mallet brothers were at their furthest point north on the Missouri, Pawnee Indians advised them to cut back southwest. They therefore crossed the Platte and Arkansas Rivers to reach Taos and

Above: Spanish cavalry men fighting Indians and intruders on the northern frontier were known as "leatherjackets." Though lances were still prefered to pistols for horse combat, this one carries both. He was painted by a fellow leatherjacket, Ramón de Murillo, to show his commanders how different frontier soldiers were.

S anta Fé is a town built of wood and without any fortification. There are about 800 Spanish and mulatto families there, and in the surrounding area are a number of villages of settled Indians, each with a Padre running the mission. There are only eighty soldiers in the garrison, poorly trained and badly armed. And there are other soldiers in this province, in the pay of the king of Spain, who transport silver every year to Old Mexico by caravan.

The Mallet brothers' report on Santa Fé, 1739

Santa Fé. For their return, the expedition was able to take a more direct route. They crossed the head of the Pecos Valley to a river, from now on to be called the Canadian, which brought them to the more familiar reaches of the Arkansas.

The French traders had received a friendly reception at Santa Fé. Although trade with foreigners was officially prohibited, Santa Fé's frontier position meant that few goods ever reached there and those that did were expensive after the long trail from Mexico. Unfortunately, the Mallets' expedition had lost its trade goods as they crossed the Saline River.

In the years after the Mallets' journey the Jumano and Comanche made peace and the route became slightly less dangerous. A trickle of Frenchmen managed to make their way through to Santa Fé. In 1741 Pierre and Paul Mallet were part of a more official but less successful expedition from New Orleans, led by Fabry de la Bruyère. They had set out to open trade links between Louisiana and Santa Fé and followed the more direct route used by the Mallets on their return in 1740. However the expedition failed to reach Santa Fé because of Bruyère's bumbling leadership and low water on the Canadian River.

In the following years various Frenchmen, including Pierre Mallet, made successful journeys to Santa Fé. But most were individual, haphazard ventures which achieved little except to put the Spanish authorities on the alert. Even these ceased as to the east French forces became involved in the great war with Britain which had begun in 1754. The peace between France and Britain, in 1763, was to change the whole power balance in the North American continent. France lost Canada to Britain, and also gave up to Spain its Louisiana territory west of the Mississippi.

The Explorations of Pierre and Paul Mallet, 1739-40

Spanish territory, 1739

French territory, 1739

Spanish settlement/mission

French settlement

Pueblo

Mallet brothers, 1739-40

Pass

Colorado Springs

Pueblo

10 July 1739
Mallets sight Spanish
Mountains in the distance

Taos

NAVAJO   20 July 1739
Church bells ring
to honor Mallets for their
overland crossing   Picuris

Albuquerque   Santa Fé

Zuñi   Acoma   NEW
MEXICO   Pecos

22 July 1739-1 May 1740
Mallets at New Mexican capital.
Of their 7 companions,
one stays and marries, one
hanged for inciting Indians

2 May 1740
Mallet party
arrive

MESCA
APAC

El Paso
del Norte   JUMANO

San Elzeario

NEW
VIZCAYA

CHIHUAHUA

MEXICO

29 May 1739
On Pawnee advice, Pierre and Paul Mallet, with 7 Illinois French traders, turn south

20 June 1739
Mallets and trading party lose horses and merchandise crossing river

30 June 1739
Mallet party finds "stones with Spanish inscriptions"

13 May 1740
3 men in Mallet party set off to "take the route of Pani Indians"

20 June 1740
Mallets abandon horses and set out in two canoes of elm bark

French hunting camps

Late June 1740
Mallets arrive, then proceed to New Orleans

1739
Pierre and Paul Mallet set out north to find route to Santa Fé via Missouri

Part IV : Ocean to Ocean

Between the northernmost point reached by Spanish ships coasting up from Mexico, and the easternmost fringe of the Russian empire, lay the longest unexplored coast in the world. During the eighteenth century, Spanish, Russian, and British ships edged their way along this broken and convoluted 5000-mile coastline, while Canadian fur traders struck out boldly across the middle of a continent that proved vaster than they had ever imagined.

By 1800, the outlines of North America had at last been established. It fell to a new century, and a new republic, to explore the interior. United States soldiers and scientists, trappers and traders, emigrants and entrepreneurs, as well as a host of map-makers, artists and photographers, pushed west across the Rockies to the Pacific, unveiling the mysteries of the Western interior.

In the eastern and southern parts of North America, exploration was steady rather than dramatic throughout the 18th century. But far away to the north and west explorers were making journeys of continental proportions. Their travels were closely associated with the demands of the fur trade, and with the continuing hope that a way might be found to the western ocean. In quest of such a route, British ships probed the ice-bound shores of Hudson Bay for an entrance to a Northwest Passage, and French canoes pushed along the river routes west of their trading empire on the St Lawrence and the Great Lakes. Indian reports of great waters just over the western horizon lured the explorers on, but they found instead the vastness of the northern plains. By the 1770s Hearne had reached the northern edge of the continent as he crossed overland from Hudson Bay to the Arctic Ocean. It was the western – or Pacific – ocean, not Hearne's polar sea, that was the objective of most explorers, but unknown to them the way was blocked by the barrier of the Rocky Mountains.

For all their flamboyant enterprise, the explorers of the north were as blind about the location of the Pacific as Cartier had been more than two centuries earlier. At the beginning of the 16th century, no European knew which direction the west coast followed, north of California. Many believed that California was an island until Kino established its connection with the mainland at the turn of the 18th century.

The Spanish made no further movement to the north until the 1760s. When they did, it was in reaction to the activities of the Russian explorers and traders who followed the tracks of Bering to the Alaskan coast. Slowly the Spaniards and Russians groped their way towards each other along the labyrinthine inlets of the northwest coast. But in the end it was an Englishman, James Cook, who closed the gap between them. In the last decades of the century, seaborne expeditions traced the outline of the mainland coast from Oregon to Alaska, penetrating beyond the screen of outlying islands.

It was in these same years that the first overland explorer arrived on the northwest coast. The outriders of the Canadian fur trade had reached Lake Athabasca in the 1770s, and Great Slave Lake in the 1780s. Then, after a false start which took him first to the Arctic Ocean, Mackenzie crossed the Rockies in 1793 to reach the Pacific "from Canada, by land."

To the south, the newly-independent United States saw its future in the vast territories that lay to the west. In the spring of 1803, President Thomas Jefferson bought Louisiana – a great tract of largely unexplored territory west of the Mississippi – from the French for 15 million dollars.

To Jefferson's opponents, the Louisiana Purchase was the "wildest chimera of a moonstruck brain." Published maps of the day displayed an almost total ignorance of the West. Leading mapmakers seemed scarcely aware of the existence of the Rockies. Americans circulated incredible tales about what these lands might hold. The President himself believed that mastodons might wander the western plains. Others told stories of gem-like "shining mountains," unicorns, giant water serpents, beavers seven feet tall, a mountain of salt, cliffs of flawless gems, silver nuggets the size of bricks.

Yet this was probably the most inspired coup of Jefferson's presidency. The following year, Lewis and Clark set off up the Missouri, over the Rockies and down the Columbia to the Pacific. It was to be the first of many military scientific expeditions that opened the West to settlement during the 19th century. Trappers and traders also played their part: John Jacob Astor's Pacific Fur Company found the South Pass through the Rockies, and trappers streamed into the Green River valley.

To the southwest, American expansion led to conflict with Spain's ailing empire and then to war with its successor, the Mexican republic. While mountain men Jedediah Smith, Tom Fitzpatrick and Joseph R. Walker, as well as Captain John C. Frémont, pioneered emigrant routes, the US Army's Corps of Topographical Engineers painstakingly recorded the dramatic terrain. As railroads took the place of wagon trains, survey teams scoured the Rockies for passes. They described, drew and photographed the landscape in meticulous detail. A new era of scientific exploration had begun.

"Yellow Mettle" and the Strait of Anian

THE TRAGIC VOYAGE OF JAMES KNIGHT, 1719

*The prospect of gold and a passage to the
West leads the veteran fur trader James
Knight and his expedition to an icy death in
Hudson Bay.*

The long bout of Anglo-French hostilities, which had begun in 1689, came to an end in 1713 with the Treaty of Utrecht. Hudson Bay and its fur-trading posts were thus restored to the English Hudson's Bay Company. In 1714 James Knight, a veteran trader who had been made the first post-war governor in the Bay arrived at Fort York. According to Knight's journals, kept over four years, he hoped not only to expand trade but also to discover a land of treasure somewhere to the northwest. The "Northern" or Chipewyan Indians, lived in that direction, fearful of the Bay area Cree and their firearms, but a potential source of information and furs.

In 1715, to make peace between the Indians and to explore the country, Knight sent William Stuart inland with a band of Cree and with a Chipewyan woman slave as their guide. Stuart was away almost a year, dependent on the Indians for survival and equipped only with a compass. He brought back ten more Chipewyan to York and a confused report which claimed he had traveled 1000 miles to latitude 67°N. This claim was exaggerated, but Stuart was the first white man to travel onto the Barrens and he probably reached the area between Lake Athabasca and Great Slave Lake.

Back at York, Knight eagerly questioned the Chipewyan who told him about "Ships in the Western Seas," rivers and straits, deposits of copper and "a Yellow Mettle" which Knight believed to be gold. He persuaded the Indians "to lay down there Rivers along Shore to the Norward they chalked 17 Rivers some of them very Large." With this information he drew up a map and convinced himself that the 17th river was the Northwest Passage.

In 1717 Knight established a new post

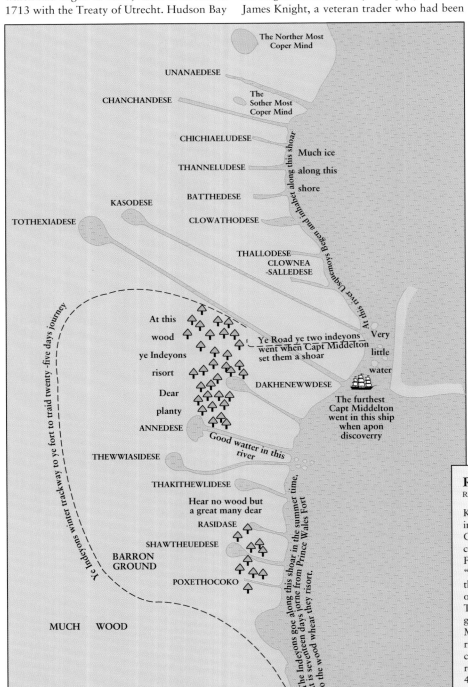

Rivers of the North
REDRAWN FROM A MAP BY JAMES KNIGHT, *c.*1716

Knight based this map on sketches and information brought to him at Fort York by Chipewyan Indians. The map shows the country north of Churchill (Prince of Wales Fort); the division between Indians and "Usquemay" (Eskimo or Inuit) territory; and the rivers as far as the Coppermine (the 16th or "Chanchandese") River.

To modern eyes its main deficiencies are that it gives no indication of the great bulges of the Melville and Boothia peninsulas, nor of the right-angled westward turn the coast makes to come round to the Coppermine River. The references to Middleton's expedition of 1741-42 (▶ *page 106*) are later additions.

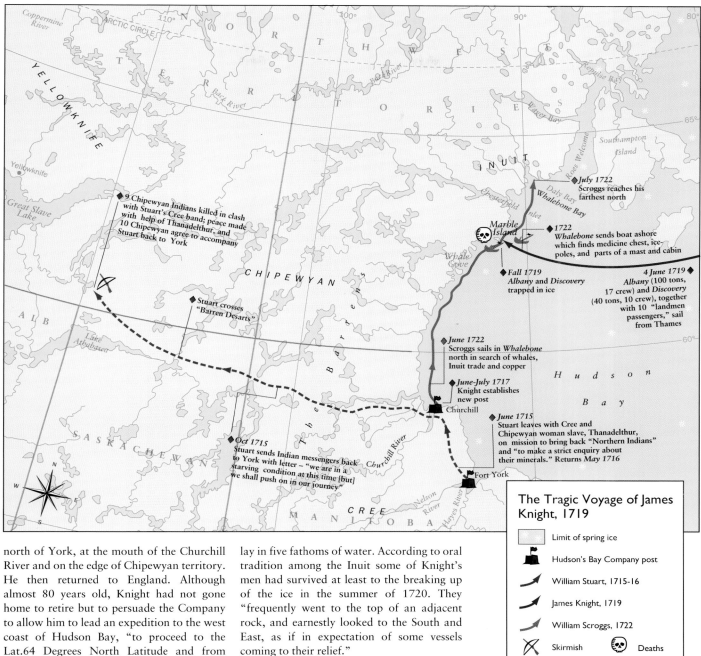

**Map labels:**

Coppermine River
ARCTIC CIRCLE
110° N
100°
NORTHWEST
90°
80°
TERRITORIES
Back River
Repulse Bay
Wager Bay
65°
YELLOWKNIFE
Yellowknife
INUIT
Southampton Island
Great Slave Lake

9 Chipewyan Indians killed in clash with Stuart's Cree band; peace made with help of Thanadelthur, and 10 Chipewyan agree to accompany Stuart back to York

Ross Welcome
Daly Bay
Chesterfield Inlet
Whalebone Bay
July 1722 Scroggs reaches his farthest north

Marble Island
1722 *Whalebone* sends boat ashore which finds medicine chest, ice-poles, and parts of a mast and cabin

Whale Cove

Fall 1719 Albany and *Discovery* trapped in ice

4 June 1719 Albany (100 tons, 17 crew) and *Discovery* (40 tons, 10 crew), together with 10 "landmen passengers," sail from Thames

Stuart crosses "Barren Desarts"

CHIPEWYAN
The Barrens

ALB
Lake Athabasca

June 1722 Scroggs sails in *Whalebone* north in search of whales, Inuit trade and copper

60°

H u d s o n
B a y

June-July 1717 Knight establishes new post
Churchill

SASKATCHEWAN

Oct 1715 Stuart sends Indian messengers back to York with letter – "we are in a starving condition at this time [but] we shall push on in our journey"

Churchill River

June 1715 Stuart leaves with Cree and Chipewyan woman slave, Thanadelthur, on mission to bring back "Northern Indians" and "to make a strict enquiry about their minerals." Returns *May 1716*

N W E S

Fort York
Nelson River
Hayes River
CREE
MANITOBA

The Tragic Voyage of James Knight, 1719

- Limit of spring ice
- Hudson's Bay Company post
- William Stuart, 1715-16
- James Knight, 1719
- William Scroggs, 1722
- Skirmish
- Deaths

---

north of York, at the mouth of the Churchill River and on the edge of Chipewyan territory. He then returned to England. Although almost 80 years old, Knight had not gone home to retire but to persuade the Company to allow him to lead an expedition to the west coast of Hudson Bay, "to proceed to the Lat.64 Degrees North Latitude and from thence Northward to find out the Streights of Anian." This expedition became one of the tragedies of Arctic exploration. Knight's two ships, *Albany* and *Discovery*, sailed in 1719 but were trapped during the fall in a small harbor at Marble Island. In that desolate spot where, a later explorer wrote, "the winds of almost perpetual winter blow in pitiless and withering blasts," every member of the expedition died.

Three years later a Company sloop off Marble Island found local Inuit with debris from the ships. Almost half a century later Company whalers came across ruins and graves near where the hulks of Knight's ships

lay in five fathoms of water. According to oral tradition among the Inuit some of Knight's men had survived at least to the breaking up of the ice in the summer of 1720. They "frequently went to the top of an adjacent rock, and earnestly looked to the South and East, as if in expectation of some vessels coming to their relief."

The Strait of Anian

REDRAWN FROM A SECTION OF J.B. NOLIN'S
GLOBE TERRESTRE, 1708

The mythical Strait of Anian, leading from Hudson Bay to the Pacific, obsessed European explorers and cartographers in the 18th century. Reports Knight received from Chipewyans at Fort York in 1716 led him to believe "there may be a Passage or Straits that parts America from Asia..."

He also heard of Indians to the west who had "a Yellow Mettle," and "every Summer see Sevl Ships in the Western Seas wch I cannot think to be Spaniards... I rather take them to be Tartars or Jappannees Vessels."

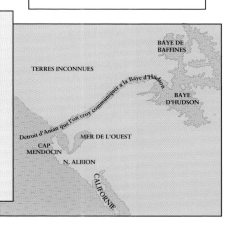

BAYE DE BAFFINES
TERRES INCONNUES
BAYE D'HUDSON
Detroit d'Anian que l'on croy communiquer à la Baye d'Hudson
MER DE L'OUEST
CAP MENDOCIN
N. ALBION
CALIFORNIE

The Search for the River of the West

FRENCH EXPLORATIONS FROM LAKE SUPERIOR TO THE SASKATCHEWAN, 1731-53

La Vérendrye presses far into the west and builds up the rich French fur trade of the Lower Saskatchewan River. The myth of a great inland sea is slowly demolished.

Part of Lake Superior

Fort Kamanestigonia

Grande Portage

Rapids
Rapids
Rapids
Rapids
Rapids

Lake Long

height of land

Lake Sesakinaga

river at bottom of Lake Superior

Monsoni nation

Lake Tecamamioness [Rainy Lake] – 3 days to cross

Cree nation

Lake of the Woods – 4 days to cross

River of the Petit Nord

prairies

River of the West

woods

prairies

Sioux of the prairies

Mississippi River

Sioux

500

400 s

300

Scale of 500 Leagues

Assiniboin

Sioux of the prairies

prairies

Lake Ouinipigon

Vermillion River

Mountain of Shining Stone

This is where the water begins to ebb and flow and is bad to drink.
The coasts of the South Sea, called in this country the Sea of the West, are not far.

After the Treaty of Utrecht of 1713, French fur traders were denied access to the sea-route of Hudson Bay. They once more turned to westward expansion along the canoe-trails beyond Lake Superior, establishing new posts and reviving old ones. In 1717 these included Kaministiquia, linking the fur trade of the west with the 1000-mile route back to Montréal. Pierre Gaultier de Varennes, de La Vérendrye, took command of these *postes du nords* in 1728. Like his predecessors, La Vérendrye was as much trader as explorer. Beyond expansion of the fur trade the French government would do no more than finance his search for a sea and river of the west.

During his first stay at the *postes du nord* the Cree brought La Vérendrye familiar reports: "they had been beyond the height of land and reached a great river which flows straight towards the setting sun, and which widens continually as it descends." La Vérendrye turned to the west. In 1731 he opened a new route to Rainy Lake by way of Grand Portage and Pigeon River. In 1732 he built Fort St Charles, a palisaded depot, at Lake of the Woods. In 1734 his sons established Fort Maurepas where the Red River of the North divided the eastern woodlands of the beaver and marten hunts from the buffalo plains of the west. Finally, in

Right: Beaver were the staple of the fur trade. This 1703 illustration shows a variety of methods used by Canadian Indians to hunt beaver with firearms, bow and arrow, nets and traps.

Auchagach's Map

REDRAWN FROM AN INDIAN MAP MADE FOR LA VÉRENDRYE, 1728-29

La Vérendrye's map was drawn from sketches made by the Cree Indian Auchagach and others. It shows the two main canoe routes west from Lake Superior, and a River of the West flowing across the prairies, past the mountain of shining stone, and on towards the western ocean. Modern scholars have suggested that if Lake Winnipeg (at this time still unknown to Europeans) is swiveled approximately 90° to its correct north-south orientation, the River of the West will flow from its northern end, and follow roughly the course of the Nelson River towards Hudson Bay.

1738 Fort La Reine was built on the Assiniboine River. It looked out to the plains and, in another direction, across "the road to the English posts" on Hudson Bay.

As the French reached the Winnipeg basin it became clear that many earlier reports about great stretches of water to the west were merely references to the Winnipeg River and Lake Winnipeg. In search of the western sea La Vérendrye then moved southwest towards the Missouri (▶ *page 96*). But he turned back north in 1738-39, disappointed by a journey to the Mandan who told him that the Blanche, or Poskioac, River (later the Saskatchewan) flowed into the western end of Lake Winnipeg.

In 1739-40 La Vérendrye's youngest son, Louis-Joseph the Chevalier, circled Lake Winnipeg and reached the Forks of the Saskatchewan, "a great crossroads of the northern fur trade, the rendezvous every spring of the Crees of the Mountains, Prairies and Rivers to deliberate as to what they shall do, go and trade with the French or with the English." The Cree told him that farther up-river there were mountains, and beyond them water which was undrinkable. But geographers were reluctant to accept that a great mountain range, rather than an inland sea, lay between the French fur traders and the ocean.

It was along the Saskatchewan River that La Vérendrye intended to make his final journey, but in 1749 he died. De Niverville attempted the journey two years later and claimed to have traveled 1000 miles upriver from Le Pas to the "Montagnes des Roches"(Rocky Mountains), where he established Fort La Jonquière. There is no hard evidence for such a claim.

Under La Vérendrye the French worked out the relationship between the Great Lakes Winnipeg, Manitoba and Winnipegosis. It was under La Vérendrye, too, that they controlled the rich fur trade of the Lower Saskatchewan. After they built Fort La Corne near the Forks, in 1753, French dominance of the interior routes seemed complete.

I t was the Chevalier de La Vérendrye who first discovered it [the Saskatchewan] and who ascended it as far as the fork... It was there that he was in the spring [1740] at the meeting of all the Cree, and where he enquired minutely, according to his father's orders, where the source of this great river was. They all replied with one voice that it came from very far, from a height of land where there were very high mountains; that they knew of a great lake on the other side of the mountains, the water of which was not good to drink.

The Chevalier's account of his discoveries of 1739-40

French Explorations from Lake Superior to the Saskatchewan, 1731-53

- English trading post
- French trading post
- Indian trade route
- Pierre de La Vérendrye and his sons, 1731-38
- Louis-Joseph de La Vérendrye (the Chevalier)1739-40
- Boucher de Niverville, 1751
- Cree rendezvous

Asleep at the Edge of a Frozen Sea

THE VOYAGES OF MIDDLETON, MOOR AND COATS, 1741-49

*A renewed search for the Northwest Passage
leads to the exploration of the remaining
uncharted coasts of Hudson Bay.*

The Hudson's Bay Company had been granted vast territories when it acquired its charter in 1670 (▶ *page 66*). But for the first 70 years of its incorporation, the Company kept to its bayside posts, waiting for Indians to come down from the interior to trade. It made little effort to send out expeditions for either trade or exploration. Nor had the Bay itself been explored to any great extent; as yet no map showed its outline accurately. In the words of Joseph Robson, a former employee, the Hudson's Bay Company had "slept at the edge of a frozen sea."

The awakening was marked by a flurry of activity in the 1740s in which exploration was pursued along the west and east coasts of Hudson Bay. It was also marked by a challenge to the Company's trade monopoly.

The expeditions to the west coast were prompted by a resurgence of hope that that elusive dream, a Northwest Passage, might yet be found. Arthur Dobbs, an Irish Member of Parliament, was fearful that the westward expansion of the French would lead them to reach the Pacific coast before the English, and that they were cutting across the hinterland of some of the Company's most profitable posts at York and Churchill. In 1741 Dobbs persuaded the Admiralty to send a naval expedition out to Hudson Bay, to search for a navigable passage to the Pacific which would outflank the French and open up new trade areas.

Commanded by Christopher Middleton, a former Company captain, this first naval Arctic expedition wintered in the Bay before exploring its west coast in the summer of 1742. Middleton was to sail farther north along the coast than any previous explorer.

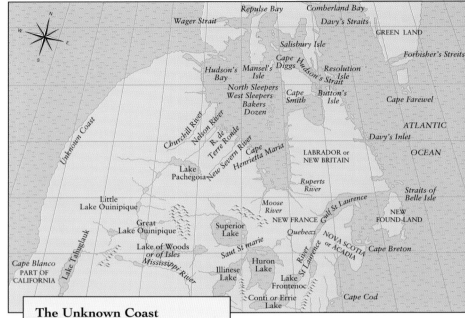

The Unknown Coast

REDRAWN FROM *A NEW MAP OF PART OF NORTH AMERICA* BY ARTHUR DOBBS, 1741

The map illustrates Dobbs's interpretation of Middleton's voyage, suggesting that three openings in the northwest corner of Hudson Bay led to an "unknown coast" which swung southwest to California. The central area is based on the travels of Joseph de La France, a "French Canadese Indian" trader. A friend of Dobbs described how La France "gave thise Description in my Dineing Room at the Golden fleece in New Bondstreet, when onto the floor we chalkt out this map."

Below: An engraving of Inuit from A Voyage to Hudson's Bay *(1748), by Henry Ellis, agent on William Moor's expedition. "These people,"* Ellis wrote, *"are of a middle Size, robust, and inclinable to be fat,... The Mens clothes are of Seal Skins, Deer Skins, and... the skins of Land and Sea Fowl; each of their Coats has a Hood like that of Capuchin... The Women have a Train to their Jackets, that reaches down to their Heels... when they want to lay their Child out of their Arms they slip it into one of their Boots."*

He discovered Wager Bay and sailed up Roes Welcome to Repulse Bay. Although his map included the main features of the west coast, Middleton omitted Chesterfield Inlet, having mistaken it for a deep bay.

Dobbs refused to accept Middleton's findings and in 1746 he organized a private expedition commanded by William Moor. Moor had been first mate with Middleton, both in the Company's service and on the expedition of 1741-42. After wintering near the Company's post at York, in 1747 Moor followed Middleton's track. But apart from entering Chesterfield Inlet he added little to Middleton's surveys. In 1762 the Hudson's Bay Company itself brought this phase of exploration to an end when one of its sloops traced the whole of Chesterfield Inlet.

The Company also carried out less-publicized explorations along the east coast of the Bay, the East Main. Since Hudson's voyage of 1610, later explorers as well as the Company's annual supply ships sailing for James Bay or points farther west kept well clear of the uncharted islands which lay off the East Main coast. What little was known of the coast and interior did not entice them to investigate. But in 1739 Indians told the mas-ter of Eastmain House that to the north there were three large lakes with plenty of wood, fish and deer visited by Indians and Inuit.

Attracted by the possibility of opening a new trade area, and anxious to determine the truth or otherwise of rumors in England that the difficult route through Hudson Strait could be by-passed by a more southerly route through the middle of the Labrador penin-sula, the Company sent two sloops to survey the East Main coast in 1744. The expedition's only discovery of note was Richmond Gulf, possibly the most westerly of the "lakes" described by the Indians. In 1749 the initial survey was followed by a more elaborate expedition. Commanded by one of the Company's senior captains, William Coats, from Cape Digges, it explored south to Little Whale River.

Coats produced detailed but unpublished surveys, of 500 miles of the East Main coast from Cape Digges southward. He also recommended that a trading post should be set up in Richmond Gulf. Richmond House was built in 1750, only to be abandoned in 1759 after its officials failed in their attempts to open trade with the Naskapi Indians and to establish a white whale fishery.

> No ship was ever pester'd with such a set of rogues, most of them having deserved hanging before they entered with me, and not three seamen among the whole number of private men, so that had it not been for the officers, who, every one of them, worked like common men, I should have found no little difficulty to get the ships to England.
>
> **Captain Christopher Middleton on the crew of the *Furnace*, August 1742**

Discovery Voyages to Hudson Bay, 1741-49

- Limit of spring ice
- Known to Europeans, 1741
- Hudson's Bay Company post
- Middleton, 1742
- Moor, 1747
- Longland/Mitchell, 1744
- Coats, 1749
- Death of explorer

To the Arctic Ocean
THE JOURNEY OF SAMUEL HEARNE, 1771-72

In one of the great journeys of North American exploration, Hearne is guided by Indians to the northernmost edge of the continent.

In 1762 when Moses Norton became factor at Prince of Wales's Fort, Churchill, he again took up the quest for a river of copper and furs. Since Knight's day (▶ *page 102*) this dream had dominated thinking about the area of country northwest of Hudson Bay. Norton, investigating Chesterfield Inlet by sloop in the summer of 1762, saw that it did not harbor the hoped-for route deep into the interior.

In the same year Norton sent two Northern or Chipewyan Indians, Mattonabbee and Idotliaze, to investigate the far country. In 1767 they returned to Churchill with exciting news. They had found a river which ran between three copper mines and a wooded country rich in furs. They illustrated these dramatic and impressive findings in a map (*opposite*).

Armed with the map, Norton sent Samuel Hearne, mate of one of the sloops at Churchill, on an overland journey in search of "the Far Off Metal River," new fur areas and the Northwest Passage. After two false starts, Hearne, with a band of Chipewyan Indians

led by Mattonabbee, pursued his task in 1771-72. They traveled on foot across the Barrens of the northern tundra, "scarcely any thing but one solid mass of rock and stones," Hearne wrote, "in general a total want of soil." The Indians lived on fish and caribou, the streams were usually too shallow for canoes, and the best time for traveling was in winter when the frozen land gave a reasonable surface for snowshoes and sledges.

In July 1771 Hearne reached the Coppermine River. He followed it downstream until he sighted the Arctic Ocean,

> ### Hearne's Route to the Arctic Ocean
> REDRAWN FROM SAMUEL HEARNE'S MANUSCRIPT MAP OF 1771
>
> The map shows the country traveled by Hearne and his Chipewyan guides in 1771-72. A dotted line traces Hearne's outward route to the Arctic Ocean; a solid one his track back to Churchill. Hearne's "Arathapescow Lake" was to be the source of much confusion; it is Great Slave Lake which here appears for the first time on a European map, but was thought for some years to be Lake Athabasca, 200 miles to the southeast. The line of trees represents the "wood's edge" – between it and Hudson Bay were the treeless Barrens.

becoming the first European to see the northern coastline of the American continent. He viewed it "with the assistance of a good pocket telescope. The ice was not then broke up, but was melted away for about three quarters of a mile from the main shore."

The Coppermine River itself was a sad disappointment, shallow and unnavigable, and offering up only a few scattered lumps of copper. Hearne placed its mouth in latitude 71°54'N, almost four degrees too far north. This was a colossal error and a reminder of the lack of training and instruments of many of the Company explorers: Kelsey, Stuart, Henday and now Hearne. Hearne's return track opened up new areas to European gaze, for Mattonabbee's band turned southwest to Great Slave Lake in search of beaver and moose. They finally returned to Churchill after a journey of almost 19 months. Hearne, traveling with his Chipewyan guides, had displayed qualities of perseverance and endurance as he crossed one of the harshest landscapes in North America.

Samuel Hearne's journal, published in 1795, showed him to be an exceptional observer of the Indians and of the wildlife of the Canadian north. His journal also significantly observed that "the Continent of America is much wider than many people imagine... When I was at my greatest Western distance, upward of five hundred miles from Prince of Wales's Fort, the natives, my guides, well knew that many tribes of Indians lay to the West of us, and they knew no end to the land in that direction; nor have I ever met with any Indian, either Northern or Southern, that ever had seen the sea to the Westward."

Hearne's journey shattered any remaining hopes that a passage for shipping might be found through the continent. He had reached its northern shoreline without crossing a strait or even a river of note. If a passage existed, it must lie still farther north, in the polar sea which Hearne had glimpsed from the mouth of the Coppermine River. This was where James Cook (▶ *page 130*) would be sent to renew the search for a passage a few years after Hearne's return.

Left: The canoes of the Chipewyan were light enough to be carried by one person. They were used to cross unfordable streams, and enabled the Chipewyan to travel long distances. They could do this in both summer and winter, when the frozen land surface allowed the use of snowshoes and sledges. This engraving appeared in Samuel Hearne's A Journey from Prince of Wales's Fort in Hudson's Bay to the Northern Ocean, *1795.*

The Continent of America is much wider than many people imagine...when I was at my greatest Western distance, upward of five hundred miles from Prince of Wales's Fort, the natives, my guides, well knew that many tribes of Indians lay to the West of us, and they knew no end to the land in that direction; nor have I ever met with any Indian, either Northern or Southern, that ever had seen the sea to the Westward.

Samuel Hearne, A Journey from Prince of Wales's Fort, 1795

Chipewyan Knowledge
REDRAWN FROM A MAP MADE IN 1767 BY
MATTONABBEE AND IDOTLIAZE

The original map seems to be a copy made and annotated by Norton in 1767-68 from "A Draught of ye Coast" drawn by Mattonabee and Idotliaze. The version here is based on a redrawing by Professor Richard Ruggles. It shows an immense area of the Canadian Northwest that was totally unknown to Europeans at the time. Its focal point is Great Slave Lake, drawn for the first time in recognizable shape, and its drainage systems.

As with Knight's Chipewyan map (▶ *page 102*), allowances must be made for proportion and direction. The coast was not a feature of great interest to inland Indians and is shown running straight north-south. It lacks the great right-angle turn above Hudson Bay which gives the Arctic coastline its east-west orientation.

Inland from Hudson Bay

FUR TRADERS ON THE CANADIAN PRAIRIES, 1754-74

Under pressure from Canadian rivals, the explorer-traders of the Hudson's Bay Company journey far into the western interior.

By 1750 French expansion into the Winnipeg basin and beyond was making a serious dent in the Hudson Bay trade. James Isham, factor at York Fort, the most important bayside post, began a series of efforts to attract the distant "Archithinues" (Blackfoot) of the prairies, who reportedly had "great plenty of the best and finest of furs."

In June 1754 a "bold, enterprizing" laborer and netmaker at York, Anthony Henday, left the post on the first major inland journey since Kelsey's in 1690-92 (▶ *page 68*). He lived and traveled with the Indians, accom-

panying the returning Cree along their canoe route from York to the lower Saskatchewan, past "a Hogstye" of a French post at Le Pas. By the end of July Henday was encountering Assiniboin, and in September saw the great buffalo herds of the plains. They were so numerous that Henday's Indians had to "make them sheer out of our way" and when they hunted the buffalo they took only the tongue and other delicacies. In October Henday's Cree band reached the horsed Blackfoot, somewhere south of Red Deer River. The "king" or "great leader" of their

impressive camp told Henday that he would not send men to trade at the Bay because his people rode horses rather than paddled canoes, and they lived off the buffalo. Henday and his few remaining Cree companions now drifted farther west and should have been within sight of the Rocky Mountains. But there is no mention of the mountains in the different versions of his journal and the map he made of his journey has disappeared.

Henday revealed that the new French posts were intercepting furs going down to Hudson Bay. But the Seven Years' War brought

Left: A plan drawing of the Hudson's Bay Company post at Fort York, by its factor James Isham (c.1750). The numbered key to Isham's plan, has unfortunately, been lost. To the top is the Hayes River, on which Indian canoes carry furs to the fort. Andrew Graham, who succeeded Isham, described York as a "handsome, well-built Fort... consisting of four bastions with sheds between them, and a breast work on which are mounted twelve small carriage guns... and on the bank's edge abreast the fort are two fascine batteries...on which are mounted thirteen heavy cannon."

We mett the Earchitinue [Blackfoot] men on horse back 40 in number they were out on a Scout from the main body... upon the top of a Hill I seed 200 tents, where they were pitched in 2 Rows, and an opening Right through the middle, and att ye farther End of the Street, their was a Large tent pitcht in front, where all the old Men were seated and their King in the middle, and in the middle of the tent was full of fatt Buffaloes flesh, and after that we had all smoakt round.

From Henday's journal, 14 October 1754

dramatic changes in North America, and Canada was ceded to Britain in 1763. The French formally relinquished their trading posts, seeming to give the Hudson's Bay Company total control of the northern fur trade.

By the mid-1760s the river routes westward from Montréal were busy again, with French canoemen and interpreters now financed by British businessmen in Canada and also the American colonies. By 1770 the "English pedlars" had reoccupied the former French posts at Le Pas and elsewhere, and the Company's trade declined sharply. Reconnaissance trips from York which covered a great arc from Churchill River to Lake Manitoba, taking Matthew Cocking well beyond the Forks of the Saskatchewan to the Eagle Hills, revealed the extent of the threat. In 1773 the Hudson's Bay Company decided on a far-reaching change of policy, ordering Samuel Hearne to establish an inland post at or near Le Pas. The next year Hearne built Cumberland House at Pine Island Lake, 60 miles beyond Le Pas, and about 700 miles by canoe from York. Though strategically situated at a crossroads of the Indian trade, Cumberland House in isolation could only offer feeble competition to the Canadians, but it was important as a symbol of the Company's new policy. Its establishment marked the beginning of 50 years of strenuous competition which was to take the rival fur traders of Hudson Bay and the St Lawrence to Athabasca, across the Rockies, and finally to the Pacific slopes.

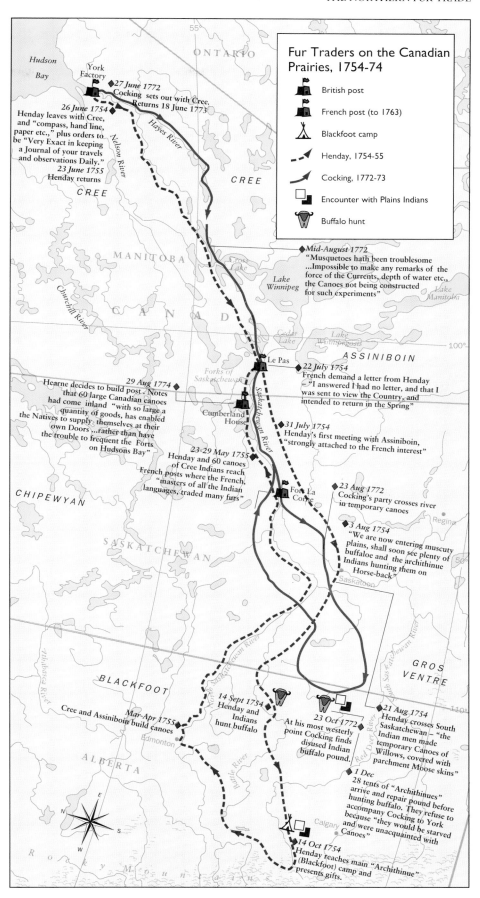

Fur Traders on the Canadian Prairies, 1754-74

- British post
- French post (to 1763)
- Blackfoot camp
- Henday, 1754-55
- Cocking, 1772-73
- Encounter with Plains Indians
- Buffalo hunt

27 June 1772 Cocking sets out with Cree. Returns 18 June 1773

26 June 1754 Henday leaves with Cree, and "compass, hand line, paper etc.," plus orders to be "Very Exact in keeping a Journal of your travels and observations Daily."

23 June 1755 Henday returns

Mid-August 1772 "Musquetoes hath been troublesome ...Impossible to make any remarks of the force of the Currents, depth of water etc., the Canoes not being constructed for such experiments"

22 July 1754 French demand a letter from Henday – "I answered I had no letter, and that I was sent to view the Country, and intended to return in the Spring"

31 July 1754 Henday's first meeting with Assiniboin, "strongly attached to the French interest"

29 Aug 1774 Hearne decides to build post. Notes that 60 large Canadian canoes had come inland "with so large a quantity of goods, has enabled the Natives to supply themselves at their own Doors ...rather than have the trouble to frequent the Forts on Hudsons Bay"

23-29 May 1755 Henday and 60 canoes of Cree Indians reach French posts where the French, "masters of all the Indian languages, traded many furs"

23 Aug 1772 Cocking's party crosses river in temporary canoes

3 Aug 1754 "We are now entering muscuty plains, shall soon see plenty of buffaloe and the archithinue Indians hunting them on Horse-back"

14 Sept 1754 Henday and Indians hunt buffalo

23 Oct 1772 At his most westerly point Cocking finds disused Indian buffalo pound.

21 Aug 1754 Henday crosses South Saskatchewan – "the Indian men made temporary Canoes of Willows, covered with parchment Moose skins"

1 Dec 28 tents of "Archithinues" arrive and repair pound before hunting buffalo. They refuse to accompany Cocking to York because "they would be starved and were unacquainted with Canoes"

Mar-Apr 1755 Cree and Assiniboin build canoes

14 Oct 1754 Henday reaches main "Archithinue" (Blackfoot) camp and presents gifts.

York Factory
Hudson Bay
ONTARIO
CREE
CREE
MANITOBA
Churchill River
Nelson River
Hayes River
CANADA
Cross Lake
Lake Winnipeg
Lake Manitoba
Cedar Lake
Lake Winnipegosis
ASSINIBOIN
Le Pas
Forks of Saskatchewan
Saskatchewan River
Cumberland House
Fort La Corne
CHIPEWYAN
SASKATCHEWAN
Saskatoon
Regina
GROS VENTRE
Athabasca River
BLACKFOOT
North Saskatchewan River
Battle River
Edmonton
Red Deer River
ALBERTA
Calgary
Rocky Mountains
N E S W

Pond and the Northwesters

THE EXPANSION OF THE FUR TRADE INTO ATHABASCA, 1778-1787

Ruthless fur trader and eccentric visionary
Peter Pond reaches and explores the Great
Slave Lake, and revives hopes of finding a
waterway to the Pacific.

By the time the Hudson's Bay Company had established its first inland post at Cumberland House in 1774 (▶ *page 110*), its Montréal rivals were sweeping past. Led by Thomas and Joseph Frobisher and the American Alexander Henry, they pushed further up the Saskatchewan and moved northwest onto English River. The further these "Pedlars" went, the harder it became for them to bring up supplies by river from Montréal, or even from the halfway station at Michilimackinac. So, to shorten their supply lines, they set up a new base at Grand Portage, at the western end of Lake Superior.

In 1778 one of the most enterprising and combative of them, the New Englander Peter Pond, did not even come down to Grand Portage from the interior. Using supplies still left in the trading areas, he followed the Indian trails to cross the height of land at the 13-mile Methy Portage and reached the Athabasca basin. His journey was a notable, if ill-defined, feat of exploration into what a contemporary described as "a country hitherto unknown but from an Indian report."

It was also a lucrative one: when Pond came out of Athabasca in 1779 he had traded twice as many fine beaver skins as his canoes

A Country Hitherto Unknown
REDRAWN FROM A SECTION OF
POND'S MAP OF JULY 1787

Pond's map was intended to be taken down to the Pacific coast and handed to Russian fur traders there for presentation to Catherine the Great. It shows the posts of the North West Company (numbered, not named); the "Lake of the Hills" (Lake Athabasca); and the Great Slave Lake, unrealistically large and about 700 miles west of its actual position. From its western end, a river flows towards "Cook's River" (Cook Inlet). The Rocky Mountains are only sketchily indicated.

could carry. His revelation of the rich fur country of Athabasca helped the formation in 1779 of a new partnership of Montréal merchants. In 1783 it adopted the name by which it became famous: the North West Company.

Meanwhile, at his post near Lake Athabasca, Pond was collecting information from the Indians about the country to the north and west, of another great lake or sea (the Great Slave Lake), of rivers and mountains. He returned to Montréal in 1784 with a grandiose scheme for a chain of posts stretching to the Pacific coast, recently explored by Cook (▶ *page 130*). He drew up a series of maps and proposals aimed at enlisting support for his plan, but they attracted little interest.

Undeterred, Pond went back to Athabasca in 1785 and organized the establishment of new posts at Great Slave Lake and on the Peace River. The evidence of his maps indicates that he also explored Great Slave Lake. This second spell in Athabasca gave Pond more evidence of possible routes to the Pacific coast which would save the exhausting two-year canoe trip back to the St Lawrence. He claimed that at Great Slave Lake he met Indians who had seen Cook's ships on the coast, and possessed articles which seemed to be of English manufacture. On the strength of these reports, he estimated that he had been "within six days travel of the Grand Pacific Ocean."

In 1787, Pond left the Canadian northwest for good. He devoted the rest of that year to drawing a series of maps intended to illustrate and promote his visionary ideas, sending them off to influential figures such as the governor of Québec and the empress of Russia. The maps show a gigantic Great Slave Lake, with a massive river flowing from its western end towards "Cook's River." The inference is clear: the two rivers were one and the same. Pond had revived the old fantasy of a navigable inlet stretching from the Pacific far into the North American interior (▶ *page 52*). Along this channel, supplies could be brought to the fur traders in Athabasca.

Pond was one of the last of the old explorers, tough in body and mind, but technically unskilled in representing where they had been or what they had seen. A ruthless, obsessive character suspected of killing two rival fur traders, Pond knew the northwest better than any other white man. But as one perceptive observer in Québec put it, Pond's longitudes seemed "to be guesswork and not in any respect accurate enough to be depended upon." Pond's theories were soon put to the test, not by himself as he once hoped, but by his young second-in-command in Athabasca, Alexander Mackenzie.

This engraving of A Winter View in the Athapuscow Lake *was based on a drawing by Samuel Hearne (▶page 108), and appeared in his* Journey... to the Northern Ocean *(1795). "The point where we crossed" Hearne wrote, "is said to be the narrowest. It is full of islands; most of which are clothed with tall poplars, birch and pines, and are well stocked with Indian deer. On some of the large islands we also found several beaver..."*

That the great Slave Lake is the most northerly large piece of water before you arrive at the Northern Ocean, and that the River which rises from that Lake empties into the Northern Pacific Ocean, and is the River that Cook discovered... another man by the name of McKanzie was left by Pond at Slave Lake with orders to go down the River, and from thence to Unalaska, and so to Kamchtaka, and then to England through Russia.

Report from Quebec on Pond's proposals, November 1789

From Canada, by Land

THE JOURNEYS OF ALEXANDER MACKENZIE, 1789 AND 1793

Traveling in harsh conditions overland Alexander Mackenzie reaches both the Arctic and Pacific oceans.

In June 1789 Alexander Mackenzie, a young Scot in the service of the North West Company, set out from Fort Chipewyan on Lake Athabasca in an attempt to reach the Pacific coast.

Mackenzie took with him three canoes and was accompanied by five *voyageurs* and five Indians, including Mattonabbee's successor as Chipewyan leader, "the English Chief." By the end of June the expedition reached the river at the western end of Great Slave Lake and found that it flowed west, as Peter Pond had predicted (▶ *page 112*). Disappointment came on 2 July, when they faced high mountains, looming "as far as we could see."

T he immense ridge, or succession of ridges of stony mountains, whose Northern extremity dips in the North [Arctic] Sea, in latitude 70 North, and longitude 135 West, running nearly South-East... to divide the waters of the Atlantic from those which run into the Pacific. In those snow-clad mountains rises the Mississippi, if we admit the Missouri to be its source, which flows into the Gulph of Mexico; the River Nelson, which is lost in Hudson's Bay; Mackenzie's River, that discharges itself into the North Sea; and the Columbia emptying itself into the Pacific Ocean.

Mackenzie's description of the Rocky Mountains, from his *Voyages*, 1801

and found that the river started to bend north, along the barrier of the Rockies. By 12 July Mackenzie had reached the tidal waters of the Arctic Ocean at America's northern coastline and produced a more accurate reading of his location, latitude 67°47'N, than Samuel Hearne had made (▶ *page 108*) 18 years before.

In September Mackenzie was back at Fort Chipewyan after canoeing almost three thousand miles in three months. "My expedition," he noted, "was hardly spoken of but that is what I expected." As with many of his predecessors, Mackenzie's journey was made possible only with the help of Indian guides, interpreters and canoemen. If the comment of a recent scholar that Mackenzie was taken on "a conducted tour" of the river soon to be named after him makes scant acknowledgement of the Scotsman's qualities of willpower and determination, it illustrates an essential truth of these expeditions.

Mackenzie had lacked adequate surveying instruments and skills on his first expedition. He acquired these in England and by the fall of 1792 returned to Fort Chipewyan to investigate a second river the Hare Indians had told him about, which flowed into the sea on the far side of the mountains.

After wintering west of Great Slave Lake, Mackenzie headed up Peace River crammed into a 25ft canoe with six *voyageurs*, two Indians and 3000lbs of goods and provisions. They soon became the first Europeans to reach

the northern Rockies from the east, where men and boat received a terrible battering from the seething waters and jagged rocks of Peace River Canyon. After they crossed the continental divide, a confusing tangle of rivers, mountains and forests almost brought the expedition to a halt. On 4 July 1793 they abandoned their canoe and, with 90lb packs on their backs, struggled towards the ocean on foot. They were on the moist western slopes, where the Indian inhabitants lived mainly on salmon and in large, decoratively-carved wooden dwellings. Passing from one Indian guide to another they reached the Pacific at Dean Channel, less than seven weeks after the arrival of Vancouver's survey boats (▶ *page 132*).

Mackenzie had not found a trade route to the Pacific, but he was the first white man to cross the American continent north of Mexico. He therefore established the true distance between Athabasca and the Pacific. He also confronted the harsh reality of the northern Rockies and while not following it far, he had found a "big river," called by Indians the Tacoutche Tesse (▶ *page 118*), which they said flowed into the sea far to the south. As Mackenzie simply inscribed on a rock on 22 July 1793, he had come "from Canada, by land."

Below: Cedar-plank houses similar to those seen by Mackenzie on the western slopes of the Rockies. This Nootka village, at Friendly Cove, was painted by John Webber, who accompanied Captain Cook on his 1778 expedition (▶ page 130).

The Journeys of Alexander Mackenzie, 1789 and 1793

- Known to Europeans, 1789
- Trading post
- Mackenzie, 1789
- Mackenzie, 1793
- Encounter with Indians
- Trading encounter
- Winter camp
- Rapids
- Tar sands

12 July Mackenzie observes rise and fall of the tide. "To the southwestward we could just perceive a Chain of Mountains extending farther to the north than the edge of the ice..."

Mackenzie meets "The Quarrellers" or Kutchin Indians, who have no knowledge of beaver or firearms

9 July

10 July Reports of nearby Inuit "dismayed my [Chipewyan] hunters...they are quite disgusted with the Voyage"

Hare Indians tell Mackenzie that "there is another large River on the other Side of the mountains which ran towards the Midday Sun"

27 July

28 July "Obliged to land to gum our Canoe. This is the first time we landed for this purpose since we left Athabasca"

Slave and Dogrib Indians try to discourage Mackenzie; tell him "we would be several Winters getting to the Sea, and that we all should be old Men by the time we would return"

5 July

2 July "At nine we perceived... a cluster of mountains stretching as far as our view could reach to the Southward, and whose tops were lost in the clouds"

Mackenzie finds entrance of Mackenzie River

29 June

23 June Mackenzie trades with Yellowknife Indians for their furs

Mackenzie reaches lake "covered all over with Ice"

9 June

"All along the River we were much troubled with Muskettows and Gnatts"

19-25 May Mackenzie's men haul canoe out of a "succession of rapids, cascades and falls"

Mackenzie meets Sekani who trade iron with Carrier Indians farther west. They in turn obtain it from coastal Indians who "trade with people like us, that come there in vessels as big as islands"

9 June

"At two in the afternoon the rocky mountains appeared in sight, with their summits covered with snow"

17 May

3 May 1789 Mackenzie sets out

Fort Chipewyan (1788)

10 Oct 1792 Mackenzie leaves for Peace River

12 Sept Mackenzie returns

1 Nov 1792-9 May 1793 Mackenzie winters among Beaver Indians

Fort Fork (temporary post)

12 June Mackenzie crosses "a low ridge of land" – the divide between the watersheds of the Mackenzie River, draining into the Arctic, and the Fraser, draining into the Pacific

21 July Mackenzie reaches sea at harbor explored by Vancouver on 5 June

19 June Canoe carried through canyon "with great difficulty"

4 July

23 June Mackenzie turns back

19 July Mackenzie glimpses sea

18 July Indians take Mackenzie's group downriver in canoes

From Hudson Bay to the Rockies

THE INLAND SURVEYS OF THE HUDSON'S BAY COMPANY, 1778-1812

In the late 18th century trained surveyors, Philip Turnor, Peter Fidler and David Thompson, map the trade routes of the Canadian West.

In 1774 the Hudson's Bay Company began to move inland. From Cumberland House, traders slowly moved their operations up the Saskatchewan River until in 1786 the Company appointed William Tomison, chief at Fort York, to reside inland. These activities signaled the beginning of a war of attrition with the North West Company which lasted until they amalgamated in 1821. For the first time the Bay posts were relegated to a subordinate status, and the extension of Company posts deep into the interior can be followed through Tomison's movements as he shifted headquarters steadily upstream on the North Saskatchewan. By 1795 he was at Edmonton House, and four years later Acton House was built on the fringes of the Rocky Mountains.

In expansion of posts, development of more flexible transport systems, and opening up of trade with the Indians of the plains and mountains, the Hudson's Bay Company had advanced far in the generation following its first tentative move inland; but it still lagged behind its rivals. Flamboyant and ruthless, the Northwesters had reached Great Slave Lake, the Peace and Mackenzie rivers and even, momentarily, the Pacific, by the time the Hudson's Bay men established their first post in Athabasca in 1802. But slowness and steadiness had compensations, and the surveyors of the Hudson's Bay Company mapped the inland routes with a thoroughness never approached by the Northwesters.

A new era in the exploration of the north began in 1778 when the Hudson's Bay Company hired Philip Turnor as "their Surveyor for settling the Latitudes, Longitudes, Courses and distances of the different Settlements Inland." For the distant London directors, it was the logical and essential consequence of the Company's shift into the unmapped interior. In the next 15 years Turnor produced detailed surveys of the trade routes, many near Hudson Bay but others as far distant as the Northwesters' run from the Methy Portage into Athabasca. The surveys of Turnor and his colleagues in 1791-92 established the position of Lake Athabasca and Great Slave Lake, and corrected the huge inaccuracies of Pond's longitudes. It was a chance meeting with Turnor in 1790 which

prompted Mackenzie to return to England to acquire the necessary skills (▶ *page 114*). Not the least of Turnor's contributions was the training of younger men, Peter Fidler and David Thompson in particular. In 1794, after his retirement, Turnor incorporated his surveys into a superb general map which formed the basis for Aaron Arrowsmith's *Map Exhibiting all the New Discoveries in the Interior Parts of North America* (1795). In Arrowsmith's words, Turnor and his associates "had laid the permanent foundation of that part of the globe." From Kelsey to Pond, the explorers of the interior until this time had been more notable for their qualities of endurance and courage than for any skill in surveying.

After David Thompson switched allegiance to the North West Company in 1797, Peter Fidler became Turnor's acknowledged successor and outdid his mentor both in years of service and in surveys accomplished. In a career of more than 30 years he traveled 48,000 miles, by canoe, on horseback and on foot, and completed 7,300 miles of surveys. He ranged across vast areas of western Canada, and became more familiar with the prairies and its Indians than any other white man. He was more than a surveyor in a narrow, technical sense, for his journals are a treasure-house of information about the regions he traversed. They include some of the earliest descriptions of the Athabasca tar sands, "great quantities of bitumen a kind of liquid tar oozing out of the banks;" as well as the eastern Rockies, described as "awfully grand... similar to dark rain like clouds rising above the Horizon in a fine summer's evening;" the destruction of the Piegan buffalo hunts, and much else. Fidler's most active period of field work ended in 1812, but by then he had made a massive contribution to the revolutionary new maps by Arrowsmith and others of the Canadian interior.

> The Buffalo are very numerous on the NE side the Red Deers River...the ground is entirely covered by them & appears quite black. I never saw such amazing numbers together before. I am sure there was some millions in sight as no ground could be seen for them in that compleat semicircle & extending at least 10 miles.
>
> Peter Fidler's journal, February 1793

The Canadian West and the Fur Trade, c.1812

Limit of spring ice

Known to people of European descent, c.1812

Hudson's Bay Company

North West Company

Post

Trade route

Portage

Fort Good Hope

Fort Norman

Great Bear River

Great Bear Lake

Coppermine River

HARE

NAHANI

YELLOWKNIFE

NORTHWEST TERRITORIES

INUIT

ARCTIC CIRCLE

Yellowknife

Fort Providence

Great Slave Lake

Slave Fort

Slave River

SLAVE

BRITISH COLUMBIA

ALBERTA

Peace River

Fort Vermilion

BEAVER

Fort Liard

Fort Wintzel

Rocky Mountain House

McLeod's Fort

Fort of the Forks

Fort Dunvegan

Athabasca River

Lake Athabasca

Fort Chipewyan

Fond du Lac

CHIPEWYAN

SASKATCHEWAN

MANITOBA

Hudson Bay

Fort Churchill

Fort Pierre-au-Calumet

Clearwater River

Fort of the Forks

Methye Portage

Fort Lac des Boeufs

Bedford House

Indian Lake House

Reindeer Lake

Churchill River

Nelson House

Nelson River

Fort York

Hayes River

Fort Severn

Lesser Slave Lake

Fort Lac La Biche

Fort Ile à la Crosse

Portage-de-Traite

Oxford House

Severn Lake House

SEKANI

Edmonton House

Beaver River

North Saskatchewan River

WESTERN WOODS CREE

Wekusko

Cross Lake House

Cedar Lake

Fort Jasper House

SARCEE

Acton House

Edmonton

Fort Vermilion

BLACKFOOT

Rocky Mountain House

BLOOD

PIEGAN

Red Deer River

Fort La Monte

South Branch House

Saskatoon

Cumberland House

Swan Lake House

Shell River House

Lake Winnipegosis

Lake Winnipeg

NAHANI

CALEDONIA

KOOTENAY

Calgary

South Saskatchewan River

Regina

GROS VENTRE DES PLAINES

Fort Esperance

Fort Qu'appelle

Portage La Prairie

Lake Manitoba

Bas de laRivière

Winnipeg

OJIBWA

ONTARIO

Fort Montagne à la Bosse

Assiniboine River

Rat Portage House

ASSINIBOIN

Brandon House

GROS VENTRE DE LA RIVIÈRE

Fort Gibraltar

Fort Pembina

Lake of the Woods

Rainy Lake

Fort William

Lake Superior

Souris River

Missouri River

Grand Forks House

Duluth

Fond du Lac

MINNESOTA

WISCONSIN

MANDAN

UNITED STATES

Traders to the Pacific

THE EXPLORATIONS OF FRASER AND THOMPSON, 1805-11

Soon after Lewis and Clark reach the Pacific overland, Canadian fur traders renew their search for a northerly route to the mouth of the Columbia River.

Early in the 19th century the North West Company was near the eastern slopes of the Rockies. Simon Fraser headed explorations to the north, planning to follow the southward-flowing "big river" down to the coast that had been found, and then left, by Alexander Mackenzie in 1793 (▶ *page 114*). Like Mackenzie, Fraser assumed this was the Columbia River.

Between 1805 and 1807 Fraser and his associates explored along and beyond Mackenzie's track. Traveling up the Peace River and among Indians who had never seen a white man, Fraser built the first trading posts on the Pacific slope. One of these, later Fort George, was the starting point for his journey to the sea in 1808. By canoe and on foot Fraser followed Mackenzie's "Tacoutche Tesse" for more than 500 miles. It could not be the Columbia, as Fraser would establish, for it ran into the sea at the Strait of Georgia. Moreover a dangerous and hair-raising sequence of rapids, cascades and whirlpools made it impossible as a trade route. It was later reported that in nine attempts out of ten the passage downriver would lead to certain death. In 1813 David Thompson, master surveyor of the North West Company, named it the Fraser River.

David Thompson, "the Astronomer," would succeed where Fraser had failed. Working first for the Hudson's Bay Company, then the better-resourced North West Company, Thompson covered in all a prodigious 56,000 miles, surveying 13,000 of them. Thompson's story of his surveys, recounted late in life, has become a classic of its kind. He mapped the country on both sides of the Canadian-American border of 1783, from Sault Sainte-Marie and Grand Portage to Lake Winnipeg, the Red River, the Upper Missouri and the headwaters of the Mississippi. He worked his way along both banks of the Saskatchewan, the Churchill River and into Athabasca. In 1801 he failed in an attempt to cross the Rockies from the Northwesters' new post at Rocky Mountain House. Thompson then turned to the south.

From 1807 to 1810 Thompson traded and explored a great arc from the Upper Columbia across the border to the Clark Fork region of Idaho. During this time, his trading activities and the hostility of the Piegan Indians stopped

> July 14th [1811] brought us to a full view of the Pacific Ocean; which to me was a great pleasure, but my men seemed disappointed; they had been accustomed to the boundless horizons of the great Lakes of Canada, and their high rolling waves; from the Ocean they expected a more boundless view... and my informing them, that directly opposite to us at the distance of five thousand miles was the Empire of Japan added nothing to their Ideas.
>
> From Thompson's *Narrative*

Above: Fort William, on the northwest shore of Lake Superior (▶ page 116), was the effective headquarters of the North West Company. When Thompson retired from the fur trade, he produced a map of the Northwest, which hung for many years in the Great Hall of Fort William. This watercolor view of the fort was painted by Robert Irvine in 1812.

his efforts to reach the ocean to the west.

In 1810 Thompson was at Rainy Lake, on his return east, when news arrived that John Jacob Astor had formed the American Fur Company and was sending a ship from Boston to the Columbia River. "I was now obliged" wrote Thompson "to take 4 canoes and to proceed to the mouth of the Columbia to oppose them."

To avoid the Piegan, Thompson followed his Iroquois guide north to make a winter crossing through the unmapped Athabasca Pass. The mountains were "far north in a rugged country" a companion noted. After three months in a miserable winter camp, deserted by most of his men, Thompson resumed his journey in April 1811. Then, threading his way through the tangled skein of rivers on the Pacific slope in June he reached the Columbia River at Kettle Falls, and became the first white man to follow the river downstream to its fork with the Snake River. From here he followed the track taken by Lewis and Clark six years earlier, past the fearsome Dalles and the Cascades, down to the sea.

There the American flag flew over Astoria, built by Astor's men three months earlier.

The Explorations of Fraser and Thompson, 1805-11

- Known to people of European descent, 1805
- North West Company post
- US post
- Fraser, 1808
- Thompson, 1810-11
- Winter camp
- Act of possession
- Rapids
- Falls
- Portage

130°   125°   120°   115°

CARRIER

Rocky Mountain Portage

Peace River

Dunvegan

28 May 1808
Fraser leaves fort with 4 canoes and 23 men

BLACKFOOT

Edmonton

30 May Atnah Indians "had heard of fire-arms, but had never seen any"

Fort Fraser

Fort George

31 May
Slave found among Indians who had been to the sea, and sketched route on oil-cloth on which "we could plainly see a confirmation of the badness of the navigation"

BRITISH COLUMBIA

Atnah Indians "are great travellers; have been at war beyond the Mountains, going by the name of Rocky Mountains, where they saw Buffaloes."

3 June

9 June "A continual series of cascades, mixt with rocky fragments and bound by precipices and mountains, that seemed at times to have no end. I scarcely ever saw any thing so dreary, and seldom so dangerous in any country"

Vancouver

26 Jan-17 Apr
Winter camp. Thompson leaves with cedar-board canoe and remaining 3 men

30 Dec 1810-10 Jan 1811
Party crosses height of land on snow-shoes and with dog-sleds

28 Oct 1810
Thompson leaves with 24 men on foot and horseback. Because of fear of the Piegan he decides on northerly Athabascan route, "which would place us in safety, but would be attended with great inconvenience, fatigue, sufferings and privation"

SHUSWAP

KOOTENAY

ALBERTA

PIEGAN

Calgary

10 June
Party cache their canoes

20 June
Take to Indian canoes at river forks. Fraser later names one fork after David Thompson

15 June
Askettish Indians ferry party across river, and draw "a chart of the Country below this to the sea. By this sketch the navigation seems still very bad, and difficult"

Nootka Island

19 June
"Thank God we arrived safe at the Ilthkoyape [Kettle] Falls of the Columbia River"

Kootenay House

14 May
"We came to the head of the Columbia River, 260 miles from our winter hunt" – they cross portage to Kootenay River

2 July 1808
"The latitude is 49° nearly, while that of the entrance of the Columbia is 46°20'. This River, therefore, is not the Columbia. If I had been convinced of this fact where I left my canoes [on 10 June], I would certainly have returned from thence"

Point Grey

26 June
"I have been for a long period among the Rocky Mountains, but have never seen any thing equal to this country, for I cannot find words to describe our situation at times. We had to pass where no human being should venture"

Pacific Ocean

CANADA

UNITED STATES

Ilthkoyape Falls

Kootenay River

15 July
Thompson canoes down to cape – "Thus I have fully completed the survey of this part of North America from sea to sea, and by almost innumerable astronomical Observations have determined the positions of the Mountains, Lakes and Rivers, and other remarkable places of the northern part of the continent"

WASHINGTON

Seattle

Spokane

Coeur d'Alene

MONTANA

14 July
Thompson arrives within sight of sea and finds "four low Log huts, the far famed Fort Astoria of the United States"

Cape Disappointment

Astoria

Cascades

Columbia River

The Dalles

Portland

Salem

9 July
Thompson reaches river junction. "Here I erected a small pole, with a half sheet of paper well tied about it, with these words on it: Know hereby that this country is claimed by Great Britain as part of its Territories, and that the N.W. Company of Merchants from Canada... do hereby intend to erect a factory at this place for the commerce of the country around"

12 July
"Walls of Rock contract the River from eight hundred to one thousand yards in width to sixty yards and less: imagination can hardly form an idea of the working of this immense body of water under such a compression, raging and hissing, as if alive"

11 July CHINOOK
"Like all the Natives along this River their living was the Salmon fishery with the Seine and Dipping nets... they informed me they had heard of white people from the sea, and warned us all to beware of the Dalles and Falls which were close below us"

OREGON

IDAHO

Helena

Butte

45°   50°   55°

N W E S

California: Island or Peninsula?

THE JOURNEYS OF FATHER KINO, 1687-1702

The Jesuit Father Eusebio Kino tirelessly journeys around the fringes of New Spain, and dispels the myth that California is an island.

Throughout the 17th century, Lower or *Baja* California lay on the very edge of the northwest frontier of New Spain. What was known of it from earlier coasting voyages was not reassuring: mountains, deserts and a forbidding coastline with few harbors, and no sign of precious metals or of populous Indian nations.

Even its basic geography was the subject of contention. Although Francisco de Ulloa's 1539 voyage to the head of the Gulf of California (▶ *page 38*) had shown that California was a peninsula, this knowledge had been obscured by later misunderstandings. Father Ascensión, who had sailed with Vizcaíno in 1602 (▶ *page 40*), claimed that beyond Cape Mendocino the coast turned northeast into the Strait of Anian, "having joined the Oceanic Sea which surrounds Cape Mendocino and the Mediterranean Sea of California." An account written in 1626 of Oñate's 1604-05 journey to the Colorado River made much the same point: "the Gulf of California is not closed, but is an arm of the sea."

During the 17th century the Spanish frontier advanced slowly along the mainland coast of the Gulf. Missions and presidios were established in Sinaloa and Sonora, and ranching activity spread north. Even so, not until the next century was it accepted that California was a peninsula. This was the individual achievement of another in the long line of Jesuit missionary explorers, Father Eusebio Francisco Kino. In the mid-1680s, he made a series of explorations across the gusty waters of the Gulf of California, and in 1685 reached the Pacific coast. Kino then moved north into the Sonoran frontier area. From the mission post at Dolores, which he founded in 1687, he pushed north to the Colorado and Gila Rivers. Accompanied by Indian guides and carriers, Father Kino made more than 50 journeys on horseback and on foot through Pimeria Alta (northern Sonora and southern Arizona) – the first exploration of the region.

By the late 1690s Kino was absorbed in the quest for a land route to California, and in 1698 described how he saw land across the head of the Gulf of California. It took another four years for Kino to be convinced of the reality of his discovery, and he himself never made the journey across the head of the Gulf

and on to the Pacific coast. But the issue of the insularity – or otherwise – of California remained unresolved. For casual callers to the coast, such as the English privateer George Shelvocke in 1721, this was proof that "the Spaniards are now grown indolent and incurious." It was not until 1747, after the voyage of Father Fernando Consag right round the Gulf of California, that the Spanish authorities publicly declared that California was a part of the North American mainland.

The Journeys of Father Kino, 1687-1702

Known to Europeans, 1687
Swamp
Sand dunes

Kino's journeys

1698   1701
1699   1702
1700

✝ Mission
Spanish ranching

◆ Frontier region with hostile Apach

Phoenix

HALCHIDOMA

Colorado River

Gila River

MARICOPA

ARIZONA

Crater Range

CALIF.

Yuma

◆ **Oct 1700**
Kino reaches junction of Gila River with the Colorado River ("the largest in all New Spain)," and learns that he is north of the Gulf of California

YUMA

◆ **Feb 1699**
Yuma Indians give Kino blue shells, only seen by him on the Pacific coast of California, suggesting an overland route from here

Nov 1701 ◆
Kino, sitting in a basket on a raft towed by Indians, crosses the Colorado to the Californian side

USA
MEXICO

Great Sand Dunes

BAJA CALIFORNIA NORTE

Altar

HOGIOPAS

◆ **Mar 1702**
Kino reaches Colorado estuary; notes that "the sun rose over the head of the Sea of California," and is satisfied that California is not an island

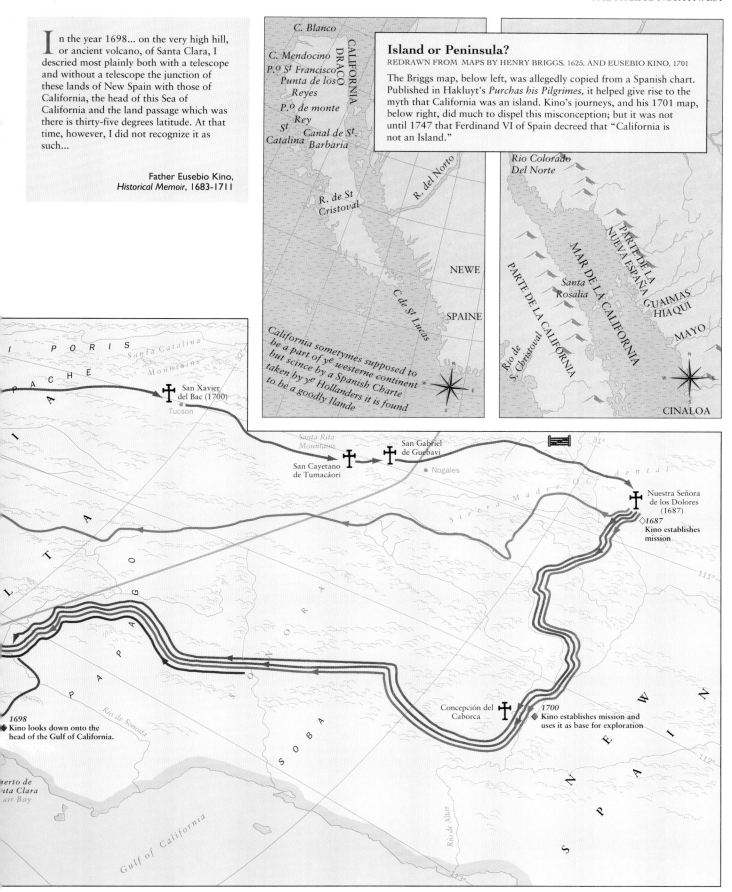

In the year 1698... on the very high hill, or ancient volcano, of Santa Clara, I descried most plainly both with a telescope and without a telescope the junction of these lands of New Spain with those of California, the head of this Sea of California and the land passage which was there is thirty-five degrees latitude. At that time, however, I did not recognize it as such...

Father Eusebio Kino,
Historical Memoir, 1683-1711

Island or Peninsula?

REDRAWN FROM MAPS BY HENRY BRIGGS, 1625, AND EUSEBIO KINO, 1701

The Briggs map, below left, was allegedly copied from a Spanish chart. Published in Hakluyt's *Purchas his Pilgrimes,* it helped give rise to the myth that California was an island. Kino's journeys, and his 1701 map, below right, did much to dispel this misconception; but it was not until 1747 that Ferdinand VI of Spain decreed that "California is not an Island."

C. Blanco

CALIFORNIA
DRACO

C. Mendocino
P.º Sᵗ Francisco
Punta de los
Reyes
P.º de monte
Rey
Sᵗ
Catalina   Canal de Sᵗ.
Barbaria

R. del Norte

R. de Sᵗ
Cristoval

NEWE

C de Sᵗ Lucas

SPAINE

California sometymes supposed to
be a part of ye westerne continent
but scince by a Spanish Charte
taken by ye Hollanders it is found
to be a goodly Ilande

Rio Colorado
Del Norte

PARTE DE LA
NUEVA ESPAÑA

MAR DE LA
CALIFORNIA

Santa
Rosalia

GUAIMAS
HIAQUI

PARTE DE LA CALIFORNIA

Rio de
S. Christoval

MAYO

CINALOA

I PORIS
Santa Catalina
Mountains

San Xavier
del Bac (1700)
Tucson

APACHE

Santa Rita
Mountains

San Cayetano
de Tumacáori

San Gabriel
de Guebavi

Nogales

Nuestra Señora
de los Dolores
(1687)

◇1687
Kino establishes
mission

31°

32°

Sierra Madre Occidental

SONORA

PAPAGO

SOBA

1698
◆ Kino looks down onto the
head of the Gulf of California.

Rio de Sonoita

Concepción del
Caborca

1700
◆ Kino establishes mission and
uses it as base for exploration

NEW
SPAIN

Puerto de
Santa Clara
Fair Bay

Rio de Altar

Gulf of California

111°

112°

113°

From Asia to America

THE VOYAGES OF BERING AND THE RUSSIANS, 1728-68

*The Russians, having expanded to the
Pacific, investigate the bolshaya zemlya
(great land) rumored to lie across the sea to
the east.*

As early as 1648, a Cossack, Semen Dezhnev,
had claimed that he had rounded the eastern
cape of Asia (now Mys Dezhneva), but his
report had been lost and his discovery
forgotten. So in 1724 Tsar Peter I ordered the
Danish seaman Vitus Bering to sail from
Kamchatka and "determine where it joins with
America." Four years later, in the *St Gabriel* (a
vessel built in Kamchatka), Bering reached the
strait now known by his name, but fog hid the
opposite shore. In 1732 Mikhail Gwosdev
reached a shoreline across the strait, although
no report of this was published.

In 1731 Bering took charge of a second,
more ambitious expedition. After years of
struggle on the long overland route from St
Petersburg and Kamchatka, he sailed from
Petropavlovsk in the spring of 1741. On the
voyage Bering's two ships became separated,
with dire results. His second-in-command,
Chirikov, sighted the American coast in
latitude 55°21'N., but there lost both his ship's
boats with their crews, and was unable to land.
Bering, meanwhile, had swung north towards
the Alaskan coast, and landed at Kayak Island.
He stayed there only long enough to take on
water, to the irritation of his German
naturalist, Georg Steller. Bering's ship, with its
crew suffering from scurvy, threaded its way
homeward, only to be wrecked on an island
near Kamchatka where Bering and many of his
crew died.

The survivors reported that the area was rich
in fur seals, foxes, and above all sea otters, and
at least 30 trading ventures sailed from
Kamchatka in the next 20 years. In crazy
vessels often held together by leather thongs,
the *promysheniki* visited the stark volcanic
islands of the Aleutian chain. They had no
interest in exploration, and killed not only sea
otters but almost exterminated the native
Aleuts, turning the intimidated survivors into
hunters. But the naval escort expeditions of
Lieutenant Synd (1764-68), and Captain
Krenitsyn and Lieutenant Levashev (1764-71),
did some useful survey work. Unfortunately,
their maps languished in the archives, and the
only published map issued from St Petersburg,
Jacob von Stählin's, was to mislead rather than
guide future explorers (▶ *page 130*).

Russian Voyages, 1728-68

	Known to Europeans, 1728
	Limit of spring ice
	Bering, 1728
	Gwosdev, 1732
	Bering, 1741
	Chirikov, 1741
	Synd, 1767-68
	Krenitsyn and Levashev, 1768
	Encounter with native people
	Shipwreck
	Death of explorer

*Above: Russian expeditions to Alaska were keen to
record both the people and the wildlife they
encountered. Levashev sketched this Aleut woman
(above), surrounded by her belongings, on Unalaska
Island in 1767.*

The Russian Discoveries
REDRAWN FROM GERHARDT MÜLLER'S
NOUVELLE CARTE, 1754-58

Published by the Academy of Sciences in
St Petersburg, Müller's map reflects the
official Russian view that all Bering's
sightings were of the American mainland.
This led him to conjecture that a vast
peninsula stretched along the line of the
Aleutian Islands towards Kamchatka.
Dreams of a passage through the
continent had lingered in the "River of the
West"and in the "discoveries"of Juan de
Fuca and Bartholomew de Fonte(▶ *page
42*). Otherwise, this was the most accurate
map of the northwest coast yet produced.

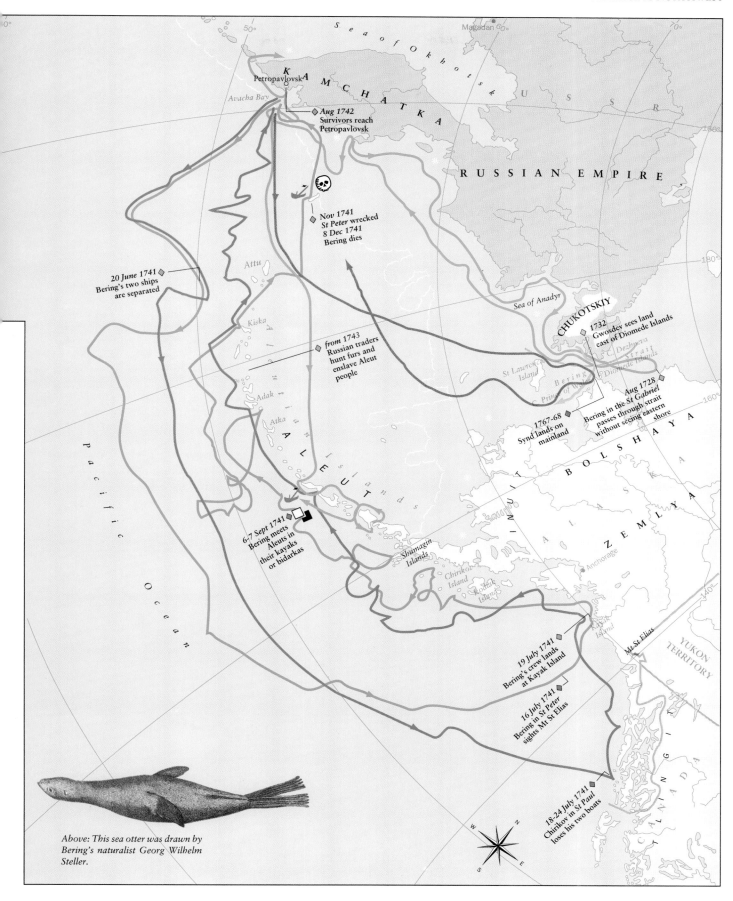

Aug 1742
Survivors reach
Petropavlovsk

Petropavlovsk

K A M C H A T K A

Avacha Bay

RUSSIAN EMPIRE

Nov 1741
St Peter wrecked
8 Dec 1741
Bering dies

20 June 1741
Bering's two ships
are separated

Attu

Kiska

Sea of Anadyr

CHUKOTSKIY

1732
Gwosdev sees land
east of Diomede Islands

St Lawrence Island

C. Dezhneva

Diomede Islands

from 1743
Russian traders
hunt furs and
enslave Aleut
people

Bering Strait

Prince of Wales

Aug 1728
Bering in the St Gabriel
passes through strait
without seeing eastern
shore

1767-68
Synd lands on
mainland

Adak

Atka

A L E U T I A N   Islands

B O L S H A Y A

Z E M L Y A

Pacific

Ocean

6-7 Sept 1741
Bering meets
Aleuts in
their kayaks
or bidarkas

Shumagin
Islands

Chirikof
Island

Kodiak
Island

Anchorage

YUKON
TERRITORY

Mt St Elias

19 July 1741
Bering's crew lands
at Kayak Island

Kayak
Island

16 July 1741
Bering in St Peter
sights Mt St Elias

T L I N G I T

C A N A D A

18-24 July 1741
Chirikov in St Paul
loses his two boats

*Above: This sea otter was drawn by
Bering's naturalist Georg Wilhelm
Steller.*

The Golden Gate

SPANISH EXPANSION INTO UPPER CALIFORNIA, 1769-1776

In a burst of military and missionary activity, the Spanish move into Alta California, where they establish missions and discover the incomparable harbor of the Golden Gate.

For a century and a half, New Spain had made no sustained attempt to advance its northern frontiers, but by the 1760s alarmist reports of Russian activity along the Alaskan coast, rumors of British expeditions to the North Pacific, and Indian uprisings in northern Sonora, prompted a change of policy.

José de Galvéz, the energetic *visitador-general* of New Spain, and Junípero Serra, Father-President of the Franciscan missions, set about extending their military and missionary activity into Alta California. The first objective was Monterey, discovered by Vizcaíno in 1603 (▶ *page 40*). In 1769, land and sea expeditions left La Paz for the north. San Diego was reached by sea in April, and by land in May. Then in a journey along hundreds of miles of shoreline never before trodden by Europeans, a party of soldiers, Indian muleteers and carriers led by the governor of Alta California, Gaspar de Portolá, headed north. Suffering from heat by day and cold by night, the expedition plodded for 11 weeks across the hilly terrain between the mountains and the shore to reach Monterey. Its open bay proved so unlike Vizcaino's flattering description – "the best port that could be desired, sheltered from all the winds" – that scouts were sent further on to see if Monterey lay to the north. Instead, they stumbled on the great bay of San Francisco. On this journey the Spaniards saw for the first time at close quarters the giant redwood trees, so vast that eight men with arms outstretched could not encircle one.

At first, the Spaniards thought that the vast expanse of sheltered water they had discovered was a great estuary, barring the coastal route to the north. In the next few years, further land approaches from Monterey to the southern and eastern shores of the bay added some piecemeal information, but the reality of the incomparable harbor was not grasped until 1775. In August of that year Juan de Ayala made the first recorded sailing through the Golden Gate, difficult to discern against the hills even in clear weather. The expedition's sailing master, Cañizares, surveyed the waters of the bay, marking numerous soundings, and on his return Ayala reported that the harbor was the best he had seen "in these seas from Cape Horn northwards." So extensive were its various bays and passages that many squadrons could anchor there without sight or knowledge of each other. The next year, a group of settlers led by an army officer, Juan Bautista de Anza, and accompanied by Father Pedro Font, arrived from Sonora to establish a presidio and a mission. Anza and Pedro Font surveyed the bay from the land side, and their maps and descriptions left no doubt about its potential.

Although San Diego, Monterey and San Francisco had been secured, and in 1771 another mission established at San Gabriel (modern Los Angeles), the Spanish position in

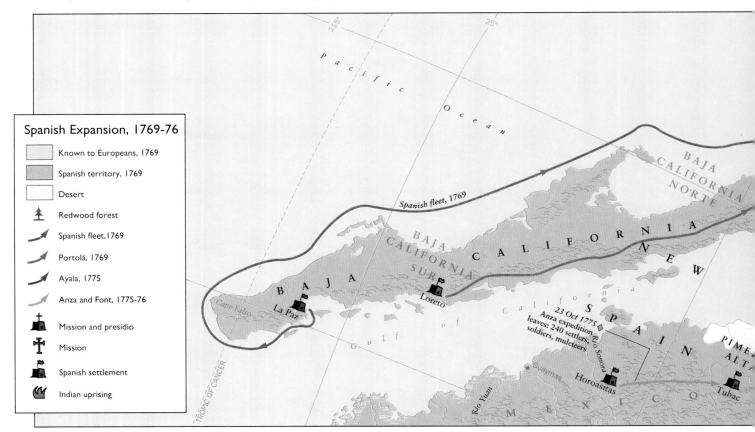

Spanish Expansion, 1769-76

Known to Europeans, 1769

Spanish territory, 1769

Desert

Redwood forest

Spanish fleet, 1769

Portolá, 1769

Ayala, 1775

Anza and Font, 1775-76

Mission and presidio

Mission

Spanish settlement

Indian uprising

Alta California was still precarious. Peninsular or *Baja* California had few resources, and supplies for the new establishments had to be brought by sea from Mexican ports. The northward voyage could take three or four months against headwinds, and the alternative of crossing the stormy waters of the Gulf of California was not an appealing one. The next stage of Spanish exploration was to find a land trail from Sonora to the Californian posts.

Right: Father Pedro Font, who accompanied Anza on his 1776 voyage, made this map of the Golden Gate the following year. "The port of San Francisco," he wrote, "is a marvel of nature, and might well be called the harbor of harbors, because of its great capacity..." Below: Along the Californian coast, the Spanish planted a string of missions. This one, the Mission del Carmelo, was painted by José Cardero in 1791 (▶ page 132).

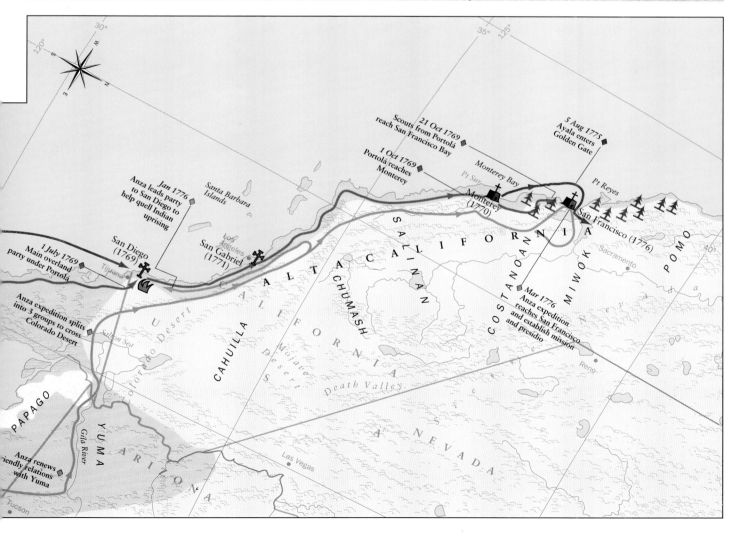

Deserts, Mountains and Canyons

SPANISH INTERIOR EXPLORATIONS, 1774-76

Spanish missionaries and soldiers reach further into the interior than any explorers since the 16th century, and discover the Great Basin.

In 1774 Juan Bautista de Anza (▶ *page 124*) and the Franciscan missionary Father Garcés led a party from Tubac to the coast. The Colorado Desert almost defeated them, but at a second attempt they skirted the waterless, trackless wastes and climbed the Sierra Nevada. From here they descended the San Jacinto Valley through the fertile Californian coastal plain, "full of flowers, fertile pastures, and other vegetation, useful for the raising of cattle," to the mission at San Gabriel.

The next year Anza proved that the route was practicable by leading 240 soldiers, settlers and muleteers, with more than 1000 animals, along it. Meanwhile Garcés searched for a more northern route which would avoid the Colorado desert. Traveling alone among the Indians, he spent much of 1775 and 1776 on or near the Colorado and Mohave rivers. He ranged as far as the Hopi pueblos, saw the Grand Canyon (the first European to do so since 1540), and reached the coast at San Gabriel. But the hardships he suffered were proof that the route was not suitable for supply expeditions. He was also the first European to enter the Great Basin that stretches from the Sierra Nevadas to central Utah, dispelling the myth of the great inland sea, the *Mer de l'Ouest*, that cartographers had placed here (▶ *page 42*).

In 1776 the Franciscan Fathers Escalante and Domínguez left Santa Fé in search of a route to Monterey. If a route could be found to the north, avoiding hostile Hopi and Apache Indians, it would strengthen the Spanish frontier which now stretched from Upper California to Texas. They failed in their main task, but the 1500-mile circle they cut through country never seen by Europeans was one of the most important interior journeys of the century. Escalante's diary tells of months of struggling with their Indian guides, horses and mules across a stark landscape of high plateaus, awesome canyons, of featureless deserts, splintered hillsides and salt lakes. Only in the quiet beauty of the Utah valley did they see any potential for future settlement. But their journey was one of the last feats of Spanish exploration, and when settlers reached the Great Basin in the next century they came from the east, and they were American.

Below: The Escalante expedition was recorded in magnificent unpublished maps drawn by its soldier-cartographer Miera y Pacheco. This manuscript shows bearded Ute Indians. A note on the map explains the growing pressures on the Spanish frontier as horsed Comanche displaced the Apache to dominate the buffalo plains.

Father Garcés is so well fitted to get along with the Indians and to go among them that he appears to be but an Indian himself. Like the Indians he is phlegmatic in everything. He sits with them in the circle, or at night round the fire, with his legs crossed, and there he will sit two or three hours or more, oblivious to everything else, talking with them with much serenity and deliberation.

From Father Pedro Font's diary, 1775

Miera notes, "The Comanche nation reaches as far as here"

Miera notes that "this mountain range is the backbone of North America, since the many rivers that are born of it empty into the two seas, the South Sea and the Gulf of Mexico"

Indians tell Escalante of lake to the north which "covers many leagues and its waters are noxious and extremely salty"

Expedition crosses Green River, named Buenaventura by Escalante

Expedition sees and kills its first buffalo

Miera proposes Spanish settlement, "for this is the most pleasing, beautiful and fertile site in all New Spain"

Expedition meets bearded Indians, Ute, some with "such long beards that they looked like Capuchin and Bethlemite fathers"

8 Oct 1776
Dispute over whether to continue search for route to Pacific; decision made to return because of "lack of provisions and the coming of winter"

28 Oct-7 Nov
Expedition searches for way across river. They eventually find Crossing of the Fathers

Crossing of the Fathers

Indian trails take expedition northeast, away from intended destination

Expedition sees "ruins of large and ancient Indian settlements"

Navajo country, all "mesas and cliffs and is much lacking in water [but] they have sheep and goats and weave fine blankets"

Expedition heads away from Colorado after Indian information about a great canyon to the south which "flows between the walls of red rock, very deep and rugged"

Moqui

Oraibi

16 Nov 1775

2-4 July 1776
Garcés turned back by hostile Hopi

Zuñi

Taos

29 July 1776
Escalante party leaves Santa Fé

Santa Fé

2 Jan 1777

Albuquerque

Acoma

14 Feb 1776
Garcés sets out alone

Yuma

Feb 1774
Anza-Garcés expedition lost long sand dunes for 11 days

Tucson

San Xavier del Bac

8 Jan 1774
Anza and Garcés set out with 30 men, mules and cattle for food

Tubac

Spanish Interior Explorations, 1774-76

	Spanish territory, 1774
	Desert
	Sand dunes
	Anza and Garcés, 1774
	Garcés, 1776
	Escalante and Domínguez, 1776
	Mission and presidio
	Mission
	Spanish settlement
	Indian settlement
	Ruins

North to Alaska

SPANISH COASTAL VOYAGES, 1774-79

To protect their settlements in Upper California from their European rivals, the Spanish sail up the northwest coast and claim new possessions.

Although the Spanish had settled far into Upper California, Antonio María Bucareli y Ursúa, the Viceroy of New Spain, was aware that Spain was vulnerable to the north. He knew the Russians were active in Alaska but was unsure how far south they had reached.

Other nations were also drawn to the northwest coast when published maps suggested a network of straits linking it with Hudson Bay and Baffin Bay. The maps showed the strait supposedly found by Juan de Fuca in 1592 as well as the one associated with Bartholomew de Fonte's imaginary voyage (▶ *page 42*). Bucareli was rightly sceptical, but sent precautionary expeditions far north along the unknown coast.

In 1774 Juan Pérez, an experienced pilot, sailed in the *Santiago* with secret instructions to take possession of all places suitable for European settlement up to 60°N. At the northern end of the Queen Charlotte Islands the Spaniards traded with Haida Indians who came out to their vessel in large, decorated canoes, beating drums and offering furs and fine wool blankets. Contrary winds and currents then forced Pérez to turn back. On the return voyage they sighted the great mass of Vancouver Island at Nootka Sound. Here the Spaniards again traded without leaving their ship; it was dark and cold, and they feared a shortage of water and the unknown coast. This was the first contact between Europeans and the Indians of the northwest coast, whose culture was very different from that of the Californian tribes.

The following year Bucareli sent two vessels north, Bruno de Hezeta in command of the *Santiago* and Peruvian-born Juan Francisco de la Bodega y Quadra in the tiny *Sonora*. As the *Santiago* coasted back south because of sickness on board, the crew sighted a large bay through which "the sea penetrates far into the land, making a horizon to the east." Lack of experience prevented them from going any closer. Hezeta thought this might be the entrance of Fuca's strait. But what he had seen was the entrance of one of North America's major rivers, the Columbia, 17 years before the American Robert Gray sighted and claimed to have discovered it.

Meanwhile, Quadra had sailed far north, becoming the first Spaniard to reach Alaska.

He was also the first Spaniard to land on the northwest coast (though not the mainland) as he searched near Bucareli Bay for signs of Fonte's supposed strait.

In 1779, hearing of Cook's arrival on the coast the previous year, the Spanish sent a further expedition to Alaska. Ignacio de Arteaga in the flagship *Princesa* and Quadra in command of the *Favorita* spent a month exploring the intricate waterways near Bucareli Bay. On their way north they took ceremonial possession of several points along the coast, including Hinchinbrook Island, the farthest north of all Spanish acts of possession in America. When Arteaga and Quadra turned back near Kodiak, they had seen neither English nor Russians, nor found any strait which might be the entrance to a Northwest Passage. Arteaga's report gave the Spanish authorities a sense of security. It would be short-lived.

Below: An Indian burial place, sketched by José Cardero, artist on Malaspina's expedition (▶ page 132). The massive wooden sculpture and architecture is typical of the northwest coast.

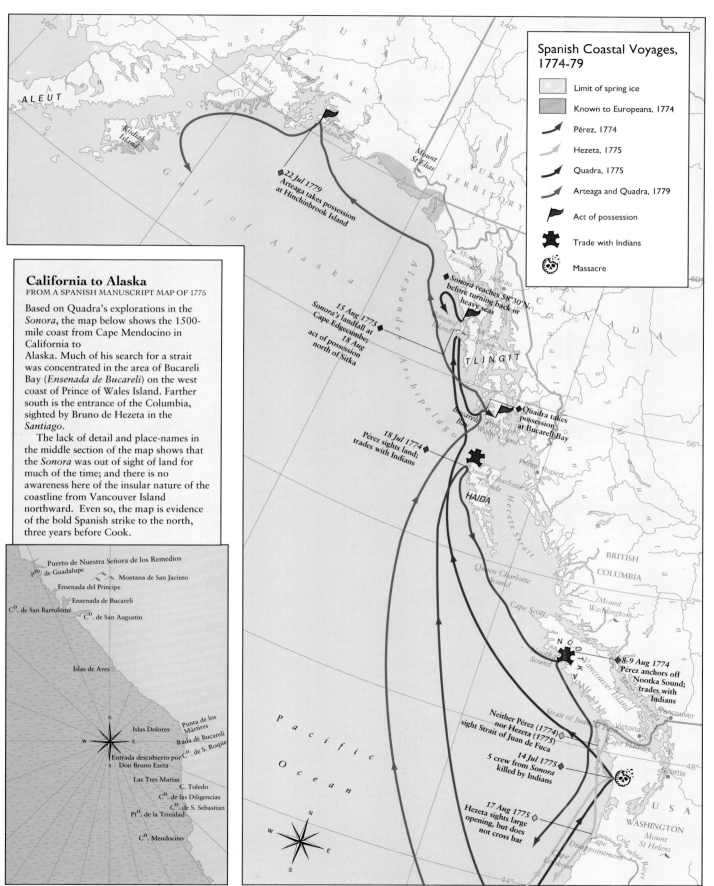

Spanish Coastal Voyages, 1774–79

- Limit of spring ice
- Known to Europeans, 1774
- Pérez, 1774
- Hezeta, 1775
- Quadra, 1775
- Arteaga and Quadra, 1779
- Act of possession
- Trade with Indians
- Massacre

22 Jul 1779
Arteaga takes possession
at Hinchinbrook Island

Sonora reaches 58°30'N.
before turning back in
heavy seas

15 Aug 1775
Sonora's landfall at
Cape Edgecumbe
18 Aug
act of possession
north of Sitka

Quadra takes
possession
at Bucareli Bay

18 Jul 1774
Pérez sights land;
trades with Indians

8-9 Aug 1774
Pérez anchors off
Nootka Sound;
trades with
Indians

Neither Pérez (1774)
nor Hezeta (1775)
sight Strait of Juan de Fuca

14 Jul 1775
5 crew from Sonora
killed by Indians

17 Aug 1775
Hezeta sights large
opening, but does
not cross bar

California to Alaska
FROM A SPANISH MANUSCRIPT MAP OF 1775

Based on Quadra's explorations in the
Sonora, the map below shows the 1500-
mile coast from Cape Mendocino in
California to
Alaska. Much of his search for a strait
was concentrated in the area of Bucareli
Bay (*Ensenada de Bucareli*) on the west
coast of Prince of Wales Island. Farther
south is the entrance of the Columbia,
sighted by Bruno de Hezeta in the
Santiago.

   The lack of detail and place-names in
the middle section of the map shows that
the *Sonora* was out of sight of land for
much of the time; and there is no
awareness here of the insular nature of the
coastline from Vancouver Island
northward. Even so, the map is evidence
of the bold Spanish strike to the north,
three years before Cook.

The Northwest Coast Revealed

THE VOYAGE OF JAMES COOK, 1778

*As the Russians and Spaniards edge towards
each other along the northwest coast, James
Cook bridges the gap between them.*

Russian and Spanish activity in the North
Pacific was interrupted by the arrival on the
northwest coast in 1778 of a British naval
expedition commanded by James Cook. The
motivation for this third Pacific voyage by
Europe's most celebrated explorer owed
much to Hearne's sighting in 1771 of the
polar sea (▶ *page 108*). This raised hopes that
a Northwest Passage might be found along
the Arctic coastline of the American
continent. Such hopes were buoyed by
fashionable theories that the polar seas were
ice-free and by publication of a map by Jacob
von Stählin. Stählin showed a wide strait
between the island of "Alaschka" and the
American continent. The optimistic plan
assumed that Cook would head north along
the northwest coast until he found the strait,
sail through it into an ice-free polar sea, and
so back into the Atlantic.

The *Resolution* and *Discovery* arrived on

the northwest coast in March 1778, from
Cook's new discovery of the Sandwich or
Hawaiian Islands. The ships anchored in
Nootka Sound on the oceanic coast of Vancouver Island, where the local Indians proved
keen traders, displayed spectacular skills in
handling their canoes, and built wooden
buildings with intricate totemic carvings. In
late April the ships sailed north, keeping well
offshore because of bad weather. On 1 May
they sighted the coast of Alaska, and the
shoreline, all dark-green forest near Nootka,
became bleaker. The scenery was dramatic,
with towering, snow-capped volcanic peaks,
including Bering's Mt St Elias a hundred miles
inland. Expectation ran high of the imminent
discovery of a strait leading north, but the
coast turned inexorably to the west. The ships
followed Prince William Sound until its shores
closed in, and traced Cook Inlet far inland.
The crews saw Alaskans in their sealskin
craft, and old Greenland hands had no doubt
that these were "Esquimaux."

Once out to sea again, the vessels were
forced away to the southwest, edging along
the tongue of the Alaskan peninsula until at
last they were able to head north through the
channel east of Unalaska Island. Aleut of Inuit
stock appeared in their kayaks, begging
tobacco and repeating the word "Russ." On 9
August the expedition finally reached a strait -

too far west to be Stählin's yet, with shores
almost in sight of each other, too narrow to be
Bering's if the Russian maps were correct.

Once through the strait the reality of polar
navigation was brought home to the crews. A
massive wall of ice threatened to crush the un-
strengthened ships. As the expedition retreated it was clear that this was indeed the

Above: The Resolution *and* Discovery *in Nootka
Sound, by the Cook expedition's artist John
Webber. The ships are surrounded by the canoes of
Nootka Indians coming to trade.*

strait reached by Bering 50 years earlier (▶
page 122). Of Stählin's strait there was no
sign, nor did the Russian fur-traders
encountered during Cook's stay at Unalaska
before he headed back to Hawaii (and his
death) have any knowledge of it.

In his final sustained feat of exploration
Cook had achieved much. In a single season
he had traced hundreds of miles of difficult
coastline, defined the Alaskan peninsula, and
confirmed the existence of Bering's strait.
While neither Cook, nor his Russian and
Spanish predecessors, had determined whether the long stretches of coastline north of
Nootka were islands or mainland, in outline
at least the shape and position of the
northwest coast of America were now known.

A Confusion of Islands

REDRAWN FROM JACOB VON STÄHLIN'S
MAP, 1774

One of Cook's officers recalled that
Stählin's map, which drew on Russian
discoveries in the northwest, was
"constantly in our hands." But its errors
– it showed Alaska as a large island and
misplaced several of the Aleutians –
proved exasperating. "Many of these
islands," Cook furiously noted in his log,
"are jumbled in regular confusion..." The
explorer dismissed Stählin's work as "a
Map that the most illiterate of his
illiterate Sea-faring men would have been
ashamed to put his name to."

18 Aug
Cook's furthest north,
lat. 70° 41' N., confronted by
"ice which was as compact
as a wall and seemed to be
ten or twelve feet high at least"

9 Aug
Ships reach Bering Strait Cook
names eastern point Cape
Prince of Wales - "the more
remarkable by being the
western extremity of all
America hitherto known"

INUIT

1 June
No sea passage to the north,
but Cook takes possession of
the region for Britain

10 Oct
Cook on Unalaska encounters
Russian fur-traders for
the first time; one claims
he had sailed with Bering

Unalaska
Island

Aleutian Islands

12 May
Ships reach Prince William Sound,
where "we had reason to expect that
by the inlet before us we should find
a passage northward" (Cook)

19 June
Natives paddle out bringing
note written in Russian: only
the dates 1776 and 1778
can be deciphered

Shumagin
Island

Chirikof
Island

Kodiak
Island

Bristol
Bay

ALEUT

CHUGACH
INUIT

Cook Inlet

Anchorage

Prince William
Sound

24 May
Ships off Cook Inlet
– "everything inspired
us with hopes of finding
here a passage northward"
(Cook)

5 May
Expedition sights peak
of Bering's Mount
St Elias, 120 miles distant

Mount
St Elias

Cape
Fairweather

TLINGIT

Mount
Fairweather

Juneau

Alexander
Archipelago

Mount
Edgecumbe

Prince
of
Wales
Island

26. Apr–1 May
Ships out of sight of land,
to Cook's regret – "we are
passing the place where
geographers have placed
the pretended Strait of
Admiral de Fonte"

Queen
Charlotte
Islands

Hecate Strait

HAIDA

BELLA
BELLA

29 Mar–26 Apr
Expedition trades sea-otter skins
from Nootka Indians under chief
Maquinna, also silver spoons stolen
from Pérez in 1774

Nootka
Sound

NOOTKA

Vancouver

22 Mar 1778
"It is in the very latitude
we were now in where geographers
have placed the pretended Strait of
Juan de Fuca, but we saw
nothing like it" (Cook)

Juan de
Fuca
Strait

Seattle

WASHINGTON

U N I T E D   S T A T E S

BRITISH
COLUMBIA

ALBERTA

YUKON
TERRITORY

NORTHWEST
TERRITORY

C A N A D A

ALASKA

SIBERIA

ARCTIC CIRCLE

Bering
Sea

C. Dezhneva

Bering Strait

C. Prince of
Wales

Norton
Sound

Chukchi
Sea

Beaufort
Sea

Arctic Ocean

Permanent pack ice

Extreme limit of drift ice

Pacific
Ocean

The Voyage of James Cook, 1778

	Known to Europeans, 1778
	Extent of permanent pack ice
	Extreme limit of drift ice
	Cook, 1778
	Encounter with native people
	Trading encounter with native people
	Encounter with Russian fur traders
	Formal act of possession

Tracing the Mainland Coast

TRADERS AND EXPLORERS, 1785-94

*Following Cook's voyage, the northwest
coast becomes the scene of intense trading,
exploring and diplomacy.*

Cook's crew reported good prices at Canton for sea-otter skins and this led to a scramble in both Europe and the new United States to fit out expeditions to the northwest coast. Their commanders soon realized that what Cook, sailing largely offshore in 1778, had assumed to be the mainland coast, was a screen of islands. Where the straits supposedly found by Juan de Fuca and Bartholomew de Fonte (▶ *page 42*) lay was still unknown.

In 1786 La Pérouse, the French explorer, had searched around Lituya Bay for signs of a strait or river leading eastward. In 1787,

George Dixon thought Hecate Strait was Fonte's strait and William Barkley, sighting an opening south of Nootka, thought he had found "the long lost strait of Juan de Fuca."

In 1792 the American Robert Gray entered the river which Hezeta had sighted from outside its bar in 1775 (▶ *page 128*). Named after Gray's ship, the Columbia River was the most important waterway of the Pacific northwest. In the next century Gray's exploit would buttress the American claim to Oregon.

By 1790 Spain and Britain had clashed over the possession of Nootka Sound and both

powers were determined to settle the rumors of a navigable Northwest Passage. During the three summers of 1790-92, Spanish vessels explored the intricate waterways inside the opening sighted by Barkley (now the Strait of Juan de Fuca). They established that far from leading inland, the passage turned back to the sea through the Strait of Georgia and Queen Charlotte Sound. Farther north, Martínez in 1788 and Fidalgo in 1790 had reached Russian trading posts along the Alaskan peninsula. In 1791 Malaspina searched the Alaskan coast for a strait supposedly discovered by Maldonado in 1588; and in 1792 Caamaño made yet another search for evidence of Fonte's strait.

By the time George Vancouver's British

> I trust the precision with which the survey of the coast of North West America has been carried into effect, will... set aside every opinion of a north-west passage... no small portion of facetious mirth passed among the seamen, in consequence of our sailing from old England on the *first of April*, for the purpose of discovering a north-west passage, by following up the discoveries of De Fuca, De Fonte, and a numerous train of hypothetical navigators.
>
> **George Vancouver, *A Voyage of Discovery to the North Pacific Ocean*, 16 April 1794**

Winter quarters of
Maquinna's people

Tahsis Inlet

Nootka

Island

Bligh Island

V a n c o u v e r   I s l a n d

Territory of Maquinna

*Nootka
Sound*

Resolution Cove
Mar-Apr 1778
Cook's ships anchor

Friendly Cove

**1789
Spaniards expel
British traders,
build own post**

San Miguel
(1798)

**1795
Nootka abandoned**

**1774
Pérez anchors**

2/Conflict at Nootka
- British trading post
- Spanish fort
- Native settlement

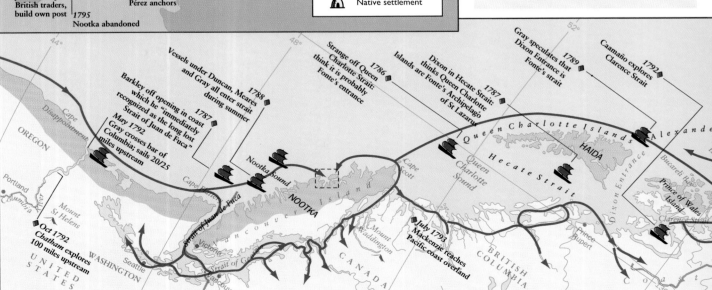

Gray speculates that
Dixon Entrance is
Fonte's strait
1789

Caamaño explores
Clarence Strait
1792

Strange off Queen
Charlotte Strait:
think it is probably
Fonte's entrance
1786

Dixon in Hecate Strait:
thinks Queen Charlotte
Islands are Fonte's Archipelago
of St Lazarus
1787

Vessels under Duncan, Meares
and Gray all enter strait
during summer
1788

Barkley off opening in coast
which he "immediately
recognized as the long lost
Strait of Juan de Fuca"
1787

May 1792
Gray crosses bar of
Columbia; sails 20/25
miles upstream

**Oct 1792
Chatham explores
100 miles upstream**

*Cape
Disappointment*

OREGON

Portland

Columbia River

*Mount
St Helens*

WASHINGTON

Seattle

UNITED
STATES

Victoria

Strait of Juan de Fuca

Cape Flattery

Nootka Sound

V a n c o u v e r   I s l a n d

NOOTKA

Strait of Georgia

Vancouver

*Cape
Scott*

*Mount
Waddington*

**July 1793
Mackenzie reaches
Pacific coast overland**

CANADA

*Queen
Charlotte
Sound*

Queen Charlotte Islands

HAIDA

H e c a t e   S t r a i t

Dixon Entrance

Alexander

Bucareli Bay

*Prince of
Wales
Island*

Clarence Strait

BRITISH
COLUMBIA

Prince
Rupert

C o a s t

Above: The port of Nootka painted by José Cardero,
who accompanied Malaspina on his 1791 expedition.

naval expedition arrived in 1792, the Spaniards were satisfied that the straits described by Fuca, Fonte and Maldonado did not exist. Yet Vancouver explored the area meticulously and his consort vessel surveyed the Columbia River for a hundred miles upstream. After three seasons of surveying, Vancouver confirmed that the Spanish were right. Any transcontinental route would be a laborious journey by rivers and lakes, portages and mountain passes. It was just such a journey that had brought Mackenzie to the Pacific coast in 1793, not far from the survey vessels of the Vancouver expedition (▶ *page 114*).

Vancouver's journal and charts, published 1798, long remained standard guides to the northwest coast. Political upheaval prevented the Spaniards from publishing theirs. Thus the Island of Quadra and Vancouver was shortened to Vancouver Island.

Martinez on coast from Prince William Sound to Unalaska
1788

La Pérouse enters Lituya Bay; takes possession of the coast for France
1786

Fidalgo explores Prince William Sound and Cook Inlet
1790

1784

1786

1793

1791 Malaspina explores Yakutat Bay and coast to north and south in search of Maldonado's strait

c.1775

I/Traders and Explorers, 1785–94

Known to Europeans, 1785

Extreme limit of drift ice

Vancouver, 1792–94

Other expeditions

Spanish

British

French

United States

Russian trading post

Forerunners of Lewis and Clark

MISSOURI EXPLORATIONS, 1792-97

The Spanish authorities send British and French traders far up the Missouri to explore the remote fringes of their dying empire.

By the late 1780s Spanish officials had long been concerned about the frontiers of their enlarged North American empire in California, New Mexico and Louisiana. Now, rumors that British traders from Canada had followed La Vérendrye's old route to the Mandan (▶ *page 96*) meant that foreigners could infiltrate or even invade the Upper Missouri. The British threat from the north, "which seemed a dream to us on account of the distance, is today at our doors."

Spanish resources were being spent on holding the Mississippi against the Americans, so their expeditions were private rather than official. They were led by French and British traders, "since no native of the country has been found with sufficient intelligence."

In 1792 the Frenchman, Jacques d'Eglise, left St Louis for the Mandan villages, "to which no one had ever gone in this direction and by this river." In 1793 St Louis merchants formed the Company of Explorers of the Upper Missouri (the Missouri Company) and sent another Frenchman, Jean Baptiste Truteau, to the Mandan villages in 1794.

With only a single pirogue of trade goods, Truteau could not get through the upper valley, past the Ponca, Omaha and Sioux. Painfully poling and paddling upriver, slipping past hostile villages at night, Truteau may have reached no farther than the Arikara villages near Grand River. But there were echoes of La Vérendrye when he asked the Indians about a river "the waters of which might possibly flow towards the setting sun."

A Scot, James Mackay, followed Truteau in the service of Spain. Mackay, an experienced trader with the North West Company in Canada, had already visited the Mandan in 1787. He was accompanied by John Evans, a remarkable young Welshman who had come to America in quest of Welsh Indians, descendants of Madoc. He hoped to find them among the light-skinned Mandan or the "White Padoucas" (Comanche).

In 1795 Mackay left St Louis with four pirogues, the largest Spanish venture on the Upper Missouri, with instructions "to open commerce with those distant and unknown nations in the upper parts of the Missouri and to discover all the unknown parts... through

West of the Mandan

REDRAWN FROM A MANUSCRIPT MAP BY JOHN EVANS, 1797

Relying on Indian information, Evans showed the Missouri west of the Mandan villages, the Yellowstone River ("River yellow rock"), the Falls of the Missouri, several ranges of mountains, and a westward-flowing river with what appears to be a European trading post. The map was taken by Lewis and Clark on their expedition in 1804.

Missouri Explorations, 1792-97

- Spanish settlement
- Indian settlement
- Eglise, 1792
- Truteau, 1794
- Mackay, 1795-97
- Evans, 1796
- Hudson's Bay Company trading post
- North West Company trading post
- Act of possession
- Encounter with Indians

Indians tell Eglise that "The Assiniboin, a wandering nation to the north of the Missouri, with whom the English traders of Canada... traffic in peltries"

1792 Indians tell Eglise that Yellowstone River is navigable, "and comes direct from the Stony Mountains but it is hard to say whether it communicates with the waters of the west"

Sept 1796 Evans reaches Mandan villages and hoists Spanish flag over British trading post
Winter 1796-97 North West Company and Hudson's Bay Company traders arrive

"The Mandans count only 300 warriors. This nation is divided into three villages, the largest ... on the west side of the Missouri and the two smaller ones... opposite"

"This river" says Truteau "is so very shallow that one cannot venture on it in a pirogue... only with boats made of buffalo skin"

Truteau: "The Sioux tribes are those who hunt most for the beaver and other good peltries of the Upper Missouri."

According to Truteau "The Sioux tribes are feared... by all of these others on account of [their] firearms... their very name causes terror"

June 1796 Evans leaves for the Mandan

Winter 1795-96 Mackay searches for Rocky Mountain Indians

Nov 1795 Mackay builds fort

Aug 1794 Truteau passes Omaha villages at night since "the policy of the savages is to prevent communication between us and the nations of the Upper Missouri [who] they keep... in a continual fear of their firearms"

Truteau describes the Niobrara as "the most abundant one in the entire continent of beaver and otter, but the waters are so swift that one is not able to either ascend or descend"

Mackay describes the Platte River: "As large as the Missouri but so shallow and... rapid that navigation is very difficult "

July 1797 Evans returns from Mandan villages, "having been so far up the Missurie that it took 68 days to come down with the furious current."

May 1797 Mackay returns from Fort Charles

May 1795 Mackay and Evans set out

that continent as far as the Pacific Ocean." Mackay built a post, Fort Charles, in Nebraska, and then sent Evans on to the Mandan country in search of trade, alliances, and a route to the Pacific. But by the time Evans reached the Mandan there was a Canadian trading post among the earth-lodges of the Indians, he was unable to travel farther west along the Missouri and he found no sign of any Welsh Indians.

Nevertheless Mackay and Evans had gathered detailed knowledge of the course of the Missouri from St Louis to the Mandan, later to be used by Lewis and Clark (▶ *page 136*). They also gleaned information from the Indians about the country to the west. As a result the Yellowstone River and the Great Falls of the Missouri appeared on the map for the first time, while Mackay and Evans began to see the Rockies as a complex series of ranges rather than a single ridge.

Across the Continent

THE JOURNEY OF LEWIS AND CLARK, 1805-06

Labels on the map:

- CHINOOK
- COWLITZ
- 18 Nov 1805 Lewis and Clark sight Pacific
- Party sees beached whale
- Fort Clatsop
- Portland
- Columbia River
- Mount Rainier
- Mount St Helens
- Mount Adams
- WASHINGTON
- Hundreds of Indians salmon fishing
- YAKIMA
- PALOUSE
- The Dalles, or Rapids of the Columbia
- WALLAWALLA
- UMATILLA
- KLIKITAT
- CAYUSE
- YAKIMA
- Mount Hood
- Coeur d'Alene
- SPOKANE 20 Sept 1805 First meeting with Nez Percé
- Lewis and Clark pause to rest before crossing rugged 165-mile Lolo Trail. Shoshone provide expedition with 29 horses and 1 mule
- Canoe Camp
- NEZ PERCE
- Wieppe Prairie
- Lolo Trail
- Lolo Pass Traveller's Rest
- Salmon River
- Clearwater River
- Bitterroot Mountains
- SHOSHONE
- 21 June - 2 July 1805 Lewis and Clark make grueling portage around Great Falls of Missouri
- Fight with Blackfoot Lewis wounded
- Marias River
- Lewis and Clark Pass
- BLACKFEET
- Ordway and Gass return
- Source of Missouri, 2500 miles above St Louis
- Jefferson Fork
- Bozeman Pass
- Butte
- Madison River
- Camp Fortunate
- BANNOCK
- IDAHO
- CROW
- Pacific Ocean
- 1805-06 Corps of Discovery spends winter
- Salt-making camp where Sacagawea first sees the Pacific Ocean
- OREGON
- Cape Blanco
- Snake River
- Boise
- Lewis and Clark build canoes to float to the Pacific
- 4 Sept 1805 Lewis and Clark meet Flathead
- FLATHEADS
- Clark reconnoiters Salmon River, later called "River of No Return"
- Camp Dubois
- Cameahwait's Shoshone village
- Ross Hole
- Beaverhead Rock
- Lemhi Pass
- Cameahwait's Shoshone village; Lewis finds large village herd, with many Spanish mules and horses, and is convinced he is on waters leading to Columbia River
- Lewis and Sacagawea's band of Shoshone are united with Clark's party
- Jackson Hole
- Hoback Canyon
- Owl Creek Mountains
- I D A H O
- Calderon Cru Rapids
- Gallatin Pass

US President Thomas Jefferson equips and sends Lewis and Clark to explore the vast tract of "wild land" he has just bought from the French.

President Jefferson had long been fascinated by the west. On 18 January 1803 he asked Congress to fund an expedition up the Missouri, stressing that the journey over Spanish soil would bring great commercial gain.

Congress agreed. Jefferson's private secretary, the young army captain Meriwether Lewis, was sent to Philadelphia to learn natural history. In the spring, Jefferson bought Louisiana from Napoleon, lending impetus to the project. Lewis asked Jefferson to appoint William Clark, his friend and former commanding officer, co-captain of the expedition. By fall, they had recruited 36 "stout, single woodsmen," a half-Indian interpreter, and Clark's black slave, York.

On 14 May 1804 Clark and the Corps of Discovery put their 55-foot, 22-oared keelboat and two pirogues (flat-bottomed dugouts) into the Mississippi at Wood River, and rowed downstream to the Missouri. Lewis joined them at Saint-Charles, a French settlement. The shallow, serpentine Missouri was filled with the green, rotting carcasses of buffalo killed by Indians. Caved-in banks and shifting sandbars lined its course. Stiff breezes and a strong current meant that the men sometimes had to get out and pull their boats through with ropes.

Occasionally they met white traders on the river. Several times they stopped to pay tribute to local Indians. Beyond the mouth of the Platte they found large numbers of buffalo, which they hunted for meat, and they regularly sighted deer, elk and antelope.

2/ The Louisiana Purchase, 1803

- United States
- Purchased by US from France
- Spanish territory
- British territory
- Lewis and Clark

In November, after high winds and the first snow, they built a winter fort, watched by curious Mandan. Toussaint Charbonneau, a French Canadian trapper who had lived for five years among the Hidatsa, arrived and Lewis and Clark hired him as an interpreter. A week later his pregnant wife, a Shoshone named Sacagawea, joined them.

Winter temperatures at Fort Mandan dipped almost 50° below zero. The hunting was poor, but the Corps built canoes and made clothes and moccasins. Lewis and Clark traded with the Indians, who told them of great waterfalls and mountains ahead.

Early in April, the keelboat, under Corporal Richard Warfington, headed back down the Missouri with specimens for Jefferson and a letter. The rest of the expedition paddled upstream. Late in May, Lewis glimpsed the distant Rockies for the first time. The explorers were in "high broken rockey" country populated by grizzly bears and bighorn sheep. On 13 June Lewis found the 80-foot waterfalls the Mandan had told him marked the Missouri, and dispatched one of his men with a letter to Clark.

For two hot weeks, the men pulled their boats up steep slopes, through rocky gullies and around great stands of prickly pear until they were back on the Missouri. They then hiked over the Continental Divide. Through rain, hail and snow they crossed the Bitterroot Range of the Rockies and along an old Nez Percé trail, the Lolo Pass, to the coastal plain.

At the Clearwater River, they left their mounts with the Nez Percé, burned out five canoes from logs, and took to the water again. Riding the rapids they followed the Clearwater, the Snake and then the Columbia River, reaching the Pacific early in November.

I/Lewis and Clark, 1804-06

US	French	
🏭 settlement	🏕	💀 Death of explorer
⛺ Indian settlement	🏕	☐ Encounter with Indians
↗ Lewis and Clark		✗ Skirmish
➤ Lewis		∿ Rapids
➤ Clark		∿ Falls
➤ Ordway and Gass		⬯ Sandstone mesa
🛶 Expedition camp		🧍 Portage
		🌵 Cactus thickets

100 buffalo forced to jump over cliff by Blackfoot. Their putrified carcasses abandoned to wolves; some carcasses float down Missouri as far as St Louis

Ordway and Gass link up with Lewis

Pompey's Pillar, a large sandstone mesa 200 feet high and 400 yards in circumference, named for Sacagawea's child

Fort Mandan

Mih-Tutta-Hang-Kush

Hidatsa and Mandan villages

8 cabins and storehouses, surrounded by wall
11 Nov 1804 Lewis and Clark meet Sacagawea here
7 April 1805 Corporal Richard Warfington and 9 men return to St Louis with journals, maps, natural history specimens; Lewis and Clark set out upriver

Arikara villages

Confrontation with Teton Sioux

Meeting with friendly Yankton Sioux

Omaha Chief Blackbird's burial hill

Aug 20 Corps member Sergeant Floyd dies of "Biliose Chorlick" (ruptured appendix)

First meeting with Indians (Oto)

La Charette

St-Charles

St Louis

Winter 1803 - 13 May 1804 Lewis and Clark assemble 36 men for expedition
14 May Clark and Corps of Discovery leave by boat
16 May Lewis joins Clark's party

Above: A page from Clark's Field Notes, written in January 1804, before setting off up the Missouri. The boat sketched here (two oars short) was purpose-built in Pittsburgh to carry the expedition's supplies and munitions right across the continent.

Here they built a winter camp, Fort Clatsop. Food was scarce, it rained nearly every day, and the men were beset by illness and injuries. On 22 March 1806, they started for home. Lewis, probably advised by the Shoshone, went overland through dangerous Blackfoot country to the Marias. He rejoined Clark at the juncture of the Yellowstone River with the Missouri and they arrived back together in September 1806.

Lewis and Clark had crossed the continent at one of its most difficult points and made contact with key Indian tribes. They returned with extensive natural history collections, field notebooks and route maps, and were able to compile several large maps. Though they exaggerated the width of the west by several hundred miles, the official account of their journey, published in 1814, showed the extent and potential of western North America. The United States had entered the imperial struggle for the continent.

The Scouts of New Spain

SPANISH TRAILBLAZERS IN THE OLD SOUTHWEST, 1786-1808

Spanish explorers forge paths between frontier posts in Texas and Louisiana. But the area they open is hotly contested by both the United States and the Plains Indians.

In 1763 the French ceded their Louisiana possessions to Spain to spite the English and suddenly the Spanish frontier advanced to Mississippi country. The Spanish bureaucracy eventually realized the value of establishing links between their remote frontier outposts. In 1786 they hired a mysterious Frenchman and former *contrabandista* or illegal trader, Don Pedro (Pierre) Vial, to blaze a trail from San Antonio to Santa Fé. Vial was a former gunsmith who had spent years living with Indians and repairing their French weapons. He crossed the plains wilderness from east to west but his diary entries were meager and much of his winding route is now conjectural.

New Mexico's governor then sent a retired corporal, José Mares, to find a more direct route. Mares was the first known explorer on the featureless plains of the Llano Estacado since the Martin-Castillo expedition of 1650. Shortly after Mares' return to San Antonio, New Mexico's governor dispatched Vial, with diarists Fragoso and Fernandez, and four com-panions, to find a direct route from Santa Fé to Natchitoches in Louisiana. On their return they found even shorter routes to San Antonio and from there to Santa Fé. Then in 1792 Vial was ordered to blaze a trail from Santa Fé to "St Louis of Illinois, province of Louisiana."

Although Spanish officials had laid out a planned interstate network of trails linking New Mexico, Texas and Louisiana, the expected trading caravans simply never materialized. When France reacquired Louisiana and sold it to the Americans, the Spanish became concerned with Anglo penetration. In 1806 Spain's frontier officials dispatched Don Facundo Malgares to intercept Zebulon Pike (▶ *page 144*). They missed him. In 1808 Lieutenant Francisco Amangual left San Antonio to make a show of force in finding a northern route to Santa Fé.

The 18th and early 19th century trailblazers of the Spanish northeast frontier covered vast distances, left significant accounts of their travels and operated with a minimum of violence. Some, like Vial, were also important intermediaries in the establishment of peaceful relations between native tribes and the Spanish.

The Spanish Southwest

REDRAWN FROM A MAP BY PEDRO VIAL, 1787

Vial's hand-drawn map shows the main Spanish settlements in New Mexico and Texas. Drawing on his own travels in the region, it represents the best Spanish knowledge of the region at the time. He shows the Canadian River, but depicts its flowing into the Red River (Rio Colorado) instead of the Arkansas (Rio de la arga).

24 Aug 1793 ♦
Vial at landing point
for traders to Pawnee

The first who met us, greeted us affectionately, shaking hands. I
asked them what tribe they were, and they told me they were
Kansas. At the same moment they took possession of our horses and
equipment, cutting our clothes with knives, leaving us entirely naked.
They wanted to kill us, at which one of them cried to the others, telling
them they should not do it with rifles or arrows but with hatchet-blows or
lances, because they had us surrounded and they might cause some
unfortunate accident to themselves. In this conflict, one of them took our
part, begging and supplicating the others not to take our lives.

Don Pedro Vial's diary, 29 June 1792

♦ *Summer 1806*
Malgares concludes
treaty, missing Pike
by a few weeks

Pawnee Republic
village

♦ 11 Sept 1792
Ransomed by French
trader and set out
downstream
by pirogue

St Louis
♦ *Sept-Oct 1792*
Hunt deer and bear

♦ 3 Oct 1792
Vial's party arrives,
after 82-day, 1100-mile journey

4 June 1793
Vial's party begin
return journey

20 Oct 1793 ♦
Midnight attack by Pawnee,
defused by Vial's
Pawnee companions

♦ *Summer 1806*
Malgares advances
into disputed new
US territory

June 1792
Vial falls ill, traveling down valley
Oct 1793
Vial back in valley
June 1808
Vial points out buffalo hunting
trail to Amangual

♦ 29 June 1792
Vial and companions captured
by Kansa. Recognized by one Indian,
who saves them from
being killed

JICARILLA
APACHE

COMANCHE

♦ Malgares's men meet 1500
Comanche; hold council
and concludes treaty

♦ 22 June 1792
Vial aims for Arkansas
River

◇ 7 April 1788
Mares climbs up to
plains and crosses again

Comanche camps

◇ 5 Sept 1787
Mares finds
French
traders
amongst Indians

♦ Vial stays Winter 1787,
parleys with Chief Leather
Cape then travels north
with Chief Zoquiné, and
July 1788, en route
to Natchioches

El Comercio
de los Franceses
Taovaya
villages

Aug 1789
Vial and Fragoso
obtain meat from
Comanche lodge on
the "in the middle of
the Llano" (possibly
first mention of Llano
Estacado)

28 Aug 1787 ◇
Mares with
friendly Comanche

◇ Feb 1788
Mares winters

♦ 15 Dec 1786
Vial, having rested
6 weeks, ascends
Brazos River
Tawakoni
village

♦ 14 Aug 1788
Sees alligators

Outlying French homes
Natchitoches

KWAHADI
COMANCHE
23 Dec 1808
Amangual returns

Ysambanbi's
Camp
Cordero's
Camp

COMANCHE

San Francisco
de Los Tejas

HASINAI
Nacogdoches

♦ 20 Aug 1788
Vial and Fragoso
arrive after 938 miles
then set out for
San Antonio

Los Adaes

Fort Rosalie

Presidio
San Saba

♦ 14 Oct 1786
Vial, ill and injured
in fall from horse, seeks
remedy from Tawakoni

TEXAS

Fort
St Louis

♦ 4 Oct 1787
Mares sees many
spring-fed streams
APACHE

♦ Nov 1788-June 1789
Vial and Fragoso rest, then
to Santa Fé with 4 Comanche

TEJAS

TONKAWA

Fort
Maurepas

New
Orleans

Pensacola

Mar 1808
Amangual leaves
for Santa Fé via
northern route, with
Comanche guide,
200 men and 800
animals

Jan 1788
Mares
departs
to find even
more direct
path

San
Antonio
de Bexar

◇ Oct 1787
Mares cuts
Vial's journey
by 300 miles

Rio San Antonio
Rio Guadalupe
Rio Colorado

Austin

Houston

Baton
Rouge

ATAKAPA

♦ *Sept-Oct 1788*
All but Vial sick with
fever and chills

Galveston
Bay

San Juan
Bautista

◇ Oct 1786
Vial first sets
out to blaze
trail to Santa Fé

Rio del Norte
Nueces
River

COAHUILA

Dec 1808
Amangual turns
back at "Las Uvas" Creek

NUEVO
LEON

Spanish Trailblazers in the Old Southwest, 1786-1808

Spanish territory, 1763	Indian settlement
Ceded to France, 1800 and sold to US, 1803	Pueblo
US territory from 1783	Spanish settlement
Spanish settlement	Spanish settlement (ruined)

Vial, 1792-93 — Trading place
Malgares, 1806
Vial, 1786-87 — Skirmish
Mares, 1787-88
Amangual, 1808 — Capture by Indians
Expedition camp
Indian camp — Pass

Pathfinders of the Old Southwest

TRAPPERS AND TRADERS IN LOUISIANA AND TEXAS, 1792-1827

US government expeditions and freelance traders and horse hunters explore the fiercely contended no-man's land between the lower Red River and central Texas.

Following the Louisiana Purchase, it became urgent for the United States to determine its uncertain boundary with New Spain. As early as 1791, Phillip Nolan, a friend of both Wilkinson and Jefferson, had penetrated Texas, trading horses with the Comanche. In 1794 he reached San Antonio. By 1800 he had led a party of filibusters who built a fort on Nolan Creek, near present-day Temple, Texas, where he was killed by the Spaniards.

Once he became president, Thomas Jefferson sent official expeditions to the region. In 1804 Scottish-born planter William Dunbar and Philadelphia naturalist George Hunter rowed up the Ouachita accumulating data on the region's geography, flora, fauna, fossils, Indian sign language and astronomical phenomena. Two years later Thomas Freeman led a party up the Red River to locate its source. Despite a 100-mile detour to avoid the log "rafts" which jammed the river, they arrived at its upper reaches before being turned back by a Spanish force under Francisco Viana.

Meanwhile a host of horse traders and gold seekers from Natchitoches contributed to knowledge of the Texas plains. Jacques Clamorgan had made his way to Santa Fé in 1807, undoubtedly invited by the Spaniards. Anthony Glass regularly led parties out onto the plains to trade with the Comanche and Pawnee for horses. So friendly was he with the Pawnee that they showed him their sacred stone, a meteorite 3 foot 4 inches long and 2 foot 4.5 inches wide. Believing that it was pure platinum, Glass stole it in 1809. In 1812 John Maley led a party up the Red River

seeking abandoned Spanish gold and silver mines. Far out on the prairie Maley and his partners were robbed by the Osage. Stripped and left with only their wallets and knives, Maley and his men wandered for nearly two grueling months before they finally staggered back into Natchitoches.

The stream of traders and trappers continued, despite frequent imprisonment by the Spanish authorities. Three civilian parties - under William Becknell, Thomas James and

Below: This oil painting by George Catlin depicts "Comanches giving the arrows to the Medecine Rock." The Comanche believed that fallen meteorites, such as the one Glass stole in 1809, had medicinal properties, and made offerings to them.

The Internal Part of Louisiana
REDRAWN FROM AN 1807 MAP BY ANTOINE NAU

Nau, a French draftsman who had served on Wilkinson's staff, based his map on a chart by Pike (▶ *page 144*). It was one of the first to incorporate the discoveries of Freeman, Dunbar and Hunter. It also shows the neutral border zone agreed by Wilkinson and the Spanish Colonel Herrera, and an 1806 confrontation between them in which armed conflict was narrowly avoided.

Hugh Glenn - were all en route to Santa Fé when Glenn met some Mexican emissaries who told him "that the mackeson province Has de Clared Independance of the mother Cuntry and is desirous of a traid With the people of the united States." With this new willingness to trade, a regular Santa Fé Trail was established by the end of 1824.

A person is mounted on a fleet horse, round the neck of which a rope is tied; and the other end of the rope is formed into a noose... and singling out one of [the wild horses], rides at full speed after him, and when he has come within the required distance, throws the noose over his head... The rider then gets off his horse and immediately mounts the other animal, and continues to ride him at full speed till he is fairly overcome, and properly broken in...

Francis Bailey, an English scientist
with Philip Nolan

Trappers and Traders in Louisiana and Texas, 1792–1827

- US territory before 1803
- Purchased by US from France, 1803
- Spanish territory

US   Spanish   Indian   settlements

- Nolan, 1792-97
- Nolan, 1800-01
- La Lande, 1804
- Dunbar and Hunter, 1804
- Freeman and Sparks, 1806
- Glass, 1808-09
- Maley, 1812
- Philibert, 1814
- US trail
- Spanish trail

- Confrontation
- Death of explorer
- Trade center
- Mission
- Trapper's fort

- Site of French fort
- Salt works
- Hot springs
- Pass

Map labels

1814 Philibert and party of trappers well received

La Lande trades with Pawnee — Pawnee villages

Spring 1804 La Lande sets out on trading trip to Santa Fé

St Louis

Kaskaskia

Fur trappers' fort, first established by Pike

c.1812-24 US trappers and traders blaze trails across prairies

La Vela Pass

Pueblo

Santa Fé Trail

Arkansas River

Raton Pass

Cimarron Cutoff

1816 Auguste Chouteau and trapping party arrested by Spanish

29 July 1806 Freeman-Sparks expedition halted by Spanish under Captain Viana

25 July 1806 Freeman and Sparks pass former French fort

Taos

Glorietta Pass

Santa Fé

Las Vegas

Albuquerque

NEW MEXICO

1812 Maley robbed by Osage

Fort Smith

Great rafts or logjams of Red River

5 July 1808 Glass and 10 people leave salt works

1804 Dunbar, Hunter and 15 others survey Ouichita River

Glass steals Medicine Rock

17 July 1809

Taovaya-Wichita villages

Comanche camp

Spanish Bluffs

Caddo villages

Principal Caddo village

El Paso del Norte

Comanche villages

Comanche villages

Soto's Post

Shreveport

Black Lake Salt Works

Fort Miro

Nogales

Jackson

CHOCTAW

1 Nov 1800 Nolan leaves on last expedition

San Elzeario

NEW VIZCAYA

1791-93 Nolan lives with Comanche

Nacogdoches

Coashutta villages

Natchitoches

NATCHEZ

Natchez

Walnut Grove Plantation

Autumn Trading

2 Mar 1801 Nolan killed by Spanish sent to arrest him

HASINA

Fort Adams

Presidio del Norte

San Antonio

1803 Becomes US trading center

New Orleans

La Bahia

KARANKAWA

1794 Nolan arrives after 3 years in Texas

19 Apr 1806 Freeman, Sparks and 23 men set off upriver to Pawnee

COAHUILA

NUEVO LEON

SPAIN

Gulf of Mexico

Vanguard of Empire

THE ASTORIANS 1810-12

John Jacob Astor's attempt to corner the north American fur trade leads to the discovery of the South Pass through the Rockies.

On 8 September 1810 John Jacob Astor launched the ship *Tonquin* on a course around Cape Horn and via Hawaii to the mouth of the Columbia River. There, under the leadership of two of his Canadian associates, Duncan McDougall and Robert Stuart, the Pacific Fur Company established Fort Astoria on the south bank of the Columbia.

Captain Thorne then took the *Tonquin* north to Vancouver Island where Salish Indians overwhelmed his ship, killing all aboard save two. One Jack Ramsay survived by jumping overboard. Another wounded sailor touched off the powder magazine, blowing up the *Tonquin* and 200 Salish, whose "arms, legs, and heads," according to Ramsay, "were flying in all directions."

Shortly after the *Tonquin* sailed from New York, Wilson Price Hunt, a St Louis clerk without any exploring experience, together with Canadian fur trader, Donald Mackenzie and 60 men, left St Louis and headed up the Missouri for the mouth of the Columbia. Hunt took with him the English botanist John Bradbury and Thomas Nuttall, a Philadelphia naturalist.

Though furnished with a map by William Clark, Hunt decided to try a shortcut to the Columbia. After suffering great hardships in the stony badlands, they eventually confronted the towering Big Horn Mountains crossing them with great difficulty. Most of the party were French Canadian rivermen – indeed, Robinson, Hoback, and Reznor were the only experienced mountain men in the party – and Hunt hoped to build canoes and cruise down the Snake to the Columbia. They should have taken note of Clark's map. They got tangled up in the rocky cliffs of Hoback Canyon, and were near starving by the time, with the help of the Shoshone, they reached the ruins of Andrew Henry's fort.

Here, Hunt made his most critical mistake. He left his few horses behind and tried to sail down the Snake. By the time they reached the rolling rapids of Calderon Linn, in present-day Idaho, the party had broken up. One detachment, led by Ramsay Crook, walked along the south bank of the Snake. Another detachment, headed by Robert McClellan, joined Hoback and Reznor and abandoned the trek to live with the Shoshone.

Meanwhile Hunt followed the north bank of the mighty Snake. Indians warned him of the 5000-foot Hell's Canyon of the Snake. He heeded their advice and later met up with Cayuse and Nez Percé Indians, who supplied the exhausted explorers with horses and pointed them toward the Columbia. At last, Hunt consulted Clark's map and realized they were in familiar country. They made their way down the Columbia. On 15 February 1812, paddling six canoes through rain and fog, they reached Fort Astoria. Mackenzie had arrived there a month earlier. Ramsay Crook, John Day and two other members of the party were robbed by Indians near the Salmon River and remained stranded until late spring when they were rescued by a party from Astoria. Dogs, horses, beaver paws, animal skins and stomach-wrenching roots were providential fare for all the explorers. Out of the 60 men who started on the expedition only 45 were to reach Fort Astoria alive.

The Astoria venture was proving to be a disaster. Few furs were taken at the fort. In July 1811 David Thompson of the North West Company arrived (▶ *page 118*), after claiming all of the Columbia River country for Britain, although the Astorians from the United States had beaten him to the mouth of the Columbia. On 19 June 1812 war was declared between Britain and the United States. By March 1813, Astoria was beseiged by the North West Company and then later by the British man-o-war HMS *Raccoon*. Macdougall and Mackenzie gave up without a fight.

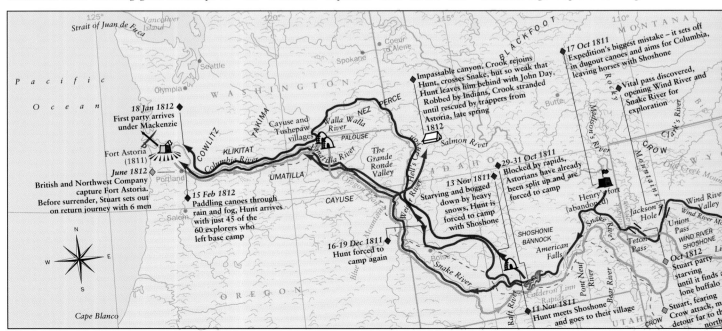

Before the surrender, on 29 June 1812, Robert Stuart and six men started the return march back across the continent. This would prove to be the most important of Astor's contributions to continental exploration. Part of their route was along what would become the Oregon Trail. The crossing was extremely difficult – even more so than that of Hunt's westbound party. John Day went insane and had to be returned to Astoria even before they crossed the Grand Ronde and the Blue Mountains of Oregon. Stuart's party avoided Hell's Canyon and followed the Snake River as it curved far south through desolate parts of present-day Idaho. Then, fearing Indians, they made a detour far to the north into Jackson's Hole. Only the shooting of a lone buffalo bull saved them from starvation.

From Jackson's Hole, they followed an Indian trail through Hoback Canyon, west of the Wind Rivers. Then they discovered the South Pass of the Rocky Mountains, soon to

Mr Crook's indisposition increased so much this afternoon that I insisted on his taking a dose of castor oil, which fortunately had the desired effect, but he... is withal so weak as to preclude all idea of continuing our journey untill his recovery... The sensations excited on this occasion, and by the view of an unknown and untravelled wilderness, are not such as to arise in the artificial solitude of parks and gardens... the phantoms which haunt a desert are want, misery, and danger, the evils of which... rush upon the mind; man is made unwillingly acquainted with his own weakness and meditation shews him how little he can sustain and how little he can perform.

Robert Stuart's journal, 1 October 1812

One of the Canadians advanced towards me with his rifle in his hand saying that as there was no appearance of our being able to procure any provisions... that lots should be cast and one die to preserve the rest... I snatched up my rifle cocked and leveled it at him with firm resolution to fire if he persisted...

Robert Stuart's journal, 12 October 1812

It was a very real pleasure for travelers harassed by fatigue to rest in quiet and be surrounded by friends after so long a journey in the midst of savages of whom it is always prudent to be wary. We had covered 2073 miles since leaving the Aricara's village.

Wilson Price Hunt's diary, on reaching Fort Astoria, 16 February 1812

become the gateway to the West, as thousands of emigrants would pass through on their way to Oregon and California.

For over a decade, however, Robert Stuart's discovery remained private, known only to Astor. It was not until 1824, that the mountain men Jedediah Smith and Tom "Broken Hand" Fitzpatrick (▶ *page 152*) rediscovered it with the help of Crow Indians.

The Astorians, 1810-12

US	Indian	
🚩	⛺ 🛖	settlement/ fort
↗		Wilson Price Hunt, 1811-12
↗		Ramsay Crook, 1811-12
↗		Donald Mackenzie, 1811-12
↗		Robert Stuart, 1812-13
▱		Winter camp
▱		Temporary camp
✳		Trade with Indians
🔥		Siege
✕		Confrontation with Indians
╲		Pass
〰		Rapids

7 Aug 1811
First sight of huge buffalo herd

12 June 1811
Expedition abandons boats and begins overland trek, with 82 horses from villages, looking for short-cut to Columbia

Arikara villages, Rhtarahe and Waho-erha

Slim Buttes

21 July 1811
Rest camp
26 July 1811
Hunt locates Cheyenne village to south; trades for more horses

5 Sept 1811
Crow Indians and renegade trader Edward Rose join party and help to make two difficult mountain crossings to Wind River

Stuart's party sets up camp for winter, but in December moves on to Nebraska

31 May 1811
Confronted by large war party of Yankton, Brulé and Miniconjou
YANKTON SIOUX

24 May 1811
Veteran mountain men Robinson, Hoback and Reznor join Hunt's party

16 Nov 1810
Robert McClellan and 14 others join expedition

21 Oct 1810
Hunt and party of 45 set out for mouth of the Columbia

South Pass (soon to become the main emigrant route over the Continental Divide)
23 Oct 1812
Stuart party discovers crucial pass, unpublicized until Crow show it to Smith and Fitzpatrick in 1824

Hunt, Bradbury and Nuttall meet aged Daniel Boone and John Coulter

Fort Osage

30 April 1813
Stuart party arrives in St Louis

The Great American Desert

THE EXPEDITIONS OF PIKE AND LONG, 1806-20

Two military expeditions cross the Great Plains to the Rockies and explore the area between Lewis and Clark's discoveries and the mysterious Spanish territory to the south.

In July 1806 General James Wilkinson, US Governor of the Louisiana Territory, sent Lieutenant Zebulon Pike to visit Osage, Pawnee and Comanche villages and to determine the source of the Red River, regarded by the US as its southern boundary. The story of Pike's expedition is the stuff of romance and intrigue. Wilkinson harbored ambitions to capture Santa Fé from the Spaniards. He gave Pike secret orders to scout out the road there, reassuring him that, as far as the Spanish were concerned, he would be "as safe as in Philadelphia," he had only hostile plains Indians to fear. But then Wilkinson, the master intriguer, leaked word of Pike's mission to the Spanish authorities, who sent Malgares out to capture Pike (▶ *page 138*).

Pike's 23 men included Lieutenant James Wilkinson, the general's own son, and a mysterious Dr John Robinson. Pike followed Malgares' broad trail towards Santa Fé. Following orders, he sent Wilkinson and five men down the Arkansas River to safety. They carried Pike's maps and final dispatches. Then Pike turned toward the Rockies, which he sighted on 15 November, 1806, looking like "a small blue cloud." Pike and his men failed in several attempts to climb what is now Pike's Peak, but he did climb Cheyenne Peak which afforded him a panoramic view of the southern Rockies. On the Arkansas the severe winter forced Pike to leave some of his men

I n regard to this extensive section of country,... it is almost wholly unfit for cultivation, and of course, uninhabitable by a people depending upon agriculture for their subsistence... The scarcity of wood and water, almost uniformly prevalent, will prove an insuperable obstacle in the way of settling the country...

Major Stephen H. Long,
General Description of the Country Traversed by the Exploring Expedition

behind. At the Rio Conejos, at the end of their endurance, Pike's men built a crude fort and awaited rescue.

Dr Robinson went on to Santa Fé, showing that Pike knew approximately where he was, but he claimed innocence when he and his men were arrested by Malgares and Spanish cavalry. At Chihuahua the Governor confiscated Pike's notes and sent him back across Texas to Louisiana. This gave Pike a matchless opportunity to spy out virtually all of New Spain and Texas. He secretly made new notes, hiding them in the barrels of his men's guns. In 1810, four years before Lewis and Clark's report, Pike made an extensive report on the Great American Desert, the road to Santa Fé, hitherto obscure northern New Spain and Texas. Wilkinson was later

tried for treason, but acquitted much to Jefferson's disgust.

In 1819, the US Secretary of War sent General Henry Rice Atkinson and 1000 men to control the Indians and drive out the British fur traders. After heading up the Missouri in five steamboats, the troops became ill and the Indians would not let them pass. Major Stephen H. Long had accompanied them, in a sixth steamboat, with scientists and army topographical engineers. After Atkinson's failure, Long was given permission to explore the Great Plains. They headed along the North and then the South Platte and, after climbing Pike's Peak, marched south. At the Arkansas River, Long sent Captain John Bell, the artist Samuel Seymour and the expedition's geologist Dr Thomas Say downriver with several riflemen. Returning, Bell's party passed through large numbers of threatening Cheyenne, Arapaho and Kiowa. Some soldiers deserted, taking most of the expedition's scientific collections and notebooks. Long continued south, at one point mistaking the Canadian River for the Red River, the boundary between United States and Spanish territory.

Originally criticized for this blunder, Long's foray is now seen to have had great merit. The US government published Long's map with "Great Desert" printed across the western prairies; a misleading description which was to deter thousands of potential emigrants. A report was privately published, with a small atlas, in 1823. It included Thomas Say's finding of marine fossils millions of years old, indicating that a great inundation had once covered the Great Plains.

The headwaters of the Red River were not discovered until 1852, by Captain Randolph Barnes Marcy, by which time they no longer had any political significance.

Left: Unlike previous expeditions, Long's had two artists. One of them, Samuel Seymour painted this view of the Rockies from Fifty miles out. Titian Peale, who also traveled with Long, illustrated the abundant wildlife to be seen on the plains. Their work provided the American public with their first visual impressions of the West.

Long's men discover mountain

July 1820
3 of Long's party for first time climb and measure Pike's Peak

Long's men try to make their way up gorge, but fail

mid-Jan
Pike leaves some men suffering from exposure and gangrene

26 Feb 1807
Pike and his men captured by Spanish cavalry at a second block-house they have built. Pike greets them innocently with "What, is not this the Red River?"

Pike climbs Cheyenne Peak to see panorama of southern Rockies

Just before making camp, Pike learns of Spanish military force sent out to intercept his expedition

Pike heads south for the Arkansas

As winter approaches, supplies run short and Pike's party builds blockhouse

Long party splits. Bell & Wilkinson head down Arkansas River, Long himself down Canadian

Long mistakes Canadian for Red River

Hostile Cheyenne, Arapaho and Kiowa confront Bell's party

Party meets up with military contingent and goes into winter quarters until spring

6 June 1820
Long's party meets enormous herds of buffalo. They pass villages of Oto, Pawnee and "Bad Heart Indians," probably Comanche

21 June 1819
Long steams upriver with a party of scientists, including John Biddle, William Biddle, Thomas Say, Augustus Jessup and Titian Peale

15 July 1806
Pike rows off with 23 men

Late August
Camp at native villages

3 of Bell's soldiers desert, taking horses, packs, rifles and most of the expedition's scientific collections and notebooks

Pike and his men are marched to Chihuahua, to governor of New Mexico

The Expeditions of Pike and Long, 1806-20

Spanish territory, 1806

US territory, 1806

US/Spanish treaty line, 1819

US fort

Spanish settlement

Spanish presidio/mission

Indian villages

Lieutenant Zebulon M. Pike, 1806-07

Major Stephen H. Long, 1819-20

Winter camp

Temporary camp

Encounter with Indians

Confrontation with Indians

Intrigue beyond the Rockies

EXPEDITIONS FROM LISA'S FORT RAYMOND, 1807-12

Drawn by the promise of riches and adventure, fur traders explore the rugged and uncharted Rocky Mountains.

In 1806, as Lewis and Clark coursed back down the Missouri, they met American fur traders heading upriver. They had been sent by Spanish-born Manuel Lisa, a brilliant St Louis entrepreneur.

Lisa was quick to grasp the potential riches of the country crossed by Lewis and Clark and dreamed of trading with Santa Fé. Denied permission by the US military governor of Louisiana, James Wilkinson, Lisa turned his interests to the north, beyond effective United States jurisdiction. In 1807 he established a trade fort at the junction of the Yellowstone and the Big Horn. His partner, Andrew Henry, headed due west and in 1810 established a trading post among the Shoshone on a fork of the Snake River. It was the first American post west of the Continental Divide. Lisa sent a number of expeditions out from his fort, including those of John Colter, George Drouillard, and Jean Baptiste Champlain; for one of Lisa's objectives was to find a route that ran west of the Rockies to Santa Fé.

The most important expedition was undertaken by Colter, one of Lewis and Clark's men. Lisa's other men always ventured out in teams, but in winter 1807 Colter headed out of Lisa's fort alone, with orders to make trade alliances with the tribes of the Big Horn Basin, notably the Absaroka, or Crow.

Colter's exact route is conjectural. Armed with only a rifle and a pack of trade goods, he made his way through Crow country. He received nothing but friendship from the Crow, who led him to the sulfurous geysers on the Shoshone, or Stinking Water, River, which were dubbed "Colter's Hell" by his incredulous contemporaries.

From there he went back through Jackson Hole and north through present day Yellowstone Park. He was the first white man to see its geysers and other marvels. Then he crossed eastward out of the Park through a pass in the Snowy Range and then moved south through Sunlight Basin back into Crow country, eventually reaching Lisa's Fort Raymond.

The following year Colter made his way to the Three Forks, source of the Missouri. He had thus located the sources of two, and possibly four, of the West's greatest rivers, counting the Snake River as it flows from

Jackson's Hole and the Green as it flows from Green Lake at the head of the Wind River Mountains. He came close to proving the contention of Jonathan Carver and Zebulon Pike that in the central Rockies was "a grand reservoir" out of which all the major rivers of the west flowed. In 1809 Colter was stripped and chased by a band of Blackfoot, and forced to run miles for his life across the Three Forks of the Missouri. Colter retired early from furtrapping and exploration but he remains a legendary figure.

George Drouillard was less lucky. He was killed by the Blackfoot at the Three Forks in 1810. Earlier, in 1808, he too explored the Yellowstone and the Big Horn Basin, though his real mission seems to have been to reach the Spaniards to the south. He believed that Santa Fé was about ten days' march away or even less via the "Salt Fork" – where the Spaniards supposedly obtained their salt. Drouillard's opinions were noted on Governor William Clark's master map of the

Lisa confronts huge party of hostile Assiniboin; "the whole prairie was red with them," he declared

Lisa confronts and pacifies the upper village Mandans

Fall 1809 Potts and Colter trapping on Jefferson Fork. Potts killed by Blackfoot. Colter runs for his life, getting to Fort Raymond in 7 days

Winter 1807 John Colter sets out alone to establish trade relations with Crow

1808 Colter crosses Snowy Range, then to Big Horn; visits Crow villages

Colter sees Stinking Water, "Colter's Hell" and Heart Mountain

1810 or 1811 Lisa sends Jean Baptiste Champlain and 23 men over Drouillard's old Big Horn route, but they head east from upper Big Horn to North Platte River

Apr 1810 Henry, Menard, & Thomas James with 80 men guided by Colter, build fort. Drouillard killed by Blackfoot

Probably where Drouillard believed "the Spaniards obtain [salt] by passing over from the river Colorado"

Drouillard looking for link with Spaniards from Santa Fé

1810 Arapaho tell Champlain about their trade with Spaniards

1812 Approximately 8 men desert party and head for Big Horn

Champlain and Porteau elect to live with the Arapaho. Nothing further is ever heard of them

Spring 1812 Champlain, Lafargue, Williams and a party reduced by attacks from Indians reach upper Arkansas and trap there, but hostile natives force them to return to Platte

Ezekiel Williams's large cache of furs just down the Arkansas from St Charles River

30 July 1812 Lafargue and three trappers reach Santa Fé, then taken to Chihuahua and imprisoned until 1815

Nobody sees clearer than I the advantages and resources of the Missouri. There is no doubt that if the means are found to exploit it, it will make someone a great fortune.

Lisa's partner Pierre Menard, 7 October 1807

Expeditions from Lisa's Fort Raymond, 1807-12

US territory, 1807

Spanish territory, 1807

US / Spanish settlement

Indian settlement

Lisa, 1807

Colter, 1807-08

Drouillard, 1807-08

Andrew Henry, 1810-11

Champlain, Lafargue and Williams, 1811-12

Trade with Indians

Spanish / Indian trading place

Confrontation with Indians

Death of explorer

Thermal springs

Salt mines

Above: An early painting of a Blackfoot Indian, a warrior of the Piegan tribe. His elk hide robe illustrates his many war "coups," including wounded enemies and stolen horses and weapons. The Blackfoot menaced trappers of the Missouri Company from the time of their first skirmish with Lewis and Clark. The artist, Karl Bodmer, traveled with an ethnologist recording Indian culture.

west, which he kept up-to-date in his St Louis office. Drouillard thus eliminated what is now Colorado and much of Wyoming from early knowledge of the west.

Champlain's expedition southward from Lisa's Fort Raymond in 1811 should have reinstated them. He headed for Arapaho country in present-day Colorado. But his company was shattered by dissension, fear and Blackfoot attacks. Seven men turned back to the Big Horn Valley. Champlain and one companion elected to stay with the Arapaho permanently and were never heard from again. Four other men from Champlain's band, led by Jean Baptiste Lafargue, actually reached Santa Fé. But only one man, Ezekiel Williams, returned. He made his way down the Arkansas River to Arrow Rock with a very large cargo of furs, only to meet the charge that he had murdered Champlain. No one knows the truth, but he was exonerated.

The Snake Country Brigades

CANADIANS IN THE AMERICAN WEST, 1818-30

*American, Canadian and British fur trappers
and traders range across the West, in search
of the lucrative beaver. They bring back
valuable information for map-makers.*

As the fur trade pushed westward across the Rockies, competition between Canadian and US trappers intensified. Thompson (▶*page 118*) had attempted to beat the Astorians (▶page *142*) to the Pacific in 1811, only to find them safely ensconced in their fort at the mouth of the Columbia River. But the network of trading posts he had set up, and the relations he had built with the Indians, paved the way for the North West Company to expand south.

Perhaps the most important of the company's explorers of the western interior was Donald Mackenzie, a huge, fat man who once stood off a party of hostile Shoshone by holding a match to a keg of powder and threatening to blow them all to pieces.

In 1818 Mackenzie organized the Snake country fur brigades for the North West Company. Sometimes numbering as many as 55 people, including Iroquois brought over from the east, Mackenzie's brigades followed the Snake River east, into the region next to the Green River. Mackenzie was one of the first white explorers to follow the Green River to its source in the magnificent Green Lake, high up in the Wind River Mountains, and he made camp in Jackson's Hole in the shadow of the Grand Tetons. In all, Mackenzie made three trips at the head of Snake country fur brigades. On one of these, he shot the rapids of Hell's Canyon of the Snake in a crude boat, a feat no white man, and probably no Indian, had done before.

Mackenzie's concept of the Snake country fur brigade was a huge success, in exploration as well as fur-hunting. He was succeeded by William Kittson, Michel Bourdon, who reached Bear Lake in Utah, and by Finian McDonald. McDonald wrote that he got "as far as the Croe Indian Cuntre on the rail Spanish river" (Green River). He also "sa the Musosoury Last fall down as far as the falls", meaning that he passed safely through Blackfoot country to the Great Falls of the Missouri River.

Still other brigade leaders from Canada followed the trails laid out by Mackenzie. Alexander Ross brought American trappers back to Flathead Post, thereby driving a rival wedge into the domain now claimed by the Hudson's Bay Company. The latter rose to the challenge, however. At the behest of Governor George Simpson, brigade leader Peter Skene Ogden set out to turn the Snake country into a "fur desert." For six years he led parties into the interior until, in 1825, he reached the country east of the Great Salt Lake. There he clashed with American trappers, though since they were below the 42nd parallel they were in Mexican territory.

Ogden also discovered and mapped the entire length of the Humboldt River, which became the main emigrant route to California. In 1829-30 he made his way from Fort Clatsop on the Columbia River south and across what is now the whole American West to the Gulf of California. Near the site of present-day Needles, California, Mohave Indians attacked his party. A pitched battle ensued in which 26 Mohave were killed.

As an explorer Ogden was second to none. Much of the information he brought back, together with that of the Canadian Snake Country Brigades and the work of explorers of the North West Company and the Hudson's Bay Company, was added to maps made by A.H. Brué in Paris and the leading map-maker of the day, Aaron Arrowsmith in London.

> O n seeing the number of their fellows who in a single moment were made to lick the dust, the rest ingloriously fled... Twenty-six remained dead on the field
>
> **Peter Skene Ogden describes his battle with the Mohave, 1829**

> T here were times when we tasted no food and were unable to discover water for several days together... our horses were reduced to great weakness so that many of them died, on whose emaciated carcasses we were constrained to satisfy the intolerable cravings of our hunger, and as a last resource, to quench our thirst with their blood.
>
> **Peter Skene Ogden in Nevada's Great Basin, winter 1829**

Left: The Kootenay River was the main route of the North West Company trappers as they headed south into the United States. Here, a supply party makes the southernmost crossing of the river, in an 1860 watercolor by James Madison Alden.

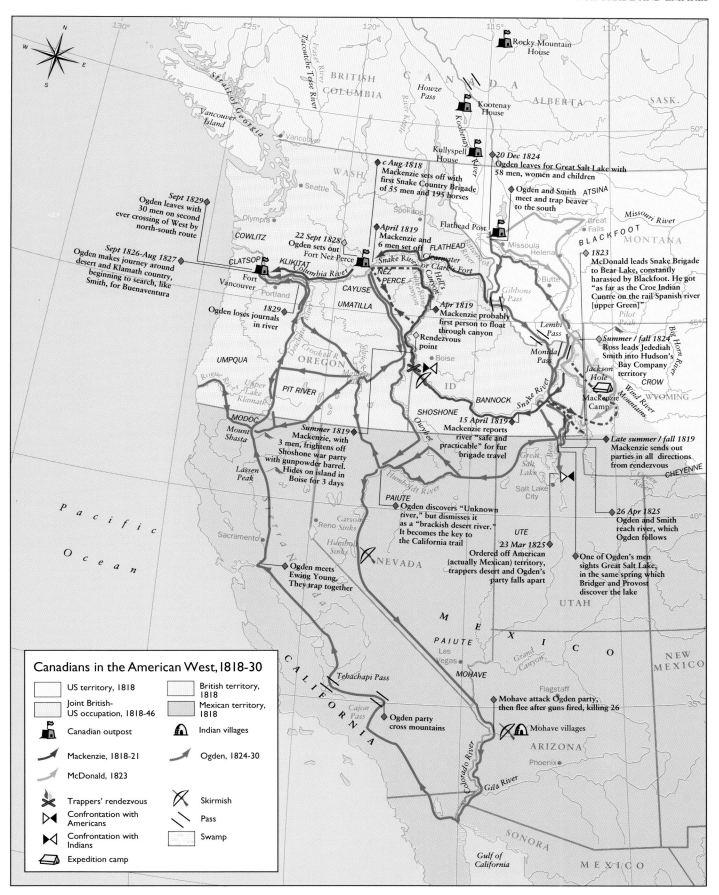

Rocky Mountain House

Howze Pass

Kootenay House

Kullyspell House

c Aug 1818
Mackenzie sets off with
first Snake Country Brigade
of 55 men and 195 horses

20 Dec 1824
Ogden leaves for Great Salt Lake with
58 men, women and children

Ogden and Smith ATSINA
meet and trap beaver
to the south

Sept 1829
Ogden leaves with
30 men on second
ever crossing of West by
north-south route

22 Sept 1828
Ogden sets out
Fort Nez Perce

April 1819
Mackenzie and
6 men set off

Flathead Post

Sept 1826–Aug 1827
Ogden makes journey around
desert and Klamath country,
beginning to search, like
Smith, for Buenaventura

FLATHEAD

BLACKFOOT   MONTANA

1823
McDonald leads Snake Brigade
to Bear Lake, constantly
harassed by Blackfoot. He got
"as far as the Croe Indian
Cuntre on the rail Spanish river
[upper Green]"

Fort
Vancouver

1829
Ogden loses journals
in river

Apr 1819
Mackenzie probably
first person to float
through canyon

Rendezvous
point

Summer / fall 1824
Ross leads Jedediah
Smith into Hudson's
Bay Company
territory

MacKenzie
Camp   CROW

WYOMING

Summer 1819
Mackenzie, with
3 men, frightens off
Shoshone war party
with gunpowder barrel.
Hides on island in
Boise for 3 days

15 April 1819
Mackenzie reports
river "safe and
practicable" for fur
brigade travel

Late summer / fall 1819
Mackenzie sends out
parties in all directions
from rendezvous

CHEYENNE

**Ogden discovers "Unknown
river," but dismisses it
as a "brackish desert river."
It becomes the key to
the California trail**

26 Apr 1825
Ogden and Smith
reach river, which
Ogden follows

23 Mar 1825
Ordered off American
(actually Mexican) territory,
trappers desert and Ogden's
party falls apart

One of Ogden's men
sights Great Salt Lake,
in the same spring which
Bridger and Provost
discover the lake

**Ogden meets
Ewing Young.
They trap together**

**Ogden party
cross mountains**

**Mohave attack Ogden party,
then flee after guns fired,
killing 26**

Mohave villages

Canadians in the American West, 1818–30

- US territory, 1818
- British territory, 1818
- Joint British–US occupation, 1818–46
- Mexican territory, 1818
- Canadian outpost
- Indian villages
- Mackenzie, 1818–21
- Ogden, 1824–30
- McDonald, 1823
- Skirmish
- Trappers' rendezvous
- Pass
- Confrontation with Americans
- Swamp
- Confrontation with Indians
- Expedition camp

All for the Seeds-Kee-Dee

TRAPPERS AND TRADERS IN THE CENTRAL ROCKIES, 1822-26

*The Green River – known to the Indians as
the Seeds-Kee-Dee – becomes a magnet for
fur trappers as they penetrate deeper into the
Rockies and discover the Great Salt Lake.*

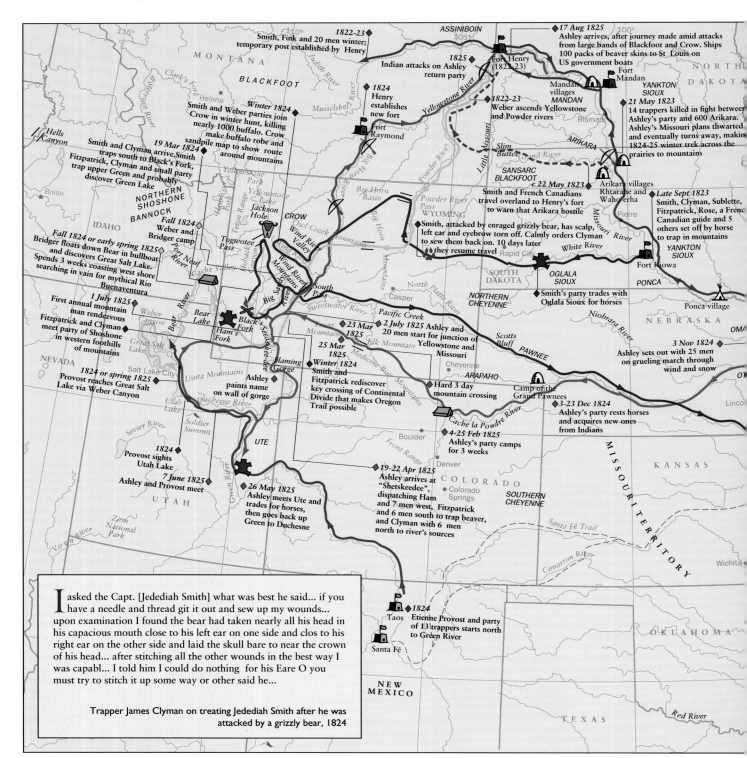

1822-23
Smith, Fink and 20 men winter;
temporary post established by Henry

17 Aug 1825
Ashley arrives, after journey made amid attacks
from large bands of Blackfoot and Crow. Ships
100 packs of beaver skins to St Louis on
US government boats

1825
Indian attacks on Ashley
return party

1824
Henry
establishes
new fort

1822-23
Weber ascends Yellowstone
and Powder rivers

21 May 1823
14 trappers killed in fight between
Ashley's party and 600 Arikara.
Ashley's Missouri plans thwarted
and eventually turns away, making
1824-25 winter trek across the
prairies to mountains

Winter 1824
Smith and Weber parties join
Crow in winter hunt, killing
nearly 1000 buffalo. Crow
make buffalo robe and
sandpile map to show route
around mountains

19 Mar 1824
Smith and Clyman arrive. Smith
traps south to Black's Fork,
Fitzpatrick, Clyman and small party
trap upper Green and probably
discover Green Lake

c 22 May 1823
Smith and French Canadians
travel overland to Henry's fort
to warn that Arikara hostile

Late Sept 1823
Smith, Clyman, Sublette,
Fitzpatrick, Rose, a French
Canadian guide and 5
others set off by horse
to trap in mountains

**Smith, attacked by enraged grizzly bear, has scalp,
left ear and eyebrow torn off. Calmly orders Clyman
to sew them back on. 10 days later
they resume travel**

Fall 1824 or early spring 1825
Bridger floats down Bear in bullboat
and discovers Great Salt Lake.
Spends 3 weeks coasting west shore
searching in vain for mythical Rio
Buenaventura

Fall 1824
Weber and
Bridger camp

1 July 1825
First annual mountain
man rendezvous
Fitzpatrick and Clyman
meet party of Shoshone
in western foothills
of mountains

**Smith's party trades with
Oglala Sioux for horses**

2 July 1825 Ashley and
20 men start for junction of
Yellowstone and
Missouri

3 Nov 1824
Ashley sets out with 25 men
on grueling march through
wind and snow

1824 or spring 1825
Provost reaches Great Salt
Lake via Weber Canyon

**25 Mar
1825**
Winter 1824
Smith and
Fitzpatrick rediscover
key crossing of Continental
Divide that makes Oregon
Trail possible

**23 Mar
1825**

**Ashley
paints name
on wall of gorge**

**Hard 3 day
mountain crossing**

**Camp of the
Grand Pawnees**

3-23 Dec 1824
Ashley's party rests horses
and acquires new ones
from Indians

1824
Provost sights
Utah Lake

7 June 1825
Ashley and Provost meet

26 May 1825
Ashley meets Ute and
trades for horses,
then goes back up
Green to Duchesne

19-22 Apr 1825
Ashley arrives at
"Shetskeedee",
dispatching Ham
and 7 men west,
Fitzpatrick
and 6 men south to trap beaver,
and Clyman with 6 men
north to river's sources

4-25 Feb 1825
Ashley's party camps
for 3 weeks

> I asked the Capt. [Jedediah Smith] what was best he said... if you
> have a needle and thread git it out and sew up my wounds...
> upon examination I found the bear had taken nearly all his head in
> his capacious mouth close to his left ear on one side and clos to his
> right ear on the other side and laid the skull bare to near the crown
> of his head... after stitching all the other wounds in the best way I
> was capabl... I told him I could do nothing for his Eare O you
> must try to stitch it up some way or other said he...
>
> Trapper James Clyman on treating Jedediah Smith after he was
> attacked by a grizzly bear, 1824

1824
Etienne Provost and party
of 13 trappers starts north
to Green River

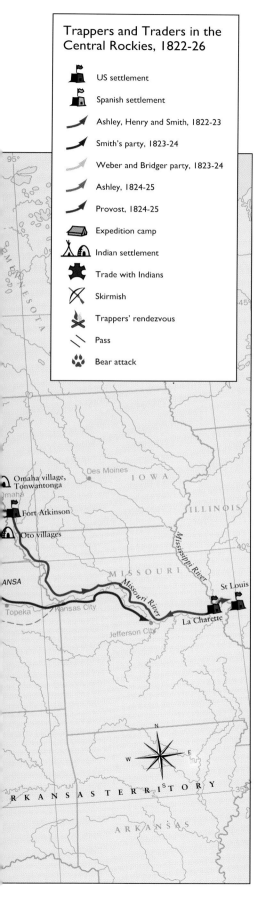

Trappers and Traders in the Central Rockies, 1822-26

- US settlement
- Spanish settlement
- Ashley, Henry and Smith, 1822-23
- Smith's party, 1823-24
- Weber and Bridger party, 1823-24
- Ashley, 1824-25
- Provost, 1824-25
- Expedition camp
- Indian settlement
- Trade with Indians
- Skirmish
- Trappers' rendezvous
- Pass
- Bear attack

In February 1822, the politician and would-be entrepreneur William Ashley teamed up with Andrew Henry to form the Rocky Mountain Fur Company. He advertised for "Enterprising Young Men... to ascend the Missouri to its source" as fur trappers: their harrowing adventures did much to create the heroic image of the mountain man.

Ashley's first keelboat sank in the Missouri, costing $10,000 in trade goods and on his second venture Arikara Indians killed 14 of his party. Andrew Henry tried to set up a post on the Yellowstone. When he took a party of trappers across the plains two more were killed by Indians. Few Indians wanted to trap furs for the white man, so Henry sent John Weber with a party to trap with the friendly Crow in the valley of the Wind River.

In September 1823 Jedediah Smith, (▶ *page 152-3*), led a second party that included James Clyman, Tom "Broken Hand" Fitzpatrick, and William Sublette. They headed out along the White River guided by a French veteran of Pierre Chouteau's Missouri Fur Company. They traded with the Sioux, but, towards winter moved west to the Black Hills of the Rockies. When Jedediah Smith was attacked by a grizzly bear, Clyman sewed his scalp and ear back on without anaesthetic.

Eventually Smith and his men joined Weber's party in the freezing Wind River valley, where they helped the Crow kill over a thousand buffalo. The Crow made a deerskin and sandpile map showing a pass over the Continental Divide. This would become the Oregon Trail, the main route for American

Alfred Jacob Miller, one of the greatest artists of the American West, painted this watercolor of trappers' annual rendezvous on Green River around 1839, just a few years before it faded into history.

emigrants heading west.

Smith and a few men went on to trap successfully on the Green River. At Henry's Fork of the Snake they met Alexander Ross with a group of Canadians. Together they reconnoitred most of what had been the prime Hudson's Bay Snake River trapping preserve.

In July, Weber and his men followed Smith's trail and eventually holed up in Cache Valley for the winter. In the late fall of 1824 or the early spring of 1825, Jim Bridger, on a bet, floated down the Bear River in a bullboat into the Great Salt Lake. The water being salty, he took it to be an arm of the Pacific. Thus Bridger was probably the first white man to discover the Great Salt Lake, although Etienne Provost, a band of Taos trappers and Peter Skene Ogden also saw it in spring 1825.

In November 1825 Ashley led a further party across the plains. Clyman was their guide as they struggled, starving, across the wintery plains to the comparative safety of the Pawnee villages at the forks of the Platte River. They eventually reached the Green River, by then the "Main Street" of the Rocky Mountain fur trappers.

Ashley immediately sent trapping parties out in all directions, while he himself set out in bull boats down the Green River past the Uinta Mountains and the Ladore canyons. Ashley met up with Provost's party and they headed toward a designated rendezvous in July 1825. He thus created the annual rendezvous or fur trade fairs, attracting free trappers, Hudson's Bay men, Taos trappers and thousands of Indians. The second, in 1826, was a bacchanal that made Ashley so rich that he quit the mountains forever, to pursue an indifferent political career.

Across Mountain and Desert

THE EXPEDITIONS OF JEDEDIAH SMITH, 1826-31

Mountain man Jedediah Smith makes a series of epic journeys from the Rockies into California, including a grueling crossing of the Great Basin.

Jedediah Smith was the greatest explorer of the American West. One of William Ashley's men (▶ *page 150*), by 1824 he had led a small brigade up the Green River and over to the Snake River. There he met Alexander Ross of the Hudson's Bay Company who had come down from Flathead Post. Ross invited Smith to accompany him back to Flathead Post, and this afforded Smith the opportunity to spy out the far reaches of the Hudson's Bay Snake Country Brigades' beaver haunts. In June 1826, Smith set out from the Cache Valley rendezvous to explore the area south-west of the Great Salt Lake. He had heard from Ute Indians that the lake had an arm to the Pacific; he thought this could be the Rio Buenaventura, much fabled by the Spanish.

In July, William Ashley sold out his interest in the Rocky Mountain Fur Company to Smith, Bill Sublette and David Jackson. Sublette went north to the Snake and encountered a large freshwater lake "one hundred by forty miles in diameter and clear as crystal." This was Yellowstone Lake, discovered almost twenty years before by John Colter (▶ *page 146*) but then forgotten.

Meanwhile Smith set out south with 18 men. In barren, rocky Black Mountain country his party subsisted largely on insects and rodents. Then in November they crossed the Mohave Desert, following an ancient Indian trade route from spring to spring and helped by Mohave Indians. After going south to San Diego, Smith returned by sea to the San Gabriel Mission in California. Here they were suspected of being spies, but eventually traveled west to the San Joaquin Valley, where they found beaver in abundance. In May 1827, far north at the American River, Smith's party failed in its first attempt to cross the snowbound Sierras. Jedediah Smith, Silas Gobel and Robert Evans then set out on what would become a great feat of exploration history. It is recounted in Smith's journal which came to light 150 years later.

The three men struggled across the vast, barren wastes of the Great Basin. After 32 days, dehydrated and near starvation, they pushed on day and night, making sometimes 40 miles in 24 hours. In July 1827 they rode down into the trappers' rendezvous in Cache Valley. "My arrival," wrote Smith, "caused considerable bustle in camp, for myself and party had been given up for lost. A small cannon brought up from St Louis was loaded and fired for a salute."

Only ten days later Smith began to retrace his route to California. The Mohave, having recently been attacked by Taos trappers, ambushed Smith's party as they crossed the Colorado. On reaching California, Smith was detained by Governor Echeandia, accused of staking an American claim to Mexican lands. A Boston shipmaster posted a $30,000 bond for Smith, but he jumped bond and sailed for San Francisco aboard an American ship. Here he was jailed and delayed again but escaped with his men and 250 horses and mules. Heading north along the western slopes of the Sierras, Smith found the head of the Sacramento and then veered west to the Umpqua River. Here Smith and two others went hunting. After narrowly surviving an attack by their Indian guides, Smith returned to find that Indians had slaughtered all but one of those left behind. Smith and his companions took to the woods, arriving safely at Fort Vancouver in August 1828. From there his Hudson's Bay rivals accompanied him back to the scene of the massacre to recover horses, equipment and journals.

In March 1829 Smith began another great journey, going far north to the heart of fur country, then turning south through the Bitterroot Valley and along a fork of the Snake. Within a year, Jedediah Smith, lonely for family and old friends, left behind the life of the mountain man. In 1830, however, he could not resist a journey over the Santa Fé trail via the Cimarron cut-off and early in 1831 he was killed by the Comanche.

I t is that I may be able to help those who stand in need, that I face every danger – it is for this that I traverse the Mountains covered with eternal snow... that I pass over Sandy Plains, in heat of Summer, thirsting for water... and most of all, it is for this that I deprive myself of the privilege of Society...

Jedediah Smith to his brother Ralph,
24 December 1829

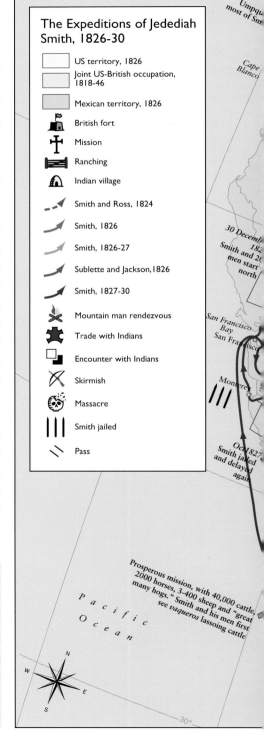

The Expeditions of Jedediah Smith, 1826-30

	US territory, 1826
	Joint US-British occupation, 1818-46
	Mexican territory, 1826
🏴	British fort
✝	Mission
⊟	Ranching
🏠	Indian village
⇠	Smith and Ross, 1824
⇗	Smith, 1826
⇗	Smith, 1826-27
⇗	Sublette and Jackson, 1826
⇗	Smith, 1827-30
⚹	Mountain man rendezvous
⬟	Trade with Indians
⬚	Encounter with Indians
✕	Skirmish
💀	Massacre
|||	Smith jailed
⟋	Pass

CANADA

ALBERTA

SASKATCHEWAN

Cape Disappointment

Seattle

Olympia

CHINOOK

Mt St Helens

Fort Okanagan

Fort Colville

1829 Smith meets David Jackson

10 August 1829 Smith given shelter by rivals from Hudson's Bay company

Fort Vancouver

COWLITZ

Portland

KLIKITAT

YAKIMA

Spokane

Flathead Post

Clark Fork

Flathead Lake

ATSINA

ASSINIBOIN

1830 Smith heads South for rendezvous then retires and returns to St. Louis and his fate on the Cimarron   BLACKFOOT

Marias River

Missouri River

MONTANA

TILLEMAUX

UMPQUA

Columbia River

WALLA WALLA

Walla Walla R

Hell's Canyon

Blue Mountains

NEZ PERCE

PALOUSE

Snake River

FLATHEAD

BLACKFOOT

Clark Fork

Helena

Butte

Sublette discovers geysers, fountains and Firehole Basin "paint pots." On return narrowly escapes Blackfoot

Musselshell River

Yellowstone River

CHEYENNE

Tongue River

UNITED STATES

12 Mar 1829 Smith leaves to scout for British fur posts

CAYUSE

UMATILLA

OREGON COUNTRY

IDAHO

Salmon River

Boise

Party divides. Sublette goes north into Yellowstone, while Jackson probably goes north towards Missouri and Flathead Post

Sublette finds sources of Snake in Jackson Hole

Sublette harassed by Blackfoot

BLACKFOOT

Teton Mountains

Yellowstone Lake

Yellowstone River

Big Horn Mountains

Powder River Mountains

CROW

Big Horn Basin

CHEYENNE

MODOC

PIT RIVER INDIANS

MAIDU

Attacked by Paiute

Deep snows prevent crossing of Sierras

Reno

WASHOE

River

Carson Pass

Ebbetts Pass

SHOSHONE

Snake River Fall 1826

Sublette party leaves rendezvous for Snake

Bear River

June 1826 Smith explores north and west shores of lake

Pierre's Hole

Jackson Hole

Wind River Mountains

Wind River Valley

Popo-Agie River

South Pass

Sweetwater River

North Platte River

WYOMING

Casper

S.D.

M.D.

NEVADA BASIN

Great Basin

Walker Lake

Wheeler Pass

Connor Pass

Salt Lake City

Great Salt Lake

Cache Valley

Bear Lake

3 July 1827 Smith arrives back for annual rendezvous

Evans collapses, Smith and Gobel leave him behind. Find spring 3 miles on. They returned and revive Evans

Smith almost drowns

Soldier Summit

Uinta Mountains

Duchesne River

ARAPAHO

Elk Mountain

Medicine Bow Mountains

MIWOK

Appelamany

Stanislaus River

Tuolumne River

Yosemite

2 June 1827 Smith, Gobel and Evans probably first people to cross Great Basin

1 June 1827 Smith, Gobel and Evans first Americans to see vast lake

25-27 May 1827 Smith finally crosses Sierras

Utah Lake

Smith meets Ute. Tries to persuade Ute to make peace with Shoshone

UTE

Green River

Castle Valley

San Rafael River

Denver

Cheyenne

Colorado Springs

Sangre de Cristo Mountains

Iron Range

South Platte River

Sukuevutnu

Wowol Yokut village

Chin-ta-che

Tulare Lake

Kern River

Kings River

PAIUTE

Zion National Park

SANPITS

Smith party meets Sanpits and Paiute. First non-Indians to notice smoke signals

UTAH

COLORADO

Nov 1826 Smith follows native trade route

Tehachapi Range

Santa Clara R

Death Valley

Las Vegas

Mohave Desert

Grand Canyon

Colorado River

MEXICO

NAVAJO

Arkansas River

San Gabriel Mission

San Pedro

Los Angeles

Santa Catalina Island

San Juan Capistrano

San Diego

Cajon Pass

San Bernadino Mountains

Mohave River

MOHAVE

Smith trades with Mohave

Mohave villages

ARIZONA

Flagstaff

Phoenix

Late 1827 Smith and party attacked by Mohave. 10 explorers 2 Mohave killed

Gila River

Santa Fé

Albuquerque

Rio San José

Rio Grande

NEW MEXICO

JICARILLA APACHE

TEX.

American smugglers tan contraband hides and keep small ranches with cattle and hogs

5 Jan 1827 Smith sails aboard brig Courier

Sept 1827 Smith sails north for San Francisco aboard US ship Franklin

MEXICO

SOUTHERN PAIUTE

SHOSHONE

PAIUTE

Southwestern Adventures

JAMES OHIO PATTIE, 1824-32

*Fur trappers explore the Southwest,
rediscover the Grand Canyon and blaze trails
into California.*

In 1825 the young James Ohio Pattie with his father, Sylvester Pattie, left Missouri for Santa Fé with Sylvestre Pratte's train. They spent the year trapping the Gila River. Although Americans were forbidden to trap in New Mexico, James Pattie was excluded from the ban for rescuing a former governor's daughter from the feared Comanche.

Late in 1825 James Pattie joined Michel Robideau and a party of 14 French Canadians heading west to the Gila and Colorado rivers. The party was soon beset by Papago Indians near present-day Phoenix. Normally friendly, the Papago left only Robideau, Pattie and one other man alive. Fortunately the three men soon met up with Ewing Young and his party of trappers. These included Tom "Peg Leg" Smith who, up on the Green River in the winter of 1827, amputated his own leg with a butcher knife.

Young's party reached the Mohave villages, previously visited in 1825 by Jedediah Smith, and then by Richard Campbell's party, who had murdered several Mohave and hanged them from trees. Young's men repeated the atrocity after Young declared that the Mohave shot arrows at his bed while he was sleeping. They then crossed the Colorado, going up along the north rim of the Grand Canyon to the Grand River and its sources. They were the first white men to see the Grand Canyon since the Spaniards nearly three centuries before (▶ *page 36*).

Pattie later claimed that they crossed over the front range of the Rockies along the South Platte, reaching the Big Horn and Yellowstone River and crossing over the Continental Divide into Flathead country. This is a somewhat incredible distance to have traveled in a single season. It is likely that Pattie was confused and that the trek was much shorter. After taking the Grand to its head, they crossed over to the South Platte, then turned south along the Front Range, crossing the mountains westward at La Vela Pass, then heading south to Santa Fé.

In 1830 the Patties made trips to the west coast of Mexico via the Gila River and down the Colorado across the baja deserts into California. But by the time the Patties reached the mission that is now San Diego, Jedediah Smith had already arrived in California. So

had the trapper Richard Campbell who, with his party of 35, had taken a more direct route. In 1830 Pattie and his father were thrown into prison in San Diego by the Spanish. His father died. After James Pattie was released he claimed to have inoculated 22,000 mission Indians and Spanish against smallpox, though the mission population was only 12,851 and the epidemic was measles. Penniless, Pattie traveled back to his home town, Cincinnati, and dictated his story to the writer-clergyman Timothey Flint. It was published in 1831.

By 1829 several routes were regularly traveled across the Southwest to California. Ewing Young and Kit Carson followed the route via Zuñi and the Gila river. Peg Leg Smith led a party down from the Green River. Manuel Armijo followed Escalante's trail of 1776 (▶ *page 126*). He went to California via a crossing north of the Grand Canyon, then via the Virgin River to Las Vegas Meadows, and finally across the Mohave Desert to Cajon Pass. This route was called "The Old Spanish Trail." In 1830 William Wolfskill followed in Armijo's footsteps but blazed a trail south, past present-day Parowan and St George, Utah. Finally, in 1832, David Jackson and 11 men swung far south through present-day Tucson, San Xavier del Bac Mission and along Father Kino's old 18th century trail to California (▶ *page 120*). California was now the magnet for trade with the Mexicans.

Meanwhile, traveling north from Taos in 1824-25, Etienne Provost met William Ashley's party (▶ *page 150*) and was among the first white men to see Utah Lake and Great Salt Lake. If he saw Great Salt Lake in the fall of 1824 then he was the first white man to do so. However this is disputed and it may have been the spring of 1825. Many other bands of trappers out of Taos followed in his footsteps as the San Juan River country became a popular trapping ground on the way to the annual Green River rendezvous.

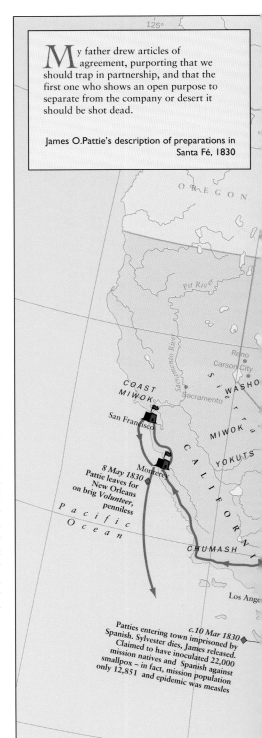

My father drew articles of agreement, purporting that we should trap in partnership, and that the first one who shows an open purpose to separate from the company or desert it should be shot dead.

James O.Pattie's description of preparations in Santa Fé, 1830

8 May 1830
Pattie leaves for New Orleans on brig *Volunteer*, penniless

c.10 Mar 1830
Patties entering town imprisoned by Spanish. Sylvester dies, James released. Claimed to have inoculated 22,000 mission natives and Spanish against smallpox – in fact, mission population only 12,851 and epidemic was measles

James O. Pattie and the Taos Trappers, 1824-30

- ☐ US territory
- ☐ Joint US-British occupation, 1818-46
- ☐ Mexican territory, 1824
- US settlement
- Mexican settlement
- ✝ Mexican mission
- Indian village

- Etienne Provost, 1824-25
- Sylvester and James Ohio Pattie, 1825
- James Ohio Pattie, Michel Robideau, Ewing Young, 1826-27
- ⚬⚬⚬ James Ohio Pattie's claimed route, 1827
- Sylvester and James Ohio Pattie, 1829-30

- Expedition camp
- Copper mines
- ✕ Skirmish
- ╲ Pass
- ☠ Death of explorer
- ⦀ Pattie imprisoned

Pattie claims to have reached the Clearwater and returned to Taos in 1827. This is doubtful

31 May 1827 Pattie claims to have taken just 11 days from South Platte, and to have traveled to Santa Fé via Clark's Fork of the Columbia, killing 16 Blackfoot and losing 4 trappers, arriving on 1 Aug

"The houses are cone-shaped like a sugar loaf. The number of lodges may amount to six hundred" (Patties)

Pawnee villages

Council Bluffs

6 Aug 1825 Party leaves camp

30 July 1825 Pratte leaves for Taos with 116 men, including Patties

Ashley visited Provost's camp

1824

20 May 1827 Pattie and Young hunt buffalo

Pattie and Young first to see Grand Canyon since Cardenas (1540)

1824 Provost sets off

23 Sept 1829 Patties set off for California

7 men desert and strip beaver before Patties, forcing them to look for other rivers

26 Oct 1825 Party arrives

Taos

Albuquerque

Santa Fé

Young claims Mohave shoot 16 arrows into his bed, none of them hitting him. As Campbell before him, kills Mohave and hangs them from trees

Mohave villages

Patties cache more furs, but stolen whilst in Santa Fé for supplies

Pattie hit by arrows in hip and breast in fight with Mescalero Apache during expedition he claimed to have made to Pecos River.

Sept 1826 Robideau and James Pattie trap before Papago kill most of party. Pattie joins Young in first expedition to cross this way to Colorado River

1825 British naval lieutenant, R. Hardy, first European to reach mouth of Colorado since Alarcon in 1540. Patties next party to reach there in 1830

Socorro

Sylvester Pattie becomes copper mine superintendant

Santa Rita del Cobre

Late Nov 1825 Patties head west with 14 men to trap on Gila

San Xavier del Bac

Mar 1830 ties reach alifornian mission

San Diego

Santa Catalina

Gulf of California

Spying Out an Emigrant Trail

THE EXPEDITIONS OF BONNEVILLE AND WALKER, 1832-34

Under the guise of fur-trading, Bonneville explores Green River country to spy out conditions for emigrants. He sends out Walker, who finds a viable central trail to California.

In May 1832 Captain Benjamin Louis Eulalie Bonneville set out from Fort Osage, near present-day Kansas City, at the head of a long train of trappers and wagons bound for the heart of the Green River fur country. He had been given a mysterious two-year leave from the army to embark on a fur trade venture that came to be known throughout the West as "Bonneville's Folly."

His route out along the Platte and over South Pass is not important, except that he was the first to take wagons over South Pass, as far as the Green River, thus proving that emigrants would also be able to make the journey. But why Bonneville was allowed to take up fur trading is still unresolved. His real purpose may have been to spy on the British in the Northwest. His twin-towered fort on Horse Creek Fork of the Green River was ideally suited to monitor the activities of British trappers and Indians, or even invading soldiers. It stood athwart the approaches to South Pass, Union Pass, Jackson's Hole, Snake River, Bear River, Humboldt River and the Great Salt Lake.

The idea is not so far fetched. Bonneville was instructed by the War Department to note all aspects of natural history and

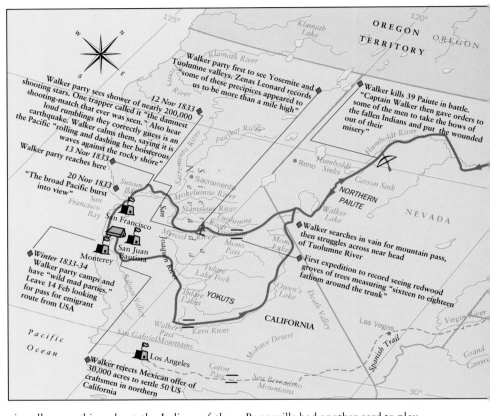

virtually everything about the Indians of the Rocky Mountains, especially their ways of making war. Indeed, General Macomb's orders enjoined Bonneville to collect "every information which you may conceive would be useful to the Government." This was all to be at his own or some mysterious private backer's expense.

By the end of the summer, Bonneville had built his fort and sent parties of trappers to Bear River. He himself moved north and east to Pierre's Hole. He then went into winter camp way up on the Salmon River. When he returned to the 1833 rendezvous at the Green River, he had little to show for his fur trapping enterprise despite the very good men working for him. His rivals scorned, but

Left: Alfred Miller's portrait of Joseph Rutherford Walker captures the romantic self-image of this ruthless mountain man. His right hand rests on his rifle, and on a gold chain around his neck, he wears a glass or silver container inscribed "Fra Diavolo," after a then-popular opera about an Italian bandit leader.

Bonneville had another card to play.

In 1833 Bonneville sent mountain man Joseph Rutherford Walker to find a feasible central trail to California. He disguised the mission, saying that Walker was scouting the western shores of the Great Salt Lake. This was perhaps because Walker was likely to travel below the 42nd parallel, thus trespassing on Spanish territory. Zenas Leonard, the clerk attached to the party, inadvertently revealed its true objective. He wrote: "I was anxious to go to the coast of the Pacific, and for that purpose hired with Mr Walker for a certain sum per year."

With California as his true destination, Walker made straight for the Humboldt River, following its great bend southward to the Humboldt Sinks near Mono Lake. Later Bonneville's map would refer to the Sinks as "Battle Lakes." It was there that Walker ordered his men to let fly a withering rifle volley at a large group of Paiute Indians. They were armed with bows and arrows but

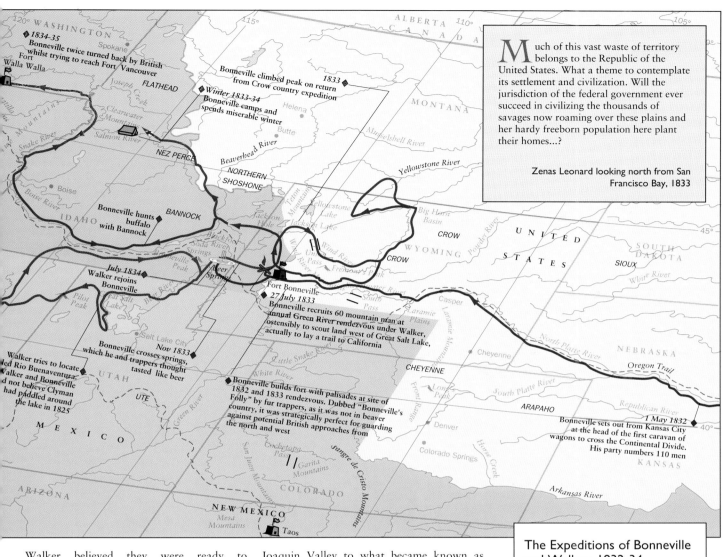

The map contains these labels:

120° WASHINGTON   115°   ALBERTA   CANADA   110°   105°

1834-35
Bonneville twice turned back by British
whilst trying to reach Fort Vancouver
Fort
Walla Walla

Spokane

FLATHEAD

Bonneville climbed peak on return
from Crow country expedition   1833

Winter 1833-34
Bonneville camps and
spends miserable winter

MONTANA

Helena

Joseph Creek

Clearwater
Mountains

Salmon River

NEZ PERCE

Snake River

Boise River

Boise

IDAHO

Beaverhead River

Butte

Musselshell River

Yellowstone River

NORTHERN
SHOSHONE

Bonneville hunts
buffalo
with Bannock   BANNOCK

Buckthorn

Soda River
Springs

Bonneville Peak

Beer
Springs

July 1834
Walker rejoins
Bonneville

Pilot
Peak

Great Salt
Lake

Walker tries to locate
fabled Rio Buenaventura;
Walker and Bonneville
did not believe Clyman
had paddled around
the lake in 1825

Salt Lake City

MEXICO

UTAH

Nov 1833
Bonneville crosses springs,
which he and trappers thought
tasted like beer

Green River

Teton
Mountains

Jackson
Hole

Yellowstone
Lake

Jackson Lake

Wind River
Mountains

Union Pass

Wind River

Fremont's Peak

Fort Bonneville
27 July 1833
Bonneville recruits 60 mountain man at
annual Green River rendezvous under Walker,
ostensibly to scout land west of Great Salt Lake,
actually to lay a trail to California

South
Pass

Little Snake

White River

Bonneville builds fort with palisades at site of
1832 and 1833 rendezvous. Dubbed "Bonneville's
Folly" by fur trappers, as it was not in beaver
country, it was strategically perfect for guarding
against potential British approaches from
the north and west

UTE

Big Horn
Basin

CROW

WYOMING   CROW

Powder River

UNITED

STATES

45°

SOUTH
DAKOTA

SIOUX

White River

Laramie
Plains

Casper

Laramie Mountains

Cheyenne

NEBRASKA

Oregon Trail

CHEYENNE

From Range

Long
Peak

South Platte River

ARAPAHO

North Platte River

Republican River

40°

Bonneville sets out from Kansas City
at the head of the first caravan of
wagons to cross the Continental Divide.
His party numbers 110 men
1 May 1832

Denver

Colorado Springs

Horse Creek

Arkansas River

KANSAS

San Juan River

Cochetopa
Pass

Garita
Mountains

Sangre de Cristo Mountains

COLORADO

ARIZONA

NEW MEXICO

Mesa
Mountains

Taos

M uch of this vast waste of territory
belongs to the Republic of the
United States. What a theme to contemplate
its settlement and civilization. Will the
jurisdiction of the federal government ever
succeed in civilizing the thousands of
savages now roaming over these plains and
her hardy freeborn population here plant
their homes...?

Zenas Leonard looking north from San
Francisco Bay, 1833

The Expeditions of Bonneville
and Walker, 1832-34

US territory
Joint US-British occupation, 1818-46
Mexican territory, 1832
US fort
British fort
Mexican settlement
Bonneville, 1832-34
Walker, 1833-34
Rendezvous
Winter camp
Skirmish
Pass
Springs
Redwood forests

Walker believed they were ready to "overwhelm" his party.

Just where Walker crossed the Sierras into California is disputed. It seems likely that he went up what became known as Walker's River, through Mono Pass and along the divide between the Merced and Tuolome rivers. They were thus the first white men to see the canyon of the Yosemite. The trip was hard but dazzling. First there was the canyon and the giant redwood trees "measuring sixteen to eighteen fathoms around the trunk," then an earthquake and a meteor shower. After coming to the arm of the great ocean at Suisun Bay, they found the beautiful coasts of the Pacific, south of San Francisco, where "they stared in amazement at stranded whales lying like helpless Gullivers washed up on a Lilliputian beach."

Walker's route back was more practicable, though the barren wastes of the Great Basin caused thirst so terrible that they drank the blood of their horses. He moved down the San Joaquin Valley to what became known as Walker's Pass, a low, easy crossing of the southern end of the Sierras. From there he turned northward in the great silent Basin. On reaching the Humboldt Sinks he again abused and murdered the helpless Diggers. He then followed the Humboldt River, but near old Fort Hall and the main trail at Bear River, branched off overland to the Snake River. At Bonneville's behest, Walker had achieved no mean feat. He had found a practicable emigrant trail to California, signaling the approaching era of Manifest Destiny.

Bonneville was recalled in disgrace and court martialed for overstaying his leave. He told the military court of secret personal instructions from President Andrew Jackson, but the General did not back him up. Whatever orders there had been to extend his leave, they had disappeared from the military records.

Beyond the Mississippi
THE SURVEYS OF LIEUTENANT FRÉMONT, 1842-48

During expeditions dogged by tragedy and political intrigue, Frémont circumnavigates the West and pioneers a new transcontinental route.

From 1842 until the Civil War, the US Army's Corps of Topographical Engineers conducted what has been termed a "Great Reconnaissance" of the American West. The Corps, accompanied by scientists and artists, sponsored expeditions to promote development and settlement and actively publicized its findings.

John Charles Frémont as a Corps member, had already explored Cherokee country in 1836 and 1837, and accompanied Joseph N. Nicollet, a French-born scientist, on expeditions to the Red Pipestone Quarry in far western Minnesota in 1838-39. He had also led his own survey of the Des Moines River in 1841. Since 1838 Frémont had been son-in-law and protégé of Thomas Hart Benton, a powerful senator from Missouri, who was keen to secure the vast Oregon Territory for the United States.

In 1842 Benton persuaded Congress to provide funds for a Topographical Corps expedition into the Rockies. Frémont arrived in St Louis by the end of May. He headed up the Missouri by steamboat, meeting Kit Carson who would become his fast friend. Frémont journeyed along the Platte on the Oregon Trail and eventually marched his men, mostly French *voyageurs*, through the South Pass and into the Wind River Mountains. Here Frémont paddled all around the lake subsequently named after him, and scaled what he believed to be the Wind River's loftiest peak, and planted a flag emblazoned with an American eagle.

In 1843 Frémont led his men from St Vrain's Fort south to the upper Arkansas. With a picked party of men Frémont crossed the Laramie Plains to the Sweetwater River. In the meantime, the others were following the Sweetwater emigrant route. Beyond the Wasatch Mountains they explored the Great Salt Lake area and then pushed on to the Columbia River and Oregon. From the Dalles, Frémont turned south for California, making one last search for the mythical Buenaventura River, and turned west into the Sierras. For 30 days his men, soon deserted by their frightened native guides, struggled through the deep snows of Truckee Pass until they reached Sutter's Fort.

After a stay in California, Frémont led his men through the San Joaquin Valley and over what they believed to be Walker's Pass (actually Tehachapi Pass) into the Great Basin.

Right: Drawing of Frémont's expedition in the Rocky Mountains by Edward or Richard Kern. It was reproduced in the publisher's prospectus for Frémont's Memoirs, 1886.

From the Las Vegas meadows, Joseph Walker led them east into Colorado's vast meadowlands.

In 1845 Frémont received orders to survey the Red River. Instead, he headed out to California where he helped instigate the Bear Flag Revolt, an action for which he was later court-martialed. He resigned from the army and, in 1848, led the first of two private expeditions to locate a central Pacific railroad route. Both expeditions became disasters. During the first, some of his best men perished in the snows of San Juan Mountains and a few fell victim to cannibalism.

Frémont had proved that no "Rio Buenaventura" ran west from Great Salt Lake and he defined the Great Basin as such. He and his men circumnavigated the whole of the American West making many scientific observations. His cartographer, Charles Preuss drew up a great map of the entire west, as well as a hugely detailed map for emigrants of the Oregon Trail.

I never was so fascinated. I never grew so fast in my life. Every scene and circumstance in the narrative was painted in my mind to last and to last forever... I fancied I could see Frémont's men, hauling the cannon up the savage battlements of the Rocky Mountains, flags in the air, Frémont at the head, waving his sword, his horse neighing wildly in the mountain wind, with unknown and unnamed empires on every hand. It touched my heart when he told how a weary little brown bee tried to make its way from a valley of flowers far below across a spur of snow, where he sat resting for a moment with his men; how the bee rested on his knee till it was strong enough to go on to another field of flowers beyond the snow... I was no longer a boy... now I began to be inflamed with a love for action, adventure, glory, and great deeds away out yonder under the path of the setting sun.

Joaquin Miller, "the Poet of the Sierras," on Frémont's ascent of the Wind River Mountains, 1842

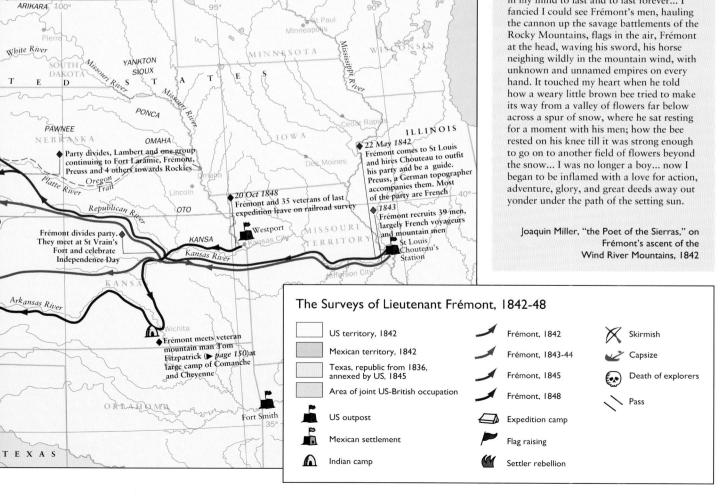

The Surveys of Lieutenant Frémont, 1842-48

US territory, 1842

Mexican territory, 1842

Texas, republic from 1836, annexed by US, 1845

Area of joint US-British occupation

US outpost

Mexican settlement

Indian camp

Frémont, 1842

Frémont, 1843-44

Frémont, 1845

Frémont, 1848

Expedition camp

Flag raising

Settler rebellion

Skirmish

Capsize

Death of explorers

Pass

**Map labels:**

ARIKARA 100°

White River

Pierre

SOUTH DAKOTA

YANKTON SIOUX

Missouri River

Missouri River

PONCA

PAWNEE

NEBRASKA

OMAHA

Omaha

Lincoln

Platte River

Oregon Trail

Republican River

OTO

Party divides, Lambert and one group continuing to Fort Laramie, Frémont, Preuss and 4 others towards Rockies

20 Oct 1848 Frémont and 35 veterans of last expedition leave on railroad survey

Westport

Frémont divides party. They meet at St Vrain's Fort and celebrate Independence Day

KANSA

Kansas City

Kansas River

Arkansas River

Wichita

Frémont meets veteran mountain man Tom Fitzpatrick (▶ page 150) at large camp of Comanche and Cheyenne

KANSAS

OKLAHOMA

Fort Smith 35°

TEXAS

MINNESOTA

St Paul

Minneapolis

WISCONSIN

Mississippi River

Cedar Rapids

IOWA

Des Moines

ILLINOIS

22 May 1842 Frémont comes to St Louis and hires Chouteau to outfit his party and be a guide. Preuss, a German topographer accompanies them. Most of the party are French

1843 Frémont recruits 39 men, largely French voyageurs and mountain men

St Louis Chouteau's Station

MISSOURI TERRITORY

Jefferson City

40°

The Soldier Archeologists

EMORY'S MEXICAN WAR RECONNAISSANCE, 1846

*Topographer Emory surveys New Mexico,
and finds the awe-inspiring ruined pueblos of
the Pecos and Gila valleys.*

During the Mexican war, the army attached
topographical engineers to most of its major
field commands. Lieutenant William H.
Emory headed the topographical unit that
accompanied Colonel Stephen Watts Kearny
and his 300 dragoons on a march of conquest
to Santa Fé. They then went on to San Diego
through southwestern territory whose

> On the hill, before reaching the
> rancheria, the Pacific opened for the
> first time to our view, the sight producing
> strange but agreeable emotions. One of the
> mountain men who had never seen the
> ocean before, opened his arms and
> exclaimed: "Lord there is a great prairie
> without a tree."
>
> **From Emory's account of the expedition's
> arrival near San Diego, 10 December 1846**

*Above: Diamond-back rattlesnakes (crotalus atrox),
found throughout the Southwest. Emory's team
recorded and classified masses of fauna and flora, and
he included pictures of many of them in his published
report .*

geography was only incompletely understood.

Emory, a career military man with strong
connections to the Coast Survey and the new
Smithsonian Institution, had an avid interest
in science. Leaving Lieutenants James W.
Abert and William G. Peck behind to map and
survey the territory of New Mexico, Kearny
rode out of Santa Fé on 25 September 1846.
With his topographical corps were two
civilians: Norman Bestor, a statistician, and
the landscape painter John Mix Stanley (▶
page 168). As Kearny and Emory headed
down the Rio Grande and west along the

upper Gila River, they found much to occupy
them in the field of natural history. Just before
Valverde, New Mexico, they met Kit Carson
on his way east with news that California had
been surrendered to the Americans. Now
Kearny sent two-thirds of his men back to
Santa Fé. The rest continued west with Kit
Carson, who reluctantly agreed to guide them
to the Pacific. Along the Gila River, Emory
found many interesting ancient ruins and
artifacts, which he first believed to be Aztec,
but later realized were remains of a distinct
native culture that had once flourished there.
He identified at least 12 aboriginal towns as
having once lined the banks of the Gila. His
most important find was the Casa Grande, or
Casa Montezuma, its pink sandstone walls
still largely standing after 400 years.

From the junction of the Gila and Colorado
rivers Kearny's men suffered immeasurably
for eight days as they marched through desert
on their way to Warner's Ranch, in the
foothills of the Sierra Nevada of California.
Just east of Warner's Ranch, near the native
village of San Pascual, Kearny's troops
clashed with Mexican soldiers in a desperate
hand-to-hand conflict. Although superior in
numbers, the Mexicans, who had been armed
mainly with lances, retired from the field first.
Nevertheless, the Americans could hardly
claim this as a victory: whereas the Mexicans
lost only 2 men, 18 Americans were killed and
13 wounded. Kearny himself was badly
wounded. Emory had proved himself a hero
when he killed the lancer about to finish off
his commander. Following the battle, the
Army of the West found itself barricaded in
what was called Snooks Ranch. On the night
of 8 December, Kit Carson, Lieutenant

6 Dec 1846
Kearny's dragoons clash with Mexican mounted lancers at native village. Americans force Mexican troops from the field, but victory hardly decisive; Kearny suffers 18 casualties, only 2 Mexicans killed

2 Aug 1846
Kearny and Army of the West march out to Santa Fé, with Emory, Abert and Peck and First Lieutenant William H. Warner

Fall 1845
Abert and Peck explore Canadian River

25 Sept 1846
Kearny marches out of Santa Fé with 300 dragoons, scouts and topographical engineers; Peck and Abert, ill, stay in Santa Fé

Abert and Peck meet Comanahe and Kiowa

Oct 1846
Peck and Abert visit ruined pueblos: "the mind recalls... those fortresses observed by the army of Cortez"

Emory examines ancient towns of Las Vegas and Pecos

Emory finds ruins of 12 ancient native towns, which he thought Aztec until he saw they were remains of distinct native culture. Casa Grande's 400-year old pink adobe walls are still standing

Kearny's men trade with members of the Maricopa and Pima tribes at their villages

6 Oct 1846
Kit Carson meets Kearny and his men, with news that California has surrendered. Kearny sends Major Sumner and 200 dragoons back to Santa Fé and continues on with 100 cavalry and the topographical unit.

Kearny's dragoons fortify themselves for a last stand.

8 Dec 1846
Carson, Beale and an Indian scout crawl through Mexican lines and make for San Diego.

Emory fixes exact location of junction of Gila and Colorado rivers using astronomical instruments

10 Dec
Gray brings forces to assist Kearny. Mexican troops retreat. Kearny continues on to Pacific

Emory learns of Mexican recapture of Santa Barbara and Los Angeles when he surprises a Mexican courier riding from California to Sonora. Kearny quickly pushes on to California to re-establish American control

At deserted copper mine worked by the Patties in 1827, Kearny meets Mangus Colorado and other Apache chieftains, who swear allegiance to the United States and offer to join fight with Mexico

Left: Giant cactus (cereus giganticus), *towering above a group of Indians, near the Gila River. Drawn by Paulus Roetter, and published in Emory's* United States and Mexican Boundary Survey Report *in 1859, giant cacti had only been seen by Indians and plainsmen in Texas, before Emory's march to the Pacific in 1846.*

High on a lofty rock of sandstone, ... sits the city of "Acoma." On the northern side of the rock, the rude boreal blasts have heaped up the sand, so as to form a practical ascent for some distance; the rest of the way is through solid rock. At one place a singular opening, or narrow way, is formed between a huge square tower of rock and the perpendicular face of the cliff. Then the road winds round like a spiral stair way, and the Indians have, in some way, fixed logs of wood in the rock, radiating from a vertical axis, like steps: these afford foothold to man and beast in clambering up.
We were constantly meeting and passing Indians, who had their "burros" laden with peaches. At last we reached the top of the rock, ... Here we saw a large church, and several continuous blocks of buildings, containing 60 or 70 houses in each block... In front each story retreated back as it ascended, so as to leave a platform along the whole front of the story ... In order to gain admittance, you ascend to the second story by means of ladders; the next story is gained by the same means, but to reach the "azotia," or roof, the partition walls on the platform that separates the quarters of different families, have been formed into steps ... Lieutenant Peck and myself ascended to the azoteas, and saw there great quantities of peaches, that had been cut in half and spread out to dry in the sun.

Lieutenant James W. Abert,
Report and Map of... New Mexico,
10 February 1848

Emory's Mexican War Reconnaissance, 1846

US territory, 1845

Mexican territory, 1845

Annexed by US, 1845-48

US outpost

Mexican settlement

Emory, 1846

Peck and Abert, 1845

Trade with Indians

Pueblo

Indian village

Ruin

Disused mine

Battle

Treaty with Indians

Pass

Edward F. Beale and an Indian scout were able to break through the Mexican lines and make for San Diego. There they recruited reinforcements, 180 sailors and marines who, under the command of Lieutenant A.V.F. Gray, marched to Snooks Ranch and finally overcame the Mexicans. Kearny's army was then able to march on to the Pacific.

Despite the military character of Kearny's expedition, Emory ensured that it fulfilled scientific objectives as well. Upon returning home, he drew the first map to portray southwestern geography accurately. His report also included topographical descriptions, lists of flora and fauna, and careful comments on the area's geology and fossil remains. Perhaps most importantly, his studies of ancient ruins pioneered the study of native ethnology through archeological remains. All in all, Emory managed to turn out a many-sided description of a very interesting and hitherto little understood area of the continent.

The Ancient Southwest Revealed

THE SURVEYS OF SIMPSON AND SITGREAVES, 1849-51

Hidden amid the canyons and mesas of the southwest, US military topographers discover the spectacular ruins of a lost civilization.

In August 1849 topographical engineer Lieutenant James H. Simpson left Santa Fé, New Mexico, with three topographical assistants. They were part of a punitive expedition against the Navajo, led by Lieutenant Colonel John M. Washington, for their raids on outlying New Mexico settlements.

Simpson marched due west and made a detailed record of the Jemez pueblo on the Rio Grande. The party then crossed the headwaters of the Puerco River, marched through a desert studded with mesas and entered the Chaco Canyon. Leading a detached reconnaissance, Simpson located the ruins of no less than ten ancient and enormous pueblos of the Anasazi, the largest complex of Indian pueblos in North America and the home of a great, lost civilization.

From Chaco Canyon, Washington led his men, including Simpson, to the foothills of the Chuska Mountains. After overcoming a group of Navajo and killing six of them, Washington's artillery moved into Canyon de Chelly, a Navajo stronghold. After a further skirmish with the Navajo. Washington was able to enforce a peace. Simpson then reconnoitred the canyon with an escort of 60 soldiers including the artist Richard Kern. They discovered spectacular prehistoric pueblos (▶ *page opposite*) and on their return march, Simpson studied further ruins in the Canyon Bonito, the village of Zuñi and Inscription Rock, a landmark carved with the names both of Indians and the Spanish conquistadors of 1605 (▶ *page 40*).

The soldiers then marched through the

Puerco Valley's pueblo towns and back to Santa Fé. Simpson reported his spectacular findings to the Corps of Topographical Engineers and, aided by information from mountain man Richard Campbell, advised that a new railroad route might run west from the Rio Grande, past Zuñi and across the Colorado into California.

In summer 1851 Captain Lorenzo Sitgreaves was assigned to assist Colonel Edwin Vose Sumner in his efforts to suppress the Navajo, and was sent to follow up Simpson's suggestion of a southern railroad route. Sitgreaves marched west out of Albuquerque with 50 infantry across present-day Arizona. He was accompanied by an army topographer, Lieutenant John G. Parke, the naturalist Dr S.W. Woodhouse, Richard

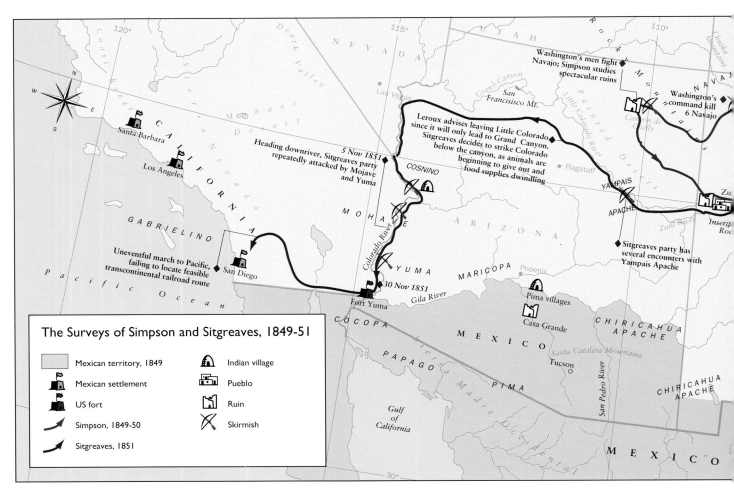

Kern, and a guide, Antoine Leroux.

Heading west in the shadow of the Indians' sacred San Francisco Mountains the party was attacked near the Colorado River by the Cosnino. They were beset by repeated ambushes. Antoine Leroux and another member of the party were wounded, Mojave wounded Dr Woodhouse and Yuma killed one straggler with war clubs. The party struggled into Fort Yuma, and eventually moved on to California.

No satisfactory railroad route to the Pacific was found but Simpson recorded the spectacular pueblo ruins he had encountered, while Sitgreaves produced valuable reports of the Wupatki ruins of Arizona, the village of Zuñi, and of his experiences with Yampais Apache and Cosnino Indians.

We had got about two miles when I came near treading on a rattle snake. I immediately jumped back and struck him on the head with my ramrod and then seized him back of the head. Unfortunately my hold was too long and he throwing round his head struck me on my finger I immediately commenced sucking it and asked for string but they had none and I pulled a buckskin string off the wallet of my compass & got Lieut P to tie it around the finger as quick as possible. I then lanced my finger well with my knife and sent off Ross for some Ammonia. I continued sucking it all the time I was walking when near the Pueblo we were met by Ross and I applied the Ammonia immediately and drank some Whiskey, on getting in the house I took some Ammonia inwardly and commenced drinking brandy. The pain when the snake first struck me was very severe and made me sick at the stomack but this soon passed away. I lanced my finger freely again and held it in warm water and it bled finely then placed it in a cup of Ammonia. They continued giving me Brandy and I was soon unconscious of every thing that was going on. How long I remained in this condition I am unable to say.

Dr Samuel Washington Woodhouse,
17 September 1851

It was somewhat exciting to observe, as we approached the valley of Chelly, the huts of the enemy, one after another, springing up into smoke and flame, and their owners scampering off in flight.

Lieutenant James Hervey Simpson,
Canyon de Chelly, September 1849

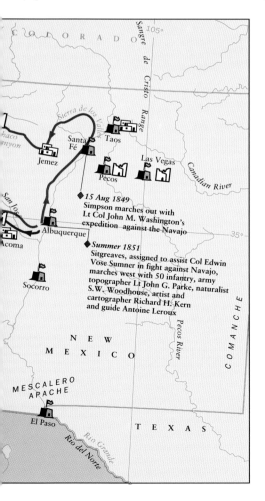

15 Aug 1849
Simpson marches out with Lt Col John M. Washington's expedition against the Navajo

Summer 1851
Sitgreaves, assigned to assist Col Edwin Vose Sumner in fight against Navajo, marches west with 50 infantry, army topographer Lt John G. Parke, naturalist S.W. Woodhouse, artist and cartographer Richard H. Kern and guide Antoine Leroux

Right: View of a ruined and ancient pueblo, spectacularly situated beneath an overhanging rock in the Canyon de Chelly. This lithograph, which was widely distributed in the mid-19th century, is based on a drawing made in September 1849 by Richard Kern, the expedition's artist and cartographer. Kern accompanied both Simpson and Sitgreaves and had previously accompanied Frémont on his ill-fated 1848 railroad survey (▶ page 158).

Grand Canyon Country

THE SURVEYS OF IVES AND MACOMB, 1857-59

The US Army, anticipating a war with the Mormons, sends its first expeditions into the Grand Canyon, in search of new supply routes into the Great Basin.

Left: Originally sent to America by the Prussian geographer Alexander von Humboldt, Heinrich Balduin Möllhausen accompanied Ives into the Grand Canyon. With Egloffstein he produced the first popular lithographs of its spectacular landforms.

Late in 1857 a topographical engineer, First Lieutenant Joseph Christmas Ives, was sent up the Colorado River to look for a water route to the Great Basin. His party included geologist, Dr John Strong Newberry, topographer, F.W. von Egloffstein, and the artist, Balduin Möllhausen.

On 1 November, at Robinson's Landing, they unloaded the prefabricated metal parts of the paddle steamer USS *Explorer*, which they assembled watched by the crews of other steamers and Cocopa Indians. On 22 December word arrived that the Mormon war had begun. Ives was ordered to assess rapidly the navigability of the Colorado. Ives' pilot, Captain D.C. Robinson, arrived a week later and that night the *Explorer* was launched.

On 8 January they entered Black Canyon, the first of the Colorado's gigantic chasms. When the *Explorer* struck a submerged rock, Ives declared they had reached the Colorado's head of navigation. With two others Ives explored the canyon in a skiff, rowing as far upriver as the Las Vegas Wash. Meantime Mormon spies attempted to persuade the area's Mohave and Paiute to attack Ives' men. This was averted by gifts and diplomacy.

Ives sent half his men back down the river on the *Explorer*. He himself left the river to search for the Mormon Road with Newberry, Egloffstein, Möllhausen, Lieutenant Tipton

and 20 soldiers. Two Hualpais guides led the party to the Grand Canyon. In April they reached its floor, near the mouth of Diamond Creek – probably the first white men to enter the canyon. Deserted by the guides, they spent two days exploring the canyon. They followed an Indian trail that led over ledges so narrow that some had to crawl along them. They finally clambered up out of the canyon onto the south rim of the Colorado Plateau.

Early in May, at the Little Colorado River, Ives split up his remaining men again, sending the supply train directly to Fort Defiance. Ives, Newberry, Egloffstein and a few others crossed the Little Colorado in boats made of canvas stretched over wooden frames. They then marched northeast across the Painted Desert to the Hopi pueblos, a peaceful community built on three sacred mesas. Despite warnings from the Hopi, they headed north hoping to reach the Colorado River again. But the desert proved too harsh and they retreated back to the pueblos. The next time they marched east. Although an increasing number of hostile Navajo trailed their party daily, on 23 May they reached Fort Defiance without incident.

Newberry was the first geologist to see the Colorado River's mile-deep canyon and his study of its geological strata greatly expanded knowledge of the formation of the whole

> Like the grand canyons of the Colorado, the broad valleys, bounded by high and perpendicular walls belong to a vast system of erosion, and are wholly due to the action of water. Probably nowhere in the world has the action of this agent produced results so surprising both as regards their magnitude and their peculiar character. It is not at all strange that a cause, which has given to what was once immense plain, underlaid by thousands of feet of sedimentary rocks, conformable throughout, a topographical character more complicated than that of any mountain chain; which has made much of it absolutely impassable to man, or to any animal but the winged bird, should be regarded as something out of the course of nature... the outlines of the western part of the North American continent were approximately marked out by areas of shallower water in an almost boundless ocean, but by groups of islands and broad continental surfaces of dry land.
>
> **John Strong Newberry on the formation of the Grand Canyon**

continent. Egloffstein invented a map-making technique, still used today, for representing physical features in sculptured relief. Ives' own expedition report was a masterpiece, combining the characteristics of a scientific paper and romantic literature.

Two years later, in 1859, another topographical engineer Captain John M. Macomb led a party into the Colorado River system. Newberry was also part of the expedition. After traveling up the Chama River he crossed the headwaters of the San Juan River and then headed west, exploring Indian ruins in the shadow of Mesa Verde. After a difficult march across the sage plain, Macomb's party became the first white men to view the intricate canyon country around the junction of the Green and Grand rivers. Newberry not only found the first dinosaur bones of the far West, he also devised an early geological concept of the entire plateau .

Great Salt Lake

Salt Lake City

Camp Floyd

Old Spanish Trail

Ives sends *Explorer* downriver
and sets off overland with
half of expedition. Hualpais
lead them to the Grand
Canyon floor

Sevier Lake

Fillmore

Late August
Macomb party first people of
European descent to
see junction of Green and Grand rivers

Macomb finds first dinosaur
skeleton in the West at
Colorado Pintado

Explorer enters canyon, and
hits submerged rock. Ives makes
camp, declaring it the furthest
navigable point

Parowan

Cedar
City

St George

Ives and his men climb back
up onto plateau and
make second descent
into canyon

Macomb's men
see Hovenweap
ruins

Macomb party discovers
ancient ruins

Ives, Captain Robinson and ship's
mate paddle skiff to Las Vegas
Wash, which Ives mistakes
for Virgen River

Zion
Canyon

San Juan River

Mesa
Verde

The Wash

Las Vegas

WALAPAI

Black Canyon

Grand Canyon

San Francisco
Mountain

11 May
Ives reaches
pueblos

HOPI

Hopi
Pueblos

NAVAJO

San Juan River

Jemez

Chama River

Taos

Las Vegas

Santa Fé

Pecos
River

25 Apr
Make camp

Flagstaff

Ives fends off Mormon-incited
attack by Mohave and Paiute

Mormon Road

Mohave
Village

Ives party met
by Mohave

Mohave River

Fort Defiance

23 May
Ives finally reaches fort

Albuquerque

1 July 1859
Macomb marches
out for Utah with
Newberry, 4 assistants
and an army detachment

MOHAVE

9 Jan 1858
Ives meets rest of party,
including groups headed
by geologist Newberry and
army engineer Taylor
11 Jan
Embark, only to run
aground almost
immediately

Colorado River

Ives divides expedition
again, leading half northeast
whilst Tipton goes southeast
to Fort Defiance

WESTERN
APACHE

Socorro

NEW

ARIZONA

Phoenix

Gila River

MEXICO

Gila River

Rio Grande

Robinson's
Landing

Fort Yuma

Tucson

El Paso

29 Nov 1857
Having sailed from San Francisco
aboard *Monterey*, Ives and his men unload
steamboat parts and build *Explorer*

BAJA
CALIFORNIA
NORTE

US. Mexican border from 1853

Ciudad Juarez

CHIHUAHUA

SONORA

MEXICO

Gulf of California

The Surveys of Ives and Macomb, 1857-59

US fort	Indian village
Mormon settlement	Pueblo
Ives, 1857-58	Ruin
Macomb, 1859	Expedition camp
Trail	Encounter with Indians
	Skirmish

The Search for an Iron Trail

THE GREAT RAILROAD SURVEYS, 1853-55

The American government spends over $1 million in search of the best railroad route to the Pacific coast. Cities along the Mississippi compete to be its eastern terminus.

The Great Pacific Railroad Surveys were set up to find "the most economical and practicable" route to the Pacific coast. Giant railroad conventions were held in St Louis, Memphis and New Orleans and after the Pacific Railroad Survey Bill in 1853, expeditions were sent out on three routes west.

The Atlantic and Pacific Railroad Company proposed a railroad west from Vicksburg, along the 32nd parallel. This "southern route" was favored by Secretary of War Jefferson Davis (later president of the Confederate states) since it would spread slavery and enable the South to dominate Congress. Senator Stephen Douglas of Illinois, an investor in the Illinois Central Railroad, favored a northerly route from Lake Superior, Chicago or Cairo, Illinois. Representative J.S. Phelps of Missouri held out for a route west from Springfield, the state capital. Others, from Hannibal and St Joseph, Missouri, favored the Oregon Trail.

Isaac I. Stevens, the new governor of Washington Territory and a former topographical engineer, explored between the 47th and 49th parallels. Lieutenant John W. Gunnison led an expedition along the 38th parallel. Gunnison and his men were killed by Ute. Lieutenant E.G. Beckwith took over and found a route over the Sierras, but his proposal was largely ignored. Lieutenant Amiel Weeks Whipple led a party west along the 35th parallel. When Congress insisted on a "southern" expedition the route was split in two. Lieutenant John G. Parke explored from San Diego to the Rio Grande; Captain John Pope from there to the Pacific. Lieutenant R.S. Williamson headed south from San Francisco and found five passes through the Sierras. He then explored northward to the Columbia with Lieutenant Henry L. Abbott.

The surveys produced a political stalemate. Ironically, Beckwith's route was the most suitable. But it had to be rediscovered by professional railroad men before northern capitalists were able to push through "the Great Central Route." Likewise it was not until a professional engineer investigated "Doc" Strong's route that the Central Pacific Railroad was formed in 1861.

The Captain's mule turned with him and plunged down the hill; and having been carried about two hundred yards, he fell from the animal, dead. The guide dismounted and prepared to fire, but finding he could not aim his rifle he succeeded in remounting and retiring down the hill. He died the next morning. The party was thrown into confusion and retreated at once... Cave died before reaching the valley, while Barling... has nearly recovered.

Lieutenant R.S. Williamson on the killing of Captain W.H. Warner in an ambush by Pit River Indians

The Great Pacific Railroad Surveys, 1853-55

Goldfields Survey, 1849

Warner and Williamson, 1849

Stevens, 1853

Gunnison and Beckwith, 1853

Williamson and Parke, 1853

Whipple, 1853

Parke, 1854

Pope, 1854

Williamson and Abbott, 1855

Proposed railroad starting

Proposed railroad destination

US fort

Pueblo

Pass

Goldfields

Massacre

Indian village

Stevens sends small parties of men off on side excursions to cover as much ground as possible. Party reunites at Fort Union

6 June 1853 Stevens leads party to find transcontinental railroad route between 47th and 49th parallels

23 June 1853 Gunnison sets out to find railroad route between 38th and 39th parallels

14 July 1853 Whipple leads party to explore the 35th parallel

Whipple's group meets Ives's party, which has orders to accompany them to California

Pope declares that a railroad can easily be built across Guadalupe Mountains and the Llano Estacado if artesian wells are sunk at strategic points.

A Topographic Romance

ARTISTS AND SCIENTISTS OF THE GREAT PACIFIC RAILROAD SURVEYS

As the cartographers of the Railroad Surveys map the American West, scientists unveil its topography and their artist colleagues record its visual splendors.

The expeditions of the Great Pacific Railroad Surveys were economically and politically inspired, but they conducted a great reconnaissance of the West. The survey reports filled 13 massive volumes, including an entire volume of maps, panoramas and pictures.

Among these was the first accurate, detailed map of the whole trans-Mississippi West, a great scientific achievement by 27 year old Lieutenant G. K. Warren. One of the important maps of American history, it was a careful composite of the numerous expedition route maps and field notes, as well as previous works by Emory and Preuss. The volume also

included three geological maps. One was by Swiss geologist Jules Marcou, who accompanied Lieutenant Amiel Weeks Whipple on the difficult route between Albuquerque and Los Angeles. A second map by W. P. Blake controverted Marcou's findings. The third geological map, by James Hall of the New York State History Survey, the "dean" of American paleontologists, was based on the work of John Strong Newberry in the Grand Canyon, of F.V. Hayden and Fielding B. Meek, as well as many other topographical engineer expeditions of the period.

Perhaps the most spectacular results of the

Railroad Surveys were the hundreds of drawings, paintings, lithographs, engravings and fold-out panoramas produced by the field artists. Highly romantic in manner, they offered the first comprehensive picture of the West. The best were by F.W. von Eggloffstein, John Mix Stanley and Gustavus Sohon, but many others joined the surveys.

The artist-naturalist Heinrich Balduin von Möllhausen had been a protegé of the great German geographer Alexander von Humboldt. In 1853 Möllhausen was also part of Whipple's expedition. Five years later he and Eggloffstein were recruited by Lieutenant

U. S. P. R. R. EXP. & SURVEYS — 47TH & 49TH PARALLELS

Stanley, Del. after Sohon.

Dearborn River   Cadotte's Pass.

MAIN CHAIN OF THE ROCKY MOUNTAINS, AS SEEN FROM THE EAST. — EXTENDING

Joseph Christmas Ives to record his venture into the Grand Canyon (▶ *page 164*). On his return to Germany, Möllhausen wrote many novels based on his American experiences, and would walk around Potsdam dressed as a mountain man.

Artists were by no means immune to the dangers experienced by the other surveyors. Richard H. Kern, a member of the Academy of Natural Sciences in Philadelphia, survived Frémont's disastrous 1848 expedition (▶ *page 158*) and his journey with Simpson and Sitgreaves into the Canyon de Chelly, where he painted the ancient pueblo (▶ *page 162*). But

he was killed by Ute Indians when on Gunnison's 1853 railroad survey – along with Gunnison, botanist Frederick Creuzefeld and five other expedition members.

Extraordinary scientific drawings by

Below: This panorama of "The Main Chain of the Rocky Mountains, As Seen From the East," combines the work of two of the most gifted artists to work on the railroad surveys. The three-panel, hand-colored foldout lithograph was engraved by John Mix Stanley after a drawing by Gustavus Sohon. It first appeared in Governor Isaac Stevens's General Report (1854).

Both men accompanied Stevens on his 1853 survey, which set out from St Paul, Minnesota with orders to find a transcontinental route between the 47th and

geologists, botanists, zoologists and amateur ethnologists portrayed the thousands of specimens they brought back with them. Their work is also part of the achievement of the Great Pacific Railroad Surveys.

49th parallels. Stevens thought Cadotte's Pass would provide the most viable route, and along with the Marias Pass, it is clearly labeled on the panorama.

Sohon and Stanley could not have seen all the topographical detail they included from any one point. The view is a composite one, put together from a number of sketches, to form a kind of three-dimensional map. This European technique was introduced to the survey by Sohon and brought to perfection by Egloffstein.

GENERAL REPORT — PLATE LII

Sarony, Major & Knapp, Lith⁵ 449 Broadway NY

Marias Pass

A POINT NORTH OF THE MARIAS PASS TO NEAR THE LITTLE BLACKFOOT PASS

Adventures on the 40th Parallel

THE SURVEYS OF KING AND WHEELER, 1867-73

*Clarence King, a brilliant young scientist,
surveys a vast tract of the American West,
Lieutenant George M. Wheeler develops
mapping techniques still in use today.*

In 1867 Clarence King, at 25 years old the darling of the scientific establishment, was appointed head of the Geological and Geographical Exploration of the 40th Parallel. With a party of hand-picked civilian scientists, he studied the alkali deserts and rugged mountains of western Nevada. His first season was hard and adventurous and many of his men came down with malaria. High up a peak, King's theodolite was struck by lightning. His right arm and side turned brown for three days.

Left: A keen climber and mountaineer, Clarence King used these skills when exploring the geology of the 40th Parallel in 1867, surveying over 100 miles in ten years. He also exposed a diamond hoax in 1872. In an attempt to con investors, two men had claimed to have found diamonds in a mesa in Colorado. They had in fact secretly "salted" the field with precious stones beforehand. King's exposure of the hoax saved not only the San Francisco Stock Exchange, but thousands of potential investors. He became the toast of San Francisco, and nationally was applauded as a "cool headed man of scientific education."

That winter King studied Virginia City's Comstock Lode and explored the mine shafts and tunnels of Mount Davidson. Timothy O'Sullivan, perhaps the West's greatest photographer, took the first pictures ever taken down a mine, and King's topographers drew detailed maps, at two miles to the inch.

During winter 1868 James D. Hague began a study of Colorado's silver mines while the main party surveyed the Great Basin. King realized that it was really composed of two ancient glacier-fed lakes, Lake Bonneville and Lake Lahonton, separated by a high mountain-studded plateau.

In 1869-70 King covered the area between the Salt Lake and the Green River, studied the mountains of the Pacific Coast and discovered a glacier at the foot of Mount Shasta, the first located in the USA. Over the next years King extended his survey east to the Front Range of the Rockies, worked the length of the parallel again, and completed his study of the Great Basin's geology.

Although King insisted that geologic change was caused by sudden catastrophes, his survey was perhaps the most sophisticated of his day. He saw to the publication of Arnold Hague's classic work, *The Mining Industry*, in 1870 and uncovered a major diamond hoax in 1872. In 1879 he was made director of the newly-created United States Geological Survey.

Lieutenant George M. Wheeler worked for the United States Geographical Surveys West of the 100th Meridian. Despite grueling experiences Wheeler never matched the flamboyant King. He and his men, including Timothy O'Sullivan who took stark and extraordinary landscape photographs, surveyed and mapped the West beyond the 100th meridian. Although falsely denied by John Wesley Powell and James Terry Gardner, Hayden's cartographer, Wheeler produced the earliest contour maps of the area.

Wheeler's parties explored and re-surveyed in California, Nevada, Utah, Colorado, Idaho, Wyoming, Montana, Nebraska and New Mexico. In 1879 Congress made Wheeler's survey part of the US Geological Survey. Wheeler's quadrant system was later adapted by Powell and remains central to the mapping of the Survey today.

The Surveys of King and Wheeler, 1867-73

▭ Area surveyed by King, 1867-73

▭ Area surveyed by Wheeler, 1867-72

▮ US fort

⛺ Base camp

📕 Expedition winters

☁ Explorer struck by lightning

↘ Mines

◣ Hoax gem strike

🛶 Boat capsizes

▪ Rescue

The route lay for more than 39 miles in light, white, drifting sand, which was traversed between 5 am and 6 pm, the center of the desert being reached about meridian. The stifling heat, great radiation, and constant glare from the sand were almost overpowering, and two of the command succumbed near nightfall, rendering it necessary to pack one man on the back of a mule to the first divide on the route, where a grass sward was reached at the end of the long sandy stretch, while the second, an old and tried mountaineer, became unconscious for more than an hour in nearly the same locality.

Lieutenant George M. Wheeler describes Death Valley

1870
King turns to study of volcanoes of the Pacific Northwest. Climbing Mount Shasta, first to discover active glacier in USA

3 May 1871
Wheeler launches survey, sending out 30 men, including two lieutenants, army surgeon, photographer, geologists and newspaper reporter. Split up to reconnoiter area around Nevada's rich mining districts

1871
King's men work out of fort, surveying country between Green and Front Range of Rockies

King struck by lightning while using his theodolite in a storm. Expedition had fanned out to survey Virginia City, Truckee and Hot Springs Mountains, and Pyramid Lake; in great heat, most get malaria and are sent to Unionville

Nov 1872
King makes way to peak just north of Brown's Hole, site of supposed gem strike, and exposes "Great Diamond Hoax"

1868
King and party continue survey from Great Basin to Great Salt Lake

Late 1867
King sends most of his men to winter in Carson City, and holes up in Virginia City with the geologist, Gardner, and O'Sullivan, studying Comstock Lode silver mines

King crawls into a cave after a grizzly bear

Fall 1871
King meets Henry Adams, soon his staunchest supporter

Spring 1869
King establishes new base camp and sends men out to work through Wasatch and Uinta Mountains and along Green River Divide

Summer 1873
One of Wheeler's survey parties, working from Denver, meets party from the Hayden survey (▶ page 178). Surveys overlap throughout summer to ire of Congress

July 1871
Wheeler leads group into valley, where they suffer sunstroke, lack of water and up to 120°F

11 Oct 1871
Wheeler loses one boat in rapids, with rations, journals, scientific instruments and collections

18 Oct 1871
Wheeler and his men finally reach mouth of creek, and meet rescue party

17 July 1867
Cavalry escort arrives and meet King and his team of topographers, geologists, a botanist, an ornithologist and a photographer at base camp

16 Sept 1871
Wheeler leads group including 14 Mohave to look for head of navigation of Colorado

OREGON
MONTANA
IDAHO
SOUTH DAKOTA
NEBRASKA
NEVADA
UTAH
COLORADO
KANSAS
CALIFORNIA
ARIZONA
NEW MEXICO
TEXAS
UNORGANIZED TERRITORY

Mount Shasta
NORTHERN PAIUTE
Truckee Mountains
Comstock Lode
Virginia City
Carson City
Glendale
Halleck Station
Great Salt Lake
Salt Lake City
WESTERN SHOSHONE
Stillwater Range
Sevier Lake
Wasatch Mountains
Green River
Uintah Mountains
UTE
Fort Bridger
Brown's Hole
Diamond Peak
SOUTHERN CHEYENNE
ARAPAHO
ARAPAHO
Santa Catalina Mountains
JICARILLA APACHE
Coast Range
Sierra Nevada
Death Valley
PAIUTE
Las Vegas
Shivwits Plateau
Grand Canyon
Great Basin
Canyon de Chelly
Chaco Canyon
Chuska Mountains
Canyon Bonito
Taos
Santa Fe
Pecos
Canadian River
Santa Barbara
Mohave Desert
Los Angeles
San Joaquin River
San Francisco Mountains
Painted Desert
Flagstaff
Little Colorado River
Puerco River
Zuni River
NAVAJO
Rio San Jose
Albuquerque
San Diego
YUMA
MARICOPA
COCOPA
Yuma
PAPAGO
Colorado River
UNITED
Phoenix
WESTERN APACHE
Socorro
Valverde
MESCALERO APACHE
Tucson
San Pedro River
Gila River
CHIRICAHUA APACHE
El Paso
Pecos River
Sierra Madre Occidental
Rio Grande
Baja California
Gulf of California
MEXICO
LIPAN APACHE
Pacific Ocean

The Mysterious Colorado

THE SURVEYS OF JOHN WESLEY POWELL, 1869-78

John Wesley Powell leads a Smithsonian expedition down the Colorado River into the Grand Canyon. He then directs a vast survey of this last unknown area of the West.

In May 1869 Major John Wesley Powell set off down the unknown Colorado River, from Green River City, Wyoming. He led a party of nine men: Powell's brother, Walter, Oramel and Seneca Howland, Bill Dunn, George Bradley, Jack Sumner, Billy Rhodes Hawkins, Andrew Hall and Frank Goodman. There was no scientist in the group, though Powell was a self-taught natural historian.

In four small boats Powell's men plunged

through dramatic canyons and braved stupendous rapids. One boat was lost early on, in a treacherous fall on the Green River, when Oramel Howland failed to see a warning signal from Powell. Later, the one-armed Powell fell from a cliff and had to cling on until he was saved by George Bradley, using his longjohns as a rope. By the end of August the party ran desperately short of rations. Finding themselves faced with the treacherous waters that would become known as Separation Rapids, the Howland brothers and Bill Dunn decided that they had had enough. They climbed out of the canyon and onto the Shivwits Plateau, where they were felled by the arrows of Shivwit Indians. The rest of the party successfully ran the remainder of the canyon and returned to a heroes' welcome.

Powell immediately began to prepare for a second trip, for which he received a federal appropriation and the position of Director of the Geographical and Topographical Survey of the Colorado River. He set out in 1871, and the following year sent a party north beyond the canyon, where they discovered the Escalante, the last unknown river in the United States, and the Henry Mountains, the last unknown range.

Powell developed an interest in the languages of the region, becoming fluent in many of them and compiling over 200 vocabularies. In 1873 Powell was appointed special Indian commissioner by the federal government. He made many proposals about ways of establishing a workable and humane reservation system. In 1874 Captain Clarence Dutton joined the survey staff (▶ *page 174*). In 1879, Powell founded the Bureau of Ethnology, for the study of Indian culture.

Powell's *Report on the Arid Regions of the United States*, published in 1878, advocated the setting up of irrigation co-operatives and the regulation of grazing and farming. His radical ideas were never implemented because of the vested interests of land speculators, water monopolists and cattle ranchers, large and small.

Left: A photograph of Powell in the Grand Canyon with a Paiute Indian, taken by Jack K. Hillers on the 1873 survey. Formerly a teamster, Hillers was originally employed by Powell as a general laborer and boatman, becoming expedition photographer during the second part of Powell's river journey.

The Surveys of John Wesley Powell, 1869-78

- Powell, 1869
- Thompson, 1872
- Expedition camp
- Boat wrecked
- Massacre
- Ruins
- Rapids

WYOMING
Leucite Hills

Great Salt Lake

Green River

Green River

Flaming Gorge

ARAPAHO

Salt Lake City

Uintah Mountains

Badland Cliffs

Provo

24 May 1869
Powell heads for the Colorado and Grand Canyon with 9 men, but no scientists, in 4 small boats

Powell's men briefly leave river to trek up Uintah to Ute Indian Agency, purchase supplies and send their first mail. English sportsman Frank Goodman leaves party

7 June
Oramel Howland, piloting the *No Name* through the canyon, does not see Powell's signal that a treacherous fall lies ahead, is swept along through the rapids and the *No Name* breaks up on an enormous boulder. All 4 passengers rescued, and next day retrieve its precious cargo of whisky and barometers

Lodore Canyon

Sevier Lake

Fillmore

UTAH E
UTE

Almon H. Thompson, Powell's second in-command, and party retrace route from Dirty Devil to Kanab
1872

Powell's men discover Escalante River and Henry Mountains, the last unknown river and range in the US

Green River

Tavaputs Plateau

Grand River

La Sal Mountains

COLORADO

UTE

UNITED STATES

28 August
Party running short of rations. Facing more rapids, Howland brothers and Bill Dunn leave party to climb canyon walls onto plateau, where they are killed by Shivwit Indians

NEVADA

Aquarius Plateau

Henry Mountains

Circle Cliffs

Escalante River

Dirty Devil River

17-21 July
Party makes camp. Powell explores surrounding high land whilst his men caulk their boats and fashion new oars

Bill Dunn names this river the Dirty Devil because it stinks of sulphur

Mancos River

San Juan River

Monument Valley

Kanab

SOUTHERN PAIUTE

Kanab Plateau

Virgin River

Zion Canyon

Las Vegas

CALIFORNIA

Callville

Separation Rapids

Shewits Plateau

Grand Canyon

Aquarius Mountains

Gerbat Mountains

Black Canyon

Kaibab Plateau

Paria Plateau

Paria River

Navajo Mountain

Painted Desert

Bright Angel Creek

Hopi Sacred Mesas

Little Colorado River

13 Aug
Party heads into Grand Canyon. They line their boats against particularly dangerous waters, braving succession of rapids

17 Aug
Find Native American artifacts and ruins at Bright Angel Creek

29 Aug
Powell and remaining men emerge from Grand Canyon and reach Callville

Flagstaff

Colorado River

Mojave Camp

YUMA

ARIZONA

Phoenix

Gila River

Gila Desert

Gila River

San Pedro River

Gila River

MEXICO

Tucson

Gulf of California

> We are now ready to start on our way down the Great Unknown. Our boats, tied to a common stake, are chafing each other, as they are tossed by the fretful river. They ride high and buoyant, for their loads are lighter than we could desire. We have but a month's rations remaining... We are three quarters of a mile in the depths of the earth, and the great river shrinks into insignificance as it dashes its angry waves against the walls and cliffs that rise to the world above...
>
> We have an unknown distance yet to run; an unknown river yet to explore. What falls there are, we know not; what rocks beset the channel, we know not; what walls rise over the river, we know not. Ah well! we may conjecture many things. The men talk as cheerfully as ever; jests are bandied about freely this morning; but to me the cheer is somber and the jests are ghastly.
>
> John Wesley Powell's diary, 13 August 1869

Into the Grand Canyon

CLARENCE E. DUTTON AND WILLIAM H. HOLMES, 1874-82

Dutton and Holmes create an unparalleled record of the spectacular landscape of the Grand Canyon.

Captain Clarence Dutton was a Yale-educated scientist. After serving in the US army in the Civil War, he was assigned to a quiet posting in upstate New York. This gave him the leisure to develop his scientific interests, and he began to correspond with James Hall, the paleontologist and geologist. By 1871, the army had reassigned Dutton to Washington. At the meetings of the Washington Philosophical Society, he met many of the most influential American scientists of the day, including Major John Wesley Powell (▶ *page 172*), who offered him a position on his Survey of the Colorado River in 1874.

In a sense, Dutton's ideas concerning geomorphology were a development of Powell's, but he added a romantic aura and a heightened literary style to Powell's thinking. Among his published works are *The High Plateaus of Utah* (1880) and *The Tertiary History of the Grand Cañon District* (1882), in which he presented his work of 1879 for the United States Geological Survey.

The immense power of the erosion that had created the high plateaus of Utah had been discovered by Dutton's colleague William H. Holmes. A veteran of Hayden's Yellowstone and Colorado surveys (▶ *pages 176–79*), Holmes joined Powell's staff in 1879. He was both an artist and a geologist, and his understanding of the underlying forms of the landscape enabled him to raise topographic art to its highest level. His unique panoramas remain the most accurate visual renditions of the Grand Canyon ever produced.

Clarence Dutton's dramatic word pictures ensured that his meticulous scientific observations were more vivid than those of any geologist of the 19th century, except perhaps his mentor, John Wesley Powell himself. Dutton's romanticism was revealed in the names he gave to the canyon's prominent features. Vishnu's Temple, for example, reflects the orientalism fashionable in the late 19th century, while American Indian names such as Kaibab Plateau and Toroweays Fault reflect Powell's ethnographic interests.

As Powell and Dutton, together with Grove Karl Gilbert, roamed over and probed the canyon country, they not only developed new skills and knowledge, they came to represent a new kind of explorer. In *The Tertiary History of the Grand Cañon District*, Dutton takes the reader on an exploring expedition over the whole of the canyon country showing how the arid lands of the West had at one time been a vast inland sea punctuated by volcanoes, fracturing and fire. Together with the work of Powell, Dutton's analysis created much of the bases for an understanding of the geological history of the continent.

As the sun draws near the horizon, the great drama of the day begins. Throughout the afternoon the prospect has been gradually growing clearer. The haze has relaxed its steely glare and has changed to a veil of transparent blue. Slowly the myriads of details have come out and the walls are flecked with lines of minute tracery, forming a diaper of light and shade... The promontories come forth from the opposite wall. The sinuous lines of stratification which once seemed meaningless, distorted, and even chaotic, now range themselves into a true perspective of graceful curves, threading the scallop edges of the strata...All things seem to grow in beauty, power, and dimensions. What was grand before has become majestic, the majestic becomes sublime, and, ever expanding and developing, the sublime passes beyond the reach of our faculties and becomes transcendent. The colors have come back. Inherently rich and strong, though not superlative under ordinary lights, they now begin to display an adventitious brilliancy. The western sky is all aflame. The scattered banks of cloud and wavy cirrhus have caught the waning splendor, and shine with orange and crimson. Broad slant beams of yellow light, shot through the glory-rifts, fall on turret and tower, on pinnacled crest and winding ledge, suffusing them with a radiance less fulsome, but akin to that which flames in the western clouds. The summit band is brilliant yellow; the next below is pale rose. But the grand expanse within is a deep, luminous, resplendent red. The climax has now come. The blaze of sunlight poured over an illimitable surface of glowing red is flung back into the gulf, and commingling with the blue haze, turns it into a sea of purple of most imperial hue – so rich, so strong, so pure that it makes the heart ache and the throat tighten. However vast the magnitudes, however majestic the forms, or sumptuous the decoration, it is in these kingly colors that the highest glory of the Grand Cañon is revealed.

Clarence E. Dutton describes Point Sublime in
The Tertiary History of the Grand Cañon District,
1882

Left: This panorama, shown in three panels, depicts the Kaibab division of the Grand Canyon, seen from Point Sublime.

Created by William H. Holmes, it was one of many published in Clarence Dutton's The Tertiary History of the Grand Cañon District, *1882.*

To draw these panoramas, Holmes spent hour after hour in the blazing sun of the canyon rim, squinting into a camera lucida. This device uses a prism to reflect the objects in front of it, in such a way that they appear to lie on the artist's paper. They can then be traced to a high level of accuracy.

Holmes managed to convey, like no other artist, the vast, scenic magnificence of the Grand Canyon in all its topographical and geological complexity.

Yellowstone's Grand Drama

EXPLORERS OF THE YELLOWSTONE, 1869-71

The marvels of Yellowstone are greeted with huge public enthusiasm. The army explores the area, and in a spectacular journey Hayden discovers the Upper Geyser Basin.

After John Colter's discovery of Yellowstone in 1808 (▶ *page 146*), trappers explored parts of the region. But it was yet to be examined by a scientific explorer and in the mid-1860s, the area was still blank on maps. There was a rumor in 1863 that Captain W.W. DeLacy entered what is now the park. But the army's western divisions sent no expedition, despite the clamor of the residents of Virginia City, Helena and Bozeman, Montana. So in summer 1869 three civilians, David E. Folsom, C.W. Cook and a ranch hand named Peterson, set off from Helena to prospect in Yellowstone. At first they remained closed-mouth on the marvels they had seen but in 1870, Folsom sold their story to the Western Monthly Magazine.

Public enthusiasm then ran so high that the army agreed that Lieutenant Gustavus C. Doane and five soldiers should explore the area, with a civilian party led by Nathaniel P. Langford and Montana's surveyor general, General Henry D. Washburn. They reached what is now the park, just west of the Absaroka Mountain, domain of the Crow Indians. A few Crow followed them closely but did not interfere. Once in the Yellowstone they found the wild beauties of the lake, thermal springs, lava flows and steam jets. They reached and named most of the great geysers including "Old Faithful." All except one was convinced that Yellowstone should never serve the purposes of any one individual. It should be a national park.

Two parties explored Yellowstone the following summer. On 11 July Ferdinand V. Hayden, head of the Interior Department's Geographical Surveys of the Territories West of the 100th Meridian, led a group from Ogden, Utah. At Fort Ellis, north of the park area, they found army Captain J.W. Barlow also preparing to lead a party to the headwaters of the Yellowstone.

On 15 July Hayden left Fort Ellis. When Barlow left a day later, he generally followed the route taken by Washburn and Doane. But by traveling south from Yellowstone Lake toward the Upper Snake River, he broke new ground and discovered Heart Lake. Hayden's reconnaissance was more spectacular. From Boettler's Ranch, they marched past the iron-red Cinnabar Mountain and the Devil's Slide and reached Mammoth Hot Springs. After exploring the ravines of Tower Creek, they ascended Mount Washburn, to view the Yellowstone basin and the Tetons. Down in the basin Thomas Moran made dozens of sketches of the Grand Canyon of the Yellowstone, which resulted in his greatest work. W.H. Jackson photographed the Grand Canyon along with Mammoth Hot Springs and the geyser basins. In August Hayden, leading three other men, headed northwest and discovered Upper Geyser Basin.

On his return Hayden joined up with Northern Pacific Railroad interests and lobbied in Washington for the establishment of Yellowstone National Park. N.P. Langford did so too, becoming known as "National Park" Langford.

Left: "The Great Blue Spring, Lower Geyser Basin of the Yellowstone," by Thomas Moran (1876). On settling in the US, the English born artist Moran had decided to "paint as an American, on an American basis." Accompanying Hayden into the Yellowstone, he and photographer William H. Jackson recorded the bizarre and breathtaking topography for an incredulous public.

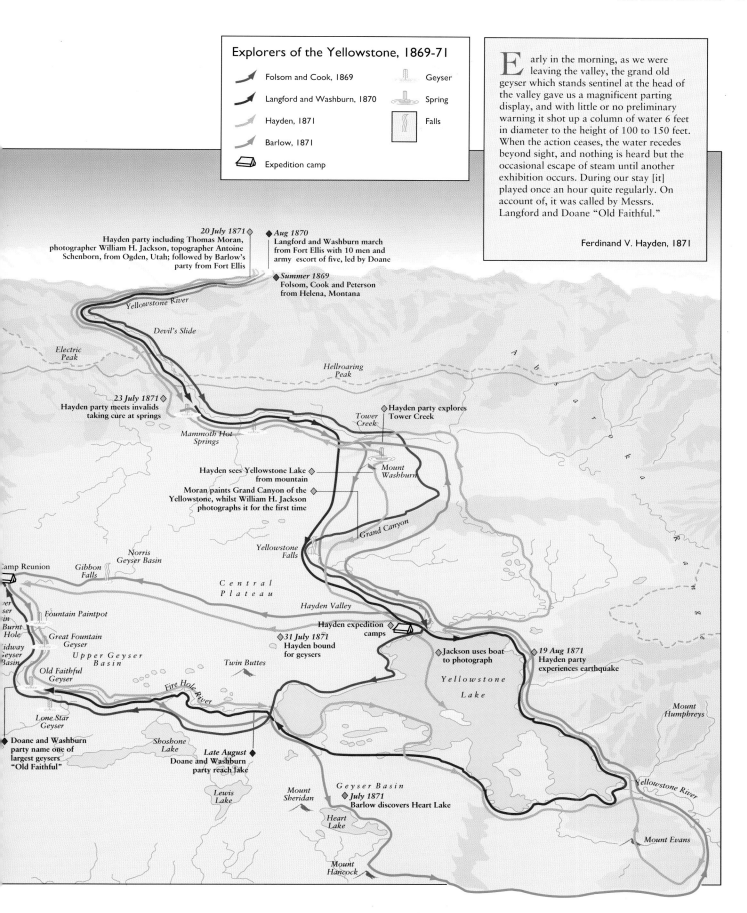

Explorers of the Yellowstone, 1869-71

- Folsom and Cook, 1869
- Langford and Washburn, 1870
- Hayden, 1871
- Barlow, 1871
- Expedition camp
- Geyser
- Spring
- Falls

Early in the morning, as we were leaving the valley, the grand old geyser which stands sentinel at the head of the valley gave us a magnificent parting display, and with little or no preliminary warning it shot up a column of water 6 feet in diameter to the height of 100 to 150 feet. When the action ceases, the water recedes beyond sight, and nothing is heard but the occasional escape of steam until another exhibition occurs. During our stay [it] played once an hour quite regularly. On account of, it was called by Messrs. Langford and Doane "Old Faithful."

Ferdinand V. Hayden, 1871

20 July 1871 Hayden party including Thomas Moran, photographer William H. Jackson, topographer Antoine Schenborn, from Ogden, Utah; followed by Barlow's party from Fort Ellis

Aug 1870 Langford and Washburn march from Fort Ellis with 10 men and army escort of five, led by Doane

Summer 1869 Folsom, Cook and Peterson from Helena, Montana

Yellowstone River

Devil's Slide

Electric Peak

Hellroaring Peak

23 July 1871 Hayden party meets invalids taking cure at springs

Mammoth Hot Springs

Tower Creek

Hayden party explores Tower Creek

Mount Washburn

Hayden sees Yellowstone Lake from mountain

Moran paints Grand Canyon of the Yellowstone, whilst William H. Jackson photographs it for the first time

Grand Canyon

Norris Geyser Basin

Gibbon Falls

Camp Reunion

Yellowstone Falls

Central Plateau

Hayden Valley

Fountain Paintpot

Burnt Hole

Great Fountain Geyser

Midway Geyser Basin

Upper Geyser Basin

Old Faithful Geyser

Twin Buttes

31 July 1871 Hayden bound for geysers

Hayden expedition camps

Jackson uses boat to photograph

19 Aug 1871 Hayden party experiences earthquake

Yellowstone Lake

Fire Hole River

Lone Star Geyser

Doane and Washburn party name one of largest geysers "Old Faithful"

Shoshone Lake

Late August Doane and Washburn party reach lake

Lewis Lake

Mount Sheridan

Geyser Basin

July 1871 Barlow discovers Heart Lake

Heart Lake

Mount Hancock

Mount Humphreys

Mount Evans

Yellowstone River

Colorado's Wonderlands

FERDINAND HAYDEN'S SURVEY, 1873-76

Hayden leads the Interior Department's Geological Survey of the Territories. He wins fame as an explorer but faces criticism as a scientist.

Ferdinand Vandiveer Hayden, in 1869 appointed survey director of the Interior Department's newly-formed United States Geological Survey of the Territories, considered his primary task was to publicize and promote the West to the American people.

In sponsoring Western exploration, the Interior Department, perhaps even more than the army, sought to open up new lands, in the first place for tourists and later for settlers. In doing so, two of its duties were to assess resources and classify land. In 1869 Hayden explored the mountains of Colorado and New Mexico from Denver to Santa Fe. In 1870 Hayden covered north-eastern Utah and southern Wyoming. He then spent two years in the Yellowstone. During the following years of the survey, 1869-78, he supervised large teams of men in the field.

Like Clarence King (▶ *page 170*) Hayden was a geologist who, as a surgeon during the Civil War, had served in the Union Army. Thirteen years older than King, Hayden came from a different generation of scientists. His training and influences were American rather than European. They came from John Strong Newberry, who made the first geological study of the Grand Canyon, and James Hall, paleontologist on the early 19th century New York Natural History Survey. Before the Civil War, Hayden had spent several years searching for fossils in the Dakotas, Montana and Wyoming, and he contributed substantially to American geology. With Fielding B. Meek he had assembled the first model of the Cretaceous horizon in the American West. After the war Hayden returned to the Dakotas searching for fossils. Then, in 1867, Hayden ran a federal government survey, county by county, of the resources of the new state of Nebraska. In 1868 he received an appropriation for an expedition to the Rocky Mountains of southern Wyoming.

Between 1873 and 1876, with James Gardner, formerly of the King survey, he led an exhaustive survey of Colorado. The painter Thomas Moran, topographer William H. Holmes and photographer William H. Jackson were important members of the survey. In 1873 Hayden, Jackson and a party discovered the Mount of the Holy Cross, a peak in western Colorado. Jackson's photographs of the snow-filled crevasses in the form of a crucifix proved enormously popular. In 1874 a party led by Jackson and Holmes discovered the ancient ruins of Mancos Canyon near Mesa Verde in Colorado.

Ferdinand V. Hayden gained considerable fame as an explorer through his work with the Survey of the Territories. Through the paintings of Thomas Moran, the photographs of William Henry Jackson, and the panoramas of William H. Holmes (▶ *page 174*), Hayden brought the wonders of the West to the American people.

However during the later years of the survey his work as a scientist came under fire, sometimes unfairly. Unlike Clarence King,

Left: Hayden's men surveying from the summit of Silverton Mountain, San Juan County, Colorado in 1874. The seated man sketching is probably the artist Holmes; the photograph is by the survey's photographer, W.H. Jackson.

Hayden's Colorado Survey, 1873-76

- Area surveyed by Hayden
- Mountain surveyed, 1873
- Mountain surveyed, 1874
- Ruins
- Confrontation
- Skirmish

WYOMING

NEBRASKA

SOUTHERN
CHEYENNE

Cheyenne

Greeley

ARAPAHO

40°

July 1873
Hayden, Jackson and other survey members discover Mount of the Holy Cross. The snow seems to form a giant crucifix

Berthoud's Pass

Long's Peak

Arapahoe Peak

The Squaw

Boulder

The Chief

Spring 1873
Hayden begins comprehensive survey. Assembles four topographic parties, photographic party led by Jackson, and topographical artist Holmes. Eventually he has eight parties working simultaneously

UTE

COLORADO

Mt Byers

Gray's Peak

Mt Powell

Mount of the Holy Cross

Mt Evans

Denver

Elk Mts

Snow Mass Mt

La Plata Mt

Mount Elbert

Twin Lakes

Pikes Peak

Colorado Springs

KANSAS

UTAH

Maroon Mt

Crested Butte

Mt Harvard

Mt Princeton

Mt Antoro

Summer 1873
One of Hayden's parties meets group from the Wheeler survey (▶ *page 170*)

Colorado River

Uncompahgre Peak

Mt Ouray

Mt Wilson

1875
Jackson and Holmes attacked by Ute; they escape a day later by clambering up deer trail to the Colorado Plateau. Jackson and party also attacked near Mancos Canyon

San Juan River

Mesa Verde

Mancos Canyon

Silverton Mt

JICARILLA APACHE

Arkansas River

Cimarron River

Sept 1874
Jackson's party discovers ruins and cliff dwellings

TEWA

OKLAHOMA

ARIZONA

Grand Canyon

NEW MEXICO

Santa Fe

Rio Grande

Canadian River

TEXAS

Amarillo

35°

110°

105°

UTE

Park Range

Dolores River

Gunnison River

Wasatch Mountains

Sangre de Cristo Mountains

Mancos River

San Juan River

---

who worked systematically through his data trying to arrive at synthesized theory, Hayden tended to publish data immediately, before fully interpreting it. After 1873, he published a *Bulletin* which included a wide variety of papers by many different scientists. Although in essence it was an important new scientific journal, it received stern criticism from academics who disliked Hayden. Yet he also published the final reports of other scientists which were often proved to be definitive works and major contributions to their respective fields.

Hayden gained fame bringing the Rocky Mountains and the Yellowstone to the attention of Americans. His map of the Yellowstone region which included a far larger tract than just the lake, the geyser basins, and the Grand Canyon. This influenced the US Congress to set aside a larger tract of the Yellowstone than they might have done, for preservation as the nation's first national park.

Just as the sun was sinking below the western walls of the cañon, one of the party descried far up the cliff what appeared to be a house with a square wall and apertures indicating two stories... The discovery... inspired us immediately... to scale the height and explore it... All hands started up, but only two persevered to the end... Up we hauled... boxes containing the camera and chemicals by... long ropes.

William H. Jackson, on his ascent to a Mancos Canyon cliff dwelling, Colorado, 1874

Part V : The Far North

By 1800, the outline of the North American continent had been explored and mapped; by the 1880s, most of the interior had been surveyed. One frontier remained: the far north. The challenge of this uniquely hostile environment was to tax the resources of governments and individuals of several nations until well into the 20th century.

Ever since John Cabot's 1497 voyage, the dream of a Northwest Passage had lured explorers to the high latitudes of the New World. By the end of the 18th century, this search, and the commercial activities of fur traders, had encompassed Lake Athabasca, Baffin Island and Hudson Bay. But much of the ice-bound wilderness of the Canadian north offered serious climatic impediments to conventional discovery and traditional European settlement.

In the first half of the 19th century, however, a series of remarkable explorers entered a territory larger than Western Europe and opened it to discovery and commerce. Naval expeditions under Ross and Parry made important discoveries in the Arctic archipelago, and John Franklin led two daring expeditions down the Coppermine and Mackenzie rivers to explore the Arctic coast. In the 1830s, George Back and Richard King set out from the Great Slave Lake down the Great Fish River, to find John Ross's naval expedition, which was missing in the Arctic.

Hudson's Bay Company agents also played a major part. In the east, Atkinson and Hendry explored the interior of the Labrador peninsula; to the north, Dease and Simpson charted missing portions of the Arctic coast; while in the west, Robert Campbell and John Bell each discovered a different overland route between the MacKenzie and Yukon drainages, linking the two major river systems of the Canadian North.

Meanwhile the Russians were busy exploring their Alaskan territory. A naval voyage under Otto von Kotzebue probed the northwest coast, while Russian fur-hunters and their creole descendents pushed up the rivers and deep into the interior.

Sir John Franklin's last expedition, which set out from Gravesend in England in May 1845, proved to be one of the 19th century's most publicized tragedies. Its disappearance in the ice-bound channels of the Canadian Arctic gripped the imagination of the public on both sides of the Atlantic, and over the next 25 years, some 50 Land and sea expeditions were sent out to find Franklin or discover his fate. Although these expeditions uncovered a phenomenal amount of new territory, their urgent priority caused them to ignore equally vast areas of the Arctic. By the time Franklin's fate became clear, the task of finding the Northwest Passage had cost the British Admiralty so much money, taken so much time, and killed so many men, that they abandoned the Arctic without actually traversing by ship any of the routes they had discovered.

In 1859 the Hudson's Bay Company's exclusive control over Canada would come up for reconsideration. Many in Britain's government believed that the vast province held more than just opportunities to trade furs. Gold had been found on the Fraser River; and the immense southern prairies might well be prime farmland that would attract European immigrants, blocking any United States expansion northwards. From 1857 to 1859, Lieutenant John Palliser surveyed the southern prairies, tabulating their natural resources, locating passes through the Rockies and mapping large areas never before recorded by geographers. Henry Youle Hinde, meanwhile, analyzed the geology of the region, laying out immigration routes to the Saskatchewan.

The Americans, meanwhile, were taking an increasing interest in Alaska. From 1865 to 1867, the Western Union Telegraph Survey charted the interior; in 1868, W.H. Dall, naturalist with the survey, learned to his delight that the United States had purchased Alaska from the Russians. Despite a series of military expeditions in the 1880s, exploration proceeded slowly until the gold rush years of 1896-98 brought thousands of prospectors and pioneers flooding into Alaska and the Canadian northwest.

In the Arctic, meanwhile, attention had shifted to the North Pole and the "Open Polar Sea" which was then believed to surround it. This was the objective of the final Arctic expedition sponsored by the British Admiralty. Commanded by George Strong Nares, its sledge team came within 399.5 miles of the Pole in May 1876. The next attempts were to be American: the ill-fated journey of Greely, and Robert E. Peary's dogged quest. The honor of completing the northwest passage, meanwhile, fell to a Norwegian, Roald Amundsen, in 1905. Another Norwegian, Otto Sverdrup explored Ellesmere Island, and the Canadians Bernier and Stefansson filled most of the remaining gaps in the map of the far north.

Peary's claim to have reached the Pole in April 1909 is the subject of controversy to this day. He was in no doubt, however, that his goal was the culmination of centuries of North American exploration. In his diary for April 1909, he wrote:

"My work is the finish, the cap and climax, of 300 years of effort, loss of life and expenditure of millions, by some of the best men of the civilized nations of the world, and it has been accomplished with a clean cut dash, spirit, and I believe, thoroughness characteristically American. I am content."

Russia Meets America

THE RUSSIANS IN ALASKA, 1790-1863

During the first half of the 19th century Russian promyshlenniki *(Siberian fur-hunters) take over the maritime fur trade and explore and settle Alaska.*

During the 1790s the Lebedev-Lastochkin Company dispatched Vasily Ivanov, a hunter, to explore the interior of Alaska. Ivanov appears to have reached the upper Kuskokwim River; a few Russian historians conjecture that he even reached the Yukon.

By 1799 the Russian American Company was chartered to gain a monopoly of the Alaskan trade. From precarious footholds on the coast it depleted the southern fur regions. So the Company gradually shifted north into the unknown heart of Alaska, enslaving hundreds of Aleut, and other tribes and placing them under *promyshlennik* supervision.

In April 1818 Petr Korsakovsky set out to cross the Alaska peninsula and spent two years trading and exploring around Nushagak Bay. Some of his men later took their own expeditions: Afanasy Klimovsky explored the Copper River in 1819; Feodor Kolmakov established the first post north of the Alaska peninsula at New Aleksandr Redoubt; Rodionov, a trader, reached the upper Kuskokwim via the Mulchatna River.

In 1816, on the northern coast of Alaska, Otto von Kotzebue took naturalists and artists to explore what became the Kotzebue Sound. In 1837 Thomas Simpson sailed from Mackenzie Bay to Point Barrow; and sailing from the west in 1838 Aleksandr Kashevarov reached 35 miles east of the point.

During the late 1820s and 1830s the Russian American Company sent a group of Russian creoles, including Klimovsky, Kashevarov, Petr Malakhov and Andrei Glazunov, to the Kronstadt Navigation College near St Petersburg. In the summers of 1829-30 Ivan Vasiliev and the Russian creole Semyon Lukin explored the Tikchik Lakes and upper Kuskokwim drainage, constantly facing down hostile natives. When Vasiliev sailed back to New Aleksandr Redoubt he received 3000 rubles from the company for his zeal in "journeying into America's interior." In 1832 Lukin and Feodor Kolmakov returned to the Kuskokwim, establishing Kolmakov's Redoubt.

In 1833 the Russians founded a post on St Michael Island, a convenient starting point for the Yukon interior. Glazunov and Lukin finally located the Yukon River from there in 1833. They returned a year later, reaching

Below: A view of the Russian settlement at New Archangel, by F.H. von Kittlitz. A former Russian army officer who had fought in the Napoleonic wars, Kittlitz visited Alaska as as artist and naturalist in 1826. The lithograph shows "the most important and crowded area of the city." An Aleut watches the Russians, on their way to the Orthodox Church, from a rock which, "according to convention ... belongs to the natives."

Kolmakov's Redoubt, but when Glazunov tried to reach Cook Inlet starvation and cold turned him back.

Malakhov left St Michael in 1838, advancing up the Yukon to the huge Koyukuk River. The following year he built a small blockhouse at Nulato. L.A. Zagoskin also left from St Michael and his travels of 1842-44 provided a rare scientific glimpse of the Alaskan interior.

By the late 1840s the Russians were facing competition from the Hudson's Bay Company.When A.H. Murray founded Fort Yukon in 1847, it served as an advance guard of English exploration (▶ *page 194*). In 1863 Semyon Lukin's son, Ivan, made a daring journey from Nulato to the new English fort: a symbolic link between Russian and Anglo-American explorers.

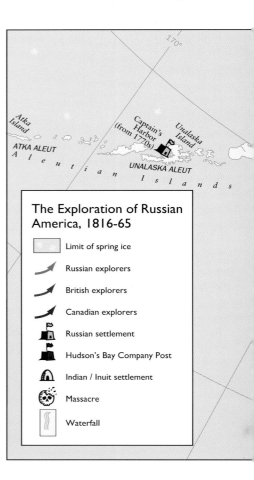

The Exploration of Russian America, 1816-65

- Limit of spring ice
- Russian explorers
- British explorers
- Canadian explorers
- Russian settlement
- Hudson's Bay Company Post
- Indian / Inuit settlement
- Massacre
- Waterfall

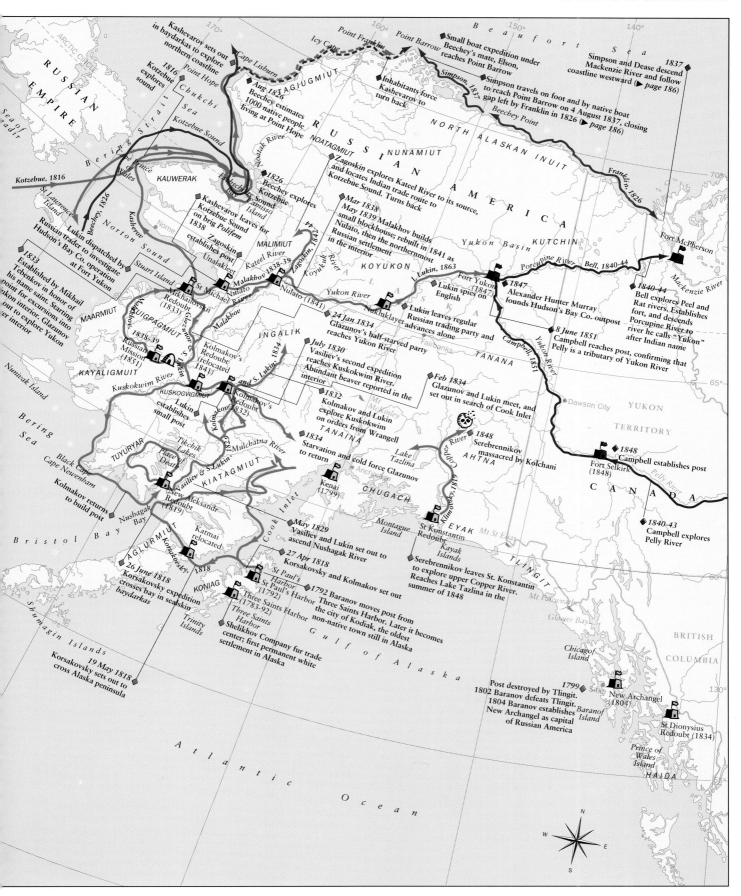

Simpson and Dease descend *1837*
Mackenzie River and follow
coastline westward (▶ page 186)

Small boat expedition under
Beechey's mate, Elson,
reaches Point Barrow

Simpson travels on foot and by native boat
to reach Point Barrow on 4 August 1837, closing
gap left by Franklin in 1826 (▶ page 186)

Kashevarov sets out
in baydarkas to explore
northern coastline

Kotzebue
explores
sound
1816

Beechey estimates
1000 native people
living at Point Hope

Inhabitants force
Kashevarov to
turn back

Zagoskin explores Kateel River to its source,
and locates Indian trade route to
Kotzebue Sound. Turns back

Kashevarov leaves for
Kotzebue Sound on brig *Politfem*
1838. Zagoskin
establishes post

Mar 1838
May 1839 Malakhov builds
small blockhouse; rebuilt in 1841 as
Nulato, then the northernmost
Russian settlement
in the interior

Lukin dispatched by
Russian trader to investigate
Hudson's Bay Co. operation
at Fort Yukon

Bell explores Peel and *1840–44*
Rat rivers. Establishes
fort, and descends
Porcupine River to
river he calls "Yukon"
after Indian name

Alexander Hunter Murray
founds Hudson's Bay Co. outpost *1847*

Lukin spies on
English

Established by Mikhail *1833*
Tebenkov in honor of
his name saint. Starting
point for excursions into
interior. Glazunov
out to explore Yukon
interior

Lukin leaves regular
Russian trading party and
advances alone

24 Jan 1834
Glazunov's half-starved party
reaches Yukon River

8 June 1851
Campbell reaches post, confirming that
Pelly is a tributary of Yukon River

July 1830
Vasiliev's second expedition
reaches Kuskokwim River.
Abundant beaver reported in the
interior

Feb 1834
Glazunov and Lukin meet, and
set out in search of Cook Inlet

1832
Kolmakov and Lukin
explore Kuskokwim
on orders from Wrangell

1848
Serebrennikov
massacred by Kolchani

Lukin
establishes
small post

1834
Starvation
and cold force Glazunov
to return

Campbell establishes post *1848*
Fort Selkirk
(1848)

Kolmakov returns
to build post

1840–43
Campbell explores
Pelly River

May 1829
Vasiliev and Lukin set out
to ascend Nushagak River

Serebrennikov leaves St. Konstantin
to explore upper Copper River.
Reaches Lake Tazlina in the
summer of 1848

27 Apr 1818
Korsakovsky and Kolmakov set out

1792 Baranov moves post from
Three Saints Harbor. Later it becomes
the city of Kodiak, the oldest
non-native town still in Alaska

26 June 1818
Korsakovsky expedition
crosses bay in sealskin
baydarkas

St Paul's
Harbor
St Paul's Harbor
(1792)

Three Saints
Harbor
Three Saints Harbor
(1783–92)

Shelikhov Company fur trade
center; first permanent white
settlement in Alaska

19 May 1818
Korsakovsky sets out to
cross Alaska peninsula

Post destroyed by Tlingit. *1799*
1802 Baranov defeats Tlingit.
1804 Baranov establishes
New Archangel as capital
of Russian America

New Archangel *1804*
(1804)

St Dionysius
Redoubt (1834)

The Land God Gave to Cain

THE EXPLORATION OF THE LABRADOR PENINSULA, 1816-43

The inhospitable wastes between Hudson Bay and the Atlantic, bypassed as the traders moved west, are finally explored by the Hudson's Bay Company.

When Jacques Cartier landed on the northern shore of the Gulf of St Lawrence in 1534, he dismissed it as "the land God gave to Cain." This was long taken to apply to the whole vast hinterland of the Labrador peninsula. As late as the beginning of the 19th century, only the coastal fringes and the more important southerly lakes and rivers had been mapped. When the Hudson's Bay Company tried to move inland it encountered formidable obstacles. Individuals could travel light over the frozen landscape in winter, despite the severe weather, but open water was essential for the canoes of the supply brigades. Many of the streams were too low to use in summer, and north of Rupert House there were no white birch trees large and straight enough to provide canoe bark. Traders had to live off the country, and in the north the boulder-strewn surface was carpeted only by lichens and mosses. There was also little reliable information about the Naskapi who occupied the northern interior.

In 1816 and 1818 George Atkinson, a mixed-blood Company servant, explored Great Whale and Little Whale rivers, and in 1820 a more far-ranging journey was carried out by James Clouston, a former school-teacher in the Company's service at Eastmain House. With Naskapi guides and hunters he crossed the central plateau, though he turned back about a hundred miles short of the sea. Clouston realized that the Naskapi were "more independent of European goods than any other Indians whom I have seen," and that the Company would find it difficult to turn them into fur-trappers.

In 1828 William Hendry, accompanied by Atkinson and Indian guides, crossed the peninsula again, and this time reached the mouth of the Koksoak River. Two years later Nicol Finlayson repeated the journey and established Fort Chimo near the sea at Ungava Bay. The little huddle of buildings, a Company factor wrote later, was "surrounded by a country that presents as complete a picture of desolation as can be imagined." It was 600 miles from the nearest

Below: Explorers in the Labrador peninsula found the rivers broken in many places by rapids. They were obliged to make frequent portages, carrying their canoes overland until they found the next navigable stretch of river.

This illustration of a portage on the Moisie River appeared in Henry Youle Hind's Explorations in the Interior of the Labrador Peninsula (1863). It was drawn by his artist brother William, who accompanied him on his 1861 expedition.

The following text labels appear on the map:

6 Jul 1828 An Indian agrees to take Hendry to Ungava Bay. His partial memory of the route is improved "by information from his mother"

Aug 1811 Moravian sloop from Okak investigates possible mission site

15 July 1828 Hendry sights sea Hope's Advance Bay

22 June 1834 Erlandson arrives at post: "When it is considered how liberal the Indians are paid... by the trader at the NW River, it will appear surprising that any of them have traded furs at Fort Chimo"

8 July 1820 Clouston turns back as signs of Inuit appear

6 Apr Erlandson sets out with 4 Indian guides

25 June 1839 McLean searches for better route to Northwest River

9 Aug 1830 Finlayson selects site for post

More than 50 portages

29 June 1828 Hendry party enters gulf, with "many narrow escapes of having the canoes stove"

1818 Atkinson reaches height of land

25 June 1820 Clouston meets 100 Naskapi who trade with Canadian posts on Gulf of St Lawrence

Jul 1839 McLean establishes post

21 May 1834 Erlandson discovers guides are taking him to Atlantic

1816 Atkinson finds no Indians or beaver

River scarcely navigable

7 May - 11 June 1820 Clouston party make canoes and wait for ice to break

6 June 1828 Hendry and Atkinson head north in canoes

17 Apr 1820 Clouston sets out on foot with Indian guides

July–Aug 1839 McLean and Erlandson seek river which Indians say flows to the sea

Aug 1839 McLean finds Grand River. Halted by "stupendous fall," which "exceeds in height the Falls of Niagara..."

10 June 1830 Finlayson and Erlandson, with 9 men, 2 Inuit interpreters and Indians leave to establish post at Ungava Bay

Place names and posts on map: Mansel Island, Cape Smith, Hudson Strait, Baffin Island, Cape Hope's Advance, Resolution Island, Cape Chidley, Fort Sivenight (1838), Torngat Mountains, Akapotak Island, Ungava Bay, Leaf Bay, Fort Chimo (1830), Leaf River, Lake Minto, Hudson Bay, Lake Kenogamisi, Koksoak River, South River House (1833), Lake Nachikapau, Okak (1776), Nain (1771), Richmond Gulf, Clearwater, Little Whale River, Great Whale River (1813), Lake Appishagamy, Lake Bienville, Fort Nascopie (1838), Fort Trial (1839), Hopedale (1782), Cape Jones, James Bay, Moar Bay, Big River, Kaniapiskau River, Lake Kaniapiskau, Kaniapiskau Post (1834), Lake Petitpiskau, Lake Michikamau, Grand Falls / Churchill Falls, North West River Post (first Canadian post 1743; Hudson's Bay Co. 1836), Hamilton Inlet, Charlton Island, Moose Factory (1673), Eastmain House (1723), Neoweskan (1793), Rupert House (1668), Lake Nemiscau, Rigolet Nichicun House (1816), Shigami River, Mingan (first Canadian post 1661; Hudson's Bay Co.1825), Grand River / Churchill River, LABRADOR, Nottaway River, Neemiscan Post (1794), Rupert River, Moise River, Sept Iles, MONTAGNAIS, Mistassini Post (1812), Lake Wasuanipi, Lake Mitasini, Anticosti Island, Gulf of St Lawrence, QUEBEC, CANADA, CREE

The Exploration of the Labrador Peninsula, 1816-43

Legend:
- Limit of spring ice
- Known to people of European descent, 1816
- Hudson's Bay Company post
- Moravian mission
- Atkinson, 1816
- Atkinson, 1818
- Clouston, 1819-20
- Hendry, 1828 and Finlayson, 1830
- Erlandson, 1834
- McLean, 1839
- Portage
- Falls

Company base at Eastmain, 200 miles across the Torngat Mountains from the Moravian settlement at Okak. Access from the sea was cut off by ice for nine months of the year.

In 1834 Erland Erlandson hoped to find a route from Chimo to the Gulf of St Lawrence, but his Naskapi guides took him instead to the head of Hamilton Inlet. In 1839 John McLean pushed south as far as the Grand (now Churchill) Falls. He supervised the establishment of a network of posts but the continuing reluctance of the Naskapi to change their way of life – "their only talk is about deer and deerhunting," – and overwhelming problems of routes and supplies, dashed all hopes. In 1843 the Company abandoned Fort Chimo until 1866, when the area could be supplied by steamer.

Despite this commercial failure, the achievement of the Hudson's Bay Company was considerable. Its traders had mapped most of the main waterways of the Labrador interior, and had established new posts on the lakes of the central plateau.

> One would need to have blood like brandy, the skin of brass and the eyes of glass, not to suffer from the rigours of a Labrador winter.
>
> James Mckenzie, 1808

The Bleak Canadian North

SEARCHES FOR THE NORTHWEST PASSAGE, 1818-45

*The British map many miles of Arctic
coastline but fail to make the missing link in
the Northwest Passage.*

After the Napoleonic wars, the British Royal Navy was left with a large officer corps. In 1818, encouraged by Cook's success (▶ *page 130*), the Admiralty sent out its first naval expedition under John Ross, to investigate three potential openings in Baffin Bay. Ross examined the entrances to Smith Sound and Jones Sound and quickly declared them closed. After sailing into Lancaster Sound, he suddenly turned and headed for home, claiming later that his path had been blocked by mountains. No-one else on board would confirm this.

William Edward Parry, Ross's second-in-command, returned to Lancaster Sound in 1819 and proved that Ross's mountains were an Arctic mirage. He then explored Prince Regent Inlet and headed west into Viscount Melville Sound. Twice he tried to complete a Northwest Passage through McClure Strait but was prevented by ice from Beaufort Sea. Parry's second voyage was less successful. He was unable to force his way through Fury and Hecla Strait, the northern passage out of Foxe Basin. On his third mission, he lost his ship, the *Fury*, before he could explore any new ground.

In 1819 Lieutenant John Franklin was sent out with George Back, John Richardson and Robert Hood. In 1820 Franklin's "British Arctic Land Expedition" established Fort Enterprise and explored from the Coppermine River delta to Melville Sound. Franklin mapped 550 miles of coast but his expedition was prey to starvation, death, murder and cannibalism. In 1825, on a second land expedition led by Franklin, John Richardson and Kendall set out east from the Mackenzie River delta. Franklin and Back turned west to rendezvous with Captain Beechey at Point Barrow, but bad weather caused them to turn back at Return Islands.

In 1829, frustrated by the lack of progress, a philanthropic gin distiller, Felix Booth, sponsored John Ross's second expedition. With his nephew James Clark Ross as second-in-command, Ross sailed down Prince Regent Sound in search of an opening to the west. The two Rosses mapped James Ross Strait and parts of King William Island and in 1831 James Clark Ross located the Magnetic North Pole. The Ross expedition then disappeared in

the ice-bound Gulf of Boothia until 1833. On a search financed by public subscription George Back and Dr Richard King reached the Thlew-ee-choh, or "Great Fish River" returning to winter at Fort Reliance. In April 1834 they heard of Ross's return after four winters in the Arctic. In June, after a difficult descent down the Great Fish River, naming Pelly, Garry, and Franklin Lakes along the way, they explored the Arctic coast.

During 1837-38 Peter Dease and Sir Thomas Simpson of the Hudson's Bay Company charted missing portions of the coast from Return Islands to Point Barrow. In 1839 they set out to the coast again, but missed the key to the Northwest Passage, Rae Strait, because it was frozen over. In 1840 another Hudson's Bay Company agent, Robert Campbell, reached the Pelly River (▶ *page 183*). The explorers of the Hudson's Bay Company were comparatively more successful than other explorers, being better adapted to the harsh conditions and developing better relations with their Inuit guides.

By the 1840s a potential Northwest Passage had been mapped along the northern coast of Canada but there was still a missing link between Lancaster Sound and Kent Peninsula. Lobbied by the Royal Geographical Society, in May 1845 the Admiralty again sent out Sir John Franklin. Already 59 years old, Franklin left with 128 men aboard the *Erebus* and the *Terror*. After two months at sea, a group of whaling ships crossed paths with Franklin near the entrance to Lancaster Sound. They were the last Europeans to see him alive (▶ *page 190*).

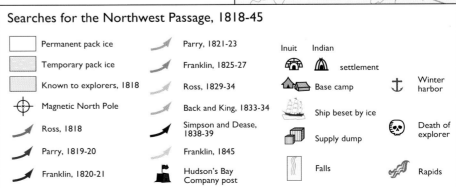

Searches for the Northwest Passage, 1818-45

☐	Permanent pack ice	🖋	Parry, 1821-23	Inuit	Indian	
☐	Temporary pack ice	🖋	Franklin, 1825-27	🛖 🛖	settlement	
☐	Known to explorers, 1818	🖋	Ross, 1829-34	🏕 🏕	Base camp	⚓ Winter harbor
⊕	Magnetic North Pole	🖋	Back and King, 1833-34	🚢	Ship beset by ice	
🖋	Ross, 1818	🖋	Simpson and Dease, 1838-39			☠ Death of explorer
🖋	Parry, 1819-20	🖋	Franklin, 1845	📦	Supply dump	
🖋	Franklin, 1820-21	🏴	Hudson's Bay Company post	🗂	Falls	〰 Rapids

30 Aug 1818 Ross abruptly turns back. Declares sound blocked by mountains. Parry does not believe him

June 1820 Parry and 10 men sledge across Melville Island

26 Jul 1845 Whaling ships last to see Franklin expedition alive

18 April 1818 Ross on HMS Isabella. Parry captains Alexander

19 May 1845 Franklin with 128 men on Erebus and Terror

Parry puts ashore. Sabine discovers they have passed over Magnetic North Pole

Prince Patrick Island

Emerald Island

Eglinton Island

Hazen Strait

Hecla and Griper Gulf

Melville Island

Cornwall Island

Grinnell Peninsula

Jones Sound

Coburg Island

Ellesmere Island

Byam Martin Island

Cornwallis Island

Devon Island

Bylot Island

Baffin Bay

28 May 1829 Ross and crew of 23 on paddle steamer Victory

Mercy Bay

McClure Strait

Cape Providence

Aug 1820 Parry stopped by ice

Viscount Melville Sound

Griffith Island

Barrow Strait

Lancaster Sound

Pond Inlet

Summer 1819 Parry in Hecla and Griper

Davis Strait

Banks Island

Cape Kellet

Prince of Wales Strait

Prince Albert Peninsula

1832 Ross's starving crew restock

Somerset Island

Prince Regent Inlet

Brodeur Peninsula

Borden Peninsula

1820 Parry completes Ross survey of Baffin Island

Amundsen Gulf

Cape Bathurst

Victoria Island

Prince of Wales Island

Creswell Bay

AGGOMIUT

Spring 1832 Victory beset by ice. Ross scuttles ship, crew heads north

Prince Albert Sound

June–July 1821 Franklin surveys coast by canoe

Gateshead Island

Victoria Headland

1 June 1831 Ross first locates Magnetic North Pole

Boothia Peninsula

Winter 1829–30 Ross sends out sledge

IGLULIK

Jens Munk Island

Wollaston Peninsula

COPPER INUIT

1831

Gulf of Boothia

Fury and Hecla Strait

Igloolik

Aug 1822 Strait blocked by ice. Parry leads party overland and confirms that passage exists. Makes 2 further attempts

ARCTIC CIRCLE

1839 Simpson encounters large encampment of "Esquimaux" near Fort Confidence

Dolphin and Union Strait

Coronation Gulf

Cambridge Bay

Alexandra

Kent Peninsula

Victoria Strait

King William Land

Queen Maud Gulf

Adelaide Peninsula

Committee Bay

Pelly Bay

Prince Charles Island

COPPER INUIT

Great Bear Lake

Coppermine River

Bathurst Inlet

Franklin turns back. They eat last of pemican and face starvation and cannibalism

NETSILIK

Simpson Strait

1839 Simpson and Dease miss the key to the Northwest Passage

Rae Strait

Melville Peninsula

Foxe Basin

DOGRIB

Sept 1821 Canoe smashed. Back and others go to Fort Enterprise for supplies

Fort Enterprise **Aug 1820**

Guided by Frederick Wentzel and Chief Akaitcho Franklin follows Yellowknife river to its source

Franklin Lake

29 Jul 1834 Back and King return to Fort Reliance

Rae Isthmus

AIVILINGMIUT

Feb 1822 Inuit visit ships. Suggest passage exists further north

BEAR LAKE

Fort deserted. Party burns floorboards and eats boiled deerskins and old bones

Lake Heeley

UTKUHIKHALINGMIUT

Back River

Repulse Bay

Wager Bay

Frozen Strait

Roes Welcome Sound

Hudson Strait

YELLOWKNIFE

Yellowknife River

"The Cascades" "First traces of Esquimaux seen here"

Lower Macdougall Lake

Lake Garry

Southampton Island

1833–34 winter quarters

Fort Reliance

Great Fish River

19 Jul 1834 "Esquimaux Tents" sighted

Aug 1821 Parry unwittingly passes into Repulse Bay

Summer 1823 Signs of scurvey among crew. Parry returns to Britain

Fort Resolution

8 Aug 1833 Back and King search for Ross

Slave River Delta

CARIBOU INUIT

1821 Parry, in Hecla and Fury, with orders to explore Foxe Basin for a passage out of Hudson Bay

Great Slave Lake

Slave River

Rat River

CHIPEWYAN

28 Aug 1833 Back discovers source of Great Fish River. Returns to winter at Fort Reliance

Hudson Bay

SLAVE

July 1820 Franklin party sets out across Great Slave Lake

Lake Athabasca

April 1834 Back and King hear Ross is safe

Fort Chipewyan

Mar 1820 Franklin and advance party arrive at fort

BEAVER

Across Canada's Plains and Rockies

THE SURVEYS OF PALLISER AND HIND, 1857-59

Palliser and Hind painstakingly chart the last gaps in knowledge of the vast prairielands of southern Canada and the Canadian Rockies.

In 1856 the Royal Geographical Society in London, through Lieutenant John Palliser, petitioned the Colonial Office to fund a two-year exploration of the wilds of southern Canada: to search out possibilities for European settlement and to block any US plans to expand northward. In 1847 Palliser, once described as "an adventurous, cheerful young Irishman," had already explored up the Missouri River, as far as the 49th parallel, hunting bear and buffalo and witnessing a battle between the Hidatsa and Sioux.

Palliser finally set off in 1857, accompanied by the plant collector Eugene Bourgeau,

magnetic observer Thomas Blakiston, geologist Dr James Hector and astronomer John W. Sullivan. They lacked only an experienced cartographer. They were to cover large areas of southern Canada, below territory previously explored by David Thompson (▶ *page 118*). They also planned to search for passes from the Canadian Rockies to the Columbia River suitable for trading parties and wagon roads, and hoped to find a railroad route through the Rockies and Cascades that would open up a Canadian port to the Pacific.

Palliser's party mapped for the first time the

vast country around the South Saskatchewan River: areas inhabited by warring Assiniboin, Blackfoot and Cree, and mostly vast prairielands covered with buffalo. In the Rocky Mountain region, they found at least four passes, one later used by the Canadian Pacific Railroad. These passes also made it possible to connect western Canada to the rest of the dominion, protecting it from US expansionists.

All year round Palliser's survey expeditions crisscrossed southern Canada. Although most strategic locations had fur trade posts with regular cart or sleigh routes in between, their experiences were tough. They dragged carts across prairie and swamp and crossed four passes through the Rockies. Narrowly staving off starvation and in freezing conditions they traveled long distances by dogsled.

Lieutenant Blakiston was the only member of the party to cause difficulty. Unable to get along with his companions he struck out on his own, albeit with some success. Palliser's party was careful to establish good relations with potentially hostile Indians. Aided by Indian guides, they mapped much new territory, and made a thorough investigation of Indian peoples, wildlife, plants, waterways and the US–Canadian frontier. But most of the Rocky Mountain passes had been

traversed much earlier by Thompson, Howze and Sir George Simpson and Palliser did not make any truly new discoveries.

Henry Youle Hind was a professor of chemistry and geology at the University of Toronto and had much in common with the great Prussian geographer, Alexander von Humboldt. He analyzed soils, described the plants, animals, Indian and European peoples of the area and he laid out shorter immigration routes to the Saskatchewan.

Neither Palliser nor Hind was optimistic about the possibilities of agricultural settlement on the great prairies. Palliser's report, published in 1863, tended to see them as much too dangerous for settlers and

ignored the rivers, lakes and woods. Hind concluded that for all the lushness of the plains and river valleys, the prairies themselves had been burned many times and were seriously short of rainfall or rivers. In fact Hind anticipated John Wesley Powell's celebrated report on the arid regions of the USA (▶ *page 172*) by over 20 years.

> Having ascended the slightly elevated ridge we then beheld our game, four or five thousand buffalo....Soon after seeing us the buffalo were in motion at a steady lope, crowding gradually into a thick black mass... the hunters came on at a steady canter increasing with the speed of the buffalo into a hand gallop... We killed seventeen cows.
>
> John Palliser at Slaughter Camp, July 1858

2/ The Surveys of Henry Youle Hind, 1857-58
☐ Area surveyed

1/The Surveys of John Palliser, 1857-59
Palliser, 1857
Palliser, 1858
Palliser, 1859
Blakiston, 1858
Hector, 1857
Hector, 1857-58
Hector, 1859

Canadian US Indian
settlement
Mission   Camp
Rapids   Falls
Pass   Gold strike
Portage   Buffalo

Cold and Tragic Shores

SEARCHES FOR FRANKLIN AND THE NORTHWEST PASSAGE, 1846-1905

The search for Franklin becomes a cause célèbre. Much Arctic territory is charted. In 1903-05 Roald Amundsen is the first to cross the Northwest passage by sea .

In 1845 when Sir John Franklin left on his last expedition, he took enough supplies for three years (▶ *page 186*). There was thus no serious concern for his expedition until early 1847. At that point, on the insistence of his wife, Lady Jane Franklin, and his friend John Ross, the British Admiralty planned the first rescue operation. It was to be the first of 50 land and sea expeditions to search for Franklin and his crew, the last of which departed in 1878.

In 1848 James Clark Ross retraced Franklin's route in the *Victory*. On entering ice-locked Peel Sound he declared it to be completely impassable and turned back. Since Franklin had been instructed to use Wellington Channel as an alternative Ross instructed the Admiralty to concentrate future search operations further north. As it was, Franklin had died the previous year, but Ross

was then turning his back on Franklin's starving crew in the process of abandoning their ice-bound ships.

In 1850 six more rescue operations began. The *Investigator* and *Enterprise*, under the general command of Richard Collinson, were instructed to search the coast of Alaska. When the two ships separated in fog near Cape Horn, the ambitious Robert McClure bypassed his commander and reached Banks' Island by early September. The more cautious Collinson turned back and spent the winter in Hong Kong.

The ice carried the *Investigator* halfway up Prince of Wales Strait, and sledge trips the following spring confirmed the strait as a possible route for the Northwest Passage. A second attempt to sail through the strait during the summer of 1851 was thwarted by

ice just 25 miles short of Melville Sound. Collinson meanwhile returned to the area and, though neither realized this, tagged two weeks behind McClure until the latter rounded the top of Banks Island. Ice kept McClure anchored in Mercy Bay for two years. When Collinson turned back to explore the southern coast of Victoria Island, he came within 40 miles of Franklin's ships.

Dissatisfied with the Admiralty's efforts, Lady Franklin hired William Kennedy, a Canadian fur trader, and Joseph-Rene Bellot, a 25-year-old French sailor, to search south of Lancaster Sound. In the spring of 1852, Kennedy and Bellot sledged across Peel Sound and circled Prince of Wales Island. They encountered a narrow gorge that separated Somerset Island from Boothia Peninsula, which Kennedy named Bellot Strait. It was a

April 25th, 1848 – HM's Ships Terror and Erebus were deserted on 22nd April, 5 leagues N.N.W. of this, having been beset since 12th September 1846. The Officers & crew, consisting of 105 souls, under the command of Captain F.R.M Crozier, landed here on Lat. 69° 37' 42" N, long. 98° 41' W. Sir John Franklin died on 11th June 1847; and the total loss by deaths in the Expedition has been to this date 9 officers & 15 men.

(signed) James Fitzjames,
Captain HMS Erebus

and start tomorrow, 26th for Back's Fish River

(signed) F.R.M. Crozier, Captain and Senior Officer

Note discovered by Lt. William Hobson in cairn at Point Victory

Left: The tombstones of three of Franklin's men lie beneath the midnight sun on Beechey Island. The seaman, stoker and Royal Marine died there during the expedition's first winter. The engraving was based on drawings by the explorer Elisha Kent Kane (▶ pages 198-201)

third possible route for the Northwest Passage.

On 15 August 1852 the last and largest of the British Admiralty's search expeditions landed at Beechey Island. The autocratic Sir Edward Belcher led five ships, sending Henry Kellett and Leopold M'Clintock off in two of them to search for Collinson and McClure. In April 1853 Lieutenant Bedford Pim found McClure at Mercy Bay. Belcher meanwhile wintered off the Grinnell Peninsula. After exploring the region by sledge, both arms of the expedition tried to rendezvous at Beechey Island. But Belcher had to abandon all four ships in the summer of 1854. Only the timely arrival of supply ships, the *Phoenix* and the *Talbot*, relieved the over-crowding on Belcher's remaining ship, the *Northstar*.

In 1853 Lady Franklin persuaded Henry

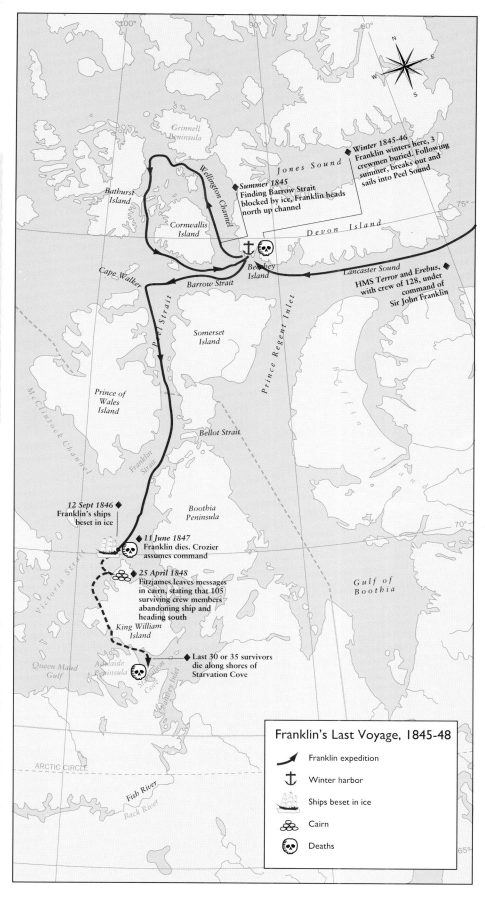

Winter 1845-46 Franklin winters here, 3 crewmen buried. Following summer, breaks out and sails into Peel Sound

Summer 1845 Finding Barrow Strait blocked by ice, Franklin heads north up channel

HMS *Terror* and *Erebus*, with crew of 128, under command of Sir John Franklin

12 Sept 1846 Franklin's ships beset in ice

11 June 1847 Franklin dies. Crozier assumes command

25 April 1848 Fitzjames leaves messages in cairn, stating that 105 surviving crew members abandoning ship and heading south

Last 30 or 35 survivors die along shores of Starvation Cove

Jones Sound
Grinnell Peninsula
Bathurst Island
Cornwallis Island
Wellington Channel
Devon Island
Beechey Island
Lancaster Sound
Cape Walker
Barrow Strait
Peel Strait
Somerset Island
Prince Regent Inlet
McClintock Channel
Prince of Wales Island
Bellot Strait
Franklin Strait
Boothia Peninsula
Gulf of Boothia
Victoria Strait
King William Island
Adelaide Peninsula
Starvation Cove
Queen Maud Gulf
Fish River
Back River
ARCTIC CIRCLE

Franklin's Last Voyage, 1845-48

- Franklin expedition
- Winter harbor
- Ships beset in ice
- Cairn
- Deaths

Grinnell to finance a search led by the American ship's surgeon Elisha Kent Kane (►page 198-201). But the first solid evidence about Franklin's expedition came in 1853 when John Rae interviewed Inuit around Pelly Bay and retrieved articles removed from the ships. Four years later, Lady Franklin sent Francis Leopold M'Clintock to follow up Rae's lead. M'Clintock forced his way to the western end of Bellot Strait, and during the spring of 1859 sent out three search teams. A party led by William Hobson discovered a cairn containing the only message left by Franklin's crew. M'Clintock's men established the final location of Franklin's ships and proved that he had died in 1847. They suggested that none of Franklin's crew of 128 had survived.

The pace of explorations slackened after M'Clintock's expedition confirmed the tragedy of Franklin's last journey. Rival interests had emerged. In particular, in 1867 the United States had purchased Alaska (► page 194).

In June 1879, American explorer Frederick Schwatka, confirmed M'Clintock's report. Traveling a record 4,000 miles overland by sledge, Schwatka gathered additional artifacts and information about the final days of Franklin's crew. In 1923, Knud Rasmussen, a Norwegian scientist, explored Starvation Cove for the first time and concluded that this was where the last survivors had died. In the mid-1980s, scientists performed autopsies on three of Franklin's crew who had been found frozen and buried on Beechey Island. They concluded that their deaths had not been caused by lead poisoning. No logbooks, journals, or diaries have yet been recovered from that fateful expedition. Nor have the sunken hulls of either of Franklin's ships been located.

When Roald Amundsen set sail from Christiania, Norway, on 16 June 1903, he was fulfilling a childhood ambition to complete what Franklin had failed to accomplish. To gain public support, Amundsen also set out to relocate the Magnetic North Pole. He succeeded in both his goals. Amundsen sailed through Peel Sound and spent two winters in Gjoa Harbor, King William Island. From there he verified that the Magnetic North Pole had shifted 30 miles to the north. The following summer he successfully navigated the last unexplored leg of the Northwest Passage, emerging from Dolphin and Union Strait early August 1905.

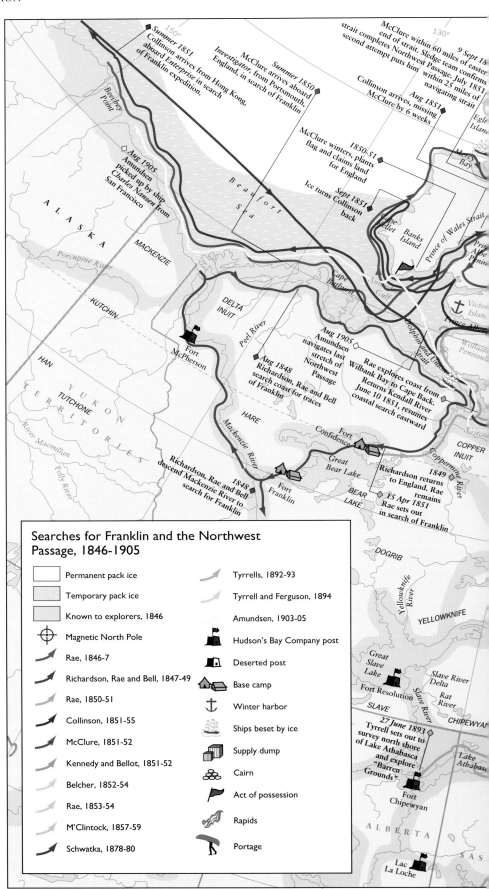

Searches for Franklin and the Northwest Passage, 1846-1905

▢ Permanent pack ice		⟋ Tyrrells, 1892-93	
▨ Temporary pack ice		⟋ Tyrrell and Ferguson, 1894	
▨ Known to explorers, 1846		⟋ Amundsen, 1903-05	
⊕ Magnetic North Pole		🏭 Hudson's Bay Company post	
⟋ Rae, 1846-7		🏚 Deserted post	
⟋ Richardson, Rae and Bell, 1847-49		⛺ Base camp	
⟋ Rae, 1850-51		⚓ Winter harbor	
⟋ Collinson, 1851-55		⛵ Ships beset by ice	
⟋ McClure, 1851-52		📦 Supply dump	
⟋ Kennedy and Bellot, 1851-52		⬡ Cairn	
⟋ Belcher, 1852-54		⚑ Act of possession	
⟋ Rae, 1853-54		⟋ Rapids	
⟋ M'Clintock, 1857-59		⛰ Portage	
⟋ Schwatka, 1878-80			

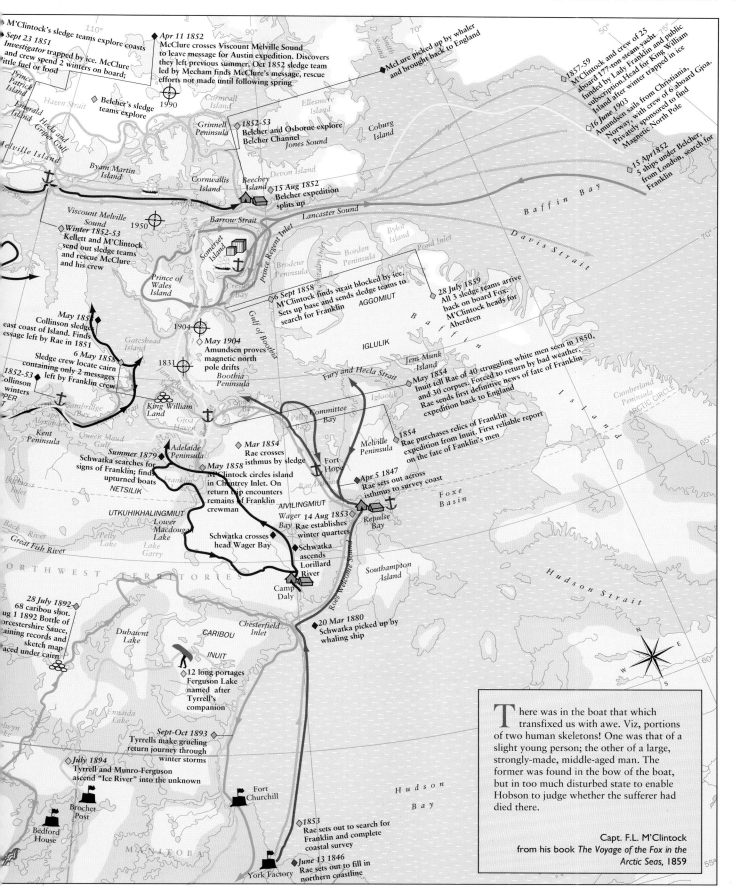

◆ M'Clintock's sledge teams explore coasts

◆ Sept 23 1851
Investigator trapped by ice. McClure
and crew spend 2 winters on board;
little fuel or food

◆ Apr 11 1852
McClure crosses Viscount Melville Sound
to leave message for Austin expedition. Discovers
they left previous summer. Oct 1852 sledge team
led by Mecham finds McClure's message, rescue
efforts not made until following spring

◇ McLure picked up by whaler
and brought back to England

◇ Belcher's sledge
teams explore

◇ 1990

◇ Grinnell   ◇ 1852-53
Peninsula   Belcher and Osborne explore
Belcher Channel
Jones Sound

◇ 1857-59
M'Clintock and crew of 25
aboard 177-ton steam yacht
funded by Lady Franklin and public
subscription. Head for King William
Island after winter trapped in ice

◇ 16 June 1903
Amundsen sails from Christiania,
Norway, with crew of 6 aboard Gjoa.
Privately sponsored to find
Magnetic North Pole

◇ 15 Apr1852
5 ships under Belcher,
from London, search for
Franklin

◇ 15 Aug 1852
Belcher expedition
splits up

◇ Winter 1852-53
Kellett and M'Clintock
send out sledge teams
and rescue McClure
and his crew

◇ 1950

◇ 6 Sept 1858
M'Clintock finds strait blocked by ice.
Sets up base and sends sledge teams to
search for Franklin

◇ 28 July 1859
All 3 sledge teams arrive
back on board Fox.
M'Clintock heads for
Aberdeen

◆ May 185?
Collinson sledges
east coast of Island. Finds
essage left by Rae in 1851

◇ 1904

◆ May 1904
Amundsen proves
magnetic north
pole drifts

◆ 6 May 1858
Sledge crew locate cairn
containing only 2 messages
left by Franklin crew

◇ 1852-53
ollinson
winters
PER

◇ 1831

◇ May 1854
Inuit tell Rae of 40 struggling white men seen in 1850,
and 30 corpses. Forced to return by bad weather,
Rae sends first definitive news of fate of Franklin
expedition back to England

◇ 1854
Rae purchases relics of Franklin
expedition from Inuit. First reliable report
on the fate of Franklin's men

◇ Mar 1854
Rae crosses
isthmus by sledge

◇ Summer 1879
Schwatka searches for
signs of Franklin; finds
upturned boats

◇ May 1858
M'Clintock circles island
in Chantrey Inlet. On
return trip encounters
remains of Franklin
crewman

◆ Apr 5 1847
Rae sets out across
isthmus to survey coast

◇ Wager 14 Aug 1853
Bay   Rae establishes
winter quarters

Schwatka crosses
head Wager Bay

◆ Schwatka
ascends
Lorillard
River

◆ 28 July 1892
68 caribou shot.
ug 1 1892 Bottle of
orcestershire Sauce,
aining records and
sketch map
aced under cairn

◆ 20 Mar 1880
Schwatka picked up by
whaling ship

◆ 12 long portages
Ferguson Lake
named after
Tyrrell's
companion

◇ Sept-Oct 1893
Tyrrells make grueling
return journey through
winter storms

◇ July 1894
Tyrrell and Munro-Ferguson
ascend "Ice River" into the unknown

◇ 1853
Rae sets out to search for
Franklin and complete
coastal survey

◆ June 13 1846
Rae sets out to fill in
northern coastline

There was in the boat that which
transfixed us with awe. Viz, portions
of two human skeletons! One was that of a
slight young person; the other of a large,
strongly-made, middle-aged man. The
former was found in the bow of the boat,
but in too much disturbed state to enable
Hobson to judge whether the sufferer had
died there.

Capt. F.L. M'Clintock
from his book *The Voyage of the Fox in the
Arctic Seas,* 1859

Seward's Icebox

US ALASKA AND THE YUKON GOLD RUSH, 1866-98

*The United States buys Alaska from the
Russians and slowly begins to explore the
vast, little-known territory it has acquired.*

In 1867 Secretary of State William H. Seward persuaded the US government to buy Alaska from the Russians. As with Jefferson's Louisiana purchase more than 60 years earlier, many thought it an act of folly to acquire a vast tract of wild and inhospitable land, and dubbed it "Seward's Icebox."

Since 1865 the Western Union Telegraph Survey had set out to link Eurasia with North America by telegraph, under Robert Kennicott and Colonel Charles Bulkley. Only a few token miles were laid and Kennicott died of a sudden heart attack in 1866, but the survey introduced American explorers to the interior. Frank Ketchum and Michael Lebarge journeyed from Nulato past Fort Yukon to Fort Selkirk. Other survey members, such as William Healey Dall and Frederick Whymper, collected natural history specimens and became experts on Russian America.

On 3 February 1868 Dall learned of the purchase of Alaska. Like the Russians (▶ *page 182*), the Americans set out to exploit their new possession by setting up the Alaska Commercial Company to rival the Hudson's Bay Company. Exploration of the interior was slow, however. In the summer of 1869 Captain Charles Raymond traveled up the Yukon on a paddlewheel steamer and at Fort Yukon calculated that this Hudson's Bay post was within US territory. In the 1870s, the US Army and the Treasury Department's Coast Survey competed over exploration of the area. In 1879 Lieutenant Henry Ray arrived at bleak Point Barrow for a long scientific mission, while John Muir, a naturalist and writer, studied the spectacular Glacier Bay.

During the 1880s the pace of interior discovery quickened. In 1883 the US Army dispatched Frederick Schwatka and George Stoney on major expeditions. Schwatka went up Chilkoot Pass – a major trail in later gold rushes – built a raft at Lake Lindeman, floated down the Yukon and eventually took an Alaska Commercial Company steamer to St Michael. While he covered little new ground, Schwatka's journey, books and lecture tours were an attempt to rouse public interest in Alaska.

From 1883 to 1885 Lieutenant George M. Stoney of the US Navy and Lieutenant John

Cantwell of the Revenue Marine openly competed in their successive travels up the Kobuk River. The US Army was active as well, launching Henry T. Allen's great expedition of 1885. Allen succeeded in penetrating the Copper River drainage where the Russian, Rufus Serebrennikov had failed (▶ *page 182*). By the end of summer 1885 Allen had explored three immense and largely unknown river systems: the Copper, the Tanana, and the Koyukuk. However his daring reconnaissance attracted little fame. That same year S.B. McLenagan explored the source of the Noatak River, and in 1886 Stoney's men accomplished a monumental journey from Point Barrow to Nulato.

During the 1890s, teams of unsung explorers from the US Geological Survey fanned out into the interior to locate the Brooks Range, calculate the height of Mt. McKinley and wonder at the geysers of Katmai Volcano. The gold rushes of 1896-98 brought thousands of prospectors and pioneers into Alaska, many eager to explore new valleys, rivers, and mountains. In little more than a century the Russian pursuit of furs and American pursuit of minerals had opened up a vast area of North America to the glory and greed of exploration and exploitation.

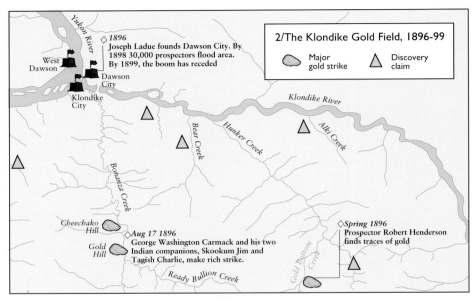

2/The Klondike Gold Field, 1896-99

⬮ Major gold strike △ Discovery claim

1896
Joseph Ladue founds Dawson City. By 1898 30,000 prospectors flood area. By 1899, the boom has receded

West Dawson

Dawson City

Klondike City

Klondike River

Bear Creek

Hunker Creek

Alki Creek

Bonanza Creek

Cheechako Hill

Gold Hill

Aug 17 1896
George Washington Carmack and his two Indian companions, Skookum Jim and Tagish Charlie, make rich strike.

Ready Bullion Creek

Gold Bottom Creek

Spring 1896
Prospector Robert Henderson finds traces of gold

Yukon River

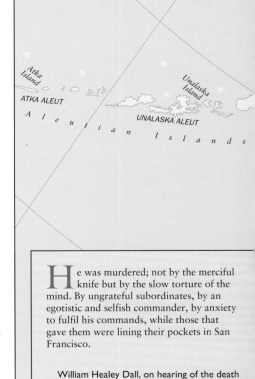

170°

Atka Island

ATKA ALEUT

Unalaska Island

A l e u t i a n   I s l a n d s

UNALASKA ALEUT

H e was murdered; not by the merciful knife but by the slow torture of the mind. By ungrateful subordinates, by an egotistic and selfish commander, by anxiety to fulfil his commands, while those that gave them were lining their pockets in San Francisco.

William Healey Dall, on hearing of the death of Robert Kennicott in 1866

Point Franklin
Icy Cape
Point Barrow

Cape Lisburne

Point Hope

Stoney, 1886

Beechey Point

B e a u f o r t   S e a

RUSSIAN EMPIRE

Sea of Anadir

Cape Prince of Wales

C h u c k c h i   S e a

Kotzebue Sound

TAREUMIUT

NOATAGMIUT

For three years Naval
Lt. Stoney makes progressive
explorations up the Kobuk River

Parties under George
M. Stoney explore
Selawik and
Colville Rivers

1886

NORTH ALASKA COAST INUIT

Noatak River

Colville River

McLenegan, 1885

KOWAGMIUT

B r o o k s

R a n g e

NUKAMIUT

Ogilvie and
McConnell
rendezvous

Kobuk Delta
Eschscholtz Bay

Stoney &
Cantwell, 1883-6

Kobuk River

Walker Lake

August 3 1885
McLenegan reaches
source of river

Fritch River

Fort McPherson

Camisso Island

Summer 1883
Stoney rediscovers
Kobuk Delta

1885
Fort Cosmos
(1885)

Stoney sets
up fort

Allen explores the upper
Koyukuk River

1869
Captain Raymond proves Hudson's Bay
Company post is in US territory

Porcupine River   Bell River

Mackenzie River

Bering Strait

Nome   1899
Gold discovered

Selawik River

MALEMIUT

Nulato
Nulato River

May 1866
Kennicott dies
at Nulato

Koyukuk River

KOYUKON

Fort Yukon

Eastern and western parties
reconnoiter telegraph route
across Alaska

KUTCHIN

Peel River

ARCTIC CIRCLE

St Lawrence Island

Norton Sound

Stuart Island

St Michael

KIKOGMIUT

Feb 3 1868
Dall learns that US
has bought Alaska
from Russians

A L A S K A

Summer 1902
Italian miner Felix Pedro
strikes rich placer gold

Western Union Telegraph Survey

Yukon River

Ogilvie, 1887

Aug 13 1887
Dawson and Ogilvie rendezvous.
Dawson returns to Chilkoot Pass,
Ogilvie continues north

YUKON
TERRITORY

Kuikpak River

MAGEMIUT

Old Ikogmiut
village

Summer 1884
Cantwell finds jadeite while
investigating a report
of a "mysterious
mountain"

Summer 1866
Ketchum, Lebarge and Lukin find
Tanana gathered for trade.
30 miles on
they meet
missionary

Bate's
Rapids

Tanana River

Fairbanks

TANANA

65°

June 26 1887
McConnell separates from
Dawson to survey northeast
to Forts Simpson and
Providence, and then down
Mackenzie River

KAIALIGMIUT

INGALIK

Mt
McKinley

Tower Bluff
Rapids

Tetlin
village

Fortymile

Dawson City

Fort Selkirk

KUSKOGVIGMIUT

TANAINA

1886
prospector William A. Dickey
names highest mountain in
North America in honor of
McKinley's nomination
for president

June 12 1885
Allen makes new
boat of caribou hides to
descend Tanana River

1896

Schwatka, 1883

Pelly River

B e r i n g
S e a

TOGIAGMIUT

KIATAGMIUT

Anchorage

Nikolai's
village

AHTENA

Fort William H. Seward

July 2 1883
Schwatka shoots
rapids on raft

Lake Lindeman

C A N A D A

Cape Newenham

Peninsula Kenai

CHUGACH

Copper
Delta

Montague
Island

EYAK

Mt St Elias

June 13 1883
Schwatka builds raft
Resolute

Major
gateway
for
prospectors

Lower
Post

Katmai
Volcano

Cook Inlet

March 29 1885
Allen at Copper Delta;
begins ascent of river

Kayak
Islands

TLINGIT

Apr 1887
Ogilvie surveys from
Chilkoot Pass to Lewes River

Chilkoot
Pass

Ogilvie, 1887

Dawson, 1887

June 1883
Schwatka dispatched by
General Miles

BRITISH

Shumagin Islands

Shelikov Strait

Kodiak
Island

KONIAGA

G u l f   o f   A l a s k a

Mt Fairweather

1879   Glacier Bay

John Muir astonished by
beauty of Glacier Bay

Juneau

Trinity Islands

AGLEMIUT

Chicagof
Island

COLUMBIA

1880 Juneau and Harris find
gold; leads to Silver Bow Basin
strike and founding of the
town of Juneau

Bristol Bay

Nunivak Island

P a c i f i c

Sitka
(1867)

Baranof
Island

Fort Wrangell
(1868)

Dawson and McConnell set
out to Survey Yukon
Territory

Apr 1887

O c e a n

130°

Prince of
Wales
Island

HAIDA

Outfitting center
during Klondike
Gold Rush

I/American Exploration of Alaska, 1865-1902

Limit of spring ice

Western Union Telegraph Survey, 1865-67

Other US explorers

Canadian Yukon Exploring Expedition, 1887-89

US settlement /fort

Hudson Bay Company Post

Indian settlement

Death of explorer

Gold strike

Rapids

Portage

The Crown of the Continent

EXPLORATIONS IN THE ARCTIC ARCHIPELAGO, 1906-18

Norwegian and Canadian explorers unveil the world's last unknown landmass – the vast archipelago of the Canadian Arctic.

The search for Sir John Franklin (▶ *pages 190-93*) had uncovered much new territory, but equally vast areas of the Arctic had been ignored. By the time Franklin's fate became clear, attention had shifted toward the "Open Polar Sea" and the North Pole. It was not until the 20th century that explorers returned to the Arctic.

The first thorough scientific survey was of the region north of Jones Sound and west of Smith Sound. In 1898 Otto Sverdrup, commander of the Second Norwegian Expedition, planned to take his ship *Fram* around the northern coast of Greenland. But ice in Kane Basin forced him to change his plan and instead he took the opportunity to survey the crown of the northern hemisphere.

Sverdrup, primarily while waiting for the summer tides to clear the ice from Smith Sound, initiated forays into the highlands of Ellesmere Island. His serious work did not begin until he moved his winter quarters into Jones Sound. Then, from his base camp in Harbor Fjord (1899-1900) and Goose Fjord (1900-02), Sverdrup sent out sledge teams. They established the connection between Greely's Fjord and Nansen Sound, discovered the islands of Ellef Ringnes and Amund Ringnes and, in spite of John Ross's claim, proved that Jones Sound was not closed off by "very high mountains." Sverdrup also came within 25 miles of circumnavigating Axel Heiberg, the island he found and named for his sponsor, the Norwegian consul.

The next phase of exploration began as Canada went about annexing the north Arctic islands. Joseph Bernier led a series of four missions to the region for the Canadian Marine and Fisheries Department. The missions carried out a variety of tasks from intensive surveys of unexplored areas to posting fines and planting Canadian flags. In 1906-07 Bernier swept through Lancaster Sound toward the Beaufort Sea, pausing just long enough at each major island to lay Canada's claim upon the soil. When ice prevented him from going farther than the eastern coast of Melville Island, he turned back to claim Victoria and Banks islands in 1908-09. That year the "impassable" McClure Strait was uncharacteristically clear of ice and had his orders allowed it, Bernier

felt confident that he could have completed the Northwest Passage. Instead Bernier finished the season dispensing whaling licences around Navy Board Inlet.

Suddenly aware that an opportunity had been missed, the Canadian government issued new orders to Bernier. In 1910-11, on his third journey, Bernier went immediately to McClure Strait but his opportunity of sailing through the Northwest Passage was lost, it was no longer open. However this third journey accomplished more original scientific work than the first two missions combined. From their winter harbor at Arctic Bay, Bernier dispatched J.E. Lavoi on two long sledge trips to survey the hitherto uncharted Brodeur Peninsula, from Admiralty Inlet to Fury and Hecla Strait. Along the way, a Mr English, the ship's geologist, located a variety of minerals, including significant deposits of sulphur. In 1912-13 on the fourth mission, Bernier explored Gifford Fjord from Foxe Basin to Admiralty Inlet.

Vilhjalmur Stefansson of Canada, an anthropologist who specialized in Arctic peoples, persuaded the Canadian government to sponsor a massive, two-pronged exploration of the region around Victoria Island and Coronation Gulf. In 1914 a trio of ships set out from British Columbia, headed for the Beaufort Sea. An easterly tide of ice separated Stefansson's team from their supply ship *Karluk*, which later sank near Wrangel Island. Undeterred, Stefansson took off across the ice wasteland north of Martin Point, Alaska, with two other men, and succeeded in his main aim – proving that the Beaufort Sea could sustain life. The party survived for three months by augmenting their meagre supplies with seals caught miles away from land.

Stefansson set up winter quarters at Cape Kellett, Banks Island, and from there continued his exploration of the Beaufort Sea and the north Arctic islands. On his long circular treks, he discovered all the remaining northern islands, making links between his own and Sverdrup's findings. He also explored the interior of Victoria Island. Over five years, Stefansson made three journeys across the Beaufort Sea.

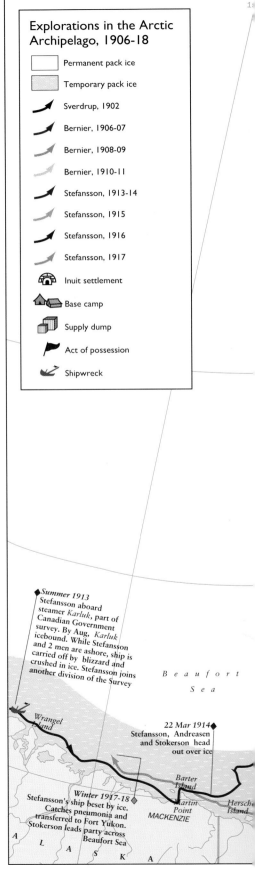

Explorations in the Arctic Archipelago, 1906-18

☐ Permanent pack ice

▨ Temporary pack ice

Sverdrup, 1902

Bernier, 1906-07

Bernier, 1908-09

Bernier, 1910-11

Stefansson, 1913-14

Stefansson, 1915

Stefansson, 1916

Stefansson, 1917

Inuit settlement

Base camp

Supply dump

Act of possession

Shipwreck

Summer 1913 Stefansson aboard steamer *Karluk*, part of Canadian Government survey. By Aug, *Karluk* icebound. While Stefansson and 2 men are ashore, ship is carried off by blizzard and crushed in ice. Stefansson joins another division of the Survey

Beaufort Sea

Wrangel Island

22 Mar 1914 Stefansson, Andreasen and Stokerson head out over ice

Barter Island

Winter 1917-18 Stefansson's ship beset by ice. Catches pneumonia and transferred to Fort Yukon. Stokerson leads party across Beaufort Sea

Martin Point *Herschel Island*

MACKENZIE

A L A S K A

7 May 1902
Sverdrup crosses Eureka Sound but fails to circumnavigate Axel Heiberg Island

11 Apr 1900
Sverdrup discovers island, names it after his sponsor, Norwegian consul Heiberg

1916
Stefansson completes Sverdrup's survey, confirming that Ringnes islands are not connected

May 1901
Sledge team of Isachsen and Hassel explore Amund and Ellef Ringnes islands

26 Apr 1917
Stefansson's furthest north. Scurvy among party prevents him continuing

1916
Arctic mirage leads Stefansson to think Borden Island is continuous

Spring 1915
Stefansson and 3 men search for additional islands

2-3 Sept 1910
Bernier fails to force way through ice pack

15 May 1914
Stefansson catches seals, proving Beaufort Sea not "lifeless"

Winter 1898-99
Sverdrup's sledge teams explore Pim and Ellesmere islands

Summer 1898
Sverdrup and crew of 15 on board specially designed ship, Fram

28 July 1908
Bernier's second voyage, aboard Arctic; 38 crew, 5 scientists

Winter 1899-1900
Sverdrup surveys fjords in small sailboat

Winter 1906-07
Bernier raises flag and leaves official messages

Summer 1906
Bernier's first voyage, aboard Arctic; 41 crew

July 1910
Bernier's third voyage, 31 crew, 4 scientists

Winter 1910-11
Bernier sends Lavoie to survey Admiralty Inlet and Brodeur Peninsula

Winter 1908-09
Bernier sends 2 sledge teams to claim Banks and Victoria islands

Spring 1917
Stokerson sledge team completes survey of Victoria Island's east coast

1906
Headwinds and ice prevent Bernier going further

Aug 1911
Ice prevents Bernier advancing to Gulf of Boothia

They had traveled eastward over the ice,...and made the journey of over a thousand miles, living on the local food supply, and had never missed a meal!...So this was the end of the enterprise which for months I had heard condemned or deplored by Eskimos and whalers and the men of arctic experience in our expedition as "one crazy and two deluded men going north over the sea ice to commit suicide!"

Science Officer George H. Wilkins, from a magazine article quoted for his book by Vilhjalmur Stefansson

The Big Nail

THE RACE TO THE POLE, 1853-1909

The dream of an Open Polar Sea is replaced by the lure of the North Pole. Robert Peary may have been first to arrive there but his claim is even now clouded by controversy.

In spring 1854 Elisha Kent Kane, an American ship's surgeon with a crew of 17, made four futile attempts to find a way to the Open Polar Sea. Like many others he was also searching for survivors from Sir John Franklin's ill-fated journey of 1845 (▶ *page 190 -193*).

In June 1854 Kane sent out four of his last six healthy men in an abortive effort to climb the massive Humboldt Glacier. The other two, William Morton and Hans Hendrik, a Greenland Inuit, cut across Peabody Bay to the top of Kane Basin. Early in July they found their path blocked by a steep cliff, Cape Constitution. Morton scrambled up, the first white man to view the northward expanse of ice-free blue water, Kennedy Channel. Convinced it led to the Open Polar Sea, Kane later wrote, "I do not believe there was a man among us who did not long for the means of entering its bright and lonely waters."

Two other Americans were frustrated in their search for the fabled Open Polar Sea. In 1860 Dr Isaac Hayes, surgeon on Kane's 1853 expedition, led a sledge team north along Ellesmere Island. After a month on the ice, Hayes believed he was above 81°N, a position that would have placed him near Lady Franklin Bay. Later explorers calculated that he only reached Cape Joseph Good. In 1871

an eccentric American explorer, Charles Francis Hall, ascended Cape Brevoort and looked across the Lincoln Sea, a sea of solid ice from Cape Joseph Henry to the horizon. Hall died in November 1871, after several weeks of illness. The official claim was that he died from a stroke but a century later, in 1968, an autopsy concluded he had been systematically poisoned by arsenic. Forced to abandon their ship the *Polaris*, some of Hall's crew shuttled between ice floes. They were eventually rescued 2000 miles south, off Newfoundland. Although he did not live to claim his achievement, Hall had effectively closed the book on the Open Polar Sea and confirmed Kane's "American route" as the path to the North Pole.

The British Admiralty's last Arctic expedition left Portsmouth in May 1875, led by George Strong Nares. He stationed the *Discovery* at a base camp at Lady Franklin Bay and continued north in the *Alert* to Cape Sheridan. In 1876 Nares launched three sledge teams. Albert Hastings Markham surpassed Parry's farthest north record of 1827 (▶ *page 186*), only 400 miles from the Pole; Lewis Beaumont reached Sherard Osborn Fiord and claimed a farthest east record; Pelham Aldrich headed north in search of a vantage point for the North Pole itself.

In 1881 the US Army used a scientific expedition to compete with the British. Adolphus Washington Greely, with two dozen men and two Greenland Inuit, established a weather station, Fort Conger, at Lady Franklin Bay. Greely then sent out two of his men, James B. Lockwood and David Brainard, who broke several records for farthest north, east and west, but Greely's expedition is best known for its disastrous end. Though stocked with plenty of supplies, Greely decided to abandon Fort Conger in August 1883 and go in search of emergency supplies at Cape Sabine. Two weeks later the ice encased Greely's four open boats near Cape Hawks and inched them southward. Greely abandoned the boats hoping to reach shore and walk the rest of the way. Halfway across the ice the current abruptly cut them adrift on a mile-wide ice floe. On hitting a stable iceberg the desperate men clambered to

safety and established Camp Clay on the north side of Pim Island. They were rescued nine months later, but only seven men, including Greely, were still alive.

To the American public, Robert Edwin Peary personified the ideal Arctic explorer. A civil engineer with the US Navy, in 1886 Peary took leave from Nicaragua to spend a few months on Greenland's icepack. He returned twice to cross northern Greenland: first in 1892 with a party of six, including Matthew Henson, his personal servant; second in 1895 when, with Henson and Hugh Ross Lee, he nearly lost his life.

The need to reach the North Pole soon became the goal of Peary's life. On his first attempt he was backed by wealthy industrialists of the Peary Arctic Club, but his ship the *Windward* could go no further than Cape d'Urville. While setting up supply depots for the journey during winter 1898-99, Peary had lost most of his toes, but they hauled supplies almost 300 miles to Cape Sheridan. He then set off from a point near Cape Hecla in spring 1902. After two weeks struggling over pressure ridges, he gave up on 21 April. He had surpassed Markham's farthest north of 1876, but failed to exceed either Nansen's record of 1895 or Umberto Cagni's record of 1900.

In spring 1906 Peary launched his second major assault on the North Pole from Cape Columbia. After a month of back-breaking work, the expedition came to a standstill on 26 March, when they ran into a river of open water, the "Big Lead." It was a week before "Big Lead" was covered by new ice. Then Peary, Henson and six Inuit headed for the Pole. On 21 April they had to abandon their goal. According to Peary's unverified calculations, they were 200 miles short of the Pole but had achieved a new all-time record of 87° 06' N.

Peary's third and final expedition departed New York harbor on 6 July 1908. This time the whole world was watching and it was the North Pole or nothing. The *Roosevelt* landed at Floeberg Beach on 5 September 1908 and they began to lay out supply depots. On 28 February 1909 the first team took off across the ice, covering 10 to 15 miles a day. On 1 April Bob Bartlett, Peary's navigator, was

> My life work is accomplished. The thing which it was intended from the beginning that I should do, the thing which I believed could be done and that I could do, I have done. I have got the North Pole out of my system. After 23 years of effort, hard work, disappointments, hardships, privations, more or less suffering, and some risks, I have won the last great geographical prize...for the credit of the United States, the Service to which I belong, myself and my family. My work is the finish, the cap and climax, of 300 years, loss of life and expenditure of millions, by some of the best men of the civilized nations of the world, and it has been accomplished with a clean cut dash, spirit, and I believe, thoroughness characteristically American. I am content.
>
> Robert E. Peary's
> personal diary for April 1909

Above: Iceberg and sea ice afloat in Melville Bay, northwest Greenland. It was through these waters that Elisha Kent Kane's party, half-dead of starvation, struggled in July and August 1855 on the way back from their unsuccessful search for the Open Polar Sea. They eventually reached the safety of Upernavik, further south along the Greenland coast, where a Spanish ship picked them up.

disappointed to be told to turn back to camp. The North Pole was still 153 miles away. Peary, Henson and four Inuit – Egingwah, Seeglo, Ootah and Ooqueah - then made their final assault. Based on progress of the previous five days, Bartlett figured it would take them eight days to reach the Pole. They made it in four. On 6 April 1909 Robert Peary took a reading at Camp Jessup which placed them within three miles of the North Pole. Peary had achieved his dream. Or had he?

When Peary returned to Newfoundland, he was to hear that Frederick Cook had reached the North Pole on 21 April the previous year. A vigorous international dispute arose. Cook's claim was accepted by Denmark but public opinion turned against him when an earlier claim that he had ascended Mount McKinley proved to be fraudulent. And when Cook was unable to produce his original North Pole records, the University of Copenhagen declared his claim "not proved." Until his death in 1940 Cook continued to defend his claim and his honor. Meanwhile, with little scrutiny, the Polar triumph officially passed to Peary.

Until recently most scholars affirmed Robert Peary as the first person to reach the North Pole, although some claims have been made for Matthew Henson, who was the first to arrive at Camp Jessup. In 1973 American astronomer Dennis Rawlins challenged Peary's unverified astronomical co-ordinates. Although Rawlins' own figures were later shown to be flawed, he had successfully rekindled the controversy.

In September 1988 the National Geographic Society reversed eight decades of support for Peary. They published a report by Wally Herbert, a British Arctic explorer, in which he suggested that the drifting ice pack might have carried Peary 60 miles off course. Also, if Peary had maintained his previous speed, he would have reached only 89° 5' N, over 60 miles short of the Pole. In 1989 scientists tried to determine whether the shadows in Peary's photographs from Camp Jessup matched a Polar position. They were hampered by cloud cover. In 1990 the National Archives released three unpublished "sunny" photographs for examination. The controversy continues.

In 1958 the nuclear submarine *USS Nautilus*, under the command of William Anderson, traveled under the North Pole and James Calvert took the *USS Skate* under the North Pole the following year. In April 1968 four amateur explorers arrived at the North Pole atop snowmobiles, the first overland expedition to reach the Pole since Peary. Wally Herbert led four men across the Pole in April 1969. Their sled journey of 14 months had been supplied by drops from the air. In May 1968, Ann Bancroft, a Minnesota school teacher, became the first woman to arrive at the North Pole, part of an eight-member team led by Will Steger. Ten days later, Jean-Louis Etienne, a French explorer, reached the same spot using only skis and pulling his own sled. The Japanese explorer Naomi Uemura arrived at the Pole alone and by dogsled in April 1978. They were all airlifted out. It was the age of the machine.

5 Mar 1909
Peary held up for 5 days
by "Big Lead"

26 Mar 1906
Peary comes to "Big Lead" but unable to cross
2 Apr 1906
Peary, Henson and 6 Inuit travel north alone

28 June 1906
Peary later claims that
from this cape he saw
"Crocker Land" along
northwest horizon

6 Mar 1906
Peary, Henson and company
depart for North Pole
from Cape Hecla

Cape
Thomas
Hubbard

3 Apr -25 Jun 1876
Aldrich leads
six men along coast

28 Feb -1 Mar 1909
Peary divides 24 men into
7 teams. Peary brings up rear

Peary's
"Crocker
Land"

Apr 21 1902
Peary abandons hi
first attempt to
reach Pole

11 May 1876
Markham's farthest
399.5 miles from Pol

Nansen Fiord

Axel Heiberg Island

Summer 1882
Greely explores Ellesmere
Island interior by sledge

Greely Fiord

Cape Brainard

May 1883
Lockwood, Brainard and Fred
mistake fiord for interior lake

Cape
Columbia

5 Sept 1908
Peary's ship Roosevelt
arrives at its 1906 base

Markham
Inlet

31 Aug 1875
Nares launches
three sledge teams

11 Aug 1881
Greely sets up Fort
Conger weather station,
with supplies for 3 years

Lake
Hazen

20 May 1854
Kane sends Hayes and Godfrey to explore
western shore in unsuccessful search for passsage
to Open Polar Sea

Grinnell Land

9 Sept 1883
Trapped in ice, Greely
abandons steamer and jolly boat.
Haul their goods across ice to
Ellesmere Island but stranded on floe

28 Sept 1883
Greely's men escape ice floe.
They suffer starvation,
frostbite and death before
rescue by USS Bear in
June 1884

Camp Cla

25 Aug 1875
Discovery made into
base camp. Nares
continues north in Alert

Ella
Bay

Discovery
Harbour

Floeberg
Beach

Cape
Joseph Henry

Cape
Sheridan

Fort
Conger

Lincoln Se

Agassiz Glacier

Cape
Frazer

Joseph
Good

Newman Bay

Sable Island

Kennedy Channel

Hall
Basin

Robeson Channel

Cape
Brevoort

Cape
Bryan

Jones Sound

Devon Island

Etah

6 Sept 1853
Blocked from
further advance,
Kane sets up base camp

Kane
Basin

Cape
Constitution

Washington
Land

9 Aug 1883
Greely heads south
in steam launch Lady
Greely and 3 small boats

July 1854
Morton and Hendrik cut across
bay. Morton climbs cape and
sees ice-free water. This later
convinces Kane that Open Polar
Sea exists

Nyeboe
Land

5 Sept 1906
Peary from New Y
City on Roosevelt

1871
Charles Francis Hall's
farthest north

Hall's
burial
place

1871

12 Jun 1881
Greely and crew of 24
from New York City
aboard steamer
Proteus. Picks up 2 Inuit,
Jens and Fred,
at Godhaven

Renselaer Bay

Smith Sound

Peabody
Bay

Humboldt
Glacier

11 May 1855
Kane and surviving crew
abandon ice-locked Advance
and drag two open boats
across ice

Natsilivik

29 May 1875
Nares from
Portsmouth in
command of two
ships, Alert and
Discovery,
instructed to
sail through Kane
Basin and reach
North Pole by
ship or sledge

30 May 1853
Kane from New York
City aboard 144-ton
brig Advance, with
crew of 17. Searches
for Franklin and
passage to Open
Polar Sea

17 June 1855
Kane expedition reaches
open water

27 Apr 1854
Kane stopped by
bad weather

June 1854
Four of Kane's men fail to
ascend glacier. Polar bears
destroy their food depots,
so they return to ship

G

R

11-18 Jul 1855
Kane waits out storm

Cape
York

Melville
Bay

Meteorite
Island

July-Aug 1855
Almost starved, Kane and his
men return to Upernavik

N
W   E
S

Alternative Peary location, based on the average rate of travel prior to 1 Apr 1909

Wally Herbert's alternative Peary locations

10. 00 a.m. 6 Apr 1909
Peary, Henson and 4 Inuit - Egingwah, Seeglo, Ootah and Ooqueah- arrive at Pole and set up camp. They stay for 30 hours

90°

North Pole 89°
Camp Jessup

87°

25 Mar 1909
Marvin turns back. Within days he is killed by one of his Inuit drivers

1 Apr 1909
Bartlett, last person capable of verifying Peary's coordinates, turns back. Peary, Henson and 4 Inuit dash for Pole

Camp Bartlett

7 Apr 1906
Blizzard pins Peary down for 7 days
14 Apr 1906
Peary makes dash for Pole

21 Apr 1906
Peary sets new record for farthest north, breaking Cagni's record of 1900

Storm Camp

9 May 1906
Peary reaches land. Inadvertently rescues support team

6 May 1906
Peary arrives back at ship from North Pole attempt

Cape Britannia
Cape Beaumont
Island
Cape Neumayer

Sherard Osborne Fiord
Cape May
Lockwood Island

13 May 1882
Lockwood, Brainard and Fred arrive at their farthest point north. Flag made by Mrs Greely placed atop 2600-foot plateau. Brainard carves "St 1860 X" in rocks to honor American brand of beer

Cape Morris Jessup

Peary Land

Independence Fiord

14 May 1882
Lockwood, Brainard and Fred arrive

6 Apr-15 Aug 1876
Beaumont and party stop short of Cape May because of poor ice conditions. Retreat to Polaris Bay

Peary, 1892

Peary, 1895

1892-95
Peary explores north Greenland, looking for jumping-off point for the Pole. He eventually rejects Greenland as a starting point, but not before proving it is an island

E
N
L
A
N
D

40°

83°

81°

79°

The ravenous, irritable conditions in which the entire party are at present cannot but have the effect of making the men morbid and suspicious. Sergeant Gardiner lately said to me that he objected very decidedly to passing Rice's ration to him, if it could be avoided. He declared that he realized the fairness of the cooks, but that, in allowing a cup of tea or a plate of stew to pass through his hands, he could not prevent himself from mentally weighing the food as it passed by, comparing it to the portion that came to himself. Such a comparison, he knew, was small and petty, but his starving condition must explain and excuse it.

Adolphus Washington Greely
Personal diary

The Race to the Pole, 1853-1909

Permanent pack ice

Temporary pack ice

Polar ice drift

Water currents

"Big Lead" river of open water

Kane, 1853-5

Nares, 1875-76

Greely, 1882-84

Peary, 1892-1902

Peary, 1906

Peary, 1909

Inuit settlement

Base camp

Camp

Supply dump

Weather station

Death of explorer

Bibliography

Bakeless, John, *The Eyes of Discovery: The Pageant of North America as Seen by the First Explorers*, New York, 1950

Brebner, John B., *The Explorers of North America 1492-1806*, London, 1933

Canada, Surveys and Mapping Branch, *The National Atlas of Canada*, Ottawa, 1982

Cumming, W.P., *The Southeast in Early Maps*, 2nd ed., Chapel Hill, NC, 1962

Cumming, W.P., R.A. Skelton and D.B. Quinn, *The Discovery of North America*, London, 1971

Cumming, W.P., S.E. Hillier, D.B. Quinn and Glyndwr Williams, *The Exploration of North America 1630-1776*, London, 1974

DeVoto, Bernard, *The Course of Empire*, Boston, 1952

Dictionary of Canadian Biography, Vols I-XII, Toronto, 1966-90

Garrett, Wilbur, and John Garver, *National Geographic Atlas of North America: Space Age Portrait of a Continent*, Washington, D.C., 1987

Gerlach, Arch C., ed., *The National Atlas of the United States of America*, Washington, D.C., 1970

Harris, R. Cole, ed. *Historical Atlas of Canada, I: From the Beginning to 1800*, Toronto, 1988

Lewis, G. Malcolm "Indian Maps," in C.M. Judd and A.J. Ray eds., *Old Trails and New Directions: Papers of the Third North American Fur Trade Conference*, Toronto, 1980, pp. 9-23

National Geographic Society, *The World of the American Indians*, Washington, D.C., 1974.

Portinario, P., and F. Knirsch, *The Cartography of North America 1500-1800*, New York, 1987

Quinn, D.B., ed. with Alison M. Quinn and Susan Hillier, *New American World*, 5 vols., New York, 1979

Ruggles, Richard I., *A Country so Interesting: The Hudson's Bay Company and Two Centuries of Mapping 1670-1870*, Montreal and Kingston, Ont., 1991

Vorsey, Louis De, "Amerindian Contributions to the Mapping of North America," *Imago Mundi*, XXX, 1978,

pp.71-78

Wheat, Carl I., *Mapping the Transmississippi West*, 5 vols., San Francisco, 1957

Part I: A Continent on the Edge of the World

THE ATLANTIC COASTS REVEALED

Asher, G.M., ed., *Henry Hudson the Navigator*, London, 1860

Biggar, H.P., ed., *The Voyages of Jacques Cartier*, Ottawa, 1924

Dodge, Ernest, *North-west by Sea*, New York, 1961

Ganong, W.F., ed. T.E. Layng, *Crucial Maps in the Early Cartography and Place-Nomenclature of the Atlantic Coast of Canada*, Toronto, 1964

Hoffman, Bernard G., *Cabot to Cartier: Sources for a Historical Ethnography of Northeastern North America 1497-1550*, Toronto, 1961

Markham, A.H., ed., *The Voyages and Works of John Davis*, London, 1880

Markham, C.R., ed., *The Voyages of William Baffin*, London, 1881

Morison, Samuel Eliot, *The European Discovery of America: The Northern Voyages*, New York, 1971

Neatby, Leslie H., *In Quest of the North West Passage*, London, 1958

Quinn, D.B., *England and the Discovery of America 1481-1620*, London, 1974

Quinn, D.B., *North America from Earliest Discovery to First Settlements*, New York, 1977

Sauer, Carl O., *Sixteenth Century North America: The Land and the People as Seen by the Europeans*, Berkeley and Los Angeles, 1971

Stefansson, Vilhjalmar, *The Three Voyages of Martin Frobisher*, London, 1938

Williamson, J.A., ed., *The Cabot Voyages and Bristol Discovery under Henry VII*, Cambridge, England, 1962

Wroth, Lawrence C., *The Voyages of Giovanni da Verrazzano*, New Haven, Conn. and London, 1970

THE SPANISH BORDERLANDS

Bannon, John F., *The Spanish Borderlands Frontier 1513-1821*, Albuquerque, New

Mex., 1974

Bolton, Herbert E., ed., *Spanish Explorations in the Southwest 1542-1706*, New York, 1916; reprinted 1959

Bolton, Herbert E., *Coronado: Knight of Pueblos and Plains*, Albuquerque, New Mex., 1964

Chapman, Charles E., *A History of California: The Spanish Period*, New York, 1921

Day, A. Grove, *Coronado's Quest*, Berkeley, Calif., 1940

Hallenbeck, Cleve, *Alvar Nuñez Cabeza de Vaca: The Journey and Route of the First European to Cross the Continent of North America*, Glendale, Calif., 1940

Hammond, George P., and A. Rey, eds. *Narratives of the Coronado Expedition 1540-1542*, Albuquerque, New Mex., 1940

Hammond, George P., and A. Rey, *Don Juan de Oñate, Colonizer of New Mexico 1595-1628*, Albuquerque, New Mex., 1953

Hodge, F.W., and T. H. Lewis, eds. *Spanish Explorations in the Southern United States 1528-1543*, New York, 1907; reprinted 1959

Holmes, M.G., *From New Spain by Sea to the Californias 1519-1668*, Glendale, Calif., 1963

Husdon, Charles, and Carmen Chaves Tesser, *The Forgotten Centuries: Indians and Europeans in the American South, 1521-1704*, Athens, Ga., 1992

Jones, Oakah L., *Pueblo Warriors and the Spanish Conquest*, Norman, Okla., 1966

Lowery, Woodbury, *The Spanish Settlements within the Present Limits of the United States 1513-1561*, New York, 1901

Maynard, Theodore, *De Soto and the Conquistadores*, New York, 1930

Mathes, W. Michael, *Vizcaino and Spanish Expansion in the Pacific Ocean 1580-1630*, San Francisco, 1968

Wagner, Henry R., *Spanish Voyages to the Northwest Coast of America in the Sixteenth Century*, San Francisco, 1929; reprinted 1966

Wagner, Henry R., *The Cartography of the Northwest Coast of America to the Year 1800*, Berkeley and Los Angeles, 1937

Wagner, Henry R., "Apocryphal Voyages to the Northwest Coast of America," *Proceedings of the American Antiquarian Society*, N.S., XLI, 1931, pp. 179-234

Part II: The Opening of a Continent

RUGGED AND LABORIOUS BEGINNINGS

Barbour, Philip L., *The Three Worlds of Captain John Smith*, Boston, Mass., 1964

Barbour, Philip L., ed. *The Jamestown Voyages under the First Charter 1606-1609*, Cambridge, England, 1969

Biggar, H.P., "Jean Ribaut's Discoverye of Terra Florida," *English Historical Review*, XXXII, 1917, pp. 253-70

Biggar, H.P., ed. *Works of Samuel de Champlain*, Toronto, 1922-36

Cell, Gillian T., ed., *Newfoundland Discovered: English Attempts at Colonisation 1610-1630*, London, 1982

Hulton, Paul, ed., *America 1585: The Complete Drawings of John White*, Chapel Hill, NC, 1984

Lanctot, Gustave, *A History of Canada*, vol. I: *From its Origins to the Royal Régime 1663*, Cambridge, Mass., 1963

Lewis, Clifford M., and Albert J. Loomie, *The Spanish Jesuit Mission in Virginia 1570-1572*, Chapel Hill, NC, 1953

Lowery, Woodbury, *The Spanish Settlements within the Present Limits of the United States: Florida 1562-1574*, New York, 1911

Quinn, D.B., ed., *The Voyages and Colonizing Enterprises of Sir Humphrey Gilbert*, London, 1940

Quinn, D.B., *The Roanoke Voyages 1584-1590*, London, 1955

Quinn, D.B., *Set Fair for Roanoke: Voyages and Colonies 1584-1606*, Chapel Hill, NC, 1985

Quinn, D.B., *Explorers and Colonies: America, 1500-1625*, London, 1990. Especially pp.257-284: "The Attempted Colonization of Florida by the French, 1562-1565"; and pp.301-320, "Newfoundland in the Consciousness of Europe in the Sixteenth and Early Seventeenth Centuries"

Rowe, Frederick W., *A History of Newfoundland and Labrador*, Toronto, 1980

Trudel, Marcel, *The Beginnings of New France 1524-1663*, Toronto, 1973

THE QUEST FOR THE WESTERN SEA

Adams, Arthur T., *The Explorations of Pierre Esprit Radisson*, Minneapolis, Minn., 1961

Biggar, H.P., ed., *Works of Samuel de Champlain*, Toronto, 1922-36

Burpee, L.J. *The Search for the Western Sea*, Toronto, 1935

Delanglez, Jean, *Life and Voyages of Louis Jolliet*, Chicago, 1948

Doughty, A.G., and Chester Martin, eds., *The Kelsey Papers*, Ottawa, 1929

Eccles, W.J., *The Canadian Frontier 1534-1760*, New York, 1969

Hamilton, N. Raphael, *Marquette's Explorations: The Narratives Reexamined* Madison, Wisc., 1970

Heidenreich, Conrad E., *Explorations and Mapping of Samuel de Champlain 1603-32*, Monograph no. 17, *Cartographica*, 1976

Nute, G.L., *Caesars of the Wilderness: Médart Chouart, Sieur des Groseilliers and Pierre Esprit Radisson 1618-1710*, New York, 1943

Kellogg, Louise P., ed., *Early Narratives of the Northwest 1634-1699*, New York, 1917; reprinted 1959

Rich, E.E., *The Fur Trade and the Northwest to 1857*, Toronto, 1967

Severin, Timothy, *Explorers of the Mississippi*, London, 1967

Thwaites, Reuben G., ed., *The Jesuit Relations and Allied Documents*, Cleveland, 1896-1901

Part III: Expanding Frontiers

TO THE MOUNTAINS AND BEYOND

Alvord, Clarence W., and Lee Bidgood, *The First Explorations of the Trans-Allegheny Region 1650-1674*, Cleveland, 1912

Bailey, Kenneth P., "Christopher Gist and the Trans-Allegheny Frontier," *Pacific Historical Review*, XIV, 1945

Bakeless, John, *Daniel Boone*, New York, 1939

Billington, Ray Allen, *Westward Expansion: A History of the American Frontier*, 2nd ed., New York, 1960

Boyd, William K., ed., *William Byrd's Histories of the Dividing Line*, Raleigh, N.C., 1929

Brown, Lloyd A., *Early Maps of the Ohio Valley*, Pittsburgh, 1959

Corkran, David H., *The Creek Frontier 1540-1783*, Norman, Okla., 1967

Crane, Verner W., *The Southern Frontier 1670-1732*, Ann Arbor, Mich., 1929; reprinted 1956

Cumming, William P., ed., *The Discoveries of John Lederer*, Charlottesville, Va. 1958

Cumming, William P., *The Southeast in Early Maps*, 2nd ed. Chapel Hill, NC, 1962

Darlington, William M., ed., *Christopher Gist's Journals*, Pittsburgh, 1893

Gehring, Charles T., and William A. Starna,

eds., *A Journey into Mohawk and Oneida Country 1634-35: The Journal of Harmen Meyndertz van den Bogaert*, Syracuse, NY, 1988

Jameson, J.F., ed., *Narratives of New Netherland 1609-1664*, New York, 1909; reprinted 1959

Johnston, J. Stoddard, ed., *First Explorations of Kentucky*, Louisville, 1898

Lawson, John, (ed. Hugh Lefler), *A New Voyage to Carolina*, Chapel Hill, NC, 1967

Leach, Douglas, *The Northern Colonial Frontier 1607-1763*, New York, 1966

Moore, Alexander, ed., *Nairne's Muskhogean Journals: The 1708 Expedition to the Mississippi River*, Jackson, Miss., 1988

Parker, John. ed., *The Journals of Jonathan Carver and Related Documents 1766-1770*, St Paul, Minn., 1976

Savage, Henry, *Discovering America 1700-1875*, New York, 1979

Thwaites, R.G., ed., *Early Western Travels 1748-1764*, vol. I [Weiser and Croghan], Cleveland, Ohio, 1904

Wood, Peter H., *et al, Powhatan's Mantle*, Lincoln, Neb., 1989. Especially pp. 6-20: Helen H. Tanner, "The Land and Water Communication System of the Southeastern Indians" and pp. 292-343: Gregory A. Waselkov, "Indian maps of the Colonial Southeast"

THE TRANS-MISSISSIPPI WEST

Bannon, John Francis, *The Spanish Borderlands Frontier 1513-1821*, Albuquerque, New Mex., 1970

Burpee, L.J., ed., *Journals and Letters of Pierre Gaultier de Varennes de la Vérendrye and his Sons*, Toronto, 1927

Caruso, John A., *The Mississippi Valley Frontier: The Age of French Exploration and Settlement*, New York, 1966

Crouse, Nellis M., *Lemoyne d'Iberville: Soldier of New France*, Ithaca, NY, 1954

French, B.F., ed., *Historical Collections of Louisiana and Florida*, New York, 1846-53. See vol. I (1846) for explorations of Joutel, Tonty; vol. III (1851) for explorations of La Harpe, Le Sueur, du Tisné

Galloway, Patricia K., ed., *La Salle and his Legacy: Frenchmen and Indians in the Lower Mississippi Valley*, Jackson, Miss. 1982

Hamilton, Raphael N., "The Early Cartography of the Missouri Valley," *American Historical Review*, vol. 39, 1934, pp. 645-62

Hoffman, F.L., ed., *Diary of the Alarcón Expedition into Texas 1718-1719*, Los

Angeles, 1935

Luebke, Frederick C., *et al, Mapping the North American Plains*, Norman, Okla., 1987. Especially ch. 2: Raymond Wood, "Mapping the Missouri River through the Great Plains, 1673-1895"; and ch. 4: G. Malcolm Lewis, "Indian Maps: Their Place in the History of Plains Cartography"

Margry, Pierre, ed., *Découvertes et Établissements des Français dans l'Ouest et dans le Sud de l'Amérique 1614-1754*, Paris, 1879-88. See vol VI, pp.455ff. for abridged journal of Pierre and Paul Mallet, 1739-40

Murphy, E.R., *Henry de Tonty: Fur Trader of the Mississippi*, Baltimore, Md., 1941

Nasatir, A.P., ed., *Before Lewis and Clark: Documents Illustrating the History of the Missouri 1785-1904*, St Louis, Mo., 1952

Norall, Frank, *Bourgmont: Explorer of the Missouri 1698-1725*, Lincoln, Neb., 1989

Pelletier, Monique, "Exploration and Colonisation of Louisiana," *Map Collector*, no. 24, 1983

Reinhartz, Dennis and Colley, Charles C., eds., *The Mapping of the American Southwest* , College Station, Tex., 1987. Especially: David Buisseret, "Spanish and French Mapping of the Gulf of Mexico in the Sixteenth and Seventeenth Centuries"

Weddle, Robert S., *Wilderness Manhunt: The Spanish Search for La Salle*, Austin, Tex., 1973

Weddle, Robert S., ed., *La Salle, the Mississippi and the Gulf*, 1987

Wood, Peter H., "La Salle: Discovery of a Lost Explorer," *American Historical Review*, 89, 1984, pp. 294-323

Part IV: Ocean to Ocean

THE NORTHERN FUR TRADE

Bliss, Michael, "Conducted Tour," *The Beaver*, vol. 69, 1989, pp.16-24. Alexander Mackenzie's Journey to the Arctic Ocean, 1789

Burpee, L.J., ed., *Journals and Letters of Pierre Gaultier de Varennes de la Vérendrye and his Sons*, Toronto, 1927

Burpee, L.J., ed., "York Factory to the Blackfeet Country," The Journal of Anthony Hendry (Henday) 1754-55, *Proceedings of the Royal Society of Canada*, 3rd series, vol. I, 1907

Burpee, L.J., ed., "An Adventurer from Hudson Bay," The Journal of Matthew Cocking from York Factory to the Blackfeet Country 1772-73, *Proceedings of the Royal Society of Canada*, 3rd series, vol. 2, 1908

Eccles, W.J., *Essays on New France*, Toronto, 1987. Especially pp.50-60: "New France and the Western Frontier"; and pp. 96-109: "La Mer de l'Ouest: Outpost of Empire"

Glover, Richard, ed., *A Journey from Prince of Wales's Fort in Hudson's Bay to the Northern Ocean... by Samuel Hearne*, Toronto, 1958

Glover, Richard, ed., *David Thompson's Narrative 1784-1812*, Toronto, 1962

Helm, June, "Mattonabbee's Map," *Arctic Anthropology*, 26, 1989, pp. 28-47

Lamb, W. Kaye, ed., *The Letters and Journals of Simon Fraser 1806-1808*, Toronto, 1960

Lamb, W. Kaye, ed., *The Journals and Letters of Sir Alexander Mackenzie*, Cambridge, England, 1970

Lewis, G. Malcolm, "La Grande Rivière et Fleuve de l'Ouest/ The Realities and Reasons behind a Major Mistake in the 18th-Century Geography of North America," *Cartographica*, vol. 28, 1991, pp. 54-87

MacGregor, James G., *Peter Fidler: Canada's Forgotten Surveyor 1769-1822*, Toronto, 1966

Morse, Eric W., *Fur Trade Canoe Routes of Canada*, Ottawa, 1969

Pentland, David H., "Cartographic Concepts of the Northern Algonquian Indians," *The Canadian Cartographer*, XII, 1975, pp. 149-160

Rich, E.E., *The Fur Trade and the Northwest to 1857*, Toronto, 1967

Ross, Eric, *Beyond the River and the Bay*, Toronto, 1970

Tyrrell, J.B., ed., *The Journals of Samuel Hearne and Philip Turnor*, Toronto, 1934

Wagner, Henry R., *Peter Pond, Fur Tracer and Explorer*, New Haven, Conn., 1955

Williams, Glyndwr, *The British Search for the Northwest Passage in the Eighteenth Century*, London, 1962

Williams, Glyndwr, "Captain Coats and the East Main," *The Beaver*, Winter 1963, pp. 4-13

Williams, Glyndwr, "The Puzzle of Anthony Henday's Journal" 1754-55, *The Beaver*, Winter 1978, pp. 40-56

THE PACIFIC NORTHWEST

Beaglehole, J.C., ed., *The Journals of Captain James Cook on his Voyages of Discovery: The Voyage of the* Resolution *and* Discovery *1776-1780*, Cambridge, England, 1967

Beals, Herbert K., ed., *For Honor and Country: The Diary of Bruno de Hezeta*, Portland, Ore., 1985

Beals, Herbert K., ed., *Juan Pérez on the Northwest Coast*, Portland, Ore., 1989

Bolton, Herbert E., ed., *Kino's Historical Memoir 1683-1711*, Cleveland, Ohio, 1919

Bolton, Herbert E., ed., *Anza's California Expeditions*, Berkeley, Calif., 1930

Bolton, Herbert E., *Pageant in the Wilderness: The Story of the Escalante Expedition to the Interior Basin 1776*, Salt Lake City, Utah, 1950

Cook, Warren L., *Flood Tide of Empire: Spain and the Pacific Northwest 1543-1819*, New Haven, Conn., 1973

Cutter, Donald C., *Malaspina & Galiano: Spanish Voyages to the Northwest Coast 1791 & 1792*, Vancouver, 1991

Fisher, Raymond H., *Bering's Voyages: Whither and Why*, Seattle, Wash.,1977

Fisher, Robin, *Vancouver's Voyage: Charting the Northwest Coast 1791-1795*, Vancouver, 1992

Fisher, Robin, and Hugh Johnston, eds., *Captain James Cook and His Times*, Vancouver, 1979. Especially pp.59-80: Glyndwr Williams, "Myth and Reality: James Cook and the Theoretical Geography of Northwest America;" and pp.99-120, Christon I. Archer, "The Spanish Reaction to Cook's Third Voyage"

Galvin, John, ed., *The First Spanish Entry into San Francisco Bay 1775*, San Francisco, 1971

Golder, Frank A., ed., *Bering's Voyages*, New York, 1925

Inglis, Robin, ed., *Spain and the Pacific Northwest Coast*, Vancouver, 1992

Kendrick, John, ed., *The Voyage of Sutil and Mexicana 1792: The Last Spanish Exploration of the Northwest Coast of America*, Spokane, Wash., 1991

Lamb, W. Kaye, ed., *The Voyage of George Vancouver 1791-1795*, London, 1984

Leighly, J.L., *California as an Island*, San Francisco, 1972

Masterton, James R., and Helen Brower, *Bering's Successors 1745-1780*, Seattle, Wash., 1948

Shalkop, Antoinette, ed., *Exploration in Alaska*, Anchorage, Alas., 1980

Wagner, Henry R., *A Cartography of the Northwest Coast of America to the Year 1800*, Berkeley, Calif., 1937

JEFFERSONIAN PATHFINDERS

Allen, John Logan, *Passage through the Garden: Lewis and Clark and the Image of the American West*, Urbana, Ill., 1974

Banda, Eldon, ed., *The Handbook of Texas*, vol. 3, Austin, Tex., 1952

Bannon, John Francis, *The Spanish Borderlands Frontier 1513-1821*, Albuquerque, New Mex., 1974

Beck, Warren A., and Inez D. Haase, *Historical Atlas of the American West*,

Norman, Okla., 1959

Benson, Maxine, ed., *From Pittsburgh to the Rocky Mountains: Major Stephen Long's Expedition 1819-1820*, Golden, Colo., 1988

Bolton, Herbert Eugene, *Spanish Exploration in the Southwest 1542-1706*, New York, 1916

Bradbury, John, *Travels in the Interior of America in the Years 1809, 1810, and 1811*, Lincoln, Neb., 1986

Coues, Elliott, ed., *The Expeditions of Zebulon Montgomery Pike*, 2 vols., 1895; reprinted New York, 1987

Coues, Elliott, *The Manuscript Journals of Alexander Henry and of David Thompson, 1799-1814*, 2 vols., New York, 1897; reprinted Minneapolis, Minn., 1965

Ferris, Robert, ed., *Lewis and Clark: Historic Places Associated with their Transcontinental Exploration*, Washington, D.C., 1975

Gass, Patrick, *Journals of the Voyages and Travels of a Corps of Discovery under the Command of Capt. Lewis and Capt. Clarke of the Army of the United States*, Philadelphia, 1911

Goetzmann, William H., *Exploration and Empire: The Explorer and the Scientist in the Winning of the American West*, New York, 1967

Irving, Washington, *Astoria or Enterprise Beyond the Rocky Mountains*, 3 vols., London, 1836

Jackson, Donald, ed., *The Journals of Zebulon Montgomery Pike*, 2 vols., Norman, Okla., 1966

John, Elizabeth, A.H., *Storms Brewed in Other Men's Worlds: The Confrontation of Indians, Spanish, and French in the Southwest 1540-1795*, Lincoln, Neb., 1975

Loomis, Noel M., and Abraham P. Nasatir, *Pedro Vial and the Roads to Santa Fé*, Norman, Okla., 1967

Moulton, Gary, ed., *The Journals of Lewis and Clark*, 7 vols., Lincoln, Neb., 1983-91. Especially vol. I: *Atlas of the Lewis and Clark Expedition*

Nasatir, A.B., *Before Lewis and Clark*, 2 vols. n.d., reprinted Lincoln, Neb., 1990

Nasatir, A.B., ed., *Three Years among the Indians and Mexicans*, Philadelphia, 1962

Newcomb, W.W., *The Indians of Texas*, Austin, Tex., 1961; revised ed. 1990

Pike, Zebulon, *An Account of Expeditions to the Sources of the Mississippi and through the Western Parts of Louisiana to the Sources of the Arkansaw, Kans, La Platte, and Pierre Juan Rivers, Performed by Order of the Government of the United States During the Years 1805, 1806, and 1807, and a Tour Through the Interior Parts of New Spain when Conducted through their Provinces by Order of the Captain-General in the year 1807*, Philadelphia, 1810

Rollins, Phillip Ashton, ed., *The Discovery of the Oregon Trail: Robert Stuart's Narrative of his Overland Trip Eastward from Astoria in 1812-13*, New York, 1935

Ronda, James, *Astoria and Empire*, Lincoln, Neb., 1990

Ronda, James, *Lewis and Clark among the Indians*, Lincoln, Neb., 1988

Wagner, Henry R., Charles Camp and Robert Becker, *The Plains and the Rockies: A Critical Bibliography of Exploration, Adventure and Travel in the American West 1800-1865*, San Francisco, 1982

Webb, Walter, ed., *The Handbook of Texas*, 2 vols., Austin, Tex., 1952

Weber, David, ed., *Albert Pike: Prose Sketches and Poems Written in the Western Country*, College Station, Tex., 1987

Wheat, Carl I., *Mapping the Transmississippi West*, 6 vols., San Francisco, 1960

FUR TRADE AND EMPIRES

Batman, Richard, *James Pattie's West: The Dream and the Reality*, Norman, Okla., 1984

Brooks, George R., ed., *The Southwest Expeditions of Jedediah S. Smith: His Personal Account of the Journey to California 1826-1827*, Lincoln, Neb., 1989

Camp, Charles L., ed., *James Clyman, Frontiersman*, Portland, Ore., 1960

Chittenden, Hiram M., *A History of the Fur Trade of the Far West*, 2 vols., New York, 1902; reprinted Stanford, Calif., 1954

Cline, Gloria G., *Peter Skene Ogden and the Hudson's Bay Co.*, Norman, Okla., 1974

Cline, Gloria G., *Exploring the Great Basin*, Norman, Okla., 1963

Clokey, Richard M., *William H. Ashley: Enterprise and Politics in the Trans-Mississippi West*, Norman, Okla., 1980

Dale, Harrison C., ed., *The Ashley-Smith Explorations and the Discovery of a Central Route to the Pacific*, California, 1941

Flores, Dan L., ed., *Journal of an Indian Trader: Anthony Glass and the Texas Trading Frontier, 1790-1818*, College Station, Tex., 1985

Gilbert, Bill, *Westering Man: The Life of Joseph Walker*, Norman, Okla., 1983

Goetzmann, William H., *The Mountain Man*, New York, 1978

Goetzmann, William H., ed., James Ohio Pattie and Timothy Flint, *The Personal Narrative of James Ohio Pattie*, 1905; reprinted Lincoln, Neb., 1984

Guild, Thelma S., and Harvey L. Carter, *Kit Carson: A Pattern for Heroes*, Lincoln, Neb., 1984

Hafen, Leroy R., *Mountain Men and the Fur Trade of the Far West*, 10 vols. Especially vols. 6 and 8, 1965

Harris, Burton, *The Original History of John Colter: His Years in the Rocky Mountains*, New York, 1952; reprinted Basin, Wyo., 1977

Irving, Washington, *The Adventures of Captain Bonneville, U.S.A., in the Rocky Mountains and the Far West*, 2 vols., New York, 1849

Loomis, Noel M., and Abraham P. Nasatir, *Pedro Vial and the Roads to Santa Fé*, Norman, Okla., 1967

Morgan, Dale L., *Jedediah Smith and the Opening of the West*, Indianapolis, Ind., 1953; reprinted Lincoln, Neb., 1964

Newman, Peter C., *Caesars of the Wilderness*, 3 vols., Markham, Ont., 1985; especially vol. 2

Oglesby, Richard, *Manuel Lisa and the Opening of the Missouri Fur Trade*, Norman, Okla., 1963

Quaife, Milo M., ed., *Kit Carson's Autobiography*, Lincoln, Neb., 1966

Sullivan, Maurice, ed., *The Travels of Jedediah Smith*, Santa Ana, Calif., 1934

The Trail Blazers, New York, Time-Life Books, 1973

Todd, Edgeley W., ed., *The Adventures of Captain Bonneville*, Norman, Okla. 1961

Townsend, John K., *Across the Rockies to the Columbia*, Philadelphia, 1839; reprinted Lincoln, Neb., 1963

Vestal, Stanley, *Joe Meek: The Merry Mountain Man*, Lincoln, Neb., 1963

Webber, David J., ed., David H. Coyner, *The Lost Trappers: A Collection of Interesting Scenes and Events in the Rocky Mountains*, Norman, Okla., 1970

Webber, David J., *The Taos Trappers*, Norman, Okla., 1968

THE GREAT RECONNAISSANCE

Abbott, Henry L., " Report upon Explorations for a Railroad Route from the Sacramento Valley to the Columbia River," *Pacific Railroad Reports*, vol. 6

Bender, Averam B., "Government Explorations in the Territory of New Mexico, 1846-1859," *New Mexico Historical Review*, vol. IX, 1934, pp. 12-13

Bender, Averam B., "Opening Routes across West Texas, 1848-1850," *Southwestern Historical Quarterly*, vol. XXXVII, 1933-34, p.119

Brandon, William, *The Men and the Mountain*, New York, 1955

Carvalho, S.N., *Incidents of Travel and Adventure in the Far West with Colonel Frémont's Last Expedition*, Philadelphia, 1954

Cooke, Philip St George, W.H.C. Whiting and Francis X. Aubrey, *Exploring Southwestern Trails 1846-1854*, Glendale, Calif., 1938

Emory, William H., "Notes of a Military Reconnaissance from Fort Leavenworth in Missouri to San Diego in California, Including Parts of the Arkansas, Del Norte, and Gila Rivers," 30th Cong., 1st sess., *Sen. Exec. Doc. 7*, 1848

Emory, William H., "Report on the United States and Mexican Boundary Survey," 34th Cong., 1st sess., *H.R. Exec. Doc. 135*, 1857

Frémont, John C., *Memoirs of My Life*, Chicago and New York, 1887

Frémont, John C., *Report of the Exploring Expedition to the Rocky Mountains in the Year 1842, and to Oregon and California in the years 1843-44*, Buffalo, NY, 1851

Frémont, John C., *Report on an Exploration of the Country Lying between the Missouri River and the Rocky mountains on the line of the Kansas and Great Platte Rivers*, Buffalo, NY, 1851

Garber, Paul N., *The Gadsden Treaty*, Philadelphia, 1923, pp. 11-12

Garrard, Lewis H., *Wah-to-yah and the Taos Trail*, Norman, Okla. 1955

Goetzmann, William H., *Army Exploration in the American West, 1803-1863*, New Haven, Conn., 1959

Goetzmann, William H., *Exploration and Empire: The Explorer and the Scientist in the Winning of the American West*, New York, 1967

Goetzmann, William H., *Exploring the American West 1803-1879*, Washington, D.C., 1982

Goetzmann, William H., *New Lands, New Men: America and the Second Great Age of Discovery*, New York, 1986

Gudde, Erwin G., and Elisabeth K. Gudde, eds., *Exploring with Frémont*, Norman, Okla.,1958

Hafen, Le Roy, *Frémont's Fourth Expedition*, 1960

Harney, W.H., "Report of the Battle of Blue Water," 34th Cong., 1st sess., *H.R. Exec. Doc. I*, 1855-56

Henry, John Frazier, *Early Maritime Artists of the Pacific Northwest Coast, 1741-1841*, Seattle, Wash., 1984

Hine, Robert, *Edward Kern and American Expansion*, New Haven, Conn., 1962

Humphreys, A.A., and G.K. Warren, "An Examination by Direction of the Hon. Jefferson Davis, Sec. of War of the Reports of Explorations for Railroad Routes from the Mississippi to the Pacific, made under the Orders of the War Department in 1853-54...," 33rd Cong., 1st sess., *H.R. Exec, Doc. 129*, 1855

Humphreys, Col. Andrew A., "Report of the Office of the Pacific Railroad Explorations and Surveys, Nov. 29, 1856," 34th Cong., 3rd sess., *H.R. Exec. Doc. I*, 1856-57, p. 212

Ives, Lt. J.C. "Report upon the Colorado River of the West," 36th Cong., 1st sess., *H.R. Exec. Doc., 90*, 1861

Jackson, Donald, and Mary Lee Spence, eds., *The Expeditions of John Charles Frémont*, 3 vols., Urbana, Ill., 1970

Kearny, Stephen W., "Report of a Summer Campaign to the Rocky Mountains...in 1845," 29th Cong., 1st sess., *Sen. Exec. Doc. I*, 1846, pp.221ff.

Macomb, Capt. John, *Report of the Exploring Expedition from Santa Fé, New mexico, to the Junction of the Green and Grand Rivers of the Great Colorado of the West in 1859*, Washington, D.C., US Engineer Dept., 1876

Madsen, Brigham D., ed., *Exploring the Great Salt Lake: The Stansbury Expedition of 1949-50*, Salt Lake City, Utah, 1989

Marcy, Capt. Randolph B., and Capt. George McClellan,*Exploration of the Red River of Louisiana in the Year 1852*, Washington, D.C., 1853

Marcy, Randolph B., "Report of a Route from Fort Smith to Santa Fé," 31st Cong., 1st sess., *Sen. Exec. Doc. 64*, 1850

Möllhausen, Baldwin, *Diary of a Journey from the Mississippi to the Coasts of the Pacific with a United States Government Expedition*, trans. Mrs Percy Sinnett, 2 vols., London, 1858

Mullan, John, "Report and Map of Capt. John Mullan, United States Army, of his Operations while Engaged in the Construction of a Military Road from Fort Walla Walla, on the Columbia River, to Fort Benton, on the Missouri River," 37th Cong., 3rd sess., *Sen. Exec. Doc., 43*, 1863

Mumey, Nolie, *John Williams Gunnison*, Denver, Colo., 1955

Preuss, Charles, *Topographical map of the Road from Missouri to Oregon... in VII Sections... from the Field Notes and Journal of Captain John C. Frémont*, Washington, D.C., 1846

Raynolds, William F., "Report on the Exploration of the Yellowstone and the Country drained by that River," 40th

Cong., 2nd sess., *Sen. Exec. Doc. 77*, 1868

Reinhartz, Dennis, and Charles C. Colley, *The Mapping of the American Southwest*, College Station, Tex., 1987

Reports of Explorations and Surveys to Ascertain the Most Practicable and Economical Route for a Railroad from the Mississippi River to the Pacific Ocean, 12 vols. in 13, Washington, D.C., 1855-1861

Rolle, Andrew, *John Charles Frémont: Character as Destiny*, Norman, Okla., 1991

Savage, Henry,*Discovering America 1700-1875*, New York, 1979

Settle, Raymond W., ed., *The March of the Mounted Riflemen from Fort Leavenworth to Fort Vancouver, May to October, 1849*, Lincoln, Neb., 1989

Simpson, J.H., "Journal of a Military Reconnaissance from Santa Fé, New Mexico to the Navajo Country Made with the Troops under Command of Brevet Lieutenant Colonel John M. Washington, Chief of the Ninth Military Department and Governor of New Mexico," 31st Cong., 1st sess., *Sen. Exec. Doc. 64*, 1850, pp. 55-168

Simpson, James H., "Report and Map of the Route from Fort Smith, Arkansas, to Santa Fé, New Mexico," 31st Cong., 1st sess., *Sen. Exec. Doc. 12*, 1850

Simpson, James H., *Report of Explorations Across the Great Basin of the Territory of Utah for a Direct Wagon-Route from Camp Floyd to Genoa, in Carson Valley in 1859*, Washington, D.C., 1876

Sitgreaves, Lorenzo, "Report of an Expedition down to the Zuñi and Colorado Rivers," 32nd Cong., 2nd sess., *Sen. Exec. Doc. 59*, 1853

Smith, W.F., "Report... of Routes from San Antonio to El Paso," 31st Cong., 1st sess., *Sen. Exec. Doc. 64*, 1850

Stansbury, Capt. Howard, *Exploration and Survey of the Valley of the Great Salt Lake of Utah*, Philadelphia, 1852

Warren, G.K., "Explorations in the Dacota Country in the Year 1855," 34th Cong., 1st sess., *Sen Exec. Doc. 76*, 1856

Warren, G.K., "Journal," Warren Papers, MS, New York State Library, Albany, NY

Warren, G.K. *Preliminary Report of Explorations in Nebraska and Dakota in the Years 1855-56-57*, Washington, D.C., 1875

Williamson, Robert S., "Report of a Reconnaissance of a Route through the Sierra Nevadas by the Upper Sacramento," 31st Cong., 1st sess., pt. II, *Sen. Exec. Doc. 47*, 1849-50, p.17

Williamson, Robert S., "Report of

Exploration in California for Railroad Routes to Connect with the Routes near the 35th and 32nd Parallels of North Latitude," *Pacific Railroad Reports*, vol. V, pp. 41-43

Woodhouse, Dr S.W., "Journals," MS, Philadelphia Academy of Natural Sciences

Ylarrequi, José S., *Datos de los trabjos astronomicos y topograficos dispuestos en forma de diario...*, Mexico, 1850, p.12. See also "Diario del Genl. Pedro Garcia Conde sobre los limites de las dos California... En relacion con los trabjos astronomicos y topograficos," MS, Archives del Ministerio de Relaciones Exteriores, Mexico City

THE GREAT SURVEYS

Bartlett, Richard A., *Great Surveys of the American West*, Norman, Okla., 1962

Dutton, Clarence E., *The Tertiary History of the Grand Cañon District with Atlas*, Washington, D.C., 1851; facsimile reprint, Santa Barbara and Salt Lake City, 1977

Goetzmann, William H., *Exploration and Empire: The Explorer and the Scientist in the Winning of the American West*, New York, 1967

Haines, Aubrey L., *The Yellowstone Story: A History of Our First National Park*, 2 vols., Yellowstone Library and Museum Association, 1977

Hayden, Ferdinand V., *Annual Reports of the US Geological and Geographical Survey of the Territory*, 12 vols, Washington, D.C., 1867-78

Jones, Capt. William A., *Report upon the Reconnaissance of Northwestern Wyoming including Yellowstone National Park, Made in the Summer of 1873*, Washington, D.C., 1875

King, Clarence, *Systematic Geology*, Washington, D.C., 1878

Powell, John W., *Report on the Lands of the Arid Regions of the United States*, Washington, D.C., 1878; reprinted New York, 1961

Powell, John W., *The Report of the Colorado River and its Canyons*, 1895; reprinted 1967

Schmeckebier, Lawrence F., *Catalogue and Index of the Publications of the Hayden, King, Powell and Wheeler Surveys*, Washington, D.C., 1904

Stegner, Wallace, *Beyond the Hundredth Meridian: John Wesley Powell and the Second Opening of the West*, Boston, 1953

Wheat, Carl I., and Dale L. Moran, *Jedediah Smith and his Maps of the American West*, San Francisco, Calif., 1954

Wheeler, Lt. George M., *Preliminary Report: Exploration in Nevada and Arizona*, Washington, D.C., 1871

Wheeler, Lt. George M., *US Geographical Surveys West of the 100th Meridian: Reports*, 7 vols., Washington, D.C., 1876-1879

Wilkins, Thurman, *Clarence King: A Biography*, Albuquerque, New Mex., 1988, revised and enlarged edition

Part V: The Far North

TO THE TOP OF THE CONTINENT

Allen, Henry T., *Report of an Expedition to the Copper, Tanana and Koyukuk Rivers in the Territory of Alaska in the Year 1885*, Washington, D.C., 1887

Back, Sir George, *Narrative of the Arctic Land Expedition to the Mouth of the Great Fish River...*, London, 1836

Bernier, Capt. J.E., *Report on the Dominion of Canada Government Expedition to the Arctic Islands and Hudson Strait on Board the DGS Arctic*, Ottawa, 1910

Berton, Pierre, *Klondike Fever*, Toronto, 1972, revised edition

Berton, Pierre, *The Arctic Grail: The Quest for the North West Passage and the North Pole*, New York, 1988

Cameron, Ian, *To the Farthest Ends of the Earth, 150 Years of World Exploration by the Royal Geographical Society*, New York, 1980

Chauncey, C. Loomis, *Weird and Tragic Shores: The Story of Charles Francis Hall, Explorer*, New York, 1971

Chevigny, Hector, *Russian America: The Great Alaskan Venture, 1741-1867*, New York, 1965

Cooke, Alan, and Clive Holland, *The Exploration of Northern Canada 500-1920: A Chronology*, Toronto, 1978

Corner, George W., *Doctor Kane of the Arctic Seas*, Philadelphia, 1972

Dall, William Healy, *Alaska and its Resources*, Boston, Mass., 1870

Dawson, George M., *Report on an Exploration on the Yukon District, N.W.T. and Adjacent Northern Portion of British Columbia*, Ottawa, 1898

Fairley, T.C., ed., *Sverdrup's Arctic Adventures*, 1959

Federova, Svetlana G., *The Russian Population in Alaska and California, Late 18th Century - 1867*, Kingston, Ont., 1973

Gibson, James R., *Imperial Russia in Frontier America*, New York, 1976

Gutteridge, Leonard F., *Icebound: The Jeanette Expedition's Quest for the North Pole*, Annapolis, Md., 1986

Herschel, Sir John F.W., ed., *Admiralty Manual of Scientific Enquiry*, London, 1851; reprinted Kent, England, 1974

Hind, Henry Youle, *Narrative of the Canadian Red River Exploring Expedition of 1857 and of the Assiniboin and Saskatchewan Exploring Expedition of 1858*, Edmonton, Alb., 1971

Kane, Elisha Kent, *Artcic Explorations in the years 1853,'54, '55*, 2 vols., Philadelphia, 1856

Karamanski, Theodore J., *Fur Trade and Exploration: Opening the Far Northwest, 1821-1852*, Norman, Okla., 1983

Lopez, Barry, *Arctic Dreams*, New York, 1986

Mirsky, Jeanette, *To the Arctic: The Story of Northern Exploration from Earliest Times to the Present*, 2 vols in 1, Edmonton, Alb., 1971

Muir, John, *Travels in Alaska*, New York, 1915

Neatby, L.H., *Conquest of the Last Frontier*, Toronto, 1966

Neatby, L.H., *In Quest of the Northwest Passage*, New York, 1958; reprinted 1962

Newman, Peter C., *Caesars of the Wilderness: The Story of the Hudson's Bay Co.*, 2 vols. Markham, Ont., 1985

Peary, Robert E., *The North Pole: Its Discovery in 1909 under the Auspices of the Peary Arctic Club*, New York, 1910; reprinted 1986

Schwatka, Frederick, *Along Alaska's Great River*, London 1883

Schwatka, Frederick, *Compilation of Narratives of Exploration in Alaska*, Washington, D.C., 1900

Sherwood, Morgan B., *The Exploration of Alaska, 1865-1900*, New Haven, Conn., 1965

Smith, Barbara Sweetland, and Redmond J. Barnett, eds., *Russian America: The Forgotten Frontier*, Tacoma, Wash., 1990

Spry, Irene M., *The Palliser Expedition: An Account of John Palliser's British North America Expedition 1857-60*, Toronto, 1963

Spry, Irene M., ed., *The Papers of the Palliser Expedition, 1857-1860*, Toronto, 1968

Stanley, George F.G., ed., *John Henry Lefroy, in Search of the Magnetic North*, Toronto, 1955

Starr, S. Frederick, ed., *Russia's American Colony*, Durham, NC, 1987

Stefansson, Vilhjalmur, *The Friendly Arctic: The Story of Five Years in Polar Regions*, New York, 1925

Thompson, David, ed., *Joseph Burr Tyrrell: A Narrative of his Explorations*, n.d.

Thomson, Don W., *Man and Meridians: The History of Surveying and Mapping in Canada*, 2 vols., Ottawa, 1966

Tikhmenev, P.A., *A History of the Russian-American Company*, trans. and ed. by R.A.

Pierce and A.S. Donnelly, Seattle, Wash., 1978

Tomkins, Stuart R., *Alaska: Promyshlennik and Sourdough*, Norman, Okla., 1945

Van Stone, James W., ed., *Russian Exploration in Southwest Alaska: The Travel Journals of Petr Korsakovskiy (1818) and Ivan Ya. Vasilev (1829)*, Fairbanks, Alas., 1988

Webb, Melody, *The Last Frontier: A History of the Yukon Basin of Canada and Alaska*, Albuquerque, New Mex., 1985

Weems, John E., *Peary: The Explorer and the Man*, New York, 1967

Wilson, Clifford A., *Campbell of the Yukon*, Toronto, 1970

Wright, Allen A., *Prelude to Bonanza: The Discovery and Exploration of the Yukon*, Victoria, 1976

Wright, Theon, *The Big Nail: The Story of the Cook-Peary Feud*, New York, 1970

Zaslow, Morris, *The Northward Expansion of Canada, 1914-1967*, vol. 17, *The Canadian Centenary Series*, Toronto, 1988

Zaslow, Morris, *The Opening of the Canadian North, 1870-1914*, vol. 16, *The Canadian Centenary Series*, Toronto, 1971

Index

Acknowledgements

20 Detail of south wall of Greenway Chapel, Tiverton Church, Devon, England. Photo by A.F. Kersting.
22 Suit of armor of a Spanish Man at Arms. M13 A.J. 1941. Fitzwilliam Museum, Cambridge, England.
24 Detail from map, "The Vatican Verrazano," Biblioteca Apostolica Vaticana, Rome.
28 John White drawing of a "Skirmish." Courtesy of the Department of Prints and Drawings, British Museum: No. P.S. 172482.
30 Jens Munk at Port Churchill. Woodcut from Munk's *Navigatio Septentrionalis*, Copenhagen, 1624. Det Kongelige Bibliotek, Copenhagen, Denmark.

Baffin Chart. Add Ms 12206 fol 5-6. *True relation of his fourth voyage for the Discovery of the North-west passage in the year 1615. A coloured chart of the ship's course between the latitude 61° 66°.* By permission of the British Library.
32 "Prickly Pear," from *Florilegium Renovatum et Auctum*, Francofurti 1641. By permission of the British Library.
34 De Soto engraving from Theodori de Bry, *America* Part V. National Maritime Museum, Greenwich, England.
36 "Indians defending a town," drawing by Diego Muñoz Camargo. Glasgow University Library, Scotland. MS Hunter 242 f 317r.

Sikyatki ceramic, Arizona, 16th century. Clay and paint. Dept. of Anthropology, Smithsonian Institution, Washington, D.C. Photo no. 155690.
38 Juan de Martinez of Messina. Detail of one of 18 "very curious geographical charts elegantly drawn on vellum in colors and gilded," 1578. By permission of the British Library. Harleian, 3450 No. 10.
40 Map by Cornelius de Jode. Courtesy Ayer Collection, Newberry Library, Chicago, Illinois. No. 135 J9 1593. Vol. 1 fol. 11 - 12.

Inscription at El Morro, New Mexico by Juan de Oñate. Photo by Jerry Jacka.
46 Jacques Le Moyne de Morgues, illustration of Fort Caroline, engraved and published by Theodori de Bry in *America* Part II, plate IX, 1598. National Maritime Museum, Greenwich, England.
48 John White drawing of Indian in war paint. Courtesy of the Department of Prints

and Drawings, British Museum: 53A.
50 Map by Nicolas de Fer, "La Peche des Mourues," 1698. Courtesy of the National Archives of Canada, Ottawa.
52 Engraving of first building in Québec. Champlain's *Voyages de Sieur de Champlain* 1613. By permission of the British Library.

Portable lead inkwell and clay pipe, c. 1624. Courtesy of the Ministry of Cultural Affairs. Québec, Canada.
54 Map by Adriaen Block, 1614. From the Algemeen Rijsarchiefdienst, General State Archives, Dept of Maps and Drawings, The Hague, Netherlands. (VEL 520).
56 The Powhatan Mantle, Woodlands Algonquin, Ashmolean Museum, Oxford, England. 1685. B.205.

John Smith's map of Virginia engraved by William Hole and published in *A Map of Virginia*, Oxford, 1612. By permission of the British Library.
58 "Champlain with his allies the Algonkians, Hurons and Montagnais, met their enemies the Iroquois on 29 July 1609." *Voyages de Sieur de Champlain*, Paris 1612. By permission of the British Library.

Montagnais Indians, from *Voyages de Sieur de Champlain*, Paris 1612. By permission of the British Library.
60 Canoes from the Codex Canadiensis. Pen and ink drawing attributed to Louis Nicolas. Thomas Gilcrease Institute of American History and Art, Tulsa, Oklahoma.

Manuscrit de Père Chauchetière. Pen and ink drawing, "Les six premiers sauvages de la Prairie viennent d'Onneiout." Archives départementales de la Gironde, France.
62 Map drawn by Père Jacques Marquette, 1673. From the Archives de la Compagnie de Jésus, St Jérome, Québec. Canada.
64 Niagara Falls after a drawing by Louis Hennepin from *Nouvelle Découverte d'un trés Grand Pays*, Paris 1697. By permission of the British Library.
66 Portrait of Charles II of England from the original charter of the Hudson's Bay Company. Provincial Archives of Manitoba, Winnipeg, Canada.

Beaver from the Codex Canadiensis. Pen and ink drawing attributed to Louis Nicolas. Thomas Gilcrease Institute of American History and Art, Tulsa, Oklahoma.

68 Engraving of buffalo from *A Discovery of a Vaste Country in America* by Louis Hennepin, London, 1698. Photo: C. Schüler, Codex Photographic Archive, London.
72 Dutch trade gun, Flemish knife and Venetian glass bead, 17th century, found on Iroquois village site. Museum of the North American Fur Trade, Chadron, Nebraska.
76 Tuscarora Indian tribunal. Pen and wash drawing by Franz Louis Michel, 1711. Burgerbibliothek, Bern, Switzerland.
78 Rawlinson Copperplate no. 29 of Virginia. Courtesy of the Bodleian Library, Oxford, England.

"The Parrot of Carolina," hand-colored engraving by Mark Catesby FRS, and published in *The Natural History of Carolina*, London, 1731. By permission of the British Library.

Frontispiece from William Gardiner, *Practical Surveying Improved*, London, 1737. By permission of the British Library.
82 Wampum belt, c.1700. Royal Ontario Museum, Toronto. No. ROM HD 6364/2B.
84 J.R. Lewis, engraving of Daniel Boone. Missouri Historical Society, St Louis, Missouri. No. POR-B-11.

Beaver trap said to have belonged to Daniel Boone. West Virginia State Museum, Charleston. Photo by M. Keller.
86 Engraving of waterfall from Jonathan Carver, *Travels through the Interior Parts of North America in the Years 1766, 1767 and 1768 etc.* Dublin, 1779. By permission of the British Library.
88 Drawing of a calumet by Minet. Pen and ink drawing over pencil. National Archives of Canada, Ottawa. No. MG, B 19.
90 L'Archévêque and Grollet's painting of ship on parchment with message, 1684-85. Archivo General de Indias, Seville, Spain.
92 Le Buteaux, "View of the camp of Biloxi," 1720. Newberry Library, Chicago, Illinois. No. Ayer MS map 147.
94 Illustration from M. Le Page du Pratz, *Histoire de la Louisiane*, Paris, 1758. By permission of the British Library.
96 La Verendrye, lead plate. Robinson Museum, South Dakota State Historical Society, Pierre, South Dakota. No. 80.125.
98 Ramón de Murillo, pen and ink and watercolor of a leatherjacket soldier. Archivo

General de Indias, Seville, Spain.

104 Beaver Pool. Engraving from the Baron Lahotan, Lord Lieutenant of the French Colony, *New Voyages to North America, Giving Full Account of the Customs, Commerce, Religion and Strange Opinions of the Savages of that Country,* London, 1703, Vol II. By permission of the British Library.

106 Engraving of Inuit from *A Voyage to Hudson's Bay by the* Dobbs, Galley *and* California *in the Years 1746-1747 for Discovering a North West Passage,* by Henry Ellis, Gent. Agent for the Proprietors in the said Expedition, London, 1748. By permission of the British Library.

108 Engraving of canoes from Samuel Hearne, *A Journey from the Prince of Wales's Fort in Hudson's Bay to the Northern Ocean - Undertaken by Order of the Hudson's Bay Company for the Discovery of Copper Mines and a North west Passage etc. in the years 1769-1772,* London, 1797. By permission of the British Library.

110 James Isham, plan of York Fort, c.1750. Hudson's Bay Company Archives, Winnipeg, Canada. G.2/5.

112 "A Winter View in the Athapuscow Lake," January 1772. In Samuel Hearne, *A Journey ...* (op. cit., **108**). By permission of the British Library.

114 James Webber, pen and ink and wash drawings of "The Indian Dwellings of Western Slopes of the Rockies." By permission of the British Library.

118 Robert Irvine, watercolor of Fort William, c.1812. Hudson's Bay Company Archives, Winnipeg, Manitoba, Canada.

123 Engraving of sea otter, from Georg W. Steller, *Auafuhrliche Beschraburg* 1753. By permission of the British Library.

Aleut woman from Unalaska 1767. From an atlas of drawings by M. D. Levashov. Photo. by A.F. Golder. University of Washington Libraries, Seattle. F.M-25.

124 Map by Pedro Font of San Francisco Bay. By permission of the British Library. Add Ms 17,651 fol 9.

Jose Cardero, watercolor drawing of La Mision del Carmelo de Monterey. Bancroft Library, Honeyman Collection, University of California, Catalog No. 615 fig. 622.

126 Map by Manuel Agustin Mascaro. "Plano general de la mision y Pueblo de Arispe" 1780. By permission of the British Library. MS 17661.

128 Jose Cardero, drawing of Pira y Sepulcros de la Familia del Actual Nakau en Puerto de Mulgrave. Museo Navale, Madrid.

130 James Webber, pen and wash drawing of the Resolution and canoes in Prince William Sound, 1778. By permission of the

British Library. Add 15514 fol 10.

132 Jose Cardero, watercolor of "Panoramica de la entrada al puerto de Nootka." Museo de America, Madrid. Collection Bouza tomo I-12 No Inv. 2..270.

136 Page from the Field Notes of William Clark for 17-20 January 1804, showing Clark's drawing for the Keelboat. Yale collection of Western Americana, Beinecke Rare Book and Manuscript Library, New Haven, Connecticut.

140 George Catlin, "Comanches giving the arrows to the Medecine Rock." Oil on canvas. National Museum of American Art/Art Resource. Smithsonian Institute, Washington, D.C.

144 L. Clarke, aquatint engraving after Samuel Seymour. Frontispiece to *Account of an Expedition from Pittsburgh to the Rocky Mountains, performed in the years 1819-1820,* London, 1823. By permission of the British Library.

146 Carl Bodmer, watercolor of Piegan Blackfeet Man, NA 148. Joslyn Art Museum, Omaha, Nebraska.

148 James Madison Alden, watercolor of the Kootenay river. Sketch no. 40, *Landscape views of the area along the North west boundary, 1857-62.* National Archives and Records Administration Cartographic and Architectural Branch, Washington, D.C.

150 Alfred Jacob Miller, pencil and watercolor of Green River Camp and Rendezvous. Yale Collection of Western Americana, Beinecke Rare Book and Manuscript Library, New Haven, Connecticut.

156 Alfred Jacob Miller, watercolor portrait of Captain Joseph Reddeford Walker. Joslyn Art Museum, Omaha, Nebraska.THE GREAT

158 Engraving called "Natural Obelisks" from a drawing by Edward or Richard Kern made during Frémont's journey through the Rocky Mountains, 1848-49. The Huntington Library, San Marino, California.

160 Two illustrations from *Report of the United States and Mexican Boundary Survey* made under the direction of the Secretary of the Interior by William H. Emory. Vol II. Washington, 1859. 34th Congress, 1st Session. Cactacea of the Boundary, by George Engelmann. View along the Gila, Cereus Giganteus, drawn by Paulus Roetter and engraved by James D. Smillie. Reptiles of the Boundary, Crotalus Atrox. By permission of the British Library.

162 Richard Kern, wash drawing of "Ruins of an Old Pueblo," Academy of Natural Sciences of Philadelphia, Philadelphia.

164 Heinrich Balduin Mollhausen, colored engraving entitled "Schluten im Hoch-

Plateau und Aussicht" from *Reisen in die Felsengebirge Nord Amerikas.* By permission of the British Library.

168 John Mix Stanley after Private Gustavus Sohon, hand-colored lithograph of the Main Chain of the Rocky Mountains, from I.I. Stephens's survey report on the 47th Parallel. Yale Collection of Western Americana, Beinecke Rare Book and Manuscript Library, New Haven, Connecticut.

170 Photo. of Clarence King mountaineering, by Timothy O'Sullivan. Bancroft Library, University of California.

172 John Wesley Powell with a Paiute Indian. Photo. Department of the Interior, US Geological Survey, Reston, Virginia.

174 William H. Holmes, "Panorama from Point Sublime" from Clarence Dutton, *The Tertiary History of the Grand Cañon District,* 1882. Department of the Interior, US Geological Survey, Reston, Virginia.

176 Thomas Moran's chromolithograph of The Great Blue Spring, Lower Geyser Basin of the Yellowstone, Thomas Gilcrease Institute of American Art, Tulsa, Oklahoma.

178 Members of the Hayden Survey team surveying from Point Sublime. Photo by Timothy O'Sullivan. Department of the Interior, US Geological Survey, Reston, Virginia.

182 Lithograph after a drawing by Alexandre Postels of the Russian colony at Novo Arkhangelsk, 1827. From *Voyage autour du Monde fait par ordre de sa Majesté l'Empereur Nicolas I.* By permission of the British Museum.

184 William G.R. Hind, "Portage on the Moisie River." Oil on board painted while on the expedition to Labrador, 1861. J. Ross Robertson Collection. Metropolitan Toronto Reference Library, Ontario, Canada.

190 The tombstones of three of Franklin's men on Beechey Island. Engraving based on a sketch by Elisha Kent Kane in 1850. Courtesy New York Public Library.

196 Icebergs and sea ice, Melville Bay, 1991. Photo: Bryan and Cherry Alexander, Sturminster Newton, Dorset, England.

Additional acknowledgements:

Special thanks are due to: Vivien Hart, Pere Joseph Cossette SJ, Carole Thibault and Michel Brassard, George Miles, Henry Spall, Felicia G. Pickering, Charles E. Hanson Jr., the staff of Royal Geographical Society Libraries.